SHAKESPEARE'S PERJURED EYE

The "Rainbow" portrait of Queen Elizabeth I, tentatively attributed to Isaac Oliver, c. 1600. By permission of The Marquess of Salisbury, Hatfield House. Photograph, Courtauld Institute of Art.

SHAKESPEARE'S PERJURED EYE

THE INVENTION OF POETIC SUBJECTIVITY IN THE SONNETS

Joel Fineman

University of California Press
Berkeley
Los Angeles
London

University of California Press
Berkeley and Los Angeles, California

University of California Press, Ltd.
London, England
© 1986 by
The Regents of the University of California

First Paperback Printing 1988

Printed in the United States of America
1 2 3 4 5 6 7 8 9 0

Library of Congress Cataloging in Publication Data

Fineman, Joel.
  Shakespeare's perjured eye.

  Bibliography: p.
  Includes index.
  1. Shakespeare, William, 1564–1616.   Sonnets.
2. Sonnets, English—History and criticism.   3. Laudatory
poetry, English—History and criticism.   4. Subjectivity
in literature.   5. Point of view (Literature)   I. Title.
PR2848.F46   1986   821'.3   85-5871
ISBN 0-520-06331-7

That is the difference between Shakespeare's plays and Shakespeare's sonnets. Shakespeare's plays were written as they were written. Shakespeare's sonnets were written as they were going to be written.

—Gertrude Stein, *Henry James*

Contents

Acknowledgments

Many people have helped me as I worked on this book, and I want here to express my gratitude and appreciation. The English Department of the University of California, Berkeley, provided a friendly intellectual atmosphere within which to carry out my research; this is something I very much value. For their advice, criticism, and encouragement, I would like especially to thank Paul Alpers and Stephen Greenblatt. My colleagues, Joel Altman, Norman Rabkin, Janet Adelman, Ann Banfield, commented on various stages of the manuscript; I owe much to their careful readings and helpful suggestions. The group around *Representations* discussed portions of the manuscript and I benefited a great deal from the responses I received. Richard Wollheim gave the final draft an exceptionally close reading; both the style and argument of the book are very much improved as a result of his generous attention. David Bevington and Coppélia Kahn also gave the manuscript a careful reading; I am indebted to them both for their many valuable criticisms. I had many useful and enjoyable conversations about the project with Hayden White, Bentley Layton, Elliot Fineman, Murray Schwartz, Rosalind Krauss, John Rajchman, Jeffrey Schaffer. Victoria Nelson copyedited the manuscript; it is much improved thanks to her efforts. I want to thank the National Endowment for the Humanities and the Regents of the University of California for grants providing free time for research and writing. I owe a special debt of gratitude to Lizbeth Hasse, who helped me to think out and to articulate the book's argument. I dedicate this book to the memory of my mother, Sylvia Malakoff, and my father, Allen Fineman.

Introduction

This book argues that in his sonnets Shakespeare invents a genuinely new poetic subjectivity and that this poetic subjectivity possesses special force in post-Renaissance or post-Humanist literature
because it extends by disrupting what until Shakespeare's sonnets is
the normative nature of poetic person and poetic persona. A large
part of this argument depends upon a characterization of the theory
and practice of epideictic poetry, for in a very general way the poetics and the poetry of praise together define the literariness
through which Shakespeare thinks his sonnets. As is well known,
the poetry of praise is regularly taken to be, from Plato and Aristotle
through the Renaissance, the master model of poetry per se; fur-
thermore, as is also well known, this is a central fact for the Renaissance sonnet, which, from Dante onward, characteristically presents itself as something panegyric. In more specific ways than are
generally recognized, however, the poetics of the poetry of praise is
important for a literary history of poetic subjectivity, for it can be
shown that the assumptions of epideixis determine in particular
ways not only the techniques and conceits of the praising poet but
also his literary personality, i.e., the way the poet presents poetic
self. This is evident in traditional lyric poetry even when such poetry only casually refers to praise. It is more especially the case in the
Renaissance sonnet, however, for this is a literary form in which an
epideictic purpose is regularly developed as primary thematic motive of poetic first person.

In obvious ways praise functions as a powerful and governing
theme in Shakespeare's sonnets, straightforwardly so, or so it appears, in the sonnets addressed to the young man, as, for example,
when the poet, praising his own poetry, tells the young man "your
praise shall still find room,/Even in the eyes of all posterity" (55).
However, when Shakespeare writes his sonnets the literary vitality

1

of such traditional epideixis—a tradition which to the late Renaissance would have seemed even more traditional than in fact it was—is to a considerable extent exhausted, and this despite many efforts to revive, through various arch and self-conscious literary means, the themes, the topoi, and the forms of the poetry of praise. This exhaustion is a decisive fact for literary history, for when Shakespeare comes to write his sonnets—long after what even Sidney, at the inaugural moment of the Elizabethan sonnet, calls "poor Petrarch's long-deceased woes"—the poetry of praise has lost so much of its original and traditional force that Shakespeare can no longer uncomplicatedly employ a poetic mode that he must nevertheless think of as orthodox. This is the general situation that leads Shakespeare to develop in his sonnets a new poetics and, along with this, a new first-person poetic posture. In what follows I am concerned with the particular ways in which these literary novelties are achieved. Specifically, I argue that Shakespeare rewrites the poetry of praise by employing (implicitly in the sonnets addressed to the young man, explicitly in the sonnets addressed to the dark lady) in an unprecedentedly serious way the equally antique genre of the mock encomium, or what I call, following traditional rhetorical terminology, the paradox of praise. ("Paradox" is here more a rhetorical than it is a logical term, though rhetoric and logic are still for Shakespeare, as is the traditional case, deeply related to each other.) This is the major thesis advanced in what follows: that Shakespeare rewrites praise through the medium of epideictic paradox and in this way invents, which is to say comes upon, the only kind of subjectivity that survives in the literature successive to the poetry of praise.

It is important to emphasize here the "re-" of "rewrite," because it is part of the point I want to make that both the novelty and the effect of Shakespeare's sonnets derive in good measure from the way they noticeably duplicate, from the way they call attention to the fact that they repeat with a difference, the epideictic tradition they succeed. This is why the paradox of praise so readily lends itself to Shakespeare's poetic purpose, for this is a genre that aspires formally as well as thematically to such different duplication; indeed, the limit and not unprecedented case of the paradox of praise would perfectly reiterate that which it parodically repeats (for example, as I mention later, the way Giordano Bruno reads Petrarch's songs to Laura as a satiric encomium of fleshly desire). To the extent that the paradox of praise, to be recognized as such, necessarily refers back in this citational way to a more straightforward poetics of praise, it is possible to say that the orthodox tradition of epideictic poetry controls in advance its own transgression, predetermining and, to some extent, anticipating the character of its own undoing. In this sense, even before they are buried, "poor Petrarch's long-deceased woes" exert a posthumous power. For the same reason, we can say that Shakespeare's sonnets, despite their novelty, are a part of the same literary history whose mutation they effect or register. This is important, for it enables us to understand how literature, as such, from its beginning, establishes exigencies that constrain literary practice. Moreover, by referring to these exigencies it becomes possible to attribute the historical success of Shakespeare's sonnets to the orthodoxy of their unorthodoxy, to their fidelity to what is, finally, a conventional literariness.

In what follows I summarize the tradition of epideictic theory by saying that praise, poetical or rhetorical, is what happens when mimesis and metaphor meet. This is an oversimple formula; it is a useful one, however, because it speaks to the fact that praise is conventionally understood to be a referential discourse that amplifies its referent by means of ornamental trope, for example, the way Aristotle identifies comparison as the distinctive formal feature of panegyric because in praise "we take our hero's actions as admitted facts, and our business is simply to invest these with dignity and nobility [*megethos kai kallos*]."[1] To say that mimesis and metaphor meet is, of course, already to speak figuratively. I do so in order to bring out the ways in which traditional poetic and epideictic theory tend regularly to describe both mimesis and metaphor in terms of the same notion of likeness: verisimilar likeness or resemblance in the first case, the likeness of figural comparison and similitude in the second. According to traditional accounts, poetry in general, but praise in particular, joins these two likenesses together in a peculiarly powerful and mutually corroboratory way, as though the likeness of the one were confirmation of—in some respects, the likeness of— the likeness of the other. Hence, according to traditional accounts, the extraordinariness of poetic language, especially as it is exemplified by praise. With metaphor added to it, mimesis becomes more than merely lifeless imitation, just as metaphor, grounded by mimetic reference, is more than extravagant ornamentation. Thus conjoined, in accord with a familiar ideal of poetic decorum—a decorum whose consequence receives sometimes more and sometimes less metaphysical inflection—mimesis and metaphor accomplish a discourse of special vividness. They generate what is often called a speech of "actuality"; in particular, a speech of epideictic actuality.

This is to summarize, somewhat heavy-handedly, a good many far more precise and nuanced formulations of traditional poetic and epideictic theory, especially as these formulations are developed, refined, and argued over by Renaissance Humanists in various literary debates and controversies. At the level of generality with which the following argument begins such a synoptic summary is at least provisionally adequate, however, for I am initially concerned with very broad issues indeed. Yet, even so, it is entirely possible that the tradition of poetic theory to which I refer—the platitudes of a conventional and a perennial poetics, whether these are reduced to generalities about mimetic and metaphoric "likeness" or whether they are taken in their full particularity—has very little to do with traditional poetic practice. Nothing assures us that the poetry of the past was in fact what its contemporary critics or its theoreticians said it was or ought to be, and even if it were possible to identify some kind of correspondence between critical dogma and poetic practice, there would still be no guarantee that the critical principles and categories thus instantiated describe significant literary features.

This is an important caveat that should always be borne in mind, if only because it is very likely that traditional rhetorical and poetic theory inadequately characterize traditional rhetoric and poetry. Even so, this is not a difficulty that must be directly confronted when discussing the relationship of praise poetics to the Renaissance sonnet. For the Renaissance sonnet (a too general label that I use only so as to stress by way of contrast the genuinely unique and novel character of Shakespeare's sonnets) is sufficiently self-conscious about its own literary practice to incorporate into itself as thematic matter what might otherwise seem merely extrinsic and prosaic speculation about poetic manner. The Renaissance sonnet, that is to say, is not only a poem *of* praise, but, characteristically, a poem *about* praise. Accordingly, the speaking first person of these sonnets will, in ways which are in fact familiar, reflect upon his epideixis, and in thus thematizing his own panegyric procedure, the sonneteering poet will himself regularly raise and foreground familiar theoretical questions regarding the way he might adequately imitate his lady or, instead, how he might make "a couplement of proud compare" (21). How, for example, can words express an excellence beyond expression? To what can one liken a *nonpareil*? How to praise what passes praise? These are common panegyric topoi, but they are so because both when such rhetorical questions are asked and when they are answered they are developed in such a way as to articulate what is a common, shared, conventional understanding of the poetics of praise. For this reason, prevailing critical orthodoxies regarding the nature of poetry possess a relevance to the Renaissance sonnet that exceeds their own critical intelligence. Such literary rubrics as mimesis and metaphor—or, for that matter, praise itself—might very well turn out to be themselves, or to presuppose, concepts that are neither useful nor coherent. Even so, it would remain the historical case that these are central themes in the practice of the poetry of praise, at least as it survives for us in the particular example of the Renaissance sonnet.

To mention the literary self-consciousness of the Renaissance sonnet, however, is already to recall what is itself a fairly orthodox and long-standing understanding of an essential aspect of epideictic rhetoric. According to theory *and* to practice, the object or the referent of panegyric is "heightened," amplified, invested with "dignity and nobility" (just as the object of invective is meiotically lowered or deflated) by means of rhetorical devices that add something to merely mimetic description. In this sense, it might seem that praise is a rhetorical practice directed toward, and deferentially subordinate to, its referential object. As early as Aristotle, however, it is recognized that the rhetorical magnification praise accords its object also rebounds back upon itself, drawing attention to itself and to its own rhetorical procedure, drawing attention, that is to say, to its own grandiloquent rhetoricity. Thus, Aristotle says, the audience for epideictic oratory functions as "observer" (*theoron*) of the speech it hears, in contrast to the way in which in the two other rhetorical genres, forensic and deliberative, the audience serves as "judge" (*kritēn*).[2] This is to specify, in terms whose literal and figurative force remain fairly constant in poetic and rhetorical theory, the circularity that makes praise a distinctive rhetorical practice. As the Greek term indicates, praise is an "epi-deictic," not a simply deictic, speech. What the prepositionally diffuse and intensifying "epi-" adds to "deixis," the root etymological meaning of which is "show forth," "bring to light," "exhibit," "reveal" (these Heideggerean themes are relevant to what follows), is precisely the rhetorical surplus that praise as a rhetorical practice adds to ordinary verbal indication. This is what makes praise into extraordinary language, for, according to traditional accounts, it is through something discursively "extra," as an effect of something registered as supplementary or "epi-," that praise becomes a showy showing speech, a pointing or indicative speech that is so in such a stagily performative way as to become a kind of theatrical oratory. At its worst, therefore, which is to say when it is most excessive—which is perhaps when praise is most itself—such epideictic ostention can turn into something ostentatious. Even restrained, however, praise is a demonstrative speech that works by showing its own showing, by pointing to its pointing. Speaking formally, that is to say—but, again, this is a traditional formal insight regularly given thematic expression in the practice of epideictic literature—praise is an objective showing that is essentially subjective showing off.

Even as a purely formal point this is important, because it suggests why praise so readily becomes the paradigmatic genre of poetical or literary language per se. The reflections of praise are also reflexive; in pointing *there* praise will also point to *here*. Praise is thus an example of language that, by its rhetorical nature, foregrounds its own rhetoricity; it is a special kind of language that, as recent formalist and structuralist theoreticians of literariness would put it (Roman Jakobson, for instance), stresses itself as merely message. Thus conceived, praise might seem, and this is a criticism that it characteristically receives, an empty language, insignificant, because caught up in the *mise en abymes* and aporias of recursive self-reference. This is to deny, however, or not to take seriously, the linguistic idealization that informs such reflexive reflection when it is either theorized or thematized. At least ideally, there is activated in praise an effective correspondence or reciprocity between objective reference and subjective self-reference, a correspondence that, at least ideally, erases the difference between objective and subjective discursive indication.[3]

The theological model for this is prayer, psalmic praise, for, as Aquinas says, in a passage I refer to later, "We need to praise God with our lips, not indeed for His sake, but for our own sake, since by praising Him our devotion is aroused towards Him, according to Ps. 49.23: 'The sacrifice of praise shall glorify Me, and there is the way by which I will show him the salvation of God.'"[4] Dante makes a point of this, as will be seen, when he identifies his own beatitude with his praise of Beatrice, his *lodano*, with *la donna*. Less grandly, but following out much the same kind of reasoning, poetry will often be defended because it is said to be an effectively exemplary praise of virtue (or invective of vice) that leads its audience to emulate (or to shun) an example that, finally, only poetry can set. The

Renaissance sonnet, not always with such piety or with such didactic intention, will characteristically exploit this formal principle of reflexive reflection in various thematic ways, frequently identifying poetic subject and poetic object, lover and beloved, by referring self-consciously to the medium of its poetic praise, a medium that thus becomes, tautologically or "autologically," the self-example of what it speaks about. Even when this identification is explicitly erotic, or intentionally comic, or otherwise less than ideal, it will still be developed as an identification guaranteed by a specific kind of idealizing speech: a speech of Cratylitic actuality in which sign and referent forcefully correspond, as in, to take high examples, the "beatitude" of Dante's "Beatrice" or the "laud" in Petrarch's "Laura."

We can therefore speak in an intelligible way of an epi-deictic subject, of a subject, that is to say, whose subjectivity is bound up in, implicated by, its panegyric indication. Praise points here when it points there, and so we grow accustomed to a praising self whose "I" and "me" depend upon their correspondence to a praiseworthy "thou" and "thee." It is not only because so many Renaissance sonnets in fact play upon this I-me-thou-thee conceit, developing a laudatory poetry of ideally mutual admiration, that I emphasize the significance of the epideictic. More specifically, in what follows I argue that the rhetoric of praise, by its formal nature, requires, or at least calls out for, precisely such conceits. The rhetoric or rhetoricity of praise, that is to say, establishes, by virtue of its self-foregrounding epideixis, a kind of grammar of poetic presence that controls the way the poet can articulate himself. The rhetorical nature of praise, the self-conscious logic of its panegyricizing logos, renders certain subjective postures rhetorically convenient to the praising poet. And the Renaissance sonnet, which is acutely aware of its own rhetoricity, and in whose history we can trace a genuinely profound meditation on the poetics of praise, develops various conceits and poetic techniques to flesh this epideictic subject out.

An obvious example is the way that praising poets manipulate deictics themselves. These pointing words, such as pronominal "I" and "you," temporal and spatial markers such as "now" and "then," "here" and "there," have always been recognized as peculiar because, speaking loosely, though their meanings are constant their referents vary: "I" on my lips means the same thing as "I" on your lips, and yet these "Is" refer to different things. For Renaissance grammarians this was a particularly vexing issue because it made for a difficulty in what was a specifically Humanist understanding of the relation of word to thing. The variable or elastic referentiality of deictics, especially of pronouns, poses a problem for any "sema-siological" or semantic grammar that wants to characterize words by analyzing their meaning rather than their formal syntactic function. In their accounts of pronouns early Humanist grammarians, e.g., Linacre and Lily—in this way distancing themselves from a more sophisticated medieval tradition—develop and commit this sema-siological fallacy, understanding the pronoun, for example, as a sim-ple substitution for the noun that it replaces. The difficulties to which this led were an important impetus—via such rhetoricians as Scaliger, Ramus, Sanctius—to the later development of formal, "logical" grammar, e.g., Port-Royal. For the sake of the following argument, there is no need to discuss in detail the history of deictic theory in the Renaissance, though the way that Humanist grammar-ians attempt to understand deixis semantically rather than syntacti-cally is relevant to the way that Shakespeare conceives the temporal relation of a speaker to his speech, a point I discuss later in relation to "Time's tyranny" in sonnet 115: "Might I not then say, 'Now I love you best.'" (So too the problems that emerge in Humanist discussion of deixis should remind us of the urgent, *because* unsettled, state of linguistic speculation contemporary to Shakespeare, not only the atmosphere of controversy and polemic regarding the nature of lan-guage, but also the sense that current linguistic theories are in the Renaissance felt to be something imperfect and transitional, not final, and for this reason a matter of pressing and topical concern.)[5]

With regard to the practice of Renaissance poetry, however, deic-tics are important not for theoretical but for thematic reasons, and this because Renaissance poets develop and deploy them in a char-acteristically self-conscious way. In a very formal sense, deictics are *always* "self-conscious" because these "shifters," as Jakobson calls them, these "egocentric particulars," as Bertrand Russell called them, acquire their reference, i.e., they identify their referent, from the point of view—personal, temporal, spatial—of the speaker who employs them. This is one obvious reason why they are common in first-person lyric. By their grammatical nature, deictics radiate out from a central space of first-person enunciation to which all refer-ence is by formal consequence itself immediately referred. By for-mal necessity, therefore, deictics are markers that, whatever they refer to, are oriented toward the speaking self who speaks them, a self who is in this way registered as present to his speech because he is the source or origin of deictic indication. Implicitly, therefore, deictics, *because* they point, always point back to the place of he who points, defining "then" by "now," "there" by "here," "you" by "I."

This is implicitly the case with the use of any deictic. But it becomes explicitly the case in a poetry, such as the Renaissance sonnet, that thematizes itself as something epi-deictic, for such poetry is thereby involved in the circular dynamics by means of which the poetry of praise becomes a praise of poetry itself. With regard to the presentation of poetic subjectivity this has specific consequences which manifest themselves in the poetic use of deixis. Characteristically, for example, the poet of the Renaissance sonnet, however much he dwells upon the past as "then," however voyeuristically he looks outside himself at "there," however selflessly he ornaments his "thee," seems always to return, almost exhibitionistically, to the egocentric particularity of the here and now of "I."[6] In this way, moreover, the poetic self of the orthodox Renaissance sonnet characteristically presents itself as a *full* self, present to itself, or potentially so, by virtue of the complementarity it discovers or hopes to discover, between objective and subjective pointing. Thus it is that in such poetry the past will regularly prefigure what the present refigures, that what the poet sees outside himself will regularly be, in fact, an image of himself, or that the poet's praise of "thee" will regularly turn out to be a praise of "me." Even when the poet takes as theme his absence from himself, this regularly induces a specifically epideictic, deictic self-inflation, as, for example, in Petrarch's *canzone* 71, where the poet sees very well "how much my praise injures you," where the poet recognizes that "if any good fruit is born from me, from you first comes the seed, in myself I am as it were a dry soil tilled by you, and the praise is yours entirely," but where, therefore, the poet's empty, solitary self finds itself concludingly foregrounded and fulfilled in an apostrophe to "Song": "Song, you do not quiet me, rather you inflame me to tell of what steals me away from myself; therefore be sure not to be alone."[7]

There is no particular novelty attaching to the claim that in the Renaissance sonnet, especially the early Renaissance sonnet, we can identify, through such topoi and through such formal devices, a strikingly powerful and resonant subjective voice. It might be said, therefore, that the epideixis to which these sonnets regularly resort is only thematically convenient for the sounding of such a voice, that this epideixis is the consequence of an increasingly subjective poetics rather than, as I argue, a governing cause. In point of fact, however, the literary history of the Renaissance sonnet does not really demonstrate an increasingly subjective poetics, not if this is understood to mean a poetry that is increasingly expressive of a personal and individuated poetic self. Quite the contrary, as the sonnet develops—as Petrarch, say, turns into Petrarchism—poetic subjectivity becomes increasingly artificial at the same time as, and in direct proportion to the way that, the sonneteering poet becomes increasingly thematically self-conscious about the rhetoricity of praise. This is why, when I speak briefly later about this literary history, it is necessary to introduce a distinction between the poetic person of Dante or Petrarch as opposed to the poetic persona of Sidney or Spenser. Though handled differently by each, praise is a central theme for these poets, as it is for the many other poets one might associate with their names. And yet, as the sonnet form evolves—in the progress, if that is what it is, from Beatrice to Laura to Stella—it can be observed that poetic first person increasingly and, it seems, deliberately presents itself in terms of what is understood to be a *merely literary* figure of a self. Quite apart from the literary history of the sonnet, this is one reason why it seems reasonable to recognize the poet's sense of praise as being prior to, and constitutive of, his literary sense of self.

My argument, however, is more particular in its claims. It is not only that the poetics of praise prescribes, in the rather formal way I have now provisionally sketched out, but whose details remain to be examined, a space and time wherein poetic subjectivity can join poetic objectivity. I want also to say that the characteristic images and motifs of the Renaissance sonnet are also predicated by the poetics of praise, especially when these images and motifs are used to characterize the character of the praising poet. I refer here to what in the text I call the "phenomenology" of praise, meaning to suggest by this that there is a particular materiality or phenomenality that objectifies the language of praise—literally the *phenomena* of an epideictic logos. Again this is to speak figuratively, but again these are not only figures that are commonly employed in the Renaissance sonnet, but, in addition, the very figures that Renaissance sonnets regularly use—sometimes seriously, sometimes playfully—to speak about their praise. Referring to a good many theoretical commonplaces, I begin by saying that praise is what happens when mimesis and metaphor meet. But mimesis and metaphor also have attaching to them an equally perennial and commonplace set of material figurations the physical properties of which evoke what is essential in such theoretical abstractions. Thus, rather famously, mimesis is transparent, or it pictures, or it mirrors, or it reflects that which like a lucid window it presents. Metaphor, in complementary contrast, is opaque, a color, shade, or shading whose dazzling, veiling brightness adds a shine or sheen to that which like a lamp it will light up. Not all such images *of* the poetical are drawn from imagery of visuality, and in the text I discuss other images as well. But such visionary motifs are especially important to a traditionary poetics of *ut pictura poesis* and "speaking picture," and they are so, I suggest, because they are themselves the illustration of a reflexive reflection the circularity of which defines the literariness of a traditional poetic ideal. When mimesis and metaphor meet, the diaphanous and the opaque join together in a twofold visibility. But this visibility is itself the objectification of an idealizing language of self-regarding "Idea." Again this is a point that is confirmed by the practice of the Renaissance sonnet. Characteristically, the poetry of sonneteering praise conceives or conceits itself as what Drayton called his sonnet sequence: *Ideas Mirrour.* Much of the following argument is devoted to extracting and to glossing the subjective and objective genitive embedded in this phrase.[8]

This point regarding the phenomenology of praise is not really very complicated. It means to understand, by taking literally, a theme that, though its provenance is ancient, receives particular emphasis and prominence in the poetry of praise: specifically, that the poet is a seer, a *vates*, who speaks a visionary speech. That the theme is ancient, and that it is particularly suited to the poetry of praise, goes without saying. Renaissance poetics especially savors the antiquity of the theme, as when E. K. footnotes Spenser's "October" in *The Shepheardes Calender*:

> This place seemeth to conspyre with Plato, who in his first book de Legibus sayth, that the first inuention of Poetry was of very vertuous intent. For at what time an infinite number of youth usually came to theyr great solemne feastes called Panegyrica, which they used every five years to hold, some learned man being more hable then the rest, for speciall gyftes of wytte and Musicke, would take upon him to sing fine verses to the people, in prayse eyther of vertue or victory or of immortality or such like. At whose wonderful gyft al men being astonied and as it were rauished, with delight, thinking (as it was indeed) that he was inspired from aboue, called him vatem.[9]

This visionary metaphor, the characterization of the poet as seer, is significant, obviously, for the way it claims for the poet a special access to the divine. "Inspired from above," as E. K. puts it, the poet,

as panegyric *vates,* possesses knowledge of an extraordinary, supra-
mundane kind. Historically, this is how the image of the praising
poet is conflated with that of the prophetic poet, the eutopic vision
of the former being readily assimilated to the apocalyptic vision of
the latter. For my purpose, however, it is the visuality of this visual
motif that is more important than the claim for Orphic, bardic wisdom. In what follows, that is to say, I am more concerned with the
poet's seeing rather than with what he sees.

Not that there is all that much difference between the two, at least
ideally. For the ideal that is ideally to be seen by the visionary poet is
itself a kind of seeing, an eye whose gaze is also origin of light, as is
attested by an ensemble of motifs and images and metaphors whose
figural development is consistent from (and before) Plato onward.
We are dealing here, clearly enough, with a motif or a metaphoreme
so central to Western thought, not only to its literary thought, that
it is difficult, probably impossible, to separate what is the history of
ideas from the concrete idea of "Idea" itself. So massive, so pervasive, so influential is the visibility of this Idea, that the figurality of
the motif is often overlooked, either because it is taken for granted
or because it is treated as a dead metaphor whose resonance requires neither explication nor commentary. And yet, in ways which
are not at all obvious, it is from this visual idea of the ideal that a
specifically visionary poetics acquires or derives its particular coherence. Before it means anything else, "idea," *idein,* means "to see,"
and this originary visual image colors in specific ways both the physics and the metaphysics of a poetics that thinks itself toward an
ideal, whether we think of the *eidola* or *simulacra,* the likenesses, of
Stoic optics, the *eidei* or essences of Plato's Forms or Ideas, or the
"species," realist or nominalist, of medieval scholasticism (from *specere,* "to look at"). Such "ideas" are, so to speak, materialized in the
poetry of praise. They are present as things or artifacts the very
physicality of which is thematically exploited, explicitly remarked,
as though through this physicality it were possible to instantiate the
rhetorical logic of an idealizing poetics based on the effective force,
the "actuality," of likeness—whether this poetics is exemplified by
the way it understands mimesis as an exercise of iconic imitation
that offers vivid pictures of that which it presents, or by the way it
understands figure as a genericizing and essentializing metaphoricity by means of which, as Aristotle said of metaphor, poets "see the
same" *(to homoion theorein estin).*[10]

It is part of my general argument, therefore—an argument that is in principle as general as this visual motif is perennial—that an idealizing language figures itself as specifically specular language because such a visual logos, in its visibility and its visuality, simulates the ideal such language speaks about. When it is thought, the ideal will be thought as a particular kind of *Sichtigkeit*, it will be imagined as a certain kind of scopic spectacularity, and, in addition, the language of Idea, *as* an ideal language, will see itself as being pretty much the same. More generally yet, I argue that that which is admired will characterize the way in which it is admired, a formula whose import will necessarily remain the same when it is put the other way around. In thematic terms the recursive circularity thus expressed is important because it establishes the truth of an idealizing speech. The knowledge (the *oida*, also from *idein*) of the ideal *is* the ideal, an identity that, applied to language, produces a discourse whose referential truth is tautologically or autologically confirmed because such language *is* the things of which it speaks. Hence the Cratylitic thematics—words the "images," the "eikones," of things—pervasive in the poetry of praise, the repeated epideictic characterizations of a special, specifically visual language whose being corresponds to its meaning, an etymological and an ontological logos in which the "truth" of speech, the *etymos* of logos, is an inherent consequence of the nature of linguistic being.[11] Again this is very general, a matter of conventional topoi and motifs. I want to stress, however, the way this generality imposes particular constraints. For the visibility of the ideal is itself reflexively reflective, on the model of the sun whose brightness is both agent and patient of both seer and seen, or of an *eidolon* whose intromissive-extromissive visibility joins beholder to beheld, or of a Platonic *eidos* or "Idea" whose metaphysical immanence will make of universal and particular the simulacra of each other. Only insofar as it compares itself to this twofold visibility can poetic language secure its epideixis. Only thus can language make the literally spectacular claim that it *embodies* its ideal.

It is in this sense that, as I put it in the text, laudatory invention possesses a limited and a particular inventory. The rhetoricity of praise is reflexively reflective, so too is the referent of praise, and, in addition, the central motifs of praise, "figures of delight," conveniently illuminate and illustrate the same reflexive reflection. As a result, characteristically comparing itself to mirror and to lamp, praise will be itself the demonstration of the things it speaks. Nowhere is this specular correspondence, simulation, eventually identification, of language and ideal, of speaking and spoken, more regularly or more consistently developed—again, sometimes seriously, sometimes playfully—than in the Renaissance sonnet. And it is this practice, which for the Renaissance sonnet is a tradition, that Shakespeare presupposes and refers to throughout his sonnet sequence, especially in the young man sequence where—even though such themes are implicitly resisted—lover and beloved are visually "fair" (*idein*, "to see"), generically "kind" (*eidos*, "form"), and epistemologically "true" (*oida*, "knowledge") in the same formulaic way that "'fair,' 'kind,' and 'true' is all my argument" (105).[12] What concerns me is the way these themes and images, which are themselves the objectification of an epideictic poetics, determine in the traditional Renaissance sonnet the subjectivity of the praising poet, the poet who, assimilating these themes and images to his poetic self, will see himself as being both the mirror and the lamp of his ideal.

Again, then, when I speak about poetic self, I mean deliberately to refer to general and conventional topoi, for my point is that such topoi enforce specific subjective consequences. Familiar conceits of intromissive and extromissive visuality argue, for instance, at several levels, for the epideictic correspondence of poetic subject and poetic object. To take one obvious example, the visual desire of the Renaissance sonnet, its traditional eroticization of *eidolon*, is image of the poetics of laudatory admiration. But when Cupid shoots his arrows through the lover's eyes into the lover's heart what is evinced is the epideictic homogeneity, the essentially self-promoting (even when self-effacing) likeness of poetic "I" and "me" to their poetic "thou" and "thee." In such ways, which must be discussed in more detail, the poetry of praise inscribes upon the ego of the praising poet the specific features of its ideal ego, and this epideictic ego ideal entails specific psychological consequences for the character or the characterology of the praising poet. At the beginning of Sidney's sonnet sequence, for example, Astrophil will look into his heart to write and see there pre-engraved or "stelled" upon it the image or *imago* of the Stella whom he loves. In this way the poet's introspection, guaranteed by extrospection, can show the poet what to write. But if Astrophil's poetic voice becomes thereby a visionary voice it is because poetic "I" becomes a speaking eye. In the same way, at least provisionally, such a stellar poetics is pressed upon Shakespearean poetic self, as when "Mine eye hath play'd the painter and hath stell'd/Thy beauty's form in table of my heart" (24); in-formed by such painterly poetics, the poet properly will "see what good turns eyes for eyes have done" (24).

It is this visionary subject, fully present to his object, to himself, and to the speech he speaks, that Shakespeare rewrites by revising the visual poetics of the poetry of praise. Very briefly, I argue that in his sonnets Shakespeare substitutes for this ideal and idealizing characterization of visionary language—"To hear with eyes belongs to love's fine wit" (23)—a different account that characterizes language as something corruptingly linguistic rather than something ideally specular, as something duplicitously verbal as opposed to something singly visual. The result is a poetics of a double tongue rather than a poetics of a unified and unifying eye, a language of suspicious word rather than a language of true vision. In Shakespeare's sonnets, I argue, the poet "give[s] the lie to my true sight" (150), and in doing so he develops, or he comes upon, a genuinely new poetic subjectivity that I call, using the themes of Shakespeare's sonnets, the subject of a "perjur'd eye" (152).

The relationship of this new poetic subject to that which it succeeds is a complicated one, and this because such a novel subject carries with it the memory of that which it displaces. The verbal word of Shakespeare's sonnets is both like and unlike the visual word, the *imago*, of the traditional Renaissance sonnet, and this because it is a simulacrum that in a double way dissimulates the likeness it bespeaks. On the one hand, Shakespeare's sonnets "give the lie to my true sight" because they truly speak against a strong tradition, not only poetic, of linguistic idealization for which words in some sense *are* the things of which they speak. On the other hand, for just this reason, compared to the iconic, autological discourse of visionary speech, compared to words that in themselves will ontologically present their referents, Shakespeare's merely verbal words, that merely represent the things of which they are the sign, will seem a kind of semiotic "lie." That is to say, because they are a discourse of the tongue rather than of the eye, because they are "linguistic," Shakespeare's verbal words are, in comparison to an *imago*, essentially or ontologically at odds with what they speak about. This is how these words are thematized in Shakespeare's sonnets, as fallen words that have lost their visionary truth. In this sense, because as speech they forswear vision, these words are what Shakespeare calls "forsworn."

According to this argument, then, two large themes govern Shakespeare's sonnet sequence: on the one hand, the theme of vision; on the other, the theme of language. But there is a kind of structural pathos built into this opposition, for the second theme, the theme of language, as it is developed in the sequence as a whole, is both like and unlike the first. Language re-presents what vision presents, and yet this repetition produces something different from that which it repeats, for the truth of language is that, compared to vision, it is false. Vision and language—visionary language and linguistic language—are thus opposed to each other in Shakespeare's sonnet sequence, but the difference between them emerges only when the latter is, as it were, so to speak, literally *so as to speak*, superimposed upon the former. It is therefore too simple to say on the one hand vision and on the other language, for language is itself, as Shakespeare develops it, at once a version of the vision it denounces at the same time that it is a perversion of the vision with which it is compared. This is how language "lies" "against" "sight." In Shakespeare's sonnets the second hand of language is indeed opposed to the first hand of vision, but this because the second hand is both these hands together both at once. As I try to show, this outlines a general structural pattern organizing Shakespeare's sonnet sequence as a whole. Characteristically a positive term will be opposed to a negative term whose negativity consists of being simultaneously that very positive and its negative. Thesis is opposed to an antithesis which is itself the synthesis of thesis and antithesis. What gives this relatively simple structure its literary interest, however, is that it is regularly referred back to the opposition between vision and language. It is a central and governing fact in Shakespeare's sonnets that the mode of likeness associated with vision is opposed to the mode of difference associated with language. As a poetic result, however, it is not simply that the difference between vision and language comes to be thematized as language itself, or that the difference between likeness and difference is registered as difference itself. Rather, more specifically, the difference between language and vision is made to seem the source of all difference, just as the difference between likeness and difference is in Shakespeare's sonnets effectively embodied in language as such.

In very general terms this paradoxical relationship between vision and language (and, again, by paradox I refer here more to a rhetorical than to a logical relation) is figured in Shakespeare's sonnets by the relationship of the poet to the young man and to the dark lady, and by the relationship of both these objects of poetic desire to each other. In Shakespeare's sonnets, we can say, linguistic difference predicates sexual difference. Thus the young man is "'fair,' 'kind,' and 'true'" (105) and the sonnets addressed to the young man regularly invoke visual imagery of identificatory likeness when they characterize their poet's desire for the young man. In paradoxical contrast, the lady, as she is given to us, is foul because both fair and foul, unkind because both kind and unkind, false because both true and false. So too the sonnets addressed to the lady regularly associate the lady with a disjunction occasioned by verbal duplicity, as when "When my love swears that she is made of truth,/I do believe her, though I know she lies" (138). To the extent that the lady is thus identified with such double speech, so too does she exemplify the difference between visionary likeness and linguistic difference, for it is explicitly *as* such difference that the lady's sexuality is regularly defined, as when her poet, looking at the lady's far too common "common place," says "Mine eyes seeing this, say this is not" (137). It is in terms of just this difference that the dark lady sonnets characterize their poet's erotic relations to the lady, in terms, on the one hand, of "eyes" that "Love put in my head,/Which have no correspondence with true sight" (148), in terms, on the other, of the way the lady leads the poet to "swear that brightness doth not grace the day" (150). Given the heterogeneity of the lady, her essential duplicity, we can say that the difference between the visually fair young man and the lying dark lady is instantiated by the dark lady herself, or, in a formula whose lusty misogyny is recognizably Shakespearean, we can say that in Shakespeare's sonnets the difference between man and woman is woman herself. But again, it is only as a figure of false speech, specifically of a false epideictic speech, that the lady comes to occupy this peculiarly charged erotic place in the sequence as a whole: "Therefore I lie with her, and she with me, /And in our faults by lies we flattered be" (138).

In Shakespeare's sonnets, therefore, the poet's various characterizations of desire very much correspond to the way he characterizes language, either as something visual or as something verbal. The homosexual thematic developed in the sonnets addressed to the young man—where language, like the desire it mirrors, is "'fair,' 'kind,' and 'true'"—exploits the specular homogeneity endlessly repeated by the orthodox Renaissance sonnet, as though this kind of eroticized sameness linking idealizing lover to idealized beloved were the homosexual truth subtending the poetics of admiration from Beatrice onward. It is important to note that the specific virtue of this ideal, homosexual desire is *not* to be erotic, and only in this sense is this desire properly Platonic. In the sonnets addressed to the dark lady, however, where we are shown a desire for that which is not admired, we come, instead, upon a heterosexual desire that is strikingly erotic at the same time that we are given the theme of a linguistic heterogeneity purchased at the cost of homogeneous visuality. This thematic innovation is decisive. I want to argue that it is only when the poet thus explicitly, rather than implicitly (as in the young man sonnets), "give[s] the lie to my true sight," only when the poet *literally* puts his suspicion of true vision into words, that lust can be a powerful theme in the Renaissance sonnet. I argue that by remarking the difference embedded in a specific kind of verbal duplicity, by speaking about a language that *as* language breaks the perennial univocity of *Ideas Mirrour*, Shakespeare's sonnets introduce into our literary tradition, they make possible for the very first time, an outspoken poetics of erotic desire. Despite the salacious profanation of the sacred in troubadour lyric, despite the often lurid pieties of the Elizabethan sonnet, I argue, therefore, that Shakespeare in his sonnets invents the poetics of heterosexuality.

I put this point strongly to point up the way that Shakespearean desire, as it is represented in the sonnets, is motivated in a way that traditional sonneteering desire is not. In the traditional sonnet the lover is drawn to his beloved by the force of her ideality. The lover's goal is a kind of narcissistic identification or unification of subject with object, the identity or unity of which is already prefigured for him in the compact wholeness of the beloved herself. Given this account, we may ask what is the source of the energy that impels the lover toward his beloved? The traditional response to such a question would be that the ideal itself exerts a power of attraction: the lady attracts the lover to herself and thereby brings the lover to himself. This is the logic of Aquinas' prayer, the way, as Psalm 49 put it, "The sacrifice of praise shall glorify Me, and there is the way by which I will show him the salvation of God." On this account, the origin or motive of desire is located in a source outside the self, outside the desiring self. The ideal operates as a kind of magnetic force (and the magnet is, of course, a familiar image of poetic inspiration that goes back at least to Plato's *Ion*—e.g., the way E. K., citing Lydgate, characterizes Chaucer as model for poetic imitation: "the Loadestarre of our language") that draws its lovers to itself.[13] Thus described, desire amounts to a gift of energy bestowed upon the self. In theological terms, this is the grace God gives to man, a grace that activates a kind of tropism toward the ideal. These theological terms can readily be naturalized, as happens, for example, in various instinct psychologies, where desire, as a kind of brute energy, given now by Nature rather than by God, motivates the movement of the self. Here again, however, though apparently internal in its origin, desire still remains extrinsic to the lover's self: it is a biological force within the person that is nevertheless impersonally conceived.

It is in contrast to this account of an impersonal desire, an account that I feel fully justified in calling orthodox, that the novelty of Shakespeare's sonneteering desire can be recognized, and this because Shakespearean desire thinks itself through, presents itself *as*, its difference from such erotic orthodoxy. Traditional desire—by which I refer to what are traditional, usually visionary, figurations of desire, whether understood as theologicized grace or as naturalized instinct—imposes itself upon the subject, determining for the subject the nature of his erotic object. When this object is presented to the subject it will satisfy desire because it answers to a want imposed upon the subject as a kind of need. Two points are worth noting about this traditional model of desire. First of all, this account begs or ignores the question of the origin of desire, referring that origin to a power outside the self, to God or to Nature, whose effective action on the self is simply presupposed. In sacred or in natural terms the motive of desire remains a Mystery. Second, however powerful the power of such a desire, however urgently or painfully experienced is the distance between the subject of desire and the object of desire, nevertheless, in principle, the want of such desire can be fully satisfied. Defined as need, desire will be answered or requited whenever it is given whatever it might want. For this reason, because it can be satisfied, such desire can cease to be desire: it can become a state of bliss. Again, therefore, we encounter a logic of desire that leads inexorably to what are familiar Christian and Neo-Platonizing idealizing themes: the end of desire conceived as the joining of erotic subject to erotic object; the end of self deriving from a perfect identification of ego with ego ideal. With regard to desire or with regard to the self, this describes a consummation that, necessarily, is *devoutly* to be wished; for this perfect, ideal, selfless, satisfying identity of the self to itself depends for its identity on the attractive, identificatory power of a deified ideal that is at once the origin, the energy, and the object of the very desire it provokes. The self that is subject to such desire depends therefore on the ideality of its desire. Emanating out of the Ideal is a desire, intromissive and extromissive, that brings the self to itself by bringing it to Itself.

The recursively circular trajectory of such an ideal Eros is fairly straightforward, as is the suitability of visual imagery to its expression. At stake is a logic or an "erotologic" of simulation and resemblance that finds its logical erotic conclusion when corresponding terms are united by and in an ultimate identity. Visual imagery of reflexive reflection—mirrors of mirrors which are also lamps—precisely figures this kind of identificatory correspondence, vividly illustrating an identity both with and of the *same*. It is a profoundly homogeneous conception of desire that is thus depicted, insofar as it presupposes the joining of kind with kind. In principle, the loving subject identifies himself with a beloved object who is, or which is, as is said of Othello, "all in all sufficient" in itself, but whose centripetal unity will also centrifugally secure and energetically promote a complementary unity in the subject, as, for example, at the end of Dante's *Paradiso*.[14] To be sure, for the moment, in the less than ideal present, such unity of subject and object exists only potentially or virtually, as teleological promise rather than as current fact. Nevertheless, even in the imperfect present it is possible to glimpse the image of the promised end. For utter perfection is already demonstrably at work within the present; even now, the attraction of the ideal is palpably experienced as the insistent pull of a desire that is as infinite in its aspiration as is its ultimate satisfaction. Hence the value of such infinite desire, the very experience of which is promissory token of its eventual fulfillment. As in Spenser's "Hymnes" to "Heavenly Love" and "Heavenly Beauty," the lover's very admiration is what elevates the lover's self. The very fact of desire realizes in advance the erotic vision that sees the subject as the replicating image of the ideal he admires. Desire itself proleptically anticipates, incipiently announces, the temporarily postponed, yet already certain, adequation of the subject to his object and, therefore, of the subject to himself:

> Love, lift me up upon thy golden wings,
> From this base world unto thy heavens hight,
> Where I may see those admirable things,
> Which there thou workest by thy soveraine might
> Farre above feeble reach of earthly sight,
> That I thereof an heavenly Hymne may sing
> Unto the god of Love, high heavens king.[15]

This is ideal desire, desire whose action is conceived ideally, conceited visually. This is the desire of an Aristotelian poetics that "sees the same," that "theorizes sameness." The desire associated with, and elicited by, the dark lady operates, however, and so too is it figured, quite otherwise, most obviously because the lady is not ideal. Moreover, so forceful is this novel and untraditional desire, so peculiar in its object and so summary in its effect—"Desire is death" (147)—that it leads the poet-lover of the lady explicitly to pose the question of desire, which is to say the question of its origin, which at the same time is the question of its force:

> O, from what pow'r hast thou this pow'rful might
> With insufficiency my heart to sway,
> To make me give the lie to my true sight,
> And swear that brightness doth not grace the day?
> (150)

Simply to ask this question is already to challenge, to make a question of, the hegemonic totality of traditional desire. For it is by virtue of her "insufficiency" that the lady provokes in the poet a desire that, lying against sight, is genuinely inexplicable in terms of a visual identification with an "all in all sufficient" ideal. So too, where desire traditionally works by joining like with like and kind with kind, it is instead the erotic predicament of the dark lady's poet "that thy unkindness lays upon my heart" (139)—a predicament which is again bound up with a language at odds with vision since it is the lady's "unkindness" that generates the poet's wish that the lady "wound me not with thine eye but with thy tongue" (139).

The difference between this and what is traditional is readily apparent, but it is important to stress the radical consequence of this difference. With her "insufficiency" and with her "unkindness" the lady introduces a fundamental heterogeneity into the tradition of erotic homogeneity. She is not, therefore, a simple alternative to that tradition, for as something other to its comprehensive sameness, as an instance of alternative alterity, she is also its undoing. Thus, in sexual terms, the lady stands for an alienating heterosexuality that, in the context of the poet's relation to the young man, intrudes upon and interrupts the poet's homosexual ideal, as happens in the cuckoldry story, where the lady steals the young man from the poet and thereby steals from the poet the ideal with which by rights the poet would identify himself: "Me from myself thy cruel eye hath taken,/ And my next self thou harder hast engrossed" (133). This cuckoldry story, however, is only a narrative account of the poet's more general experience of a divisive lust, a dramatic acting out of the way, as the narrative develops, the poet moves, as I will want to characterize it, from the unity of *folie à deux* to the duality of *ménage à trois*. For in committing his heart to the "unkind" lady the poet already identifies himself, not with that which is a unity, but with that which is duplicitous. Instead of identifying himself with what is like himself, the poet instead identifies himself, not only with what is unlike himself, but with what is unlike itself—"By self-example mayst thou be denied" (142). As a result, but as a highly paradoxical result, no longer joined to a sameness which is the same as itself, the poet is joined instead to an irreducible difference, to an essential otherness, whose power consists in the way it thus disrupts the logic and erotics of unified identity and complementary juncture. The poet-lover of the dark lady in this way identifies himself with difference. He identifies himself—but how can this be?—with that which resists, with that which breaks, identification, which is why as lover of the lady the poet experiences a twofold—what Troilus calls a "bi-fold"—desire. To love the lady is to be alienated from affection *by* affection, to be the subject of a heterogeneous desire constituted by its own division, an "unkind" desire double in the poet's self because double in itself. This is why the poet has "Two loves . . . of comfort and despair" (144), because desire *in* itself is equal to "one angel in another's hell" (144).

I argue that the lady acquires this "power" of "insufficiency" (150), which is the heterogeneous power of heterosexual desire, from the language that she speaks and the language she inspires, a double language—whose linguistic nature is defined as being half linguistic and half visual—that, *as* language, speaks against the unified identities of a visual ideal. The duplicitous sexuality of the lady, what the poet calls her "Will" (135, 136) and "common place" (137), embodies, as it were, the voice of such a language, a language *of* desire because a language of linguistic and erotic "lie."

This is why it is important that the very *look* of the lady, because defined as something double, is what renders her excessive to the visionary poetics of a unified ideal. Characteristically, the lady is shown *to be* that which is not what it is, as in a good many sonnets whose theme is that the darkness of the lady is somehow other than at first it appears. Either the lady's foul is really fair—"In the old age black was not counted fair" (127)—or her novel fair is really foul—"For I have sworn thee fair, and thought thee bright,/Who art as black as hell, as dark as night" (147)—but in either case the specular truth of the lady is that she is both fair and foul at once. It is this double darkness of the lady that makes her an *imago* of what cannot be imagined by a poetics based on visionary likeness. As the poet says, "My mistress' eyes are raven black" (127), and this is why, as the poet also says, "My mistress' eyes are nothing like the sun" (130). But if the darkness of the lady is unlike an ideal likeness, if her "eyes are nothing like the sun" which is itself the image of an ideal likeness, then the lady can be likened only to the way comparison has failed, which is why the only fit comparison for the lady is that she is "as rare/As any she belied with false compare" (130). As I try to show when I discuss the so-called anti-Petrarchanism of sonnet 130, the irrational ratio of this formula defines the peculiarity of the lady: logically, as well as grammatically, she is a "she" who is both subject and object of "false compare." However, if this peculiarity is what makes the look of the lady into something beyond comparison, into something beyond the poetics of comparison, so too does it associate this look with a novel poetic *voice*. For the way the lady *looks* is precisely like the "belying" double way that language *speaks*, which is why the lady's raven eyes are such that they will thrust the poet out of the poetics of a simulating vision and into the poetics of a dissimulating speech, making him, as at the end of sonnet 127, not a poet of the "eye," but, instead, a poet of the "tongue": "Yet so they mourn, becoming of their woe,/That every tongue says beauty should look so."

As Ulysses says of wanton Cressida, therefore, "There's language in her eye."[16] But this is the case only insofar as we register, as does the poet in sonnet 127 (which is the first dark lady sonnet) the "mourning" that the lady's verbal eyes will thus put on display—"Yet so they mourn, becoming of their woe"—for it is because they thus are image of the loss of vision that the lady's eyes acquire a significance that gives them their erotic charge. When the poet looks at the lady's raven eyes he sees not only their blackness but also their difference from what, with regard to the fair young man, he calls "that sun, thine eye" (49). It is in this way that the lady, from the very beginning of the sonnets addressed to her, is an image that calls forth what it is not, a signifier of an absence rather than a signifier of itself. To look at the lady is thus for the poet to see the difference *between* the fair and foul, a difference that writes itself out temporally in sonnet 127 as the difference *between* the poet's deictic *now* and *then*, the difference between, on the one hand, a present in which "black" is "now" the "name" of "beauty," and, on the other, an "old age" as well as an old poetics, in which "black was not counted fair." In this way the visual present of the dark lady sonnets is experienced as the aftermath of an ideal past, and this because "now is black beauty's successive heir." From the very beginning, therefore, what the poet sees in the lady's eyes is thus the true-false "name" of "beauty," and for this very reason the very present and the very presence of the lady, exemplified by the "mourning" language in her eye, effectively will situate the poetics of ideal visionary presence in a retrospective past, marking it as something which exists "now" only as an imaginary ideal *after which* the poet lusts.

This is the complicated, yet effective, consequence that derives throughout the dark lady sonnets from the thematic compact of a "perjur'd eye." Representation carries with it its regretting difference from that which it presents, provoking a desire for that which, as representation, it necessarily absents. Looking at the lady, the poet therefore discovers the loss of a visual ideal, but at the same time this inspires a guilty desire to recover what is lost. As erotic object the lady thus determines an erotic project, for her very presence will elicit a desire that her very presence at the same time will frustrate. With regard to a traditional account of desire two points are here relevant. First, this Shakespearean desire no longer originates in a source outside the self. Insofar as the lady, with her "false-speaking tongue" (138), is presented as herself the figure of such speech, the poet's desire is now determined as an effect occasioned by the language that *he* speaks: "On both sides thus is simple truth suppress'd" (138). That is to say, from the first moment that the poet becomes a poet of the word rather than a poet of the *imago*, when he passes, as I will put it, from a poetics of *ut pictura poesis* to a poetics of *ut poesis poesis*, his desire is imposed on him, not by God or by Nature, but by poetry itself, for every word the poet speaks effectively presents to him the loss of his ideal. Second, this novelly verbal desire, a desire now *of* language, not only motivates itself but also is determined as its own regret. Such desire has the power to generate its own desire, for lust is always lusting after the love that lust has lost, in accord with a structure of continuous erotic nostalgia whose yearning is continually refeeding itself *because* "consum'd with that which it was nourish'd by" (73). As a result, however, because it motivates itself, so too does such desire characteristically accuse itself, assuming responsibility for the loss of its ideal. In the end, therefore, in an unprecedented way, desire is *motivated* by the economy of its own regret, as "th' expense of spirit in a waste of shame" (129).

I emphasize here the twofold nature of this Shakespearean desire not because this is the only theme of Shakespeare's sonnets but because this helps to explain the novel pathos of their poet's self, the way, that is, Shakespeare's sonnets give off a powerful and, in the tradition of the Renaissance sonnet, a genuinely new effect of subjectivity. In contrast to the deictic and epideictic first-person "I" of the traditional sonnet, the speaking eye of a visionary poetics, the poet of Shakespeare's sonnets is instead the subject of a "perjur'd eye," a poet who, because he speaks, is poised between a visionary and a verbal self.[17] In the traditional sonnet the poet presupposes or anticipates the correspondence, ultimately the identification, of his ego and his ego ideal: he is therefore a full self, incipiently or virtually present to himself by virtue of the admiration instantiated by his visionary speech. In profound contrast, Shakespeare's sonnets instead record the difference between their vision and their speech, and they therefore situate their poet in between his ego and his ego ideal. In this way the language that the poet of Shakespeare's sonnets speaks manages to place the poet's image of identification, his ideal of identification, in an imaginary past, making both image and ideal into something retrospective. Accordingly, because the poet identifies himself with this retrospective identity, both a space and a time will open up *within* the poet for subjective introspection. It is not too much to say, therefore, that the subject of Shakespeare's sonnets experiences himself *as* his difference from himself. His identity is an identity of ruptured identification, a broken identity that carves out in the poet's self a syncopated hollowness that accounts for the deep personal interiority of the sonnets' poetic persona. This "hole" within the "whole" of the poet—and also without (see the discussion of sonnet 134)—circumscribed by the heartbreak of a "perjur'd eye" (a phrase that we can think of, therefore, as a "Shakespeareme," i.e., the smallest minimal unit of Shakespearean self) accounts for the personal interiority that, as many critics have remarked, is the most conspicuous and distinctive feature of Shakespeare's sonneteering mode. Again, I want to show that the qualitative phenomenology, the "feel," spatial and temporal, of this interior and psychologized "withinness," is specifically determined by, and gains its literary force from, the way it materially redoubles, with a difference, master images of sameness that traditionally objectify the poetics of the poetry of praise. Assimilating such images to their poetic person, Shakespeare's sonnets in this way manage to give off the subjectivity effect required by a postidealist literariness.

It is for all these reasons that I understand Shakespeare's sonnets to represent a highly significant moment in the history of poetic subjectivity. In these sonnets we see what happens to poetic person when true vision is captured by false language. To use another general formula, in Shakespeare's sonnets we see how a novel literary self is precipitated when the deictic and epideictic "I" and "eye" of a traditional poetics find themselves at odds with their poet's "Will." To refer to this "Will" is, of course, to refer to what is Shakespeare's special pun, a gift that language gives to him and that, for this reason, is idiosyncratic to himself. Nevertheless, in the several sonnets that play upon the propriety of his proper name Shakespeare manages, I argue, to write a general end to a literary epoch that from its beginning is thoroughly dominated by the deictic self-promotion of an epideictic subject. With his puns on "Will" Shakespeare shows, first, how a literary tradition, unfolding itself through a Cratylitic idealism that leads from "Beatrice" through "Laura" to "Stella," exhausts a poetics centered on the visionary fullness of subject and object; second, when he introduces this nominal subject, the subject of a name, Shakespeare shows how this tired tradition will subsequently be revived when it turns into a poetics centered instead on the resonant hollowness of a fractured verbal self. It is not only the tradition of the sonnet that is thus rewritten, for Shakespeare's "Will" occasions a revision of any pietistic literature that grounds its first person in a visionary ideal. In Langland's *Piers Plowman*, for example, "Will" is tutored by "Ymagynatif," and turned thereby to the salvation of God.[18] In Shakespeare's sonnets, however, it would be truer to say that "Will" subverts imagination, thereby inverting a familiar faculty psychology which is itself the allegorical image of a transcendent self.

For Shakespearean "Will," as I argue in chapter 5, is the name of a linguistic desire, the name of a desire *of* language, which is at once more personal and more painful than it is structurally possible for any visionary poetics of ideal (and therefore desireless) desire even to imagine: "Make but my name thy love, and love that still,/And then thou lovest me, for my name is *Will*" (136), As *double* double entendre "Will" denominates both the "prick" (sonnet 20) which is the mark of homogeneous sameness as well as the "cut" (Elizabethan slang for "cunt") which is the mark of heterogeneous difference, joining these together in the verbal intercourse of heterosexual "whole" and "hole," as happens, for example, in the cuckoldry conceit of sonnet 134, where the poet plays upon the difference thus occasioned by the presence or the absence of a double-U and double you: "He pays the whole, and yet am I not free".[19] It is this "Will," a name that dares to speak its love, that the poet becomes when he becomes his name: a subjectivity thus puffed up with the "(w)hole" in "(w)hole"; a subjectivity materially imagined, for reasons that I will develop later, as the four-term copulation of the "pricked prick" and the "cut cunt." So too, in contrast to the self-referring deictics of ideal epideixis, whose pointing elsewhere always points back to the self, whose deictics always identify their poet's first and second persons, Shakespearean "Will" denominates instead a split and slippage *in* the poet that differentiates his "I" and "you." "Will" in this *effective* fashion designates the way the poet's visual being (the ideal correspondence of "I" and "you," of poetic ego and ego ideal) is constitutively disrupted, spatially and temporally, by the verbal meaning that identifies poetic self (the constant, personal reference of a proper name): "Swear to thy blind soul that I was thy *Will*" (136). I argue that when the poet in this way becomes his "Will" he becomes *to* himself an absent third person whose nowhere is what stands between, as missing connection, his otherwise identical first and second person. More generally, I argue that in the elaborate, which is to say in the recognizably *over*-elaborate, sonnets devoted to "Will" Shakespeare manages not only to characterize the verbal density and texture—what I call the "languageness" of language—that distinguishes all his sonnets and gives them their peculiar literary quality, but, also, that he thereby takes up the specific consequences for poetic subjectivity that such linguistic self-consciousness, such a passage of person *into* language, necessarily entails within the context of traditional literariness.

That Shakespeare was sensitive to such "languageness" goes, perhaps, without saying. But the point is that in the "Will" sonnets Shakespeare does not let this go without saying. Quite the contrary, he instead gives a *personal* name to this linguistic palpability, as though in this way to specify its personal effect. This emphasized subjective register is what obliges us to think of "Will" as Shakespeare's name for the *way* his sonneteering poetic person works, and this is why it is important to investigate the various thematic and figurative ways in which "Will" presents and imports into the person of the poet the specific materiality of absence that regularly defines what is *in* a Shakespearean name. For in Shakespeare's sonnets "Will" is designated as the proper name of the person of the poet, as the generic name of poetic person. For this reason, it becomes possible to understand through "Will's" inflection how the literariness that Shakespeare associates with his poetic name (i.e., the rhetoricity of the paradox of praise), coupled with the logical paradox that Shakespeare also associates with naming (i.e., the class of all classes that do not classify themselves, the universal quantifier that quantifies itself as lack: "Among a number one is reckon'd none," 136) together determine the corresponding psychological paradox that makes the "willful" and "will-filled" poet—"*Will* will fulfill the treasure of thy love" (136)—into a One that is not one: "Think all but one, and me in that one *Will*" (135).

With regard to a larger literary tradition, it is worth recalling in this connection that it is Oscar Wilde who makes a strong and final issue out of the thematic tension in the sonnets that obtains between a verbally hollow and a visually "hallowed" *name* (108). It was Wilde who, picking up an old conjecture, reads between the sonnets' lines and names the poet's catamite "Willy Hughes," doing this in order to draw out the important pun on "you's" and "hues" (also "use" and "views"), a pun that specifies both the form and content that in Shakespeare's sonnet sequence govern the triangular quarrel between visual deictic and verbal name. Wilde's *The Portrait of Mr. W. H.* is the only genuinely literary criticism that Shakespeare's sonnets have ever received, and part of the reason for this circumstance is that, like Shakespeare's sonnets, it too is caught up in the literary problematic that derives from the effort to imagine a visible language, a language in which there would be no difference between the *imago* of presentation (the "Portrait") and the *sign* of representation ("W. H.")—as though it were possible to paint a picture of language that would not be an emblem of the limits of vision. This is not only epigrammatically the case in the novella's title; so too is it the controlling logic of a story that narrates the progress from an initially false picture to a concluding false letter. We see much the same in *The Picture of Dorian Gray*. So too, in the same Shakespearean fashion, Wilde takes up in *The Importance of Being Earnest* the paradoxical relationship of a person to his proper name, showing the way the meaning or "import" of a personal name is acquired at the cost of any univocal idealization of personal "Being." It would be fair to say that by developing this theme in *The Importance of Being Earnest* as straightforward farce Wilde puts an end to a tradition of theatrical subjectivity that begins, at least in the tradition of English drama, with Shakespeare's *The Comedy of Errors*—a tradition that is by no means restricted to farce, though it begins and ends as such.[20] All this is important, however, not because it establishes Wilde's "Jack-Earnest" as the only authentic revenant of Shakespearean "Will," but, instead, because it evidences the historical continuity of Shakespeare's sonneteering self, a self whose paradoxical construction *through* language remains in this way a thematic constant from the popular literature of the late Renaissance through to what we can plausibly think of as the end of a literature based on the effect of the personal. That is to say, Wilde's evacuating clarification of Shakespearean characterology, his "Bunburying" of Shakespearean person, supports my argument that with their "Will" Shakespeare's sonnets inaugurate and give a name to the modernist literary self, thereby specifying for the future what will be the poetic psychology of the subject of representation.

All this refers, however, only to what might be called the thematics of the poet's represented persona—his divided and dividing desire, his sense of broken internal space and also his sense of broken time. Though such psychologistic thematics are important, they could not by themselves establish the literary authority of Shakespeare's sonneteering self. Very obviously, the subjective effect of Shakespeare's sonnets depends quite as much upon the sonnets' formal poetic procedures, which determine tone and mood, as it does upon the sonnets' characterizations of poetic self. For this reason, for the sake of my argument regarding Shakespearean subjectivity, it is also necessary to understand how Shakespeare's sonnets express and inflect poetic voice. This is especially important given the fact that it is often a theme of these sonnets that speech says more "than niggard truth would willingly impart" (72).

The most general literary category that I use to characterize the poetic or rhetorical mode of Shakespeare's sonnets is the paradox of praise, i.e., the mock encomium, traditionally a comic mode that offers ironic praise to an object that by orthodox propriety should instead receive invective. The category is an appropriate one for several reasons, but not because all of Shakespeare's sonnets are themselves examples of the paradox of praise (though some in fact are such, especially those that develop the virtues of the lady's vices, which is why, as I explain later, I prefer to call the dark lady sequence para-Petrarchan rather than anti-Petrarchan). Rather, I employ the category because Shakespeare's sonnets are written as though by a poet who has already essayed the paradox of praise, who has tried it out in misplaced earnest, and who now draws from this appropriate and consequent conclusions: "For I have sworn thee fair, and thought thee bright,/Who art as black as hell, as dark as night" (147).

I discuss in the text the complicated relationship of Shakespeare's sonnets to the paradox of praise. As preparation for that discussion, however, it is good to have a relatively simple example at hand. Accordingly, I take the following from Marston's *The Dutch Courtesan*; this is Freevill's panegyric on prostitution, his response to Malheureux' invective of lust:

> Alas, good creatures, what would you have them do? Would you have them get their living by the curse of man, the sweat of their brows? So they do. Every man must follow his trade, and every woman her occupation. A poor, decayed mechanical man's wife, her husband is laid up; may not she lawfully be laid down when her husband's only rising is by his wife's falling? A captain's wife wants means, her commander lies in open field abroad; may not she lie in civil arms at home? A waiting gentlewoman that had wont to take say to her lady miscarries or so; the court misfortune throws her down; may not the city courtesy take her up? Do you know no alderman would pity such a woman's case? Why, is charity grown a sin? Or relieving the poor and impotent an offense? You will say beasts take no money for their fleshly entertainment. True, because they are beasts, therefore beastly; only men give to loose because they are men, therefore manly; and, indeed wherein should they bestow their money better? In land, the title may be cracked; in houses, they may be burnt; in apparel, 'twill wear; in wine, alas for pity, our throat is but short. But employ your money upon women, and, a thousand to nothing, some one of them will bestow that on you which shall stick by you as long as you live. They are no ingrateful persons; they will give *quid* for *quo*. Do ye protest, they'll swear; do you rise, they'll fall; do you fall, they'll rise; do you give them the French crown, they'll give you the French—O *justus, justa, justum!* They sell their bodies; do not better persons sell their souls? Nay, since all things have been sold—honor, justice, faith, nay, even God Himself—[21]

I cite this at such length because it is important to have a feel for the rhetorical excess that is characteristic of praise paradox, the way it delights in its own copiousness, adding example to example, piling one outlandish illustration on top of another, so as thus to show off its own rhetorical ingenuity. This rhetorical extravagance, the stress on its own verbal facility, is the most prominent feature of the mode, and it is this excess, registered as such, that distinguishes praise paradox from the equally rhetoricized, in many ways equally stylized, and yet nevertheless more straightforward praise it mocks. I have already referred to the self-referring *ostentatio* of epideictic rhetoric, oratory that calls attention to itself, that puts its rhetoricity on display. In the rhetorically self-conscious tradition of sonneteering praise, this will be reflected in the enthusiasm for Petrarchist artifice, the striking oxymorons, the catachretic imagery, the ornamental diction, the formal and the complicated syntax with which radical conceits are developed through and to their bold conclusions. For all its staginess, however, for all the often comic self-regard implicitly informing such rhetoric, the poetry of praise, especially of sonneteering praise, for the most part idealistically commits itself to its rhetorical posturings, collating speaker with speech in such a way that the poet's rhetoricity, however flamboyant, is nevertheless consistent with the poet's ideal image of himself. Even when it is elaborately artificial, the rhetoricity of the poetry of praise is understood authentically to express poetic intention, to do so in a straightforward way, for, finally, its laudation is understood to define its poet's purpose. In contrast, the paradox of praise deliberately distances itself from the rhetoricity to which it draws attention, belying itself by means of a hyperrhetoricity whose ironic intention is most fully realized when understood to mean something other than what it seems to say. This is the oddity of paradoxical intention. The speaker of such a mock encomium appears to be at one remove from his laudation, as though his speech were somehow independent of his speaking, or were being presented to his audience as a kind of demonstration of the fact that speaking well is not the same as speaking true. Like praise, therefore, the paradox of praise is a speech for us to consider and to observe rather than to be persuaded by; unlike praise, however, the paradox of praise shows off a rhetoricity that speaks against itself.

Such ironic, comic speech will therefore add an extra wrinkle to the traditionally self-conscious rhetoricity of epideictic speech. In the mode of Petrarchist admiration, for example, a speaker, turning a phrase, might very well tell us how he "gives to lose," and then draw out from this *contentio* any number of oxymoronic arguments that show the ways such losing gifts might make a gain of loss. In Freevill's paradoxical declamation, in contrast, "men give to loose," and with the sexy pun thus added to *contentio* the balanced phrase is somehow thrown off balance, pointing up in this belying way the very rhetoricity on which the wit of the phrase depends, as though such rhetoricity were itself the answer to the rhetorical question "Why, is charity grown a sin?" Much the same might be said of all Freevill's rhetorical flourishes, the repetition of words to different semantic and syntactic purpose (*commutatio, refractio, heratio*), the redeployment of sententia, the archly counterbalanced, isocolonic sentence structure—all of which show off a language whose pleasure seems to be to be at odds with itself, a language that plays upon its own figurality and on its own formal resources in so elaborate a way as to render relatively unimportant the truth of what it speaks about. The lady's husband is "laid up" and so the lady can be "laid down," and this because "her husband's only rising is by his wife's falling." The captain "lies in open field abroad," and therefore the captain's wife can "lie in civil arms at home."

To respond to this kind of verbal repetition, a device or trope that is technically called *copulatio,* it is necessary to hear the several "lies" in "lay" and the "lays" in "lie," and to recognize the extralinguistic correspondence thus developed as a fact occasioned more by language than by that which language here refers to. It is to hear, as a kind of independent force, language itself, the "languageness" of language, as it hovers above and in some sense determines the way its speaker speaks. Related to this is the typically vivacious energy of the mock encomium, the verveful, almost delirious forward-thrusting movement of the *amplificatio,* the rapidity with which clauses are balanced off against each other, the speaker's impulsive rush from topic to topic, the rhetorical questions that are posed only so as to be answered with yet more rhetorical questions (*antipophora, rogatio*), the free-associating logic—all of which produces the sense of a discourse given over to its own discursivity, a discourse that is at once formally controlled, a set and polished rhetorical performance, at the same time as it seems to bristle with a kind of immediate rhetorical self-awareness and linguistic spontaneity, as though its speaker were genuinely interrupting himself with tropes suggested to him by his own rhetorical bravura, a speech, in this sense, that takes on a life of its own.

Such exercises, and they are very common in Elizabethan and Jacobean drama, presuppose a very sophisticated rhetorical consciousness in their audience, for the pleasure they offer is not simply the result of their comic logic—"because they are beasts, therefore beastly," "because they are men, therefore manly." Rather, the wit of such paradoxical rhetorical performances derives from the way their speaker plays with language, forcing upon his audience the realization that it is the speaker's single intention to employ all the standard, well-known arts of language so as not to mean the things he seems to say. In such speeches a univocal satiric purpose is expressed by a deliberately equivocal locution whose irony emerges when the equivocation is maximally implausible and captious yet minimally arbitrary and capricious, when the irony, that is to say, is

straightforwardly and palpably oblique. It is because their paradoxical effect depends upon the way they thus maintain a careful balance of propositions which seem simultaneously logical and illogical that it often happens that these mock encomia suddenly seem to
take themselves very seriously indeed, as though the speaker,
caught up in his speech, or caught up by it, no longer playing upon
language, but, rather, being played upon by it, were suddenly persuaded by the force of his sophistic argument, or as though his
equivocation had suddenly struck him as something univocally
plausible. Not infrequently, therefore, the irony of paradox will turn
into a surprised earnestness, its initially satiric intention turning bitter, as happens here in Freevill's declamation, where the good-hu-
mored swipe at the proverbially lecherous alderman leads to the
more urgently repulsed and heartfelt tonalities of "since all things
have been sold—honor, justice, faith, nay, even God Himself."

The variability, the brittle instability, of paradoxical intention
points up the way the formal properties of the mode render certain
themes or topics convenient to it. In principle, of course, praise paradox gives high praise to things that are low. Thus there are the famous examples from antiquity, orations in praise of hair, lice, fleas,
and the like, all of which stand as precursors to such Renaissance
examples as, say, Harington's praise of privies or Nashe's praise of
the red herring. In such cases the wit derives from the way the praise
of unworthy things is implicitly compared to the praise of worthy
things, or, rather, since comparison is the primary trope of praise,
the way a set of paradoxically amplifying comparisons is implicitly
compared to the more familiar comparative procedures of laudatory
amplification. In principle, therefore, paradoxical praise, to be
noted as such, must noticeably allude, even if only indirectly, to
straightforward praise, citing this as the model which it mocks. In
practice, however, paradoxical citation of the orthodox turns out
rather regularly to be far more explicit than it is implicit, for the most
expedient way to elevate the low ironically is comically to compare it
to the high, explicitly exchanging the low term for the high term by
means of a substitution that reworks familiar conceits to novel effect. For this reason, while praise paradox can in principle select for
development any topic whatsoever, it tends to feature or to fasten
upon topics or themes that can be brought into effective contrast
with official ideals. A selection procedure, governed by the principle
of antithesis, proposes folly as appropriate complement to wisdom,

blindness to sight, poverty to riches, lust to love, for these are topics that, because they are the opposite of ideals, most fully lend themselves to paradoxical treatment.

The point is an obvious one, but it illustrates the fact that Freevill's "Will" is not so free in its concerns as might appear. Paradoxical praise, as a mode that compares itself to straightforward praise, and as a mode whose rhetoricity tropes comparison, turns its attention, by a kind of necessary logic, to issues and themes whose development establishes, stipulates, even exaggerates, the black and white, positive and negative polarities organizing strong cultural values. It does this, however, in a way that leads it also to foreground similarities subtending these cultural extremes. Paradoxical praise, therefore, is a comic mode whose rhetorical form exigently leads it to eke out and to amplify ambivalences attaching to highly charged cultural antitheses, and this ambivalence, however comic its development, is capable of acquiring at any moment a force of its own, a force that threatens to put the proper hierarchy of official contrasts and polarities—positive v. negative, high v. low—into question. This is what happens, to some extent, in *The Dutch Courtesan*, whose *argumentum* Marston summarizes as follows: "The difference betwixt the love of a courtesan and a wife is the full scope of the play."[22] In one sense, no other rhetorical mode is more suited than praise paradox for pointing up such erotic "difference," for praise paradox works by contrasting perverse and ideal admiration. Thus it is perfectly fitting that whereas the good "wife" to which the argument refers—her name is "Beatrice"—enters the play reading aloud from the idealizing love sonnet Freevill has written to her, the courtesan instead receives Freevill's paradoxical praise of lust. In another sense, however, no other rhetorical mode is ultimately more inimical to the maintenance of such "difference," for the paradox of praise works to subvert just those contrasts and oppositions to which it draws attention—and indeed, the question raised by Freevill's paradox (the play begins with the passage I have quoted, so that its paradox colors all that succeeds it) is how to reconcile Freevill's subsequent sonneteering praise of Beatrice—"Purest lips, soft banks of blisses,/Self alone, deserving kisses"—with the totalizing disgust of "Nay, since all things have been sold . . ."[23]

I mention this not because I want to argue that *The Dutch Courtesan* has as its misogynist purpose or effect the radical subversion of either the poetics or the thematics of Petrarchist admiration. It does not.[24] What is important, however, is that we notice the way

Freevill's paradox acquires, almost in spite of itself, a frenetic seriousness or urgency which is excessive to its initial comic purpose. This energy does not really derive from Freevill's arguments, from the logical reasoning he advances, as though the speaker, commissioned to argue *in utramque partem*, had suddenly fallen prey to *parti pris*. Rather, as I have suggested, the energy of Freevill's speech derives from the way his language seems itself to ape straightforward admiration, to mime it, however, in a way that leaves us genuinely uncertain, at least for a moment, as to whether we should take its irony for real. This is the ultimate peculiarity of praise paradox: only the excessive animation of its language distinguishes it from the praise it mocks, so that the more powerful such paradoxical language the more such language will belie itself—to a point, however, where this derisive imitation of the ideal becomes itself a kind of truth. Hence the subversive power that praise paradox always possesses with regard to the orthodox praise to which it holds itself up as mirror. Speaking ideally, there is supposed to be a correspondence in praise rhetoric between laudatory signifier and laudatory signified. So too, therefore, in Freevill's paradox, but in a way that undercuts this ideal, as when we hear his language lie in the same way that the lady "lies." Similarly, in deference to a universalizing ideality, the themes and figures of praise will characteristically draw out an ideal complementarity between the high and low. So too, therefore, does Freevill's paradox of praise, but more radically and invidiously so, as when it yokes "laid up" to "laid down," or when the gentlewoman thrown down by court misfortune is taken up by city courtesy, or when, with burlesque gesture, Freevill assures us: "Do you rise, they'll fall; do you fall, they'll rise."

I will argue that such parodic imitations of ideal imitation, such mimic versions of linguistic correspondence, lead Shakespeare in his sonnets to what I call a limit case of Cratylism, to a second, ironic degree of the sympathetic relation of speaking to bespoken, whereby language, stressing itself *as* language, truly demonstrates, effectively instantiates, rather than merely asserts, the fact that it is false. For now it is enough to realize that, though the wit of Freevill's paradox is unambiguously transparent, the difference between what is serious and what is parodic depends here on our registering the hyperrhetoricity with which language makes a mockery of ideal rhetorical forms and themes. It is language itself, the "languageness" of language, that distinguishes praise from paradox, at the cost, however, of linguistic idealization. It is language itself, heard as such and added on to praise, that subtracts from praise its approbation, as when the merest bit of Latin makes a syphilitic tit-for-tat out of an otherwise laudably reciprocal "*quid* for *quo.*" In the same way, everything that we might mean by "just" is translated, and thereby reduced, by Freevill's paradox into something merely nominal, into "words, words, words," or into a licentious and infectious "French," when broken down into merely verbal grammatical cases: "*justus, justa, justum*" (this paradigm might very well be the shortest and the most efficient epideictic paradox in the history of rhetoric, if we recall that the Greek word for "justice," *diké,* stems from the same Indo-European root as does "deixis"—or, for that matter, as does "para-digm"—*deig,* "to show." In this sense, "paradigm" is always "paradox").

For Marston, such epideictic paradox is an appropriate comic device with which to establish the tone and mood of a play that in its prologue he himself calls "slight." *Turpe est difficiles habere nugas* is the epigram from Martial that Marston takes as epigraph for his comedy, a tag that also epitomizes the traditional response to praise paradox, and one whose opprobrium Marston seems quite content to accept, at least with regard to the shame that comes from having accomplished the particular trifle which is *The Dutch Courtesan.*[25] The poet of Shakespeare's sonnets, however, seems to take both the turpitude and the trifling nonsense of praise paradox in a far more serious way, being deeply troubled by a "Muse" that "spend'st . . . thy fury on some worthless song./Dark'ning the power to lend base subjects light" (100). In such thematic ways the paradox of praise will register itself in Shakespeare's sonnets as something neither trivial nor comic, just as traditional topoi of the paradox of praise will cease to be in Shakespeare's sonnets a laughing matter (e.g., the association of female speech with female sexuality, which is a familiar subject for mock encomia in Renaissance literature from *The Wife of Bath* to Jonson's *Epicoene,* it being relatively easy to see in the linguistic excess of the one the operative logic of the erotic excess of the other).

The question arises, therefore, as to how and why a literary mode that is traditionally marginal and unimportant comes to acquire in Shakespeare's sonnets such unprecedented urgency and force, as though the paradoxing of praise were now suddenly something consequential. Sketching out the answer developed in the text, we can say in a preliminary and oversimple way that, in response to a larger failure of visionary poetics, the languageness of language traditionally displayed in the paradox of praise comes in Shakespeare's sonnets to impose itself on the more sober literariness of the sonnet, and that it does this in so powerful a way as to erase the heretofore secure

difference between praise and its subversive simulation. As a consequence, in Shakespeare's sonnets the self-belying palpability of language works to transform or to translate the most straightforward
instances of praise into their own parodic instrument. The result is
neither praise nor paradox, but, instead, a novel and peculiar kind of
lyric literariness that stands unhappily between the two. I refer here
more to tone than to theme. It is possible to identify many conceits in
Shakespeare's sonnets—some of these nothing but traditional—that
emphasize the way a self-remarking language truly speaks, despite
itself, against itself, as in the various Liar's paradoxes that the sonnets
like to flirt with, e.g., "Those lines that I before have writ do lie,/Even
those that said I could not love you dearer" (115). Such themes acquire
their force, however, not from what they say but from the particular
way that they say it, from the way Shakespeare's sonnets regularly
employ a specific rhetoricity that resists the most idealizing assumptions of the poetics and the poetry of praise.

For if paradox is the mocking double of praise, then so too will its
rhetoric or its rhetoricity trope the trope of praise, doubling it so as to
divide it. The identificatory comparisons through which epideictic
rhetoric "sees the same" and develops its amplifying logic of dual
unity—the epideictic correspondence of "I" with "thou" and "thee"
with "me:" "thou mine, I thine" (108)—will find themselves expressed
by and exampled by a mode whose rhetorical duplications are designed to break such ideal dual unity in half. Rhetoric gives many
names to this troping of trope—*syneciosis, antimetabole, metathesis, con-
trapostum, conjunctio, commistio, chiasmus*—all of which refer to some
way that language manages noticeably to redouble with a difference
the complementary similarities of a figurality based on likeness. The
term I will use, however, because it seems most precisely to characterize Shakespeare's practice in the sonnets, is the "cross-coupler,"
which is Puttenham's playful translation of *syneciosis,* and which Puttenham defines thus:

> Ye have another figure which me thinkes may well be called (not much
> sweruing from his originall in sence) the *Crosse-couple,* because it takes
> me two contrary words, and tieth them as it were in a paire of couples,
> and so makes them agree like good fellowes, as I saw once in Fraunce a
> wolfe couple with a mastiffe, and a fox with a hounde.[26]

I discuss cross-coupling in the text: the way its miscegenating
mixture of figurative "kinds" is convenient to the paradox of praise,
the way it makes for a rhetoric that remarks itself with its own surplus repetition, the way it lends itself first to Petrarchan and then to

para-Petrarchan complaint, the way it informs the psychology of Shakespeare's sonneteering poetic self. Again, however, it is good to have an example before us that does not come from the sonnets, and I take as a relevant illustration Tarquin's indecision at the moment he decides upon his rape.

> Away he steals with open list'ning ear,
> Full of foul hope, and full of fond mistrust;
> Both which, as servitors to the unjust,
> So cross him with their opposite persuasion,
> That now he vows a league, and now invasion.
>
> (*RL:* 283 –87)

The interest of the example derives from the way Shakespeare makes a certain kind of figurality itself the figure of subjective motivation. We recognize, presumably—and if we do not, the narrator makes the point explicit—that Tarquin is here "crossed" between two coupled oxymorons. The "foul hope" of his lust is poised off against the moral reservation of his "fond mistrust" in a conjunction that reverses the normal connotations of all four terms. As a result, because the positives become negatives and the negatives become positives, Tarquin is left suspended between a foul fondness and a hopeful mistrust, a rhetorical indeterminacy that serves, at least initially, to illustrate his hesitation between a peaceful "league" and an aggressive "invasion." This is a general formal device of *The Rape of Lucrece,* characteristic of the characters' diction as well as the narrator's, as, for example, when Lucrece defensively appeals to Tarquin's better nature and tells him not to let a tiny spot of lust "stain the ocean of thy blood./If all these petty ills shall change thy good,/Thy sea within a puddle's womb is hearsed,/And not the puddle in thy sea dispersed" (655 –58), a conceit that asks us to imagine the inside on the outside and the outside on the inside, as though the infinitely small were larger than the infinitely large and the "boundless flood" containable "within a puddle's womb"—a conceit whose titillating resonance and contours seem uniquely ill-designed to accomplish Lucrece's chastening, prophylactic rhetorical purpose.[27]

In general this kind of invaginating, inside-out rhetorical device is prominently featured in both of Shakespeare's two long narrative poems, *Venus and Adonis* and *The Rape of Lucrece*—two poems which are complementary in that the former, with the example of hunter-Adonis, illustrates the male's desire for violence, whereas the latter, which is also the later, illustrates, with the example of Tarquin, the violence of male desire (at stake in both is the coupling of Mars and

Venus). So too, both poems (which are contemporary with the sonnets) are conceived and structured as dramatized arguments *in
utramque partem*—between love and lust, between honor and desire—but with the opposition between the two arguments somehow more complicated than at first appears. Recognizing this, it
seems reasonable to say that Shakespeare tries to energize his experimental efforts at erotic *epyllion* by seeing what happens when
antithetical arguments are cross-coupled with each other—an experiment he conducts, of course, more subtly and with more consequence in the plays.[28] More interesting, however, is the way, even in
these relatively early efforts, the rhetorical form of cross-coupling,
which is a form that seems especially congenial to Shakespeare's
imagination, is intuitively and powerfully assimilated by Shakespeare to the stuff or to the matter, as well as to the formal manner,
of a specific kind of desire. We can see this if we follow out the example of Tarquin's indecisive lust.

The poem does not give us a graphic description of Tarquin's rape
of Lucrece, at least not of the actual "invasion," this being passed over
by the poem in a single discreet stanza (680 – 86). Instead, beginning
where the lines on "foul hope" and "fond mistrust" end, the poem
projects the details of the rape onto a description of Tarquin's progress
towards Lucrece's bedroom, his movement through the passageways
of her castle to her "chamber door" (337) being developed as a kind of
pornographic *effictio*. In the course of this movement—it is fair to say,
in the intercourse of this movement—three obstacles bar Tarquin's
progress, three hindrances stand "between her chamber and his will"
(302). First, there are a series of locked doors, "each one by him enforc'd retires his ward" (303). Then, "as each unwilling portal yields
him way" (309), "the wind wars with his torch to make him stay" (311).
Finally, there is "Lucretia's glove, wherein her needle sticks" (317),
which, when Tarquin picks it up, "the needle his finger pricks" (319).
All three of these things, the doors, the wind, the glove, slow Tarquin
down, as though the material world conspired to retard the rape. All
three, however, are at the same time, and very obviously so, precisely
rendered images *of* the rape, its physical objectification: the doors
whose locks are "enforc'd" and which "unwilling" "yields him way";
the wind, which "through little vents and crannies of the place" (310)
"wars with his torch . . . And blows the smoke of it into his face"
(311–12); the fetishistic glove "wherein her needle sticks." Moreover,
not only is each one of these things, in the resistance that it offers, an
image of the rape that it repulses, but so too does each one of these
bars to Tarquin's desire manage also to spur the rapist on. The "his" of

"retires his ward" refers both to Tarquin and the door. The wind that blows out Tarquin's torch also inspires "his hot heart, which fond desire doth scorch,/[to puff] forth another wind that fires the torch" (314–15). So too with the clitoral "prick" of the glove that "pricks" the rapist on: "'This glove to wanton tricks/Is not inur'd'" (320–21).

All this does not go by unnoticed, either by the narrator or by Tarquin. With regard to the hindrances to Tarquin's desire, the narrator observes: "He in the worst sense consters their denial:/The doors, the wind, the glove that did delay him,/He takes for accidental things of trial;/Or as those bars which stop the hourly dial,/Who with a ling'ring stay his course doth let,/Till every minute pays the hour his debt" (324–29). The narrator's image is of a clock whose hour hand, connected to a spring mechanism, builds up potential energy when its movement is restrained by protuberant minute markers. At successive intervals the hour hand bursts past each momentary "let" in an explosive jerky movement that measures time and brings the marker of the hours to its next repulsing and propulsing impediment. It is an image of inviting resistance, of an impetus that is derived from its frustration, and as such illustrates not only the way "the doors, the wind, the glove that did delay him" promote what they postpone, but also illustrates the rape itself, the way, that is, that Tarquin "consters" Lucrece's "denial."

It is, perhaps, an obvious point, for Tarquin draws the same moral for himself, immediately repeating—indeed, sharing—the narrator's image of the temporal "let":

> "So, so," quoth he, "these lets attend the time,
> Like little frosts that sometime threat the spring,
> To add a more rejoicing to the prime,
> And give the sneaped birds more cause to sing."
> (330–33)

However, even if the erotic psychology thus enunciated is proverbial, and its sententious phrasing makes it seem as though it is, it is important to notice that the erotic psychology of the "let," as well as the material phenomenology of the doors, the wind, and the glove, unpacks the cross-coupling formal rhetorical logic of "foul hope" and "fond mistrust." That is to say, when Tarquin was indeterminately suspended between oxymorons, when he was "crossed" by "their opposite persuasion," he was already, *even* in his indeterminacy, embarked upon his rape. This is important because it shows us that the cross-coupler, as Shakespeare employs it, is not a neutral

trope; it is instead the trope of a specific desire whose hindrance is
what gives it leave to go. Specifically, it is the tropological structure
and expression of an eros whose *contrapposto* energy simulates the
action of a rape—and of a rape, moreover, that, rendered genially
pastoral by the "little frosts that sometime threat the spring,/To add
a more rejoicing to the prime" offers itself as general model for the
motivating and the consummating *friction* of heterosexual desire per
se. This, at any rate, seems to be both the erotic and the rhetorical
logic of *The Rape of Lucrece*, a logic of "let" that links Lucrece to Tarquin and that makes Lucrece responsible for her rape by virtue of
the energetic and energizing resistance that she offers to it. Lucrece
herself, that is to say, becomes a "let," because, as Tarquin says, in
response to her cross-coupling entreaties:

> "Have done," quoth he, "my uncontrolled tide
> Turns not, but swells the higher by this let.
> Small lights are soon blown out, huge fires abide,
> And with the wind in greater fury fret."
> (645–48)

Given such a logic, the "sneaped birds" of which Tarquin speaks
are by necessity kinds of Philomels, with no more to sing about than
Lavinia in *Titus Andronicus*. Given such a logic, all women, if they
are desired, are erotic "lets". By the same cross-coupled token, however, neither does Tarquin have great reason to rejoice. With his
rape he "hath won what he would lose again" (688). Like the hour
hand that has lost its momentum, his "hot desire converts to cold
disdain" (691). If Lucrece is image of a wounded woman, so too is
Tarquin image of a wounded man: "A captive victor that hath lost in
gain,/Bearing away the wound that nothing healeth,/The scar that
will despite of cure remain" (730–33).

In more than patent ways, this logic of the "let" is very like the
rhetorical and the erotic logic of Shakespeare's sonnets, with their
"expense of spirit in a waste of shame." So too, this corresponds to
the structure of time in the sonnets, their sense of a temporality that
is *not* successively and homogeneously "like as the waves make towards the pibbled shore" (60). So too this cross-coupling mode, linking a certain kind of language to a certain kind of desire, and then
objectifying this link both in material things and in dramatic psychology, is very like what happens in the plays. Consider, for example, the inside-out language, desire, and glove of *Twelfth Night*:

CLOWN: A sentence is but a chev'ril glove to a good wit. How quickly the wrong side may be turn'd outward!

VIOLA: Nay, that's certain. They that dally nicely with words may quickly make them wanton.

CLOWN: I would therefore my sister had had no name, sir.

VIOLA: Why, man?

CLOWN: Why, sir, her name's a word, and to dally with that word might make my sister wanton.[29]

With regard to my principal concern here, however—the "subject" of Shakespeare's sonnets, the impression of person or persona that is conveyed by Shakespeare's lyric voice—it is the difference between *The Rape of Lucrece* and the sonnets that is more significant than the similarity. For no one could plausibly suggest that the subjective effect given off by Tarquin or by Lucrece or, for that matter, by Venus or by Adonis, is in any way comparable, in degree or in kind, to that which is given off by the sonnets or by certain characters in Shakespeare's plays. And the reason for this, I suggest, is that while the narrative poems employ a cross-coupling mode in a very obvious, perhaps too obvious, way, they do not flesh this mode out with the large thematic motifs of Shakespeare's paradox of praise, with the motifs that I will identify as vision and language, and whose force and propriety we can understand to derive from the way these motifs, joined together, paradoxically reduplicate the poetics of admiration.[30] In the sonnets, but also in the plays, Shakespeare presents a material logic of the person—as well as a rhetorical, formal, and psychological logic of subjectivity—that possesses enormous power in our literary culture because, though it breaks with an epideictic tradition that is central to our literature from antiquity through the Renaissance, it nevertheless continues to develop this tradition in a way that coherently and materially registers and responds to the failure of epideixis.

This, then, is the largest assumption I make, an assumption that I justify by referring to the self-consciously retrospective literary thematics of the sequence as a whole: namely, that Shakespeare's sonnets understand themselves to inherit the debts of a bankrupt poetic tradition, but that they also understand this legacy, which is the burden of literary history itself, to impose specific constraints upon poetic practice, constraints that are particularly compelling with regard to the presentation of poetic subjectivity. Recognizing the powerful canonical status of Shakespearean subjectivity in literature successive to the Renaissance, the enthusiastic and continually reiterated claims made for the characterological authenticity both of the sonnets and of the plays, I conclude that Shakespeare's literary intuitions were in this respect singularly acute. For this reason, however, I say also that Shakespeare in his sonnets invents the *only* kind of literary subject that survives in the aftermath of the poetry of praise.[31]

It will be recognized that this argument, operating as it does on several levels—historical, rhetorical, psychological, thematic, each of these related to each of the others—is, whatever else it is, a complicated one. In what follows, for the sake of clarity, the argument is presented in incremental segments rather than synoptically, its related aspects initially kept separate lest they be confused with each other. As a result, I will often return to a poem that I have already discussed so as to see how the poem fits into a new stage of the argument. So too it will often happen that initial critical formulations are revised in the light of later complications. This recapitulatory exposition entails a certain amount of repetition, justified, I hope, not only by whatever clarity is gained thereby, but also because, as I try to show, Shakespeare's sonnets, taken individually and in sequence, are written so as to call forth this kind of rereading. In chapter 1 I begin to discuss the way the sequence of sonnets addressed to the young man and the sequence of sonnets addressed to the dark lady are usefully opposed to each other in terms of the difference between praise and its paradox. In chapter 2 I discuss in a very general way the tradition of visionary epideictic language and the relation of this to the representation of poetic person. In chapter 3 I discuss the way the young man sonnets are also inflected by the paradox of praise. Here I introduce the thematic opposition of vision to language, and I try to show that an important difference between the young man sonnets and the dark lady sonnets is that while the first sequence is implicitly suspicious of its visionary mode the second sequence explicitly puts those suspicions into words. This explication by the dark lady sonnets of the young man sonnets' implications effects, I argue, a specific poetic consequence. In chapter 4 I discuss several formal ways in which epideixis is cross-coupled in the sonnets addressed to the young man. In chapter 5 I discuss some of the ways in which this cross-coupling form is fleshed out by specific subjective affects; here I discuss in greater detail the poet's personal sense of space, time, and desire, and the way all three of these join together in his puns on "Will." Finally, in a very brief epilogue, I suggest how this argument regarding Shakespeare's sonneteering self might be applied to a discussion of Shakespeare's dramatic form. Here I am concerned with the way different subjective effects are given off by the early comedies, the high tragedies, and the late romances.

It remains for me to say something about critical method, for the reader will no doubt already have noticed that this account of Shakespeare's sonnets, even with its simplifications regarding metaphor and mimesis, is very much informed by recent philosophical, psychoanalytic, and hermeneutic theory of a kind that has come somewhat simplistically to be labelled structuralist and poststructuralist. My concern with the way Shakespeare's sonnets stress the languageness of language is related in an obvious way to discussions of literariness as exemplified by such formalists as Roman Jakobson, Gérard Genette, Michael Riffaterre.[32] The rhetorical form that I call crosscoupling is related in equally obvious ways to A. J. Greimas's semantic square, to Paul De Man's chiasmus, and also to Jacques Lacan's "schema L," which Lacan draws as a quaternary "Z."[33] So too my account of the disruption of the metaphysics of "kind" by a low "unkind," though it goes back to Socrates' observation in the *Parmenides* that there is no ideal form for mud, is in many ways like, certainly it is in many ways indebted to, Jacques Derrida's essays in deconstructive phenomenology.[34] Most obviously, and most importantly, my account of a subjectivity precipitated by the paradoxical relationship of language to vision, my understanding of a language of desire and a desire of language, is very much influenced by Lacan's psychoanalytic account of the capture of what he calls the Imaginary by what he calls the Symbolic (this itself but an elaboration of Freud's distinction between visual *Sachvorstellungen* and verbal *Wortvorstellungen*).[35]

I want to acknowledge these debts here as strongly and emphatically as possible, for in the text I deliberately avoid explicit citation of these or any other contemporary theoreticians. There are two reasons for this. First, and least important, it seems possible and even likely that the specialized vocabulary and concerns of these authors will be unfamiliar to many, if not to the majority, of Shakespeareans to whom this book is addressed. Perhaps this is an unnecessary worry, for what is unfamiliar today has the uncanny ability to turn into quite the opposite tomorrow. Even so, there seems no good reason to complicate further an already complicated argument by introducing terms of art taken from discourses and disciplines foreign to the argument's anticipated audience. A certain amount of precision and also of concision, especially with regard to phenomenological matters, is lost by thus forgoing the resources of several technical nomenclatures. Such precision, however, would be overdelicate given the level of generality at which the argument I present here is designed to operate. So too such precision would be self-defeatingly obfuscatory if attained at the cost of general accessibility.

There is another consideration, however, more important than that of rhetorical *claritas*, that leads me to avoid directly employing what can be called, as I write now, contemporary theory. This has to do with the historical status and situation of such theory. For it would be very possible to trace out in recent theoretical discussion, especially discussion of subjectivity, a development very similar not only to the development that we can discern in Shakespeare's sonnets, as they move from the sonnets addressed to the young man to the sonnets addressed to the dark lady, but similar also to the larger literary development within which we can locate the historical significance of Shakespeare's sonnet sequence as a whole. For example, responding to Husserl's Dantesque phenomenology of *Ideas*, to Husserl's concern with eidetic reduction and a transcendental Ego, Sartre developed a psychology of imagination whose logic and figurality very much resemble the paranoiac visionary thematics of at least some of Shakespeare's young man sonnets.[36] The subjective optics of the Sartrian "gaze" and its melodrama of mutually persecutory master-slave relations, subsequently received in the thought of Merleau-Ponty, especially in late works such as "Le Oeil et l'esprit" and *Le Visible et l'invisible*, an ironically comic revision whose chiasmic marriage of subject and object is reminiscent of more than a few of Shakespeare's most genuinely poignant sonneteering conceits; it was Merleau-Ponty, after all, who introduced "chiasmus" into recent critical discourse, as a way to explain the way Cézanne paints the trees watching Cézanne.[37] Lacan, Merleau-Ponty's friend, broke with Merleau-Ponty on just this point, seeing in the fully lived "flesh" and "visibility" of Merleau-Ponty's chiasmus a psychological and a phenomenological sentimentality. Instead, Lacan developed an account of the way human subjectivity is born in the place where chiasmus breaks.[38] Lacan's anamorphic gaze, very different from *le regard* of Sartre or of Merleau-Ponty, along with Lacan's account of the way language potentiates and inherits this rupture of the visual imaginary, rather perfectly repeats the formal as well as the thematic logic of Shakespeare's "perjur'd eye."[39] In this context, we can add, it is significant that Derrida's subsequent attempt to rupture Lacan's rupture, Derrida's putatively postsubjective account of supplemental *différance*, seems, from the point of view of Shakespeare's sonnets, nothing but another "increase" that "from fairest creatures we desire" (1), a subjective indeterminacy, that is to say, which is already predetermined, as was Tarquin's rape, by the exigencies of literary life. (I am here assuming in advance the wrinkle, literally the "crease," that Shakespeare introduces into the perennial poetics of copious "increase"; see chapter 5.) More generally, I argue that what Derrida calls "writing," the thematics of the deconstructive "trace" that Derrida associates with *écriture*, is not beyond Shakespeare's sonnets but is instead anticipated and assimilated by them to the theme of language, with the two of these together being opposed to the theme of vision. Even more generally, I argue that the "photologocentric" metaphysics that Derrida opposes to writing already contains within its collation of vision and language a historically significant and essentially orthodox, deconstructive dynamic; see, for example, the discussion of *Ha Shem* in Fludd's diagram in chapter 2, and the relation of this to "correspondence" in sonnets 44 and 45; see also the discussion in chapter 5 of the "stelled" logic of "an ever-fixed mark/That looks on tempests and is never shaken" (116).[40]

Recognizing these homologies, which could be developed further, and which are by no means restricted to the continental philosophical-psychoanalytic tradition to which I here allude, it seems at least possible that contemporary speculation about subjectivity repeats in a theoretical mode (and the visual etymologies that impose themselves here are important, for "theory" too begins as "seeing") what literature accomplishes toward the end of the Renaissance. The essentially Cartesian problematic of the self with which all these thinkers contend is a problematic that not only first emerges in the Renaissance, but one whose subsequent articulation is prescribed by powerful Renaissance models of subjectivity. This is very general history of ideas indeed. However, if such a history of the subject of subjectivity were ever to be written, Shakespeare would necessarily occupy a privileged place within it, not only because Shakespeare invents strong characters, but also because those characters have come subsequently to pose themselves to theoreticians of subjectivity as pressing problems to be solved. I am thinking here especially of Freud, who gives us the fullest account of subjectivity that we possess and to whom Lacan wants to serve as faithful annotation. One example can stand for many. In the letters Freud writes to Fliess, just prior to the announcement of the discovery of the Oedipus complex, Freud quotes Shakespeare. Soon after, armed with the Oedipus complex, Freud analyzes Shakespeare, sketching out for Fliess the outlines of Freud's famous reading of *Hamlet*. Reading these letters, hearing the Shakespearean echoes coalesce into science, it is difficult to determine who is accounting for whom.[41] Perhaps the question is by now familiar: Is Shakespeare Freudian or is Freud Shakespearean?

I do not really mean to answer this very large question, and I raise it only to explain why, in what follows, even when I talk about "Will," I do not invoke the psychoanalytic account of desiring subjectivity—from Freud's theory of castration to Lacan's *objet a*—by which I am in fact very influenced. The reason is this: there is at least the possibility that modernist—and, for that matter, postmodernist— theories of the self are not so much a theoretical account or explanation of subjectivity as they are the conclusion of the literary subjectivity initially invented in the Renaissance. If this is the case, we might want to say that Shakespeare marks the beginning of the modernist self and Freud—not Wilde—its end, the two of them together thus bracketing an epoch of subjectivity. However, if this is the case, it is so in a way that assures us that neither will tell more about the other than he will about himself. (Even if this is not the case, it remains difficult, in several respects, to distinguish between Freud's strongest theoretical concepts and the theory of rhetorical trope from which, it is possible to argue, they derive.)

This is to make Shakespeare's name denominate a very general and a very broad event in the history of literature and in the history of ideas. In what follows I am, frankly, more concerned with specific literary attributes of Shakespeare's sonnets, and with the relation of these to the plays, than I am with this broad history. For this reason, at least in what follows, literary history and the history of ideas are significant only to the extent that in his sonnets Shakespeare seems to regret that he repeats them with a difference. This sense of repetition, however, is itself a distinctive mark of Renaissance sensibility, especially of a good many literary minds for whom the project of their present is to give rebirth to the past. The very great Humanist, Leone Ebreo—precursor to Spinoza and in this way an important influence on Freud—in his dialogue *D'amore e desiderio* distinguishes—the topic is an old one—between love and desire on the grounds that love is an emotion one feels for that which one possesses, whereas desire is the emotion one feels for that which one does not possess.[42] Returning to the subject sometime later, in a dialogue call *De l'origine d'amore*, Ebreo emends his original distinction, reformulating it on the grounds that even that which one possesses, because it is possessed in transient time, carries with it, even at the moment of possession, a sense of loss.[43] This possession of loss, an emotion which is half love and half desire—what we might call a desire for love, but what we cannot call a love of desire—grows increasingly strong when the later and post-Humanist Renaissance returns to rethink a good many other topics relating to the origin of love. In time, in Shakespeare's sonnets, the rebirth of the Renaissance turns into the death of remorse, for in Shakespeare's sonnets "desire is death" (147) *because* "now is black beauty's successive heir" (127).[44]

This is one aspect of Shakespeare's sonnets, however, that is surely of more than merely local interest. In Shakespeare's sonnets we hear how a literature of repetition, rather than a literature *De l'origine*, explains its desire to itself. With regard to the matter of poetic person this is important because it allows us to understand how Shakespeare's response to secondariness leads him to introduce into literature a subjectivity altogether novel in the history of lyric, or, as Shakespeare puts it, "since mind at first in character was done" (59). For this very reason, however, the constitution of Shakespearean poetic self necessarily recalls the imperatives of a literariness larger even than the Shakespearean. Consider sonnet 59:

> If there be nothing new, but that which is
> Hath been before, how are our brains beguil'd
> Which laboring for invention bear amiss
> The second burthen of a former child!

"The second burthen of a former child" very well characterizes the subjectivity fathered in the late Renaissance by the burden of a belated literariness. In what follows there will be good reason to compare the rebirth of this aborted subject that "invention bear[s] amiss" with "Death's second self, that seals up all in rest" (73). However, to the extent that it is not only Shakespeare who looks, as sonnet 59 puts it, "with a backward look" to see "your image in some antique book," the revolutionary question raised by such Shakespearean retrospection will continue to retain the ongoing urgency of a perennial and, it seems fair to say, since even Shakespeare now is "nothing new," an increasingly important literary commonplace:

> That I might see what the old world could say
> To this composed wonder of your frame,
> Whether we are mended, or whe'er better they,
> Or whether revolution be the same.
>   O, sure I am the wits of former days
>   To subjects worse have given admiring praise.

·I·

One thing expressing, leaves out difference.
(Sonnet 105)

The sonnet begins as a poetry of erotic praise, as though it goes without saying that the poet is a lover who desires only that which he admires. As the form develops, blending troubador courtly courtship lyric with Christianizing and Neo-Platonic elaborations of the object of desire, this epideictic attitude of the poet toward his love remains a constant and becomes, in fact, a characteristic theme. Almost from the beginning, the sonneteering poet makes his loving praise into the matter as well as the manner of the sonnet's approbation, as though the height of praise were fully realized when praise comes in this reflexive way to speak about itself. As early as Dante's *La Vita nuova*, for example, in a passage that Dante will later remember as inaugurating the *dolce stil nuovo*, the "beatitude" *(beatitudine)* of the poet, which is to say "the goal of [his] desire," is not only expressed by, but is explicitly identified with, "those words that praise my lady" (*In quelle parole che lodano la donna mia*).[1] And the same with Petrarch, in whose sonnets the collation of desire and praise, and the Cratylitic identification of *lodano* with *la donna*, though less overtly theological than for Dante, continues to define the subject and the object of the poet's project, as the repeated puns on "Laura," "laud," and "laurel" consistently insist.[2]

Into this tradition of the praise of love, whose metaphysical and rhetorical roots go back to the *Symposium* and the *Phaedrus*, and whose abiding English literary vitality we can recognize in Sidney or in Spenser, Shakespeare in his sonnets introduces something novel. To begin with, Shakespeare writes his sonnets as something to conclude with. That is to say, writing, for the most part, after the sonnet-sequence vogue has passed, Shakespeare will, at least in the sonnets addressed to the young man, casually recapitulate almost all the laudatory themes and postures and amatory psychology that make up the poetry of erotic praise, alluding to the conventionality of these conventions (such allusion being itself, to some extent, con-

49

ventional) at the same time as he employs them.[3] Apart from those sonnets in which the theme is implicitly stipulated, praise is the central topic of about one quarter of the 126 sonnets in the young man sub-sequence, principally because the young man's poet repeatedly will speak about the way he wants to make the young man "much outlive a gilded tomb,/And to be prais'd of ages yet to be" (101).[4] And yet, despite the prominence they give the theme, indeed, as though there were something morbid in the very practice of the poet's eternizing purpose—"Your monument shall be my gentle verse" (81)— these sonnets' many references to praise are often colored by an elegaic mood that would be more appropriate for a funereal remembrance of things past than for a celebration of things current.

To take just one example, consider sonnet 106, where the poet sees a rather ghostly image of the praiseworthy present in the panegyric past:

> When in the chronicle of wasted time
> I see descriptions of the fairest wights,
> And beauty making beautiful old rhyme
> In praise of ladies dead and lovely knights,
> Then in the blazon of sweet beauty's best,
> Of hand, of foot, of lip, of eye, of brow,
> I see their antique pen would have express'd
> Even such a beauty as you master now.

For the young man's poet, such ancient "blazon of beauty's best," the kind that "their antique pen would have express'd," is that to which "such a beauty as you master now" must now be retroactively compared. Given the comparison, itself an old one, between today and yesterday, the young man, by convention, necessarily gets the better of it. As the poet says, using what is a familiar epideictic topos, "all their praises are but prophecies/Of this our time, all you prefiguring" (106).[5] And yet, however much the young man thus fulfills the promise of all ancient panegyric, a kind of odd and self-conscious literary retrospection attaches to the way this leads the poet to conclude: "For we which now behold these present days/Have eyes to wonder, but lack tongues to praise" (106). The "lack" to which the poet here refers introduces a paradox whose wit is not entirely benign. What the poet says in his dumbfounded "wonder" leaves the reader wondering just how it is the poet manages to say it. And this is a problem that the reader will resolve only when he then concludes that what the poet is saying here is somehow not the same as praise.

Taken by itself, this is a small and casual example, and there are many other kinds of consequences that follow from the way Shakespeare's sonnets, rather frequently, confusingly collate the use and mention of their epideictic practice. It is a valuable example, however, because it illustrates how readily and regularly the poet of the young man sonnets will situate himself—sometimes wittily but often reluctantly and regretfully—posterior to the praise he presupposes. The poet of the young man sub-sequence seems always to reflect upon as much as he repeats the literary assumptions he invokes, and for this reason the sonnets that he writes in "these present days" characteristically present themselves as the most up-to-date item "in the chronicle of wasted time," as though they were themselves a current version of "beauty making beautiful old rhyme." Such sonnets are to their poetic past as they say the future is to the young man's present; in ways that are genuinely surprising, they and their "now" are after the ideal epideictic fact, as in the prospective retrospection of sonnet 104, where the poet tells "thou age unbred:/Ere you were born was beauty's summer dead."

This is the initial peculiarity of Shakespeare's young man sonnets, a peculiarity that affects the tonality with which their most conventional sentiments are expressed. Shakespeare's sonnets— even if some of them are written as early as the 1580s—begin both where and when the tradition of sonneteering admiration ends, as though Shakespeare or, more precisely, as though the poet-lover of the young man, means to consummate, by representing or reenacting, the original intentions of a bygone poetry of praise. This is a peculiarity that should not be overlooked. The young man sonnets explicitly conceive themselves as something metaleptic. Their poet explicitly rewrites what he says has long ago been written by an "antique pen" (106), just as he rereads "your image in some antique book" (59). Accordingly, because the poet "makes antiquity for aye his page,/Finding the first conceit of love there bred,/Where time and outward form would show it dead" (108), the young man's poet's "best is dressing old words new,/Spending again what is already spent" (76). From such a perspective, with the sonnets looking backward at their literary past, even the characteristic literary self-consciousness of traditional epideictic poetry, its characteristic emphasis on its own rhetoricity—as early as Aristotle praise is defined as a rhetoric of self-display—begins itself to seem self-conscious. Moreover, given the fact that the lyric sonnet is a poetic form that characteristically stresses the personal voice of its speaking first person, it seems especially significant that in Shakespeare's sonnets this personal self-consciousness, which is also frequently thematized or spoken about in the conventional laudatory sonnet, becomes itself yet more self-conscious—so much more so, I will want to argue, as to produce not only a novel thematization of, but also a novel impression of, poetic self.

In sonnet 62, to take another preliminary example, the poet begins by reporting how "sin of self-love possesseth all mine eye." Proceeding then to demonstrate the point, the poet recounts in the octave the panegyric that his self-love gives him leave to write or think about himself:

> Sin of self-love possesseth all mine eye,
> And all my soul, and all my every part;
> And for this sin there is no remedy,
> It is so grounded inward in my heart.
> Methinks no face so gracious is as mine,
> No shape so true, no truth of such account,
> And for myself mine own worth do define,
> As I all other in all worths surmount.

It is understood, of course, from the very beginning of this sonnet, that the poet here praises himself—"no face so gracious is as mine"—only because he here identifies himself with the young man. Such identification of praising subject with praised object is a staple in the repertoire of praise and, for this reason, long before the poet makes the point explicit, we understand that the poet's self-applauding laud is the reverse of something solipsistic. But then, if we thus understand the octave, we do not fully understand what follows it, or we do not do so in the same conventional way. For what is striking in the succeeding quatrain is the harshness and abruptness with which the poet interrupts this comic praise of his own self:

> But when my glass shows me myself indeed,
> Beated and chopp'd with tann'd antiquity,
> Mine own self-love quite contrary I read;
> Self so self-loving were iniquity.

However we take this quatrain—as another piece of wit or as a new kind of regret—it should be clear that its effect is radically different from, for example, Dante's self-conscious identification of his own beatitude with his praise of Beatrice, or Petrarch's identification of his laurel and his laud. For the poet's concessive point in sonnet 62, brought out by the genuinely poignant "but," is that when he looks into his mirror what he sees are the ways in which his identification and his identity do not coalesce. Moreover, the poet's identification and identity are sundered at the very place and at the very moment in which the laudatory mania of the octave and the deprecating melancholy of the sestet meet—which is to say, both where and when the conclusion of the octave, which is the height of praise ("As I all other in all worths surmount") modulates into the beginning of the sestet, which is the poet's vision of himself ("But when my glass shows me myself indeed"). By putting octave and sestet together in this way, the difference between them stressed and elided by the poet's "but"— and the sestets of Shakespeare's sonnets characteristically turn upon the octave in just this poignant counterpointing way—the sonnet makes it seem as though the poet were himself the difference between the youth and age of praise. And this, in fact, is the burden of the sonnet's couplet, where the poet, expressing a conflicted consciousness of self, makes a rueful joke about the invert, deictic, epideictic way in which "'tis thee (myself) that for myself I praise,/Painting my age with beauty of thy days."

Recognizing both the humor and the pathos of sonnet 62, we can say that there is something irreducibly unfamiliar and unconventional about the reticent nostalgia expressed by the sonnet's reference to the poetry of praise. In the poetic voice of such a sonnet we sense a kind of freshly guilty longing—"Self so self-loving were iniquity"—for a self that would not find itself so thoroughly departed from its ideal self. Yet even so, if this amounts to something new in the poetry of praise—and it is the young man sonnets' tone or mood, more than any single one of their conceits, that initially strikes a reader as novel—it seems reasonable to assume, at least provisionally, that this is so only insofar as it is something late or retrospective. Stylizing their own traditional style, thematizing their own well-worn themes, the young man sonnets seem nevertheless profoundly loyal to the poetry of praise, concerned more to fulfill, rather than to reject, the historical, formal, and thematic impulses of the epideictic model to which they regularly refer. For example, because the young man sonnets can assume a tradition in which praise bespeaks desire and desire calls up praise, no special or corrosive irony necessarily attaches to the way the poet-lover of the young man will first praise his love and then proceed to love his praise. In the young man sonnets such literary playfulness, or such playful literariness, can develop itself as the expression of a purified and an idealized rhetorical narcissism, as in the sort of conceit that leads to such easily answered rhetorical questions as: "What can mine own praise to mine own self bring?/And what is't but mine own when I praise thee?" (39). And, however self-consciously conducted, the young man sonnets seem straightforwardly to develop the circularity of this progression—from praise of love to love of praise, from praise of "thee" to praise of "me"—in accord with a conventional logic of epideictic desire whose proprieties and provenance not only anticipate and predicate such reversals, but which also give to love and praise alike their operative poetic force.

For just this reason, however, because the literary tradition of the sonnet as a whole and the sonnets to the young man in particular both regularly and regulatively assume that love and praise self-consciously entail each other, the sonnets addressed to the dark lady present themselves as something strange—as something more outspokenly peculiar, more explicitly unusual, than anything we might associate with the troubled tonalities sounded by the epideictic sonnets addressed to the young man. For the explicit complaint of the second sub-sequence is that the poet's dark lady is an object of desire who is equally an instance of disdain or, in a profoundly complicated way, that she is spur to a desire that knows better than itself. Hence the invert blazon and *effictio* with which the dark lady sonnets consistently reverse epithets and attributes of Petrarchist and *stil nuovo* approbation, as though to code the lady's charming beauty as conventionally unconventional in contrast to the emphatically familiar beauty of the fair young man. So too, also in contrast to what happens in the young man sub-sequence, desire in the dark lady sonnets is explicitly defined—and in a way that seems more permanently bitter than is the custom in traditional complaint—by its regret: "My love is as a fever, longing still/For that which longer nurseth the disease,/Feeding on that which doth preserve the ill" (147).

These are contrasts or differences—and, as we compare the two sub-sequences, others soon become apparent—that make for a disturbing set of problems. To begin with, how does it happen, and why does it seem more than an accidental aspect of the sonnets' narrative, that the poet who first loves the fair young man comes subsequently to lust after the dark lady?[6] Given the idealizing formulas and values, both physical and metaphysical, of the poetry of praise, it makes, perhaps, a certain sense that if the poet's "mistress' eyes are nothing like the sun," that then the poet's love will register itself as "an expense of spirit in a waste of shame." But if the poet of the young man sonnets is thus given the assumptions of the poetry of praise—and we know that he employs them in a considerable number of his sonnets—why does the poet of the dark lady sonnets proceed in turn to give them up? Thinking only of the psychology of the sequence as a whole—of the sequence, that is, which is composed of these two separate and unequal parts—the contrast leads us to wonder what kind of ugliness can fairly substitute for beauty, and what kind of eros is compact of its own disgust? Correspondingly, thinking instead of the literary novelty of the sequence as a whole, and remembering that the sonnet begins as a poetry of erotic praise, we ask what happens to the sonnet when its poet ceases to admire that which he desires?

These are questions to which the sonnets themselves will give direct expression, for the sonnets often make a kind of apocalyptic, epochal literary history out of their different "loves" "of comfort and despair." On the one hand, the poet sees the young man as the consummating height of praise. In effect, because "all their praises are but prophecies/Of this our time, all you prefiguring" (106), the young man is presented as the Messiah of the poetry of praise: he is the panegyric figure *after* all "prefiguring" who puts an end to epideictic history simply by his immanence. On the other hand, for just this reason, poetry, in what is therefore now the aftermath of praise, must henceforth develop a postepideictic poetics so as in this way to record the final consequence of its past panegyric. Accordingly:

> In the old age black was not counted fair,
> Or if it were it bore not beauty's name;
> But now is black beauty's successive heir,
> And beauty slander'd with a bastard shame.
> (127)[7]

This is the first of the sonnets addressed to the dark lady, and it argues, reasonably enough, in favor of unadorned black beauty because such is the only guarantee of honesty in a cosmeticizing age where "each hand hath put on nature's power,/Fairing the foul with art's false borrow'd face" (127).[8] The sub-sequence of sonnets addressed to the dark lady in this way introduces the blackness of the lady as appropriately witty "mourning" for the artificiality of present beauty. The lady's disfiguring blackness "postfigures," we might say, what ancient praise heretofore "prefigures," and in this sense, because black is now "beauty's successive heir," the lady's darkness constitutes a convenient (and certainly not an unprecedented) figure for the so-called anti-Petrarchan reaction to Petrarchan epideictic artifice (e.g., du Bellay's "Contre les pétrarquistes"):

> Therefore my mistress' eyes are raven black,
> Her eyes so suited, and they mourners seem
> At such who, not born fair, no beauty lack,
> Sland'ring creation with a false esteem.[9]

Read in this way (assuming we forget, for the moment, that if this is anti-Petrarchanism, it is of a sort that Petrarch himself might have written), the black beauty of the lady becomes, as sonnet 127 says, a refreshed and revivifying version of a fair and prior beauty that has died—a playful variation on the post-mortally resplendent transcendentalism of dead Beatrice or Laura.[10] As the sub-sequence develops, however, it turns out that appearances are not at all deceiving, and that the conventions of Petrarchanism are truer than the poet had initially iconoclastically supposed. For the lady's black exterior is, in fact, an honest sign of her interior evil, just as the corruption of her spirit corresponds exactly to the ugly way she seems. Back on the outside, so too is the dark lady black on the inside, as any orthodox Petrarchan would have known at first abhorrent sight.

The question thus remains: why does the poet first praise what is ugly, and then, even after recognizing the folly of this praise, why does he continue to desire something he contemns? On the one hand, having "put fair truth upon so foul a face" (137), it is the false-praising poet himself, more than any painted lady, who throughout the dark lady sequence "slanders" beauty with a "false esteem:" "Thy black is fairest in my judgment's place./In nothing art thou black save in thy deeds,/And thence this slander as I think proceeds" (131). On the other hand, a second hand that knows the error of the first, the poet of the dark lady describes an ongoing desire that knowingly continues to commit the same indecorous mistake: "In faith, I do not love thee with mine eyes,/For they in thee a thousand errors note,/But 'tis my heart that loves what they despise,/Who in despite of view is pleas'd to dote" (141). Acknowledging the doubly disgusting nature of the lady—that she is black, that she is false—we therefore ask, along with the poet, what makes the poet, with his unconventional praise, "give the lie to my true sight" (150), and what makes the lover, with his unprecedented desire, "love what others [including the lover himself] do abhor" (150)? The point to recognize is that these are pressing questions *for* the poet: "O, from what pow'r hast thou this pow'rful might/With insufficiency my heart to sway" (150)?

A reader accustomed to the conventions of Renaissance poetry may be tempted to eliminate such questions altogether, either by justifying the dark lady sonnets' exclamations of disgust or by discounting the terms of their peculiar praise. In either case—speaking with the lover against his dark desire, or with the poet against his novel panegyric—the reader can stress the coarse and fleshly sexuality of the poet's relation to the lady, and then contrast this with the thematically ideal, ascetic eroticism of the poet's relation to the man. It thus becomes possible to fit the two sub-sequences together by referring them both, in a conventional and reassuring way, to the Neo-Platonic tradition of the double Venus, with the young man taken to be the image of spiritual and intellectual desire as opposed to the dark lady's embodiment of the material corporeality of lust.[11] This would give a proper philosophic context to the different genders, since for Renaissance Neo-Platonism the love of man for woman is more vulgarly appetitive than that of man for man.[12] Taken thus, the sequence as a whole becomes a kind of exaggerated and radical repetition, in reverse, of such cosmological allegories of desire as Spenser's *Fowre Hymnes*, the sequence as a whole instructively, even upliftingly, sliding down the great chain of being via its initial laudatory description of celestial love and beauty and its subsequent concluding invective of their more earthly manifestations.[13] The very guiltiness of the poet's love for the lady would in this way reconfirm by its regret, just as his unconventional praise of her would reapprove by being false, his first and pristine love and praise for the young man.[14]

The difficulty, however, with situating the sonnets within such a familiar literary context, or with immediately applying to them the moral, ontological, or psychological valuations that such "Farewell, Cupid" literature presupposes—quite apart from the fact that the young man is not particularly angelic, just as Spenser's earthly love is not really very carnal—is that, in perfectly inverse proportion, the more despicable the desirable dark lady, the less ideal is the young man. For the great irony built into Shakespeare's sonnets is that the young man, like the poet, loves the lady, and to the extent that he does so the admiration of the poet for the man is correlatively undercut: "my female evil/Tempteth my better angel from my side,/ And would corrupt my saint to be a devil" (144). We might want to say that this sordid cuckoldry story, which shows us "one angel in another's hell" (144), a story that is considerably different in tone or consequence from similar stories we hear about in the young man

sub-sequence (e.g., sonnets 40–42, 92–93), is the way that the misogynist poet "realizes" his masculine ideal—the dark lady being
thus defined as the material conclusion of an originally immaterial
imagination, the loathsome heterosexual object of an ideally homosexual desire. However, it is more than the real that is thus established as disgusting. Insofar as the young man, "in another's hell,"
thus finds himself embarrassingly and realistically "incarnate," he
loses the legitimacy of his own moral force. Specifically, the ideal,
being "in another's hell," is no longer, in itself, ideal. And, as a result,
the young man no longer deserves either his poet's Petrarchan
praise or his lover's Neo-Platonic love.

This is bad enough, but if the man is not praiseworthy, by what
measure is the lady to be blamed? "The power of beauty," says Hamlet to Ophelia, in a passage to which I will later return, "will sooner
transform honesty from what it is to a bawd than the force of honesty can translate beauty into his likeness. This was sometime a paradox, but now the time gives it proof. I did love you once" (3.1.110–
14). With the young man thus "transformed," where is the honesty
with reference to which we might indict the bawdiness of beauty?
With the man "translated" to the false "likeness" of the lady, how do
we determine which is worse—or, really, thinking of the contents
and the contours of what Iago calls "the beast with two backs,"
which is which? This is the dilemma, half rhetorical and half sexual,
generated by the coupling of the first sub-sequence with the second,
by the coupling of the young man with the dark lady. Like the "rascal
beadle" in *King Lear*, the dark lady's poet "hotly lusts to use her in
that kind/For which thou whipst her" (4.5.162–63), and because he
desires that which he condemns, his severe appraisal of the lady
only serves to demonstrate the way the judge himself is literally
wanting in his judgment.

All this brings out the fact that there is a difference in kind, rather
than degree, between the poet's loves "of comfort and despair," and
that the difference is purchased dialectically—measure for measure—at the "expense of spirit." Unlike Spenser, for whom the lower
Venus is, as such, an ennobling image of the higher Eros, the dark
lady is for Shakespeare conceived as the undoing of that which she
attracts. She is not a negative version of, nor is she an alternative to,
conventional sonneteering ideals. Instead, being dark and (so it
seems) being a lady, she is specifically and constitutively presented
as the perversion of any such idealization, not simply the lowest
rung on the ladder of love, but a power that kicks the ladder out

altogether. This is not only unfortunate, but, in the tradition of erotic praise, essentially inexplicable, for just as there is no good reason for the poet to praise what he says is not praiseworthy, so too we cannot understand why the poet desires what he says is not desirable. The question remains: "O, from what pow'r hast thou this pow'rful might/With insufficiency my heart to sway" (150)? The difficulty here is structural in that the dark lady sub-sequence first posits the very values that it subsequently both remembers and subverts, a double bind that leads in turn to both a poetry that writes against itself and to a desire for that which is abhorred. At stake here, therefore—in both a praise and love at odds with their best selves—are the most fundamental assumptions of the poetics and the erotics of Renaissance literary admiration, at least as these are characteristically thematized in Renaissance poetry. Moreover, since the poetry of love characteristically writes itself out as the love of poetry, what is also at stake here is the Renaissance attitude toward poetry itself.

We should be clear about the difficulty, for it arises not as a simple consequence of, or reaction to, the intrinsic merit of the young man or of the lady, as though were either man or lady better than either he or she is the poet-lover's poetic and erotic problems would thereby disappear. As many critics have pointed out, almost from the beginning of the young man sonnets no one is more certain that the object of his praise is unworthy of encomium than the author, or the represented author, of the young man sonnets himself. The tone of disillusion, the sense of betrayal, the failed idealism, the almost Proustian suspicion—all this is sounded very strongly throughout the sonnets addressed to the young man. This is so much the case that, at a certain point, the young man's poet takes the apparent discrepancy between his ideal manner and his less than ideal matter as his explicit theme. But, though the young man does not deserve the poet's praise, this does not prevent the poet from heaping panegyric on him. Even when the young man sonnets take up the young man's faults, they, like the poet's rival poets, "cannot dispraise but in a kind of praise" (95). In a sense, this is analogous to the way the dark lady sonnets "put fair truth upon so foul a face" (137). Yet, though the parallel with the dark lady is exact and even stressed—"so shall I live, supposing thou art true,/Like a deceived husband" (93)—the poet, when he addresses the young man, does not entirely regret his exercise of "false esteem." Indeed, the way the poet overlooks the young man's scarcely hidden flaws, the way he "play[s] the watchman ever for thy sake" (61), to some extent defines the conventional virtue of such epideictic poetry. For what allows the poet to commit himself to what is, at least in some respects, a cosmeticizing, *because* idealizing, rhetoric is that this poetry is itself intended, as it itself says, to make up for, rather than to point up, the distance between what is its ideal and what is the mundane actualization of its ideal. It is in this sense, but only in this sense, that the poet of the young man can honestly say, taking advantage of the grammatical ambiguity that links him to his love, that "both truth and beauty on my love depends" (101).

Here, as elsewhere, the young man sonnets evoke or repeat what I have already suggested is a typically reflective and reflexive movement of Petrarchan poetry, especially as it develops in England from Wyatt through Sidney, whereby the poet, ruefully disappointed in his object, turns his poetry round upon itself, so that the poetry, by taking itself as its own subject, turns out to make itself its own ideal. In this circular way poetry presents itself as truth despite the fact that what it represents is false: "So are those errors that in thee are seen/To truths translated, and for true things deem'd" (96). The self-conscious posturings of this kind of oblique poetry of praise, as well as the justifications for them, are familiar enough because they are themselves built into the tradition of the poetry of praise: the poem will be itself a model to the lapsed beloved who is ostensibly its model; poetry will draw out a vision of perfection, of which it is itself the best and most precise example, in order to redeem by reference to itself discovered imperfection in the person it addresses, as when, to take a high example, the poet of the young man sonnets assumes a compensating reciprocity between the immortality of his verse and the ephemerality of the young man's beauty.[15] Hence the egocentric, narcissistic thematics frequently observed in such a poetry, where the voice of the poet takes precedence over that which it bespeaks, as when Sidney at the opening of *Astrophil and Stella* looks into his own heart to read there what he ought to write, or as when Spenser tells his lady to leave her "glasse of christall clene," "and in my selfe, my inwarde selfe I meane/most lively lyke behold your semblant trew."[16] These are common motifs, common epideictic gambits—with a fully developed psychology of love, a theory of imaginary vision, and a rhetorical genealogy to back them up—and this explains why the poet-lover of the young man will so frequently base his own poetic and erotic integrity on just such literary self-regard. This is why, for example, assuming we ignore the tonal irregularities to which I have already alluded, "Sin of self-love possesseth all mine eye" (62) can be supposed to find its orthodox expiation in the identificatory ideality of "'tis thee (myself) that for myself I praise" (62).[17]

The rhetorical and recuperative self-reflection that governs Shakespeare's praise of the young man is, therefore, at least in terms of theme, something fairly conventional and would have been recognized as such by Shakespeare's contemporaries, especially those with a sophisticated or learned literary sensibility. From antiquity, or at least from late antiquity, this kind of turn upon itself is the way that a poetry or oratory of praise has typically defended itself against the charge of being merely a poetry of obsequy and flattery. Moreover, as is well known, in the Renaissance this traditional defense of poetic panegyric—with poetry the flattering mirror held up to image tarnished nature with its own ideal reflection—was enthusiastically revived and amplified by various types of Neo-Platonic Humanism, beginning with Petrarch himself, and more and more emphatically repeated by Erasmus, Sidney, Spenser, among many others, as well as in the rhetorical handbooks themselves.[18] So too, this kind of Platonic exemplarism—poetry as operative imitation of the ideal—coupled with a Horatian "profitable" instruction—poetry as pleasingly didactic guide to proper action—constitutes a set of moralizing aesthetic assumptions subtending the entire mood of so-called courtly poetry—a mode or vogue with which Shakespeare's "patronizing" sonnets have obvious affinities—and is what gives to that deliberately theatrical poetry of self-display a seriousness that is the consequence of, rather than the alternative to, its witty and stylized artificiality.[19] In this sense, Shakespeare's sonnets are courtly *manqué* in the same way that the poet is epideictic *malgré lui*. The praise initially accorded the young man is conducted with pointed reference to a well-established poetic and rhetorical context that Shakespeare changes only by raising to the status of an especially self-conscious theme. The praise of the young man therefore gains its meaning or its value, on this account, not for being praise but for being stagily poetic praise, a praise of poetry rather than a poetry of praise, and in this way, despite the young man's faults, remains ideal: "His beauty shall in these black lines be seen, / And they shall live, and he in them still green" (63).

But again, for all the authority and convenient familiarity of this epideictic tradition, when we come to the dark lady sonnets (leaving to the side, for now, the various ways in which the young man sonnets resist these themes) we discover neither the simple repetition nor the negation of such self-confidently self-idealizing, almost self-congratulatory, literary admiration, but, instead, an imitation of praise that, in a strange way, is its own antithesis. And this is the case not only because the dark lady provokes as much desire as she does disgust—and in a way that makes it seem as though the one were the cause as well as the price of the other—but also because when the poet elects to criticize his lady he does so not with a rhetoric of invective, but, in fact, with praise.

This is an obvious fact, but one whose pervasiveness and consequence is often and significantly overlooked. All the dark lady sonnets, for example, that have been customarily called anti-Petrarchan (and then, since Sidney Lee, equally customarily called Petrarchanly anti-Petrarchan)—"In the old age black was not counted fair," "My mistress' eyes are nothing like the sun," 131, and 132, to take the most clear-cut cases—open up a method of panegyric that proceeds by purposefully reversing conventional images and epithets of approbation so as markedly to produce conventionally unconventional praise.[20] These sonnets do not exactly blame the lady for being whatever it is she is and is not, but they nevertheless employ, and make a point of saying that they employ, a kind of upside-down praise that is both tonally and thematically very different from the apparently straightforward rhetoric of compliment that the poet invokes, and makes a point of saying that he invokes, for the young man.

It is no doubt right to remember that such reversals of orthodox panegyric are neither unusual nor profoundly anti-Petrarchan. The Petrarchan habit of oxymoron—black snow, icy fire—lends itself to such witty reversal, and there are more than enough literary precedents for dark erotic women, going back to the Queen of Sheba, so as to force us to temper any claims for novelty with regard to Shakespeare's nut-brown old maid.[21] But, however we choose to characterize these sonnets or the woman they describe—both of them coded as traditionally untraditional—they and their reversals introduce and blend into a yet more radically rhetorically inverted set of dark lady sonnets in which we hear a more ambiguous invective, an invective that is the product of the way these other sonnets paradoxically couch the terms of their regret in praise. The famous example, of course, is sonnet 138—"When my love swears that she is made of truth,/I do believe her, though I know she lies"—where the lady's "false-speaking tongue" is matched precisely by the poet's: "On both sides thus is simple truth suppress'd" (138). But we find similarly inverted panegyric in sonnets 135 or 136, where the lady's abundant treasury of sexuality speaks as much against her as the poet does for her, or the way sonnets 137, 141, 147, and 152 are happy to admit, or are unhappily obliged to confess, the poet's impulse "to put fair truth upon so foul a face" (137). In these sonnets the duplicity of the lady is both countered and delimited by the duplicity of the language with which she is described. And this is the subject of these sonnets, something they directly talk about, in the same way that the young man sonnets talk about the way—and thereby stylize and frame the way—they talk about the man.

Again, there is nothing unusual or novel about such rhetorical inversion and again there are antique precedents for this kind of blame by praise that go back at least to Gorgias' praise of Helen or to Isocrates' praise of Busiris.[22] This is the tradition of paradoxical praise—"The Wonderer," as Puttenham called it—whereby something low and base receives elaborate praise that it does not deserve.[23] This is a deliberately comic rhetorical form, an ostentatiously self-deflating rhetorical practice, that takes as its topoi such things as hair or baldness or poverty or riches or anything, really (including nothing, as in Dyer's or Cornwallis's "Prayse of Nothing"), which is of such a kind as to admit of underhanded compliment.[24] Here too the panegyric vileness of the lady can claim its own historical authority, since the traditional duplicity of woman renders her a perennially and peculiarly convenient topic, as "Honest Whore," for an epideixis that takes as its rhetorical project the pretending of a praise it does not mean (so authoritatively convenient that the sober-minded Giordano Bruno could only make moral sense of Petrarch's frenzied love sonnets to a flesh-and-blood Laura by reading them as instances of comic praise).[25] Here too, though the rhetorical tradition is an ancient one, we approach what is another contemporary vogue, for this kind of comic praise, *para-doxical* in the specifically rhetorical, not logical, sense of being beyond or to the side of *ortho-doxa*, has enormous popularity in the Renaissance—is an "epidemic," in Rosalie Colie's well-known phrase—and we can cite innumerable employments of the mode, high and low, serious and comic—from Erasmus' *Praise of Folly* to Nashe's "Prayse of the Red Herring," to Rabelais's praise of debt, to Harington's praise of privies—all these being cases where the author learnedly acknowledges the tradition of rhetorical duplicity on which his rhetoric depends.[26]

As with straightforward, demonstrative praise, this kind of paradoxical praise is necessarily reflexive, designed more to show off the
rhetorical skill of the poet than the virtues or, for that matter, the vices
of the object he describes. Yet there is a crucial difference, both of
affect and of effect, between the self-reflexive reversals of straightforward praise, such as we see them in the young man sonnets, and the
way that paradoxical praise folds over upon itself, inverting, rather
than reversing, the direction of its praise, turning its approbation inside out rather than back to front or upside down. In the former case,
at least at the level of its explicit thematization of itself, the honesty of
poetry, for all its reversals, continues to survive even if the honesty of
what it speaks about does not: the praise of the young man exemplifies itself *as* truth almost, it seems, *because* the young man is deliberately defined, at least in part, as false, but in doing so the praise continues to hold out the image of an ideal to which the young man, like
the reader, might aspire: "I love thee in such sort, / As thou being mine,
mine is thy good report" (96). In contrast, in the yet more ironical case
of a yet more ostentatiously rhetorical praise—the case, we might
want to say, of *merely* rhetorical epideixis—the doubleness of paradox
comes to suffuse the language as well as the object of the praising
poet—"Then will I swear beauty herself is black" (132)—and this produces a yet more complicated rhetorical decorum than what we find
with praise per se because here the poetry presents itself as simultaneously true *and* false precisely because, and not in spite of the fact
that, its object is duplicitous: "When my love swears that she is made
of truth, / I do believe her, though I know she lies" (138). Here not even
the persona of the poet survives the failure of his idealization, or,
rather—because a poetic self survives, albeit an unambiguously unhappy one—the integrity of the poet's first idealized self-representa-
tion turns out to be itself undone by the realized dishonesty of the
beloved object on whom the poet staked his admiration and his self-
representation in the first place: "In loving thee thou know'st I am
forsworn, / But thou art twice forsworn, to me love swearing" (152).

An obvious logic therefore informs the progress from the early
sonnets to the later ones, with the sequence as a whole tracing out a
rhetorical opposition between a poetry of praise that praises poetry
and a praising poetry that calls praise into question. As Shakespeare
develops it—in individual sonnets and in the narrative of the sequence as a whole, with its story of a mathematically complete adultery, whereby the poet is permutatively betrayed not only by both
his objects of desire but by each with each—this general logic in turn

supplies the Ciceronian decorum that justifies the collation of the one rhetorical mode with the ideal young man and the other with the clearly less than ideal dark lady. In a complicated way, that is, the poet's several matters do indeed go very aptly with his several manners, even when, and sometimes because, he says that they do not, and every reader recognizes this consistent appropriateness even if he cannot articulate the grounds of the rhetorical propriety to which he uncritically responds. Yet however starkly formulated is the difference between the two rhetorical modes, still this difference, even sketched out in this perfunctory and schematic way, does not constitute a simple antithetical contrariety, and, for this reason, the progress from the early sonnets to the later ones fails to trace the simple black and white, or foul and fair, rhetorical opposition that might have been produced had Shakespeare chosen to contrast his panegyric of the man with a straightforward invective of the lady. Paradoxical praise is not simply the negation of straightforward praise, but, instead, its peculiar imitative double, a rhetorical doubling that, by including praise within itself—in the same way that we find the young man "in" the dark lady's hell—becomes the parody, rather than the opposite, of what it duplicates.

This is both the cause and the point of the difference between Shakespeare's conventional reversals of praise, which simply put a disclaiming negative before the positives of straightforward praise, and what I have characterized as his more radically paradoxical inversions, which fold praise over upon itself, du-plicating it, so as in this way to subtract from praise its approbation.[27] There will be good reason to return to this notion of a "folded" or a "bi-fold" rhetorical admiration whose wrinkles correspond to an erotic "fold" as well; I will later want to argue that it is precisely this fold that joins the poet's "Will" to the lady's "common place."[28] For now, it is enough to note that paradoxical praise, either as a witty figure in itself or as the rhetorical occasion and frame for Shakespeare's reflections upon the consequences of such wit, does not simply reverse the rhetorical procedures of the praise it mocks; it repeats them, rather, in such a way as to register those procedures as themselves merely rhetorical. And the result is something quite different from the circular idealizations by means of which the poetry of praise self-referentially confirms itself in the sub-sequence of sonnets addressed to the young man. There, in a familiar way, poetry turned to itself, spoke of itself and of its own perfection, when what it spoke about belied the force of its poetic truth. Here, though poetry again foregrounds the rhetoricity of its rhetoric, poetry turns out itself to be the measure, cause, and instance of the very failure it bespeaks. Raising its paradoxically praising rhetoric to the status of a theme, poetry will now itself become its own regret:

> My thoughts and my discourse as madmen's are,
> At randon from the truth vainly express'd;
>> For I have sworn thee fair, and thought thee bright,
>> Who art as black as hell, as dark as night.
>>> (147)

This may seem a roundabout way of saying—indeed, of laboring—something that, perhaps, is so obvious that it might properly go without saying. But the formal rhetorical distinction between praise and its paradox, though it is not itself a distinction based on differences of topic or of style (since the most successful paradox of praise will necessarily be the one perceived to replicate most perfectly the pristine praise it presupposes and repeats, as, for example, in Bruno's paradoxical reading of Petrarch), nevertheless produces a systematic explanation of topical as well as stylistic differences between the young man sonnets and the dark lady sonnets. I have said that paradoxical praise empties praise by doubling it, mocking it with imitation. This is a characterization that I will want in time to refine and to redefine, for to some significant extent it is too simple. However, in the same way that Shakespeare's paradoxical rhetoric of praise in the dark lady sonnets seems in a formal way ironically to echo the straightforward praise of the young man sonnets, so too does Shakespeare seem regularly to redouble in the dark lady sonnets themes and images that in the young man sonnets he had initially presented as univocal and homogeneous. That is to say, the dark lady sonnets will frequently repeat a theme or an image or a word from the young man sonnets, and, moreover, when they do so they will often stress the fact that this involves a repetition. Sometimes the dark lady sonnets will even stress the fact that this effectively amounts to a deliberately parodic quotation. At the same time, however, when the dark lady sonnets thus recall and reemploy an item from the young man sonnets they succeed (and "succession" is itself a theme that finds itself thus problematically repeated, e.g., the way the theme of legitimate, procreative "succession" [2] in the opening young man sonnets is subsequently troped in the first dark lady sonnet when we discover that "now is black beauty's successive heir"), they will also frequently accompany it with, and sometimes fuse it with, its own inverted imita-

tion. In another oversimple formula, whatever the young man sonnets present, the dark lady sonnets characteristically re-present, but
they do so not simply by repeating what has come before, but, in
addition, by developing those initial themes and images as though
they were themselves peculiarly refracted, as though they were their
own internal repetition, as though they were a kind of mimic version
of their former unitary selves.

To take a central instance, consider the way the dark lady sonnets
develop the image of the sun. It is not just that sunlight reappears in
the dark lady sonnets, after having been elaborately developed as an
image, at least on the shining face of it, of simple and honest illuminating brightness in the sonnets addressed to the young man. Rather,
this second sunlight, this dark lady sunlight, is developed by Shakespeare in these sonnets as a brightness which is itself double, thematically double, not only measured by its power to darken transitively, as
in the buried suntanning imagery of sonnet 132 (which repeats the
way the young man's poet in sonnet 62 is "beated and chopp'd with
tann'd antiquity"), but as a general motif of reduplicated lucidity the
internal contradictions of which stand as physical correlative to the
metaphysical and moral duplicity of the dark lady herself.[29]

The sun is by no means the only image that the dark lady sonnets
take up from the young man sonnets and develop in this odd citational way, as though its very being were divisively inflected by its
presence in a context of quotation. But the sun is a particularly important image to consider in this connection, first, because it is so
very prominent a motif throughout the sequence as a whole, second, because both sub-sequences rely upon perennial conceits that
make the light and motion of the sun into an image of specifically
poetic speech. Because the sun possesses this strong value—because it functions as both a central poetic image and as an image of
the poetical—the difference between the way the sun is characterized in the young man sonnets, on the one hand, and the way it is
characterized in the dark lady sonnets, on the other, can help to
specify the different kinds of materiality Shakespeare associates
with the poetry of praise and with the poetry of praise-paradox. In
turn, this can help to explain the subjective psychology that informs
the by no means simply antithetical contrast that the sequence as a
whole develops between the young man's poet and the dark lady's
poet. Given the different ways the sun, which is the light of poetry
itself, shines in the world of the young man and the world of the dark
lady, we can begin to understand why the young man is an old-fash-

ioned ideal who appears to the poet's "imaginary sight" (27) as a brightness that "makes black night beauteous, and her old face new" (27), whereas the lady manifests a kind of double and a novel darkness that leads the poet "to make me give the lie to my true sight,/ And swear that brightness doth not grace the day" (150).

Following out the example, therefore, which is one to which I will return in later chapters, it is worth noting how vividly Shakespeare imagines an original and praiseworthy sunrise in the world of the young man:

> Lo in the orient when the gracious light
> Lifts up his burning head, each under eye
> Doth homage to his new-appearing sight,
> Serving with looks his sacred majesty.
>
> (7)

or, more famous yet:

> Full many a glorious morning have I seen
> Flatter the mountain tops with sovereign eye,
> Kissing with golden face the meadows green,
> Gilding pale streams with heavenly alcumy.
>
> (33)

The imagery of both these openings—of an idealizing, clarifying light, transparent even in its burnishing luminosity—is familiar enough, whether we refer ourselves outside the young man sonnets to the conventions of Petrarchan or *stil nuovo* lyric, where the lady shines as golden light to her lover (e.g., Petrarch's sonnet 348, to cite one of many, or Dante's apostrophe to light at the end of the *Paradiso*, or Spenser's invocation to Elizabeth at the opening of *The Faerie Queene:* "Great Lady of the greatest Isle, whose light/Like Pheobus lampe throughout the world doth shine"), or whether we think to the ensemble of associations carried by other references to light in the sonnets addressed to the young man, for example: "For who's so dumb that cannot write to thee,/When thou thyself dost give invention light?" (38). This is the characteristically golden light of a poetic style and period that the tradition of literary criticism has itself come to call "golden" (with delighted enthusiasm, as, for example, by C. S. Lewis, or, instead, with disgust, as, for example, by Yvor Winters, with his pejorative "aureate"), as though to label the poetry in terms of those essential physical properties without which such poetry simply could not be imagined.[30] We see here also both the fundamentally *visual* modality of such idealizing epideictic poetry—"ideal" deriving from *idein*, "to see"—as well as the agency of vision, the kind of light, that gives a sight for such an ideality to see.

Later I will discuss the genuinely darker side of the young man sonnets and at that point it will be necessary to consider the provenance and the context, as well as the formal rhetorical assumptions, responsible for making such a golden light convenient to a poetry of praise. The habitual appearance of this idealizing sun in idealizing poetics and idealizing poetry is neither an accidental nor a natural fact, and the fixed epideictic value of such poetic heliocentrism constitutes an important question for literary history, a question that source criticism simply begs or postpones when it derives Shakespeare's sun from Spenser's, Spenser's from Petrarch's, Petrarch's from Dante's, and so back to Plato or the Psalms. Even putting this question to the side, however, and looking just to the lines themselves, the reader cannot fail to note the "gracious" quality of the young man's light, with all the religious connotations the phrasing carries (sun-son), as well as the latent theme of sanctified political and cosmological order conveyed by the description of a majestic sun done courtly homage by all who look upon it. The poems present an atmosphere of ideal visuality where glory presupposes courtly praise (or even flattery) in the same way that majesty calls up eyes, which is to say that they assume a world of visually imaged truth, where darkness comes from intervening clouds and not from light itself, and where, as Stephen Booth remarks, at least one pertinent meaning even of "stain," as in the couplet to sonnet 33, refers more to outshining than to fading: "Yet him for this my love no whit disdaineth:/Suns of the world may stain, when heaven's sun staineth."[31]

In contrast, if we turn to a dark lady sonnet such as 132, we find a sun that shines both as a blackness at the break of day and as a brightness at the break of night:

> Thine eyes I love, and they as pitying me,
> Knowing thy heart torment me with disdain,
> Have put on black, and loving mourners be,
> Looking with pretty ruth upon my pain.
> And truly not the morning sun of heaven
> Better becomes the grey cheeks of th' east,
> Nor that full star that ushers in the even
> Doth half that glory to the sober west,
> As those two mourning eyes become thy face.
> O, let it then as well beseem thy heart
> To mourn for me, since mourning doth thee grace,
> And suit thy pity like in every part.[32]

Here again the general conceit of the poem, with its frustrated lover addressing his pitiless, disdaining beloved, is a Petrarchan commonplace, going back beyond Petrarch to the *rime petrose* of Arnault Daniel. Equally common is the intricate development of imagery of sympathetically erotic vision. In this sense, we are here given the same poetics that the poet presupposes in the young man sonnets, where, for example, he can speak familiarly of "that sun, thine eye" (49) precisely because a long-standing tradition of metaphysical and sexual allegory authorizes an iconographic equating of the two.[33] In an insistent way, however, sonnet 132 further plays upon or tropes this convention and these traditional light-sight metaphors when, as a result of comparing the beloved's eyes to the sun, it turns out not that her eyes are lamps, but that the sun to which they are compared is therefore black. This too is, in part, conventional (e.g., Stella's eyes are black), but what concerns us is the stressed contrast to what has come before. In the sonnets addressed to the young man, the morning is "sacred," "new-appearing," "golden," and "green." Here, instead, "the morning sun of heaven" is obscuring complement to "the grey cheeks of th' east," shining in the morning like the evening star at night, because it is a brightness in an encroaching darkness of which it is itself the cause and sign.[34] Where in the sonnets addressed to the young man the sun is a "gracious light" to the morning, here, instead, the morning is a "mourning" whose inversion is a darkening "grace": "since mourning doth thee grace." This pun on "mo(u)rning," which explains why in general in the dark lady sonnets "brightness doth not grace the day," is the kind of motivated homophone for which Shakespeare is often either faulted or appreciated, either the sort for which, as Johnson complained, he threw away the world, or the sort with which he generates the resonant ambiguities that critics like to list. But the point emphasized by the sonnet is that the pun, which must be noticed as such for it to work its poetic effect, does in little what the poem does rhetorically as a whole: repeating itself *in* itself so as to undo itself with its own echo, discovering and producing its own loss at the very moment of calling to the reader's attention the way language, theme, and image displace themselves by folding over upon themselves. So too this is precisely the self-remarking, mourning "paradox" of what is epideictically orthodox, for which the poem will sadly say that it was written: "Then will I swear beauty herself is black,/And all they foul that thy complexion lack" (132).

In obvious ways, all this—morning *and* melancholia—results in something much more complex than a simple reversal of Petrarchan themes and images, and for this reason the poem produces a tonality more complex than that which we associate with even the most self-consciously witty Petrarchan lovers' complaints. The system of logical oppositions and conventional antitheses into which we might be tempted to organize the sonnet's courtly courtship argument falls to pieces as soon as the sonnet brings antithesis into play. Just as the lady's eyes by turning black express a pity occasioned by her heart's disdain, so too does the poet thematize the fact that he here expresses his heart's desire with a language of disdain. In the same way that the stain of the lady's eyes is both image of and answer to the disdain of her heart, so too does the poet amplify the lady's beauty by fouling the conventional images of fairness. The relationship between the lady's eye and the lady's heart, or of the poet to the lady, is a matter, therefore, neither of similarity and contrast nor of pity and disdain, and, for this reason, there is no univocal way in which either poet or lady might "suit thy pity like in every part." As the sonnet develops them, pity is a figure of disdain just as morning is a version of the night, each of them the homeopathic mirror of the heteropathy of the other. As a result, with likeness emerging as the instance, rather than the antithesis, of difference, with pity the *complement* to disdain, we deal with oddly asymmetrical oppositions, both rhetorical and emotional oppositions, whereby each polarized side or half of every opposition that the sonnet adduces already includes, and therefore changes by encapsulating, the larger dichotomy of which it is a part. With regard to the lady, this means that she *cannot* treat the poet either with pity or disdain or even with an oxymoronic combination of the two. For her "charm" consists precisely of the way these two apparently antithetical modalities, empathy and antipathy, turn out each of them to be, within their singular propriety, the contrary double not only of the other but also of itself, the two together thus precipitating a double doubling whose reduplicating logic forecloses the possibility of ever isolating either modality *in* itself. With regard to the poet, this means that he *cannot* speak of his lady (of her pitying black eyes or of her pitiless fair heart) with a simple rhetoric of similarity and contrast, for his language undercuts the logic of its opposites even as it advances them and their contrarieties.[35]

As I have already suggested, I want to make the general claim, which I will subsequently modify, that this is a distinctive feature of the language, argument, and imagery of the dark lady sonnets. These sonnets characteristically undo the oppositions to which they call attention by means of a rhetorical strategy of chiasmus that serves both to reverse and to invert what initially appear to be more simple binary relations. This can be understood as a general application and amplification of what ancient rhetorical theory would call *syneciosis,* the trope that Puttenham translates as the "cross-coupler."[36] But if this pattern of doubling reversal and inversion describes the stylistic manner and the thematic matter of the dark lady sonnets, it is necessary also to realize that it gains its specific significance within Shakespeare's sonnet sequence as a whole from the fact that the young man sonnets regularly speak—at any rate, they seem to speak—against any such admixture of cross-coupling antithesis. In the first sub-sequence, for example, the young man's poet will write, summing up motifs that run through much of the poetry addressed to the young man, a matching pair of sonnets where eye and heart are alternately enemies and friends. The first sonnet of the pair begins: "Mine eye and heart are at a mortal war,/ How to divide the conquest of thy sight" (46).[37] In contrast, the second sonnet, relying on a "verdict" that "is determined" at the conclusion of sonnet 46, begins: "Betwixt mine eye and heart a league is took,/ And each doth good turns now unto the other" (47). Taken together and in sequence, the two sonnets, 46 and 47, in this way compose an argument *in utramque partem,* with their poet placing himself on both sides of a rhetorical question that is a commonplace in the tradition of the Renaissance sonnet. Despite the conventional opposition, however—and it is precisely this convention that the eye-heart conceit of sonnet 132 presupposes—the two young man sonnets confidently argue to what is the same, and equally conventional, conclusion: namely, that their poet's eye and heart do "good turns now unto the other" (47). Thus, in the first sonnet, after meditating on the war between his eye and heart, the poet syllogistically and Neo-Platonically derives the moral that: "As thus: mine eye's due is thy outward part,/ And my heart's right thy inward love of heart" (46). In turn, in the second sonnet, from thinking on the amity between his eye and heart, the poet reassuringly discovers that "thy picture in my sight/ Awakes my heart to heart's and eye's delight" (47). Taken together and in sequence, therefore, the two sonnets respond to the question that they raise by juxtaposing a *concordia discors* and a *coincidentia oppositorum* each against the other. Both sonnets speak to the fact that their poet's eye and heart, however much they differ from or with each other, are equally "delighted"; in both sonnets eye and heart will peacefully "divide the conquest of thy sight," as though, from the ideal perspective shared by the two sonnets, eye and heart are complementary and coordinated aspects of each other.

In an obvious fashion, the rhetorical wit of these two young man sonnets consists of thus hendiadistically arriving, from different starting points, at a common destination, for in this way the two sonnets manage to resolve, or to beg the question raised by, a traditional *débat*. Yet, however witty, the poems take very seriously the equivalence of the conclusions that they share. In both cases the relationship of eye and heart, whether initially antipathetic or sympathetic, leads immediately, via complementary antithesis, to a recuperative and benign assessment of yet other differences adduced. In war or peace the sonnets' several binaries combine to generate a clarity of eye and purity of heart whose own discrete proprieties in turn reciprocally establish, or are established by, the integrity and integration of the other categorical oppositions to which the poems refer. In sonnet 46, for example, the difference between "outward" and "inward" is secured and reconciled because the vision of the eye and the "thinking" of the heart can be harmoniously apportioned out between the clean-cut opposition of "the clear eye's moiety and the dear heart's part." In sonnet 47 the absence of the beloved is converted or transmuted into presence because:

> With my love's picture then my eye doth feast,
> And to the painted banquet bids my heart;
> Another time mine eye is my heart's guest,
> And in his thoughts of love doth share a part.
> So either by thy picture or my love,
> Thyself away are present still with me.

This systematic complementarity, whereby opposites either are the same or, as opposites, still somehow go compatibly together, reflects a general—I will say later a generic—homogeneity subtending both sonnets, something that informs them more deeply than the thematic heterogeneity that the two sonnets only provisionally or momentarily evoke. In the first sonnet it is the difference between eye and heart that establishes the concord between them, whereas in the second sonnet the concord derives from their similarity. But this difference, which is the difference between difference and similarity, turns out not to make much difference. In both sonnets the eye is "clear" and the heart is "dear" by virtue of a governing structure of likeness and contrast, of identity and difference, of similarity and contrariety, that both sonnets equally and isomorphically employ.

What these two young man sonnets share, therefore, thematically and formally, is the sameness of their differences, what joins them together is a structural identity, or a structure of identity, that is yet more fundamental and more powerful than their apparent opposition.[38] In terms of poetic convention and in terms of poetic psychology, this produces the Petrarchan commonplace whereby the poet's eye and heart, which is to say his vision and desire, come instantly to complement each other, moving from war to peace, from antipathy to sympathy, in a progress that constitutes a kind of shorthand summary of the amatory assumptions of ideal admiration—whether we look to Petrarch's "cruel lady who with her eyes, and with the bow whom I pleased only as a target, made the wound about which, Love, I have not been silent to you," or whether we remember the tradition of visual desire that goes back to *Le Roman de la Rose*, where Cupid's arrows go directly through the lover's eyes into his heart.[39] The difference between this and what happens in sonnet 132 is pointed enough. Where the two young man sonnets, sonnets 46 and 47, see both eye and heart as each the figure and occasion of the other, the dark lady sonnet instead both literally and figuratively describes a desire at odds with itself because at odds with what it sees. Where the two young man sonnets bring out the syncritic identity built into their differences, the dark lady sonnet instead brings out the diacritical difference built into its identities. Where the young man sonnets develop an ideal logic of sympathetic opposition, the dark lady sonnet gives us instead what is the paradoxical opposite, if we can call it that, to such a logic of sympathetic opposition.

Generalizing from all of this, we are tempted to formulate very simple formal and thematic criteria with which to distinguish the young man's poet from the dark lady's poet. Speaking formally, we might want to say that whereas the first sub-sequence tends to derive similarity out of difference, the second instead tends to derive difference out of similarity. Correspondingly, in terms of major themes, we might say that whereas in the young man sonnets the poet's eye and heart are equally "delighted," in the dark lady sonnets, in contrast, the desire of the poet's heart is such that it distorts his vision, just as what the poet sees is quite enough to break his heart: "O cunning Love, with tears thou keep'st me blind,/Lest eyes well seeing thy foul faults should find" (148). Such formulas, however, are at once too abstract and too general adequately to distinguish between the poet's loves and poetries of comfort and despair. In what follows it will be important, for example, to see how the kind of difference *in* identity that the dark lady sonnets render explicit in terms of unhappy desire and blind vision is effectively, albeit silently, present in the young man sonnets too, as, for example, in sonnet 62, where, as I briefly noted, the poet's identity and identification do not coalesce "when my glass shows me myself indeed."

Having said this, however, we must also realize that, specifically *in general*, the poet-lover of the young man will define his own identity—his "I," but also his "eye"—as poet and as lover, in terms of his visual identification with the young man—"In our two loves there is but one respect,/Though in our lives a separable spite" (36), or "Now see what good turns eyes for eyes have done" (24)—whereas, in pointed contrast, the poet-lover of the dark lady will discover both himself and his poetry in the loss produced by the fracture of this ideal identification:

> Me from myself thy cruel eye hath taken,
> And my next self thou harder hast engrossed:
> Of him, myself, and thee I am forsaken,
> A torment thrice threefold thus to be crossed.
> (133)

There is a strong parallel, that is to say, a parallel that is emphasized by its exaggerated and repeated generalization, between the way, on the one hand, the homogeneous figurality—linking like with like—of the young man sonnets turns into the heterogeneous figurality—linking like at once with like and unlike—of the dark lady sonnets, and the way, on the other, the narcissistic, homosexual, and ideal desire of the poet for the young man is "transformed" and "translated," to use Hamlet's words of "paradox," into the selflessly "crossed," cross-coupled, heterosexual desire of the poet for the lady: "In things right true my heart and eyes have erred,/And to this false plague are they now transferred" (137).

In at least one sense, this repeated matching of the object of desire to the language of desire merely continues and expands a theme that is endemic to the poetry of praise. Just as Petrarch makes Laura the objectification of laud and laurel, of praise and poetry, just as Dante identifies *lodano* with *la donna*, so too do the dark lady sonnets make the dark lady the figurative equivalent of the paradox of praise and, by extension, of the paradox of poetry. If the first sub-sequence equates the true poetry and true love that goes with the young man—"O, let me, true in love, but truly write" (21)—so too does the sub-sequence addressed to the dark lady correlatively associate lying with language with lying with woman: "Therefore I lie with her, and she with me,/And in our faults by lies we flattered be" (138). But if both sub-sequences in this way stress and thematize the correspondence of their manner with their matter—the correspondence, that is, of their poet's language of desire with that which the poet says that he desires—it remains the case that the poetics and the erotics of the second sub-sequence can only be thought out *in* and *as* the aftermath of the poetics and erotics of the first. The poet's love for the lady is equal to his loss of the young man in the same way that the paradox of praise is an imitation of praise that renders praise passé. The poet's saint is chiasmically "corrupted" "to be a devil" when the purity of the fair young man is displaced by being placed within the duplicitous fair-black dark lady—"I guess one angel *in* another's hell" (144)—in the same way that the univocity of praise is ironized within the equivocality of paradox.

Such relations, stated in this way, are simple homologies, with no necessarily causal connection linking the language of desire to the object of desire. But the dark lady's poet will regularly make a point of relating the one to the other by referring to the novel duplication built into the way he speaks, a duplication, moreover, that the dark lady's poet consistently associates with the paradox of praise. Thus the poet in sonnet 132 resolves to "swear beauty herself is black" when he unpacks his pun on "mo(u)rning." The witty point of the poem is that the content of "mourning," what is literally *in* it, *is* the loss of "morning," insofar as the two of these together are what spell the loss of one. By itself, this is nothing but a trivial equivocation; even so, the pun, once noticed, means univocally that "morning" proper ever after will never be the same, since its use will always thus be put in question by the contradictory mention that is sounded by the pun. And, as sonnet 132 develops it, this particular conflation of use and mention is powerfully consequential, since it is by means of this confusion that neither "the morning sun of heaven" nor its complementary twin, "that full star that ushers in the even," will do more "glory" to the lady's face than her "two mourning eyes," which in turn is why, from this point onward, the poet means to take as his peculiar theme the ways in which "they [are] foul that thy complexion lack." "Mo(u)rning" is perhaps an overly compressed instance of the paradox of praise. It illustrates, however, how in the dark lady sonnets the undoing of praise by its paradox is not just the medium of but is presented also as the *explanation* of the poet's double erotic disappointment. The paradox of praise is not simply the rhetorical consequence of the poet's divided desire but its operative logic: "*So* him I lose through my unkind abuse" (134), "*Therefore* I lie with her, and she with me" (138), "*For* I have sworn thee fair" (147, 152).

What is new in the dark lady sonnets, therefore, is not the identification of the language of desire with the object of desire. Such identification is a conventional feature and theme of the poetry of praise, as when the young man is fair, kind, and true precisely because "'fair,' 'kind,' and 'true' is all my argument" (105), a premise whose collateral metaphoric assumptions I will discuss in more detail in subsequent chapters. Rather, the explicit novelty developed in the dark lady sonnets consists of a desire that is constitutively derived from the disruption, and, therefore, the "corruption," through thematized repetition, of this rhetorical-sexual identification. The poet's lust for the lady *is* the forswearing, cross-coupled relationship that emerges between his desire and its expression, and it therefore registers itself *in* and *as* the slippage between what the poet wants to say and what the poet says he wants. In this way the peculiarity of the poet's panegyric speech explicitly becomes the gloss of what the poet speaks about. On the one hand, the poet will discover through his paradox of praise the loss of an ideal that he desires; on the other, the double speech the poet speaks about in turn inspires an equally peculiar desire to recover through such speech the loss that it bespeaks. I have already suggested a way to put this point arithmetically—and I did so because this numerical conceit is one that Shakespeare seems to savor: "Among a number one is reckon'd none" (136)—when I said that the paradox of praise forfeits the signifieds of desire by paradoxically reiterating the signifiers of desire. It is possible now to follow out at least some of the logic that informs this calculation. The doubling of praise by paradox subtracts from praise its approbation, and this because epideictic signifiers, thus redoubled, survive as their own unhappy surplus, Like "Will" in sonnet 135, which bears the burden of excessive "overplus"—"Whoever hath her wish, thou hast thy *Will*, / And *Will* to boot, and *Will* in overplus"—they are ideal signifiers lacking ideal signifieds.

In this very general way—and it will be necessary now to flesh this generalization out—the sonnets to the dark lady introduce into the tradition of the sonnet a new desire and a new poetics, both of them new in that they understand themselves to be the ruin of that which they succeed, structurally novel insofar as they are cause and consequence of the loss that they lust after and that they elegiacally lament. "Mourning" their "morning," paradoxing their praise, the dark lady sonnets divide the original bright desire and golden poetry with which the sequence begins by means of a duplication whose repetition undoes both erotic and rhetorical identification. It is for this reason that I have so far characterized the relationship between the young man sonnets and the dark lady sonnets in terms of praise and its paradox, in order thus to emphasize, using themes the sonnets themselves stress, this consistently more and less than dialectical relationship between what the sonnets themselves characterize as something old and something new. In the poetics of the sequence, at the level of its rhetorical figures, the dark lady sonnets break the amatory metaphorics of "two distincts, division none" (*The Phoenix and the Turtle*) by substituting for such a unitary duality a tropic system of triangular, "cross-coupling" duplicity: "A torment thrice threefold thus to be crossed" (133). In the narrative the sequence tells, this figural double duplication, which brings out the difference built into binary identities, is materially embodied in the ambiguously duplicitous dark lady—darker and older, almost by structural necessity, than the fair young man—and then projected into the double-cuckoldry story itself, the sequence as a whole moving from the unity of *folie à deux* to the duality of *ménage à trois*. In terms of the sonnets' own literary self-consciousness, there is an analogous contrast, again thematic, between the traditional poetry of erotic idealization addressed to the young man and the mimic undoing of that tradition by means of the radically *anti-* or, rather, the *para*-Petrarchanism addressed to the dark lady. Finally, however, because the self-conscious tradition of the poetry of praise assumes that the language of desire is itself identical with the object of desire—which is why the orthodox poetry of love writes itself out as a love of poetry—the dark lady sonnets' paradox of the orthodox poetry of praise will also bring out even the difference built into the identity of literary and sexual admiration, and by reference to this will not only describe, but will also explain, a poetic desire whose *eros* and *logos* are themselves thematically out of joint.

I will treat these figural and thematic relationships and associations as distinctively Shakespearean, indicative of what for Shakespeare's imagination is habitually poetically convenient. The formal proportion of praise to its paradox can serve as a *ratio* with which to organize and to coordinate apparently separate accounts of what I have so far clumsily called "the poet-lover of the young man" and "the poet-lover of the dark lady" within the confines of a single Shakespearean sensibility or subjectivity that is itself divided by its registration of the difference built into its two rhetorical and erotic identities. Praise and its paradox being Shakespeare's subject-matter, so too would they define his subjectivity, leaving us to situate the specifically Shakespearean subject in the space of differentiated identity or self-difference traced out by the slippage circumscribed by the characterology of the poet-lover of the young man and the characterology of the poet-lover of the dark lady. Responding to the tonality of personal presence in the poems, recognizing their strong affect of individuated interiority, we would thus plausibly read the sonnets as psychological documents, taking them and the conflicts they express as the historical record with reference to which an accurate portrait of the person, rather than the plural personae, of the sonnets' poet might be drawn. Reading them in this complicated but still authentically autobiographical way, we could say, as Wordsworth said, that Shakespeare in his sonnets offers us a key with which to unlock his idiosyncratic heart. But if so, if the sonnets are for us simply evidence of the biographical Shakespeare, then, as Browning said in response to Wordsworth's romantic reading, "the less Shakespeare he," and, in addition, the less Shakespeareans we. And this not because there is any good reason to assume an effective discrepancy between the private man and his public work—especially with regard to work so minimally public as Shakespeare's sonnets—but because, though such a reading might succeed in describing a singular historic Shakespeare, it would fail even to acknowledge, still less to account for, either Shakespeare's general historical literary appeal or his historical literary influence.[40]

For the Shakespearean subject—as subject matter or as subjectivity—however particular, informs and founds the canon of representational subjective literature as it has evolved since the Renaissance, marking both the effective beginning of a literature of deep subjective affect as well as standing to that tradition as validating, psychologistic touchstone. Shakespeare's famous capability, negative or not, to develop "real" characters, his ability to remake out of stock, conventional types—either lyric or dramatic—figures of such distinctive "personality" as to have themselves become, by virtue of their very specificity, abstract instances of the universal—the Hamletian, the Leontene, the Othelloesque—is, of course, itself a determinate literary effect, a literary feature or function associated with only a few kinds of literature and, for that matter, with only a very few of Shakespeare's dramatis personae. We know that the taste for such a literature of personality emerges only relatively recently—if not with Shakespeare, then in the Renaissance, when an allegoricizing literature begins to rewrite itself in a more densely textured mode—a taste, moreover, that it is reasonable to suspect may have already died out. Yet this is a taste that has always been fed by the Shakespearean, in the sense that even Shakespeare's most thinly developed dramatic characters, his Hermias and Helenas, have always been seen to participate in, and to accommodate themselves to, a theater organized by a logic of personality—a theater of psycho-logic as opposed to an Aristotelian theater of logical action—whose subjective intelligibility and authority have been uniformly remarked by the entire tradition of Shakespeare criticism, and not only by romantic critics of character.[41]

This is one reason why—quite apart from their literary merit, which has at times been questioned—Shakespeare's sonnets have historically been so interesting, even to periods or tastes that regret their "personality"—from Benson's genteel emendations of the sonnets' scandalous and embarrassing "he's," to Ransom's and Winters's icy disdain for the poet's too obviously fiery self. Being the genre of first-person discourse, Shakespeare's sonnets necessarily sound to their readers as Shakespeare's most subjective or personal voice, the very opposite, of course, to the zero-person voice that is heard—or, rather, by formal necessity, that cannot be heard—in Shakespeare's plays, and a voice possessing considerably more personal presence than that evinced by the third-person speaker of the narrative poems. Connecting the neutral, dramatic Shakespeare to the personal, lyric Shakespeare, readers often assume that the "deep" characters in the plays are projections, total or partial, of this more palpable, because lyric, Shakespearean subject whose voice we hear at sonnets. From this it seems to follow that Shakespeare's characterological effects in his plays—his joining of particularized passion to particular person, of singularized characteristic to singular character—are effective because of Shakespeare's verisimilar insight, conscious or not, into how personality—his own, but, by projection, all—authentically expresses itself. In short, summarizing a good many critical assumptions, the Shakespearean is thought to be successfully personal because personality is thought to be, in essence, Shakespearean. This is a mode of reasoning that psychoanalytic criticism renders explicit when it attempts to account for Shakespeare's popularity. But the same psychologistic assumptions implicitly underlie more formalist approaches, as when Frye explains Shakespearean dramatic structure by reference to mythic forms and cross-cultural

archetypes which are the consequence and expression of global human necessity.[42] In either case, the general appeal of Shakespeare's
characters eventually becomes evidence of Shakespeare's psychological acumen, and then, reversing the argument, Shakespeare's
psychological sophistication becomes in circular turn the explanation of his literary appeal.

But—and these are the caveats that will constrain the argument
that follows—even if there is such a thing as a psychology that can lay
claim to being universal, still the literature of personality is itself historically particular, flourishing only at certain times in specific literary
genres, concerning itself only with certain personality types and particular literary psychologies. Correspondingly, even if it is the case
that Shakespeare has left us in his sonnets the palimpsestial record of
a personality peculiar to himself, still that particular personality has
historically established itself as the hallmark and the all-encompass-
ing paradigm of literary subjectivity in general. Dryden makes the
point with regard to the plays, but it is yet more relevant to the "character" of the sonnets: "If Shakespeare be allowed, as I think he must,
to have made his Characters distinct, it will easily be infer'd that he
understood the nature of the Passions; because it has been prov'd
already, that confus'd passions make undistinguishable characters."[43]
For this reason, recognizing both the historical particularity and the
generality of the Shakespearean subject, its literary specificity and its
literary commonality, I want to argue that it is Shakespeare's specifically *literary* insight, his insight into literature rather than his psychological acumen, that makes his psychology effective, and that his
characters are persuasive, when they are persuasive, not because
they are the imitation of a real human nature, but because they enact
the *only* logic through which subjectivity can be thought or represented in our literary tradition insofar as our literature commits
itself to being what it traditionally understands as literary. (It follows as a corollary, though one that is not very relevant to my argument, that Shakespeare's characters are psychologically authentic
only to the extent, which may, of course, be considerable, that natural humans reenact the literary representation of human nature.)

This is why the poetics of praise, which from Aristotle to the Renaissance supplies the formal model, the material topology, the rhetorical tropology, for *all* of literature, seems so important. For the
poetics of praise, as will be discussed in subsequent chapters, not
only determines the values of the praising poet but also, and in very
particular and determinate ways, his proper poetic persona as well.

Accordingly, if Shakespeare elaborates something new in the literature of the self, this is because he rethinks—and not only in the sonnets—the subjective exigencies of the poetry of praise, thereby
opening up for the first time—by rethinking the form, the matter,
and the tropes of literature—the possibility of a literature of subjective depth. This is why I will come finally to say, despite the bizarre
enormity of the claim, that the Shakespearean subject is *the* subject
of our literature, the privileged and singular form of literary subjectivity since the Renaissance. And this in turn will suggest why it is
that Shakespeare's canon has historically been institutionalized by
and within a larger literary canon for which subjectivity, as authorial
presence, novelistic characterology, introspective interiority, has always seemed—or, at least, has always seemed since Shakespeare—
a significant literary feature.

By the Shakespearean subject, therefore, I do not refer to an actual
or biographical Shakespearean personality—"sweet" or "upstart" as
the case may have been—of a kind that historical critics look for in
literary and extraliterary archives; still less do I propose to seek out in
Elizabethan chambers originals for the young man or the dark lady.
Neither do I identify the identity of the Shakespearean subject either
with any of the individual, or with the sum of all the individual, characters who figure in what too graphically is called the "corpus," as
though it were possible, by invoking an ultimately incoherent notion
of "negative capability," to flesh out a Shakespearean personality
from the indicators of character who enact the action of the plays.
Rather, by the Shakespearean subject I mean to refer, to begin with,
very simply, to the way that Shakespeare's poems and plays will occasionally, by no means always or even frequently, induce the literary
effect of a subject. If I were here concerned with the plays and the
theatrical formation of such a Shakespearean subject, it would be
necessary to discuss stylistic and dramatic techniques quite as much
as characterological psychology or motivation, if only because the
subjectivity of a theatrical character is as much a function of the dramatic atmosphere in which he acts as it is of his own personality—
Claudio, Othello, Posthumus, and Leontes, for example, being characters whose jealousies are equally illegitimate but who nevertheless
live out their fantasmatic cuckoldries to quite different affective and
theatrical consequence.[44] If this were done with any success and with
enough plays, it would be possible to distinguish between a character's destiny and his density so as thereby to bring out what is
uniquely Shakespearean in the relationship between the generic
mode of a play, the diegesis of its plot, and the motivating psychology

of its theatrical subject. In principle it should be possible to describe what are characteristic formal and phenomenal features of Shakespearean dramatic characterology and in this way to develop a "personal account" of the stylistic and thematic evolution of the canon from the early comedies through the high tragedies to the late romances. In an epilogue I will refer very briefly to what I think are especially significant generic distinctions in the subjectivity effect given off by Shakespeare's major theatrical personae.

With regard to Shakespeare's sonnets, however, the subjectivity *in* the sequence is already its literary subject matter. The sonnets themselves explicitly take up the relationship between the way they speak, and what they speak, and the figured first person who is ostensibly the speaker of their speech. For this reason, the sonnets are themselves already a literary account—an account *in terms of* literature—of the formation of the Shakespearean subject, advancing their own manipulation of the rhetorical conventions of the sonnet—which is to say of the poetics of amatory praise, which is to say of the literary proprieties of the language of desire—as explanation of the sensibility informing the sequence as a whole. This is why it is necessary to approach the novelty of the Shakespearean subject through the sonnets' paradox of what is epideictically orthodox, through the way the dark lady sonnets trope the conventional epideictic tropes of the young man sonnets, for this is the way the sonnets themselves explain what is new about their poet's person.

For just this reason, however—because Shakespeare's sonnet sequence exists not only as an example of but also as an explanation of the way, at a certain moment in the history of the sonnet, an orthodox poetic persona suffers a significant mutation—I believe that a practical criticism or reading of Shakespeare's sonnets will also make a theoretical point about the literary history of the sonneteering self. By convention, the first person of a sonnet sequence is operatively defined, as in the young man sonnets, on the one hand, as a poet, on the other, as a lover: these two hands joining together, like Romeo's and Juliet's when the lovers first meet and speak their sonnet, in a poetry of love whose admiration expresses itself as a love of poetry. All this Shakespeare's sonnets characterize, however, and make a point of characterizing, as something old: old in the sense of being prior to that which comes later, old, that is, because written when poetry was young, early because passé. In contrast, I have suggested that Shakespeare's later sonnets, i.e., the ones that come late in the sequence, are something new, and that they describe themselves as such, because they rewrite these old conventions by repeating them, thus developing a new poetics and a new desire at odds both with each other and with themselves, and thus developing, at the same time, a new poetic persona at odds with its self. This new persona, novel and novelistic, emerges not as a break with the past but as the regretful foreclosing or retrospective forswearing of what has come before—an "aftermath," I have said, meaning to convey by this term the memorializing nostalgia for an older or original ideal self whose loss is structurally inherent in such revisionary self-constitution. Only as my argument develops will it be possible to determine how specifically and canonically Shakespearean is this new subject born as the souvenir of its own admiration in the split between its desire and speech. But it is precisely the precipitation of such a subject, disrupted, at the same time as it is constituted, by its doubled language and its divided desire—"In loving thee thou know'st I am forsworn,/But thou art twice forsworn, to me love swearing" (152)—that seems to initiate the very possibility of a powerful subjectivity effect.

It is, of course, a commonplace of Renaissance literary criticism to see in the sonnet vogue itself the evidence of an increasingly personal or personalizing literature, an incipiently psychological literature of subjective interiority whose self-conscious conventions evince the contours and preoccupations of a recognizably modern "self." This literary mode and mood—Augustinian in tone, Petrarchan in theme—of which Shakespeare's sonnets can be taken as radically symptomatic, is in turn commonly connected to what seem to be analogous Renaissance impulses to individuation—from the solitary piety of Reformationist meditation to the redevelopment (delayed in England) of unifocal linear perspective in theater and painting, from the revival of solipsistic Pyrhonnic skepticism, as, for example, in Montaigne, to the formulation of the Cartesian *cogito*, from the rise of a frankly middle-class ethics to the organization of the centralized nation state, *et alia*—all of which, taken alone or taken together, are said to testify to the emergence—sometime between the beginning of Italian Humanism and the founding of the Royal Society, between the revival of Greek and the decline of Ciceronianism, between the invention of the printing press and the codification of the enclosure laws, *inter alia*—of privatized, bourgeois, psychological identity.

However this may be—and the chronological as well as the methodological objections to so unnuanced and synthetic a history of ideas have often been noted—it would be a mistake too quickly to identify the Shakespearean subject with what is too loosely called the "Renaissance self." Such a generically ideal, Burckhardtian, Renaissance "first person"—historically manifesting its self, perhaps, like Shakespeare's panegyric self, only in potentiating, apprehensive anticipation of its own loss—may well be a great simplification of the lineaments and dynamics of Renaissance literary subjectivity (certainly, for famous example, the banalities that are said to define Petrarchan sensibility do little justice to Petrarch).[45] Leaving this larger question to the side, it will be necessary to distinguish very carefully between the subject of Shakespeare's sonnets and the idealized self of the traditional laudatory sonnet, and this precisely because the tradition of erotic praise seems so characteristically and so characterologically to present a self.

For in the same way that Shakespeare's young man sonnets begin where the official panegyric tradition ends, distancing themselves from the epideictic conventions of that tradition by noisily foregrounding them, so too does the self immanent in Shakespeare's dark lady sonnets retract by retracing the official personality of the Petrarchan poet-lover, as, for example, in sonnet 132, where, as we have seen, the poet apes but yet inverts the self-promoting figures of Petrarchan seduction. What concerns us, therefore, is the way the self-conscious conventions of Petrarchist amatory poetics will originally produce, or seem to produce, an idealizing poetry of an idealized self, but then, when those conventions become themselves yet more self-conscious, will produce instead a paradoxical poetry of a self derived not only from the loss of its ideal but also from the loss of itself. This is the subjective paradox, a paradox *of* subjectivity, that stands as psychological corollary to the problematic themes, imagery, and literary self-criticism of the dark lady sonnets. In general, the question is how a literary logic determines a corresponding psycho-logic. Specifically, the question is why an identity articulated in its disappointed difference from itself becomes at once and persuasively the subjective instrumentality of a poetry that writes against itself, of a love for that which is abhorred, and of a praise for that which is despised. This leaves open the further question, which I want also to address, as to why this forswearing subject, which takes flight in Petrarchan dusk, seems both more personal and more "Shakespearean" than that which it "forswears."

·2·

Cambio is chang'd into Lucentio.
(*The Taming of the Shrew,* 5.1.123)

I have so far distinguished the sub-sequence of sonnets addressed
to the young man from the sub-sequence of sonnets addressed to
the dark lady by calling the one a poetry of praise and the other a
poetry of praise paradox. This is a generic distinction; it speaks to
the fact that, at least on the face of it, the young man sonnets characterize the young man as something praiseworthy, just as they characterize their own poetic purpose in terms of the poetics of praise,
whereas, in contrast, the dark lady sonnets either characterize the
lady's traditional foul as something novelly fair or they develop a
blame of the lady through mock encomiastic amplification of the
lady's vices or, reacting to this blame, they explicitly remark and
regret the import of their novel panegyric: "For I have sworn thee
fair, and thought thee bright,/Who art as black as hell, as dark as
night" (147).

In addition, referring both to their themes and to the poetic forms
they employ, I have further distinguished the two sub-sequences, one
from the other, by saying that whereas the young man sonnets tend to
derive similarity out of difference, the dark lady sonnets instead derive difference out of similarity. Like the distinction between praise
and its paradox, this was a distinction that involved an interrelationship between the two terms distinguished, for I argued that the second sub-sequence discovers the specific differences that it develops
when it chiasmically reduplicates, when it "cross-couples," precisely
those dual unities that are initially developed and foregrounded in
the first sub-sequence. I further suggested that these distinctions between the two sub-sequences— generic, formal, and thematic—are
important because they are effectively related both to large narrative
events in the sequence as a whole—for example, the double cuckoldry story—and also to the way the sequence as a whole manifests
what in the context of the conventional Renaissance sonnet is a strikingly peculiar poetic first person. The principal illustration for all of

86

this was the way the heterogeneous relation of eye and heart that is developed in sonnet 132 seems systematically to undo and to subvert the homogeneous relation of eye and heart that is presented in sonnets 46 and 47.

These initial distinctions and relations must now be further refined, for many of the features, though not all, that I have provisionally associated with the dark lady sonnets are operatively present in the young man sonnets as well. To recognize this, however, does not take away from the fact that the sequence as a whole regularly emphasizes the homogeneity-heterogeneity distinction to which I have referred. This is especially evident with regard to the visionary themes and motifs that the poet plays with in sonnets 46 and 47. To the extent that the young man sonnets characterize themselves as a poetry of praise, as a poetry of admiration, they characteristically develop a homology or correspondence between their poet's vision and their poet's desire: "thy picture in my sight/Awakes my heart to heart's and eye's delight" (47). In contrast, to the extent that the dark lady sonnets characterize themselves in terms of the paradox of praise, it is just this correspondence that they put into question:

> O me! what eyes hath Love put in my head,
> Which have no correspondence with true sight,
> Or if they have, where is my judgment fled,
> That censures falsely what they see aright?
> (148)

In the sequence as a whole this contrast is given special prominence; so too the motifs through which it is elaborated are specific and consistent. In the young man sonnets the young man is an emphatically visual ideal: "And more, much more than in my verse can sit,/Your own glass shows you, when you look in it" (103). In ways that are utterly conventional, the young man is at once the active and the passive principle of sight, both the subject and the object of the poet's admiration: "The lovely gaze where every eye doth dwell" (5). So too, as both complement and compliment to this visual ideality, the poet's poetry is itself conceived, also conventionally, as something visual, as the panegyric picture-image of the young man's beauty: either cloudedly so, as when "'tis thee (myself) that for myself I praise,/Painting my age with beauty of thy days" (62), or with a delighted brightness, as when "his beauty shall in these black lines be seen,/And they shall live, and he in them still green" (63) or when "this miracle have might,/That in black ink my love may still shine bright" (65) or when "so long as men can breathe or eyes can see,/So long lives this, and this gives life to thee" (18), or when "your praise shall still find room,/Even in the eyes of all posterity" (55) because "you live in this, and dwell in lovers' eyes" (55).

In contrast, when the dark lady's poet looks at the lady, his "eyes . . . behold and see not what they see" (137). The poet's eyes are such that though "they . . . see where it lies,/Yet what the best is take the worst to be" (137). So too, if the poet loves the lady, it is not a desire motivated by visual admiration—"In faith, I do not love thee with mine eyes,/For they in thee a thousand errors note" (141)—or if it is a visual desire, it is so only insofar as "all my best doth worship thy defect,/Commanded by the motion of thine eyes" (149). Finally, the dark lady sonnets do not characterize themselves as something visual, but, instead, as something verbal, as something of the tongue rather than of the eye, as when "every tongue says beauty should look so" (127) or as when the poet resolves "then will I swear beauty herself is black" (132). Moreover, this speech the poet speaks about *as* speech seems, for just this very reason, effectively to speak against—indeed, effectively to "lie" against—the poet's vision, as when "mine eyes seeing this, say this is not" (137).

In subsequent chapters I will be concerned with the way the sequence as a whole develops and amplifies these various differences, differences that can be summarized by saying that whereas the young man's poet, motivated by his admiration, wants to employ a visionary language with which to "write the beauty of your eyes" (17), the dark lady's poet, instead, stimulated by his lust, seems obliged to speak a verbal speech that "give[s] the lie to my true sight" (150). In general terms I will argue that the homogeneous-heterogeneous distinction that divides the two sub-sequences one from the other—like the distinction between homosexual love and heterosexual lust—finds itself not only exampled by, but also explained by, the paradoxical relation of vision to speech that is developed in the sequence as a whole. Along with this, I will argue, first, that the dark lady sonnets present their speech as the cross-coupling reduplication of the unitary (though already problematic) vision of the young man sonnets, and second, that this is how Shakespeare fleshes out and gives characterological depth to his sonneteering persona.

In the context of the typically visual laudation of the conventional Renaissance sonnet—indeed, in the context of a literary tradition for which all poetry is a poetry of visionary praise—this Shakespearean disjunction between poetic word and poetic vision is something profoundly new. It is so, I will argue, because it is stressed and, in the strongest sense, *realized* by being explicitly thematized, i.e., by being put into words in a very direct and straightforward way. At the same time, however, it is important also to realize that, for all its novelty, this disjunction is something both the conventional Renaissance sonnet and, speaking broadly, conventional literature anticipate in very specific ways. The final point I will want to make, therefore, is that though Shakespeare in his sonnets invents a new poetics of the "word," this verbal poetics is something already virtually present in, and therefore something Shakespeare does indeed literally come upon when he rethinks, the visual ideality characteristic of what would have seemed to Shakespeare traditional literature and traditional literariness. I will argue that it is because traditional poetry and poetics in this way prepare in advance—generically, formally, but also thematically—a place, which, as will be seen, is a conventional "no place," for Shakespearean invention, especially a place for Shakespeare's novel poetic persona, that Shakespeare's sonnets possess their historical force and significance. To understand how this place is prepared and anticipated, however, it is necessary for us first to rehearse in very general ways the central role of the poetry and poetics of praise in the literary tradition Shakespeare inherits. This review will allow us to recall the central role of vision within the tradition of the poetics and the poetry of praise; this in turn will make it possible to see how the literature of such a visual tradition mutely imagines the verbality it cannot bring itself to speak about.

The importance of praise (or, more generally, the "epideictic," praise or blame) in traditional poetics is of course well known and cannot be overestimated. In the literary tradition Shakespeare receives, both practical and theoretical, praise is not simply one among the many kinds of poetry but is instead the ideal kind to which all other kinds aspire to be like, at once the formal and the functional model for poetry as a whole. That praise is the noblest form of poetry because it imitates the noblest things, and that all of poetry should therefore imitate praise, defines a claim, or a presumption, or an aesthetic, that goes back to Aristotle, who derived all of poetry from the first, primal, epideictic imitations, and the ideal goes even further back than that, if we remember that the only poetry Plato allows into his ideal Republic is "hymns to the gods and praises of virtuous men." So too this very general idea, formulated at the very beginning of systematic reflection on the nature of the literary, is one whose force seems never really to wane, being developed yet further in antiquity by, for example, Isocrates, Quintilian, Cicero, Hermogenes, Menander, being subsequently reformulated and repeated by Donatus and Fulgentius, eventually being most dogmatically and influentially asserted by Averroes in his twelfth-century paraphrase of Aristotle's *Poetics*, where Aristotle is made to say, more summarily than in fact he did, that all of poetry is a version of praise. As is well known, the particular topoi, the schemes for exposition and amplification, the stylistic exigencies, along with the general aesthetic principles of praise, are all codified and popularized by the early Florentine Humanists in the form that, soon after, will be transmitted to England through the medium of such critics as Scaliger and Minturno.[1]

Throughout, the reasoning of these philosophers, rhetoricians, and literary critics is consistent and profound, and the poetic logic they invoke continues to inform and to motivate the conventions of the Renaissance sonnet both in England and on the continent. To begin with, in the mimetic tradition in which Shakespeare writes, it is axiomatic that praise is historically the first, and conceptually the highest, form of poetry because it is the form of poetry that imitates the first and highest things. This is the basis of Renaissance genre theory, which again goes back to Aristotle, where the hierarchy and decorum of poetic kinds is established by declining, as Puttenham puts it, "the subject or matter of poesie" downward to invective from "the laud honour and glory of the imortall gods."[2] This is also the basis for the various Renaissance didactic defenses of poetry, all of which make poetry something morally valuable by referring to its specifically epideictic mimetic effect—by referring, that is, to the way that poetry promotes on the part of its audience a virtuous emulation of the model it panegyrically mimes or, taking the negative, repulsing case of invective, by referring to the way that poetry induces in its audience an equally virtuous, but now allotropic or apotropaic, emulation of the object it, again mimetically, blames. (This argument is reversed, of course, but the same reasoning maintained, when poetry is attacked either for inducing an imitation of vice or for satirizing virtue.)

In the most general sense, all poetry is understood to be epideictic because all of it is understood to be morally mimetic in this way, all of it, in Sidney's famous words, "fayning notable images of vertues, vices, or what els, with that delightful teaching, which must be the right describing note to know a Poet by."[3] But because it is with praise that poetry most obviously and most effectively sets a good example, the better and more serious poet, the exemplary poet, will restrict himself to "hymns at heaven's gate" (29), taking his praise, as does Shakespeare in the sonnets addressed to the young man, as the particular poetic example of poetry per se. This is one reason why the poetry of praise so readily becomes the praise of poetry as a whole, because this is the generic explanation or "apologie" of poetic "profit and delight." As Sidney says, here repeating more than one ancient commonplace, "Poesie . . . is an arte of imitation, for so Aristotle termeth it in his word *Mimesis*, that is to say, a representing, counterfetting, or figuring foorth: to speake metaphorically, a speaking picture: with this end to teache and delight" (*AP*, 158). And this is why even false praise is understood to possess its own poetic virtue. Even when it is flattery—"sweet flattery" (42), Shakespeare calls it—praise remains the sincerest and highest form of poetic imitation, the emulate genre, as it were, of mimesis itself.

This mimetic dimension identifies the ethical value of poetry, for, on the one hand, through its imitations poetry teaches an ideal knowledge that is worth the knowing, and, on the other, by virtue of its praise, poetic imitation elicits a worthy mimetic response from its audience. By itself, however, this principle of poetic imitation (related, of course—though, as we will see, problematically related—to the way poets are supposed to imitate exemplary poetic precursors) does not fully explain how poetry is able to move its audience to imitate the praiseworthy examples poetic imitation epideictically depicts. It fails to explain the poetic *effect* of poetic panegyric. Here is where "delight" enters the poetic picture in a specific way, as the sugar wrapped around the presumably bitter pill of teachable doctrine.

Again the point is nothing but a commonplace. Poetry has an energy, an *energeia*, and a vivacity, an *enargia*, that animates poetic imitation. Poetry is not simply a verisimilar imitation of the real, nor is it a sermonizing rehearsal of the ideal; it is instead a lively and an enlivening representation of the real *through* the ideal. Unlike "the meaner sort of Painters, who counterfet onely such faces as are sette before them," the poet, says Sidney—here again echoing familiar claims—"bestow[s] that in cullours upon you which is fittest for the eye to see" (*AP*, 159). "These bee they," Sidney goes on to say, "that, as the first and most noble sorte, may justly be termed *Vates*" (Sidney's epideictic examples are either scriptural, e.g., "*David* in his Psalmes, *Salomon* in his song of Songs . . . *Moses* and *Debora* in theyr

Hymnes," or classical, e.g., "*Orpheus, Amphion, Homer* in his hymnes"); they deserve the "name of Poets: for these indeede . . . imitate both to delight and teach, and delight to move men to take that goodnes in hande, which without delight they would flye as from a stranger" (*AP*, 159).

In this way "delight" informs or supplements poetic mimesis, making poetry into something that is more than merely lifeless imitation. Sidney is quite emphatic with regard to the ethical importance of "delight": "that mooving is of a higher degree then teaching, it may by this appeare, that it is well nigh the cause and effect of teaching" (*AP*, 171). This is why, for example, the truth of poetry is more edifying than either the "precept" of the philosopher or the "example" of the historian. On the one hand, the philosopher's "precept" is "abstract and generall" (*AP*, 164) and so lacks rhetorical force; on the other, the historian's example "is so tyed not to what shoulde bee but to what is, to the particuler truth of things and not to the general reason of things, that hys example draweth no necessary consequence, and [is] therefore a lesse fruitfull doctrine" (*AP*, 164). In contrast, the delightful, lively, vivid, vivifying, imitations of the poet "goe beyond them both" (*AP*, 163), and this because, "illuminated or figured foorth by the speaking picture of Poesie" (*AP*, 165), the poet marries precept to example, philosophy to history, generalized ideal to particularized real:

> Now dooth the peerlesse Poet performe both: for whatsoever the Philosopher sayth shoulde be doone, hee giveth a perfect picture of it in some one, by whome hee presupposeth it was doone. So as hee coupleth the generall notion with the particuler example. A perfect picture I say, for hee yeeldeth to the powers of the minde an image of that whereof the Philosopher bestoweth but a woordish description: which dooth neyther strike, pierce, nor possesse the sight of the soule so much as that other dooth.
>
> (*AP*, 164)

Again, all this is nothing but familiar. Sidney's *Apology for Poetry* is a representative document because its syncretic blend of Aristotle and Plato, Horace and Cicero, gives expression to what are the commonplace generalities, even the banalities, of Humanist poetics. Sidney is being thoroughly orthodox when he says the poet does not merely copy Nature, but, rather:

> the poet, disdayning to be tied to any such subjection, lifted up with the vigor of his owne invention, dooth growe in effect another nature, in

making things either better then Nature bringeth forth, or quite a newe, formes such as never were in Nature.

(AP, 156)

In this way, "ranging . . . within the Zodiak of his owne wit," the poet makes a "golden" Nature out of what would otherwise be a "brasen" Nature (*AP*, 156), eking nature out through the "Ideality" of his imagination:

> for any understanding knoweth the skil of the Artificer standeth in that *Idea* or fore-conceite of the work, and not in the work it selfe. And that the Poet hath that *Idea* is manifest, by delivering them forth in such excellencie as hee hath imagined them. Which delivering forth also is not wholly imaginative, as we are wont to say by them that build Castles in the ayre: but so far substantially it worketh, not onely to make a Cyrus, which had been but a particuler excellencie, as Nature might have done, but to bestow a Cyrus upon the worlde, to make many Cyrus's, if they will learne aright why and how, that Maker made him.

(AP, 157)

Here is the high Renaissance conception of poetic vocation. Guided by his "Idea," the poet becomes a maker like the divine Maker. In accord with a metaphysical aesthetics of "formal" imitation that goes back to Plotinus, if not to Plato (and whose negative Gnostic versions motivate the first great Christian heresies), the poet becomes a demiurgic demigod:

> Neyther let it be deemed too sawcie a comparison to ballance the highest poynt of man's wit with the efficacie of Nature: but rather give right honor to the heavenly Maker of that maker, who, having made man to his owne likenes, set him beyond and over all the workes of that second nature, which in nothing he sheweth so much as in Poetrie, when with the force of a divine breath he bringeth things forth far surpassing her dooings.

(AP, 157)

I quote these famous passages for several reasons. First of all, it is important to recall the ways in which the ethical defense of poetry is regularly couched in terms of panegyric. It follows directly from the principle of "teach and delight" that poetry is praiseworthy only insofar as it is a poetry of praise. This is why, whatever else it might seem to do or might seem to be about, poetry is always essentially epideictic, is always a blazon of a paragon's perfection, an idealizing laud of an idealized Cyrus, as, for example, when the *Aeneid* is read as praise of Aeneas.

Second, these passages from Sidney's *Apology* recall the consistently visual metaphors and images through which such epideictic idealization is typically conceived. These metaphors originate, perhaps, with the visuality that is etymologically embedded in the Neo-Platonic "Idea" to which Sidney refers (again, from Greek *idein*, "to see") or perhaps with the "light" that shines in "delight." They acquire a more specific inflection, however, when developed so as to illustrate the general and perennial assumptions of the poetics of *ut pictura poesis*. Thus, using an ancient formula, and relying on the faculty psychology of imagination that derives from Aristotelian and Stoic anatomies of the soul, poetry is a "speaking picture," a "perfect picture," whose "image" "strikes," "pierces," "possesses the sight of the soul" more powerfully than the "woordish description" of the Philosopher. So too, presupposing and blurring the "eikastic"-"phantastic" distinction that derives from Plato's *Sophist*, poetry is "fayning notable images of vertues, vices, or what els," and this "fayning" has value and effect because its "images" are "illuminated or figured foorth by the speaking picture of Poesie." Such visual or visionary motifs are given special emphasis in the characteristically epideictic vocabulary of Humanist poetics, in the theoretical language of *specchio exemplare, pictura, eikon, idea, imaginem, eidolon*. So too these are the master metaphors by means of which the Renaissance sonnet will characteristically idealize itself, as when Drayton alternately calls his sonnet cycle either *Ideas Mirrour* or *Idea*.

Finally, these regularly anthologized passages are important because they illustrate how readily and generally it happens that poetic "delight," understood in terms of poetic effect on the one hand, is assimilated to poetic ideality, understood in terms of poetic content or doctrine on the other, i.e., as "well nigh the cause and effect of teaching." The way the poet pleases, his delightful manner, is not only decorously compatible with, but is somehow conducive to, the substantive doctrine or matter that the poet teaches. Thus the poet amplifies, vivifies, energizes, his referents because he "bestow[s] that in cullours upon you which is fittest for the eye to see." These colors are specifically "delightful." But this ornamental amplification, which is what sets the poet off from "the meaner sort of Painters, who counterfet onely such faces as are sette before them," is also the means whereby the poet passes over from the particular real to the universal ideal, from the historical to the exemplary Cyrus. This is what Sidney means, for example, when he says that the poet "manifests" the "Idea" "by delivering them forth in such excellencie as hee hath imagined them." Such imaginative "delivering forth" "is not wholly imaginative"; it is not, Sidney insists, building "Castles in the ayre." Rather, "imagination" works "substantially," "not onely to make a Cyrus, which had been but a particuler excellencie, as Nature might have done, but to bestow a Cyrus upon the worlde, to make many Cyrus's, if they will learne aright why and how that Maker made him."

The last point is important because it speaks to the way poetic manner and matter are regularly understood in traditional rhetorical theory to complement each other, as though poetic idealization of the real were at the same time a realization of the ideal. Such complementarity can receive a very metaphysical elaboration; in the extreme it can become or provoke a kind of Hermetic word magic. In practical terms, however, what is at stake here is a defense of poetic exaggeration, insofar as this is generated by poetic figurality and ornamental trope. When Sidney says "Poesie . . . is an arte of imitation, for so Aristotle termeth it in his word *Mimesis*, that is to say, a representing, counterfetting, or figuring foorth: to speake metaphorically, a speaking picture: with this end to teach and delight," there is some question as to whether the first colon in the passage establishes "to speake metaphorically" as apposite equivalent to "representing," "counterfetting," "figuring foorth," or whether, instead, the colon functions to mark "to speake metaphorically" as a kind of "as it were" introducing the extravagant metaphor of the "speaking picture" whose "end [is] to teach and delight."[4] The confusion or the ambiguity reflects the fact that the mirror of "*Mimesis*," if it is to be either effective or ideal, must somehow augment, but in doing so it must thereby distort, its verisimilar imitation of the real. If it turns out that such "counterfetting" and "figuring foorth" of the literal are not to be trusted, if the effect of the ideal is achieved by means of a traducement of the real, then there is either a noticeable discontinuity built into, or an increasingly severe judgment unfolded by, the series with which Sidney unpacks the *Mimesis* he takes from Aristotle, namely: "representing, counterfetting, or figuring foorth: to speake metaphorically, a speaking picture."

This is of course a general problem for all of poetry, for what is in question is the veridical force of poetic figure. It is metaphor, understood in the most general way, that is the instrument of lively "figuring foorth," and the issue raised by Sidney's "fayning," or by his "counterfett," or by his either literal or metaphorical "to speake metaphorically" is, therefore, precisely, how it is that any kind of veracity whatsoever attaches to metaphoric "delight." If the question is a general one, however—how to relate the poet's mimetic mirror to his metaphoric lamp—it is one that is especially acute with regard to, and one that is traditionally foregrounded in discussions of, epideictic literature, and this because such hyperbolic amplification of the real—whether as panegyric idealization or as deprecatory invective—is traditionally understood to be the most distinctive tropic feature of the genre. Again, as does the association of the epideictic with primal mimesis, this goes back to Aristotle, for whom such augmenting "comparison" is the singularly characteristic, the "most suitable," figural feature of epideictic speech:

> the comparison [*sugkrinein*] should be with famous men: that will strengthen your case; it is a noble thing to surpass men who are themselves great. It is only natural that methods of heightening the effect [*auxeisis*] should be attached particularly to speeches of praise [*eulogos*]; they aim at proving superiority over others, and any such superiority is a form of nobleness. Hence, if you cannot compare your hero with famous men, you should at least compare [*paraballein*] him with other people generally, since any superiority is held to reveal excellence. And, in general, of the lines of argument which are common to all speeches, this heightening of effect [*auxeisis*] is most suitable for declamations [*epideiktikois*], where we take our hero's actions as admitted facts, and our business is simply to invest these with dignity and nobility.[5]

So too, and again as with the association of the epideictic with the mimetic, it would be possible to follow out the ways in which subsequent rhetorical theory regularly repeats and yet further generalizes this initially Aristotelian observation. From antiquity up through the Renaissance, from Quintilian and Aphthonius to such rhetoricians as Scaliger, Brandolini, Erasmus, there is shared agreement, first, that praise proceeds by means of amplifying comparisons, second, that such epideictic comparisons characterize any discourse that means to specialize and to charge itself with the rhetorical color and heightening generated by the use of figures of speech.[6]

In traditional rhetorical and poetic theory there is of course no real suspicion regarding the truth of poetic figure, not if figure is handled properly. Quite the contrary, as in Sidney, the colors of rhetoric are the means whereby the poet manifests and actualizes his "Idea." This is the case, however, only because the primarily epideictic poetics of *ut pictura poesis* presupposes a profound consonance, a mutually confirming compatability, between mimesis and metaphor, these being the two most fundamental modal terms of traditional poetics. Thus when Sidney speaks about "Mimesis," he is obliged not only "to speake metaphorically" about it, but also to speak of the metaphoricity, of the "figuring foorth," that mimesis requires to eke out its real with efficacious "delight." Correspondingly, when Sidney speaks about metaphor, so too is he obliged to speak about it mimetically, to ground it in terms of mimetic likeness, lest it turn into Asiatic, artificially euphuistic ornament. This is why, for example, Sidney will object in the *Apology* to poets who, "more careful to speak curiously then to speak truly," use too many "similitudes," and who use them, moreover, in absurd and overconceited ways (*AP,* 202–3). In the same way, Sidney will speak of "Matron Eloquence apparelled, or rather disguised, in a Curtizan-like painted affectation: one time with so farre fette words, they may seeme Monsters, but must seem straungers to any poore English man" (*AP,* 202). So too, in the voice of Astrophil, Sidney mocks those poets who "ennoble new found Tropes with problemes old," and who "with strange similies enrich each line."[7] In contrast to such artifice, as opposed to the exotic ways in which "*Pindare's* Apes, flaunt they in phrases fine,/Enam'ling with pied flowers their thoughts of gold," Astrophil is proud to say instead that he speaks nothing but the plain mimetic truth: "then all my deed/But Copying is, what in her Nature writes."

Such comments, however ironically they may sometimes be delivered (it is Astrophil's wit, for example, regularly to Ape the far-fetched tropes of "Pindare's Apes," e.g., the pun on Penelope Rich's name in "enrich each line"), reflect very traditional notions of poetic decorum, namely, that mimesis and metaphor, if they are properly deployed by the poet, will exemplify and support each other. One consequence of this is that in the same way Sidney understands mimesis to be a kind of figurative "figuring foorth," so too does he understand rhetorical figurality or metaphoricity to be a kind of truthful mimesis. For Sidney, and not only for Sidney, tropes themselves are functions of resemblance, for they derive both their effect and their veracity from the way they identify a formal likeness or sameness underlying the apparently dissimilar terms that they connect. Again, this reduction of trope to similitude is familiar and Aristotelian. This is what Aristotle means, for example, when he says that metaphor—which for Aristotle is the essential dictional feature of poetry, "the greatest thing by far"—amounts to the capacity "to see the same" (*to homoion theorein estin*).[8] So too, this is the logic of Aristotle's famous formal definition of metaphor, as it is given succinct formulation in the *Poetics:*

Metaphor [*metaphora*] consists in giving the thing a name [*onomatos*] that belongs to something else; the transference [*epiphora*] being either from genus [*genos*] to species [*eidos*], or from species to genus, or from species to species, or on grounds of analogy [*analogon*].[9]

The definition stipulates the essential homogeneity of a classical metaphor, and it leads immediately to Aristotle's "proportional" theory of metaphor (as A is to B, so C to D, and therefore as A to D) insofar as it characterizes the generic or special similitudes that, because they subtend comparable differences, enable the poet to transfer "names." This is why metaphors conceived in Aristotelian terms are metaphors of taxonomic "kinds." For Aristotle and for the tradition of figurative theory that derives from Aristotle, metaphors identify by name the elementary "sameness," the *homoion*, that different things share. This "sameness" is what the poet "sees," or "theorizes," either as formal *eidos* (also from *idein*, "to see") or, using the Latin, as "species" (from *specere*, "to look at"). As in a simple ratio, these atomic, elemental comparisons factor things by least and common "denominators"; they articulate essential relationships, relationships *of* essence, because they admit no incommensurability of terms. By definition, such "trans-ferring," such "meta-phoring" or "epi-phoring," of analogizable "names" leaves nothing over as irrational "remainder." The names are commutable and distributive, one to and with another, because they are divisible by, and reducible to, the categorical unity or oneness, the sameness or likeness, that links them each to each.

These are very general remarks both about mimesis and about metaphor, and there is no need really to labor the point that traditional rhetorical theory understands the likeness of the one to be, at least in some respects, like the likeness of the other. Almost platitudinously, it is assumed that when poetry is at its best, which is to say when it is both most truthful and most forceful, the resemblance of mimesis and the similitude of metaphor will manifest themselves as aspects of each other. This is a conventional understanding of the way poetry acquires both its profit and delight. If these are general remarks, however, it is important to recognize the specifically epideictic consequence they entail, for if it is poetry in general, then it is praise in particular that happens when mimesis and metaphor meet. This is important because it explains why praise, as such, is consistently accorded a privileged generic place in the mimetic-metaphoric conception of poetry and of the poetical that governs literary theory from antiquity through the Renaissance. Praise is taken to be a paradigm for poetry, the master genre through which all other genres are thought, the exemplary instance of an exemplary poetics, because it is in praise or, better, *as* praise, that mimesis and metaphor, most generally conceived, most thoroughly conjoin, with the verisimilar likeness of epideictic imitation weighting poetry toward the real at the same time that the figurative likeness of epideictic comparison raises or links the real to the ideal.

The courtly "marigold" of Shakespeare's sonnet 25, which looks "at the sun's eye," a flower that "spread[s]" its "fair leaves" like "great princes' favorites," would be a good example. The marigold is a commonplace figure in the poetry of praise, and so too is the marigold a commonplace figure *of* the poetry of praise. This is the case, however, because the marigold's mimetic matter exemplifies its metaphoric manner. On the one hand, the marigold is like the sun that it admires, for like an icon it transparently instantiates the image it reflects. On the other hand, the marigold is equally a "figure of delight" (98), for its troping or its turning is what motivates its imitation, adding something metaphorically *enargic* to a merely lifeless imitation. In a straightforward way, therefore, the marigold mimetically embodies the sun that it resembles, but so too does its metaphoric troping imitate the turning of the sun. This is a simple example, but it accounts for the special and the specifically *epideictic* value of the marigold, or of any other such heliotropic flowers of fancy in the gardens of dainty poetic devices. The marigold looks like the sun that it looks at; its turning animates its imitation, its imitation is itself a kind of troping, and so it shows the panegyric way in which the likeness of poetic metaphor and the likeness of poetic mimesis reciprocally will vivify and realize the ideal substance of each other.[10]

If the courtly marigold, which looks both like and "at the sun's eye," is a convenient illustration of the epideictic way traditional poetics understands metaphor and mimesis to be mutually imbricated each in the other, so too does it again recall the specifically visual imagery with which this mimetic-metaphoric compact is regularly imagined and expressed in the traditional poetics of *ut pictura poesis* and "speaking picture." Again, such visuality is built into the "idea" of "Idea," just as it calls forth the idealizing "light" in "delight." So too, vision is the medium through which the Aristotelian metaphorician "see[s] the same"—or, as Giordano Bruno will say, sight is the faculty of comparison—just as poetic mimesis is typically characterized in terms of optical *eidola* and *simulacra*.[11] So too poetry has force, *vis*, because it has vision, *visum*, just as what distinguishes the vatic poet is, precisely, his "imagination," for, as Aristotle says, and the etymology is regularly repeated by Renaissance rhetoricians, "As sight is the most highly developed sense, the name *phantasia* [imagination] has been formed from *pháos* [light] because it is not possible to see without light."[12]

In familiar ways, therefore, such visual motifs govern poetic theorization; moreover, they define the ways in which the poetical is perennially and generally imagined in poetic practice as well. It would be a great mistake, however, to say that this is the case because poetry is in fact something visual or visionary. Simply to reemploy such traditional imagery fails to explain its traditional use, not only because poetry is a verbal, not a pictorial, medium, but, more to the point, because neither poetry in general, nor epideictic *ekphrasis* in particular—with its characteristically generic iconography and its typically abstract hyperboles—very much depends upon realistic or particularizing representation of physical, visible detail. This is obvious, but it is important to emphasize the specific metaphoric values of such visual imagery, for it then becomes possible to ask why and how visual imagery so readily presents itself as illustration of poetic speech. In a broad sense, the answer to this question is also obvious. Even so, even in a broad sense, it has particular consequences both for the theory and the practice of traditional poetry, especially for the theory and practice of epideictic poetry.

Speaking very generally, therefore—but again, it is only as something general and perennial that these metaphoremes possess historical significance—we can say that imagery of vision is characteristically employed either to represent what is figuratively understood to be the transparent reflection of poetic mimesis, or, equally figuratively, the illuminating, shining colors of poetic metaphor. A convenient example of the former would be Quintilian's characterization of the way poetic representation presents things to the eye, the way in which the vivid verisimilitude of mimesis actualizes reference:

> There are certain experiences which the Greeks call *phantasiai*, and the Romans *visions* [*visiones*], whereby things absent are presented to our imagination with such extreme vividness that they seem actually to be before our very eyes [*per quas imagines rerum absentium ita repraesentantur animo, ut eas cernere oculis ac praesentes habere videamur*].[13]

A convenient example of the latter would be the way Aquinas defends scriptural figurality, because such metaphors render divine truth vivacious, because the "color" of figurative imagery idealizes mundane "likeness":

> The ray of divine revelation [*radius divinae revelationis*] is not extinguished by the sensible imagery [*figuras sensibiles*] wherewith it is veiled [*circumvelatur*], as Dionysius says [*Cael Hier.* i]; and its truth so far remains that it does not allow the minds of those to whom the revelation has been made, to rest in the metaphors [*in similitudinibus remanere*], but raises them to the knowledge of truths [*ad cognitionem intelligibilium*]; and through those to whom the revelation has been made others also may receive instruction in these matters.[14]

This is to distinguish the reality effect of the mimetic and the idealization effect of the metaphoric one from the other. The point brought out by such quotations, however, is that neither the clarity of the mimetic nor the heightening veil or color of the metaphoric will be thought, or conceptualized, without the other. Puttenham's account of the "double vertue" of "ornament Poeticall," where grave and sententious *energia* finds itself yet further delighted by the "lustre and light" of dictional *enargia*, is a good example of the way neither the referential likeness of mimesis nor the figurative likeness of metaphor is imagined as an independent function by itself. For Puttenham, "ornament Poeticall"

> is of two sortes according to the double vertue and efficacie of figures . . . one to satisfie and delight th'eare onely by a goodly outward shew set upon the matter with wordes, and speaches smothly and tunably running: another by certaine intendments or sence of such wordes and speaches inwardly working a stirre to the mynde: that first qualities the Greeks called *Enargia*, of this word *argos*, because it geueth lustre and light. This latter they called *Energia*, of *ergon*, because it wrought with a strong and vertuous operation; and figure breedeth them both.[15]

We see here the characteristic and frequently remarked overlap of *energia* and *enargia* in traditional theory. The distinct significations of these two terms regularly fuse, but this fusion corresponds to the way the vivid actuality of the one will regularly presuppose or call forth the vivacious actuality of the other.[16] Aristotle does much the same, for example, when he speaks to the force of a "smart," "polite," "witty," or "dainty" (his word is *asteia*; this the closest thing in Greek to the Renaissance sense of courtly "wit") metaphor: "I mean that things are set before the eyes [*pro ommaton*] by words that signify actuality [*energounta semainei*]."[17]

Not only the ideas that are expressed in such quotations, but also the visual imagery with which such ideas are expressed amount to a poetic orthodoxy. Poetry is more than lifeless imitation, and so too is it more than ornamental trope, and this because these two are joined together by means of a decorum that works synergically to vivify them both. The relatively simple point to make about this is that visual imagery presents itself as especially appropriate illustration of such mimetic-metaphoric complementarity because vision is itself understood to operate by means of just such colored clarity. "Light," says Aristotle," is a sort of color [*chroma*] in the transparent [*diaphanous*] when made transparent in actuality [*entelecheia diaphanes*] by the agency of fire or something resembling the celestial body."[18] The same kind of physical reasoning informs Stoic and later medieval optics—the science of *eidola, species, simulacra,* and the like—for here too light is understood to be a kind of transparent spectacularity, a twofold lucidity, manifesting utter diaphaneity, on the one hand, and, on the other, dazzling, even blinding, opacity.[19] For this reason, therefore, because light, like poetry, is double in itself, the color *of* transparency, it serves as a convenient image of—in effect, as the objectification of—the mimetic-metaphoric compact built into the poetics of *ut pictura poesis* and "speaking picture." The light whose luminosity consists of limpid iridescence presents itself, because it has this "double vertue," as illustration of the way poetic metaphor applies its lustrous shine or veiling sheen to the transparently mimetic.

Again the point is obvious, but if we recall that it is specifically as praise, as something epideictic, that mimesis and metaphor most perspicuously combine, we begin better to understand why the language of praise so readily characterizes itself with the same specular imagery it invokes for what it speaks about. We understand better, that is, why the rhetoricity of idealization is imagined as materially equivalent to its idea of its "Idea." Such material equivalence is, in fact, built into the etymology of "epideictic," from Greek *epideiknunai,* "to show," "display"; in the middle voice, "to show off" or "display for oneself." The Indo-European root is **deik,* with variant **deig,* "to show," which gives Greek *diké,* "justice," and the verb *deiknunai,* "bring to light," "show forth," "represent," "portray," "point out," "show," leading to English "deictic," "paradigmatic," "apodeictic," and so on. So too *deiknunai* is also closely related to *deikeilon,* "representation," "exhibition," "reflection," "image," "phantom," "sculpted figure."[20] This semantic field characterizes, on the one hand, the figuratively visual ekphrastic manner of the epideictic, the way it "exhibits," "reflects," "images," in short, the way it "brings to light." By the same token, however, to the extent that this defines an epi-

deictic manner, so too does it define an epideictic matter which is
itself a matter of display. For it is light that epideixis brings to light,
an exhibition that it exhibits, a painting that it paints, a sculpture
that it sculpts. These are not trivial correspondences. What is at
stake in these factive, cognate accusatives (all of which are regularly
exploited by the Renaissance sonnet) is the recursive structure of
epideictic showing, a circularly deictic indication whose displaying
is somehow the same as that which it displays, a Cratylitic representing that duplicates whatever it presents because whatever is
presented is itself already an image of its own representation. This is
the peculiarly tautological relationship between epideictic manner
and epideictic matter that the figurative language of traditional rhetorical theory characteristically enforces. The epideictic is epiphanic
because, like light itself, this speech displays its referent by self-
displaying itself. And this has special referential force because an
epideictic or praiseworthy referent does pretty much the same.

This is to speak figuratively, but the point to recognize is that
these are constitutive or enabling figures *of* the poetical, necessary
or inevitable figurations through which a poetics based on *effective*
likeness will think its own semiotic coherence. Only by imagining
itself in terms of such figures, in terms of a light whose showing and
showing forth are one and the same, does epideictic speech "bring
to light" the *pháos* or light that emanates out of the *phai-nomena* about
which it speaks. Thus Aristotle will distinguish epideictic oratory
from the two other kinds, forensic and deliberative, on the grounds
that in the former the audience serves as "observer" (*theoron*), whereas in the latter two the audience serves as "judge" (*kritén*).[21] It is a
distinction that refers, of course, to the primarily ceremonial, theatrical function of praise performance in the Athenian *polis*, and this in
turn recalls the origins of theater—the *thea*-trical, the seen—in ritu-
alized and sacred, panegyric hymns. But it also characterizes what
to Aristotle is the essential, formal peculiarity of epideictic rhetoric.
For Aristotle's point, brought out by his distinguishing between a
rhetoric addressed to vision and a rhetoric addressed to judgment,
is that epideictic or demonstrative oratory, as distinct from the invisible language of the law courts or the assembly, is a rhetoric both of
display and of self-display, a spectacular speech that we "observe"
precisely because its manner calls attention to itself, a rhetorical
"monstration" that works reflectively but also reflexively to demonstrate itself.

Speaking less figuratively, we can say that the visibility Aristotle associates with the epideictic identifies the way that praise fore-grounds its own rhetoricity, and this, in fact, is a commonplace observation in later rhetorical theory, where epideictic speech will regularly be characterized as ostentatious speech.[22] To the extent that such ostentation dominates ostention, the objective showing of epideixis amounts to a subjective showing off. This is what Sidney is objecting to when he speaks about poets who are "more careful to speak curiously then to speake truly"; so too, this is why Astrophil complains about the way "*Pindare's* Apes, flaunt they in phrases fine,/Enam'ling with pied flowers their thoughts of gold." Correspondingly, to the extent that the epideictic is merely deictic, i.e., merely ostensive, it turns into what Sidney calls the forceless and pallid "woordish description" of the philosopher, "which dooth neyther strike, pierce, nor possesse the sight of the soule." Speaking ideally, however, a specifically epideictic speech will manifest a decorous conjunction of showing and showing forth, a conjunction that makes the one into the proof of the other.

Thus Mazzoni, to take another example, when he defends the truth of poetic "imagination," will cite a cryptic aphorism by the Stoic Chrysippus that he finds in pseudo-Plutarch:

> Fantasy [*phantasia*] is a passion [*pathos; una passione*] born in the mind which represents both the thing demonstrated and the demonstrating thing [*en deiknumenon heauto kai to pepoieokos*, sic; *che rappresenta la cosa demonstrata, e la demonstrante*].

Glossing this, Mazzoni quotes Plutarch again:

> For just as light shows both itself and the thing that it illuminates [*gar to phos auto deiknisi kai ta alla ta en auto periechomena*, sic; *il lume mostra se stesso, e le cose, ch'egli illumina*], so fantasy reveals both itself and the things that make it [*kai hei phantasia dieknisin eauto, kai to pepoieikos auto*, sic; *la Phantasia mostra se stessa, e le cose, che la fanno*].[23]

For Mazzoni, this is a justification of those fantasies that are generated spontaneously in or by the mind, rather than inspired by impressions that the mind receives from things external to itself. His point (part of his defense of Dante's "vision," which he understands to be a function of Dante's panegyric purpose, and relating, as does Sidney's discussion of "Idea," to an old question as to whether poetry must necessarily treat historical events) is that even purely internal fantasies are true because they not only show the unreal things they show, but, also, at the same time, show them *as* phantastic.

From one perspective such a true depiction of the imaginary mode of representation would be a limit case of representation (that which takes itself as its own object); from another, it would be the most general, representative case of all (that which takes all objects as example of itself). In either case, however, the reflexive reflection of the conception will determine or call out for a specific set of images, *generically* visionary, that illustrate this deictically circular correlation of the showing and the shown. Thus, for example, it is not only the principle but a particular material imagery of reflexive reflection that governs the relationship of the sonneteering panegyric poet to his beloved, as in sonnet 66 of Spenser's *Amoretti*, where what links the lowly poet to his high ideal is the way he is a matching, praising mirror to his lady's self-illuminating lamp:

> Yee whose high worths surpassing paragon,
>   could not on earth have found one fit for mate,
>   ne but in heaven matchable to none,
>   why did ye stoup unto so lowly state?
> But yet thereby much greater glory gate,
>   then had ye sorted with a princes pere:
>   for now your light doth more it self dilate,
>   and in my darkness greater doth appeare.
> Yet since your light hath once enlumind me,
>   with my reflex yours shall encreased be.

So too such reflexive reflection will be itself exampled with a set of conventional laudatory items, mimetic and metaphoric both at once, that, as objects *of* praise, itemize the substantial body of a formal ideal, as in sonnet 9 of the *Amoretti*, where, by *expeditio*, the lady is the sum of all the wondrous things that she is not:

> Long while I sought to what I might compare
>   those powerful eies, which lighten my dark spright,
>   yet find I nought on earth to which I dare
>   resemble th'ymage of their goodly light.
> Not to the Sun: for they doo shine by night;
>   nor to the Moone: for they are changed never;
>   nor to the Starres: for they have purer sight;
>   nor to the fire: for they consume not ever;
> Nor to the lightning: for they still persever;
>   nor to the Diamond: for they are more tender;
>   nor unto Christall: for nought may them sever;
>   nor unto glasse: such basenesse mought offend her;
> Then to the Maker selfe they likest be,
>   whose light doth lighten all that here we see.

What these Spenserian examples bring out is the formulaic nature of the phenomenology of praise. There is a specific materiality that illustrates what metaphor and mimesis look like when they join together. The physical things that Spenser here lists are, taken together, a summary image of epideictic likeness, at once the likeness of Idea and an idealization of likeness. These are images of, but they are also the media of, the "sameness" that the poet "sees." These images acquire their poetic value precisely because they embody in this Cratylitic way the rhetoricity with which they are expressed. They are the images of traditional poetic imagination, the *phai-nomena* of an epideictic logos. It is no accident, therefore, that the poet who wonders "to what I might compare/those powerful eies, which lighten my dark spright" proceeds to imagine those eyes in terms of objects the concatenated physicality of which works, in the phrase Mazzoni takes from Plutarch, to "represent both the thing demonstrated and the demonstrating thing." Such circularity defines the essential phenomenality of the epideictic, the kind of being immanent to its rhetorical meaning. This is the material palpability, the *stuff*, of praise: a reflectively reflexive palpability that can be generalized in terms of a shining "light" that "doth lighten all that [deictically] here we see," but which acquires a more particular inflection when unpacked as a materialized homogeneity by reference to which the intromissive and the extromissive, the transparent and opaque, the hot and cold, the solar and the lunar, the brittle and the pliable, the naked and the clothed, the stony and the liquid, are all of them but complementary aspects of the same.

It is in this sense, because what one admires must also characterize the way one admires, that laudatory invention possesses a very limited and a very particular poetic inventory. The rhetorical decorum of praise requires that its matter be an illustration of its manner, and for this reason the figures of praise necessarily function as the figured *of* praise: "figures of delight,/Drawn after you, you pattern of all those" (98). There is a particular epideictic materiality that lends itself to the physical, as well as to the metaphysical, realization of this idealizing tautology, and for this reason such materiality is rhetorically "convenient" to the language of praise. There are things which are specifically *epideictic* things, arti-facts of praise, and they regularly appear in the literature of praise because they serve as self-exampling gloss and instance of panegyric literariness.

Later, it will be necessary to speak more carefully and precisely about the phenomenal qualities of these things of praise. For now, however, it is enough to realize that it is not simply because the visual, as such, is beautiful or picturesque that imagery of the visual so characteristically figures in a poetry that thematizes itself as a poetry of admiration. Rather, this imagery is called forth because it serves a specific panegyric purpose; it functions to objectify the rhetorical self-consciousness, the self-showing ostention, that is formally endemic to—and often thematically foregrounded in—the literary genre of the epideictic. One further Spenserian example will make the point again, and will also recall the way in which such imagery, coded as imagery of a particular literariness, is regularly assimilated to the psychology of the praising poet.

In the "Hymne in Honour of Beautie" Spenser begins by addressing the "Love" or Venus who has inspired him to write his praise of Beauty. Like the Love, the inspiration works in a typically circular way:

> Whylest seeking to aslake thy raging fyre,
> Thou in me kindlest much more great desyre,
> And up aloft above my strength doest rayse
> The wondrous matter of my fyre to prayse.
> (4–8)

In the rest of the poem Spenser develops familiar Neo-Platonist and Petrarchist themes and topoi, mostly so as to explain why:

> these faire soules, which have
> The most resemblance of that heavenly light,
> Frame to themselves, most beautiful and brave
> Their fleshly bowre, most fit for their delight.
> (120–24)

As these quotations suggest (and as is the case in all of Spenser's *Fowre Hymnes*), the "Hymne in Honour of Beautie" is organized around large schemes of visual imagery, this imagery being as standard and orthodox as is the idealist doctrine that it is used to illustrate. The following stanza, the ideas of which go back directly, through Ficino, to the *Phaedrus*, is a representative example of what happens in the poem as a whole:

> But gentle Love, that loiall is and trew,
> Will more illumine your resplendent ray,
> And adde more brightnesse to your goodly hew,
> From light of his pure fire, which by like way
> Kindled of yours, your likenesse doth display,
> Like as two mirrours by opposd reflexion,
> Doe both expresse the faces first impression.
> (176–82)

There is perhaps no real need to elaborate the way in which a Love that "illumine[s] your resplendent ray,/And adde[s] more brightnesse to your goodly hew" simulates the way in which the spectacular display of epideictic metaphor is traditionally understood to augment the specular reflections of epideictic mimesis: "rays[ing]/The wondrous matter of my fyre to prayse." Nor is there any need to stress the way in which such a fiery light, which is at once transparent and opaque—the color of transparency, as Aristotle has it—serves as image of a self-displaying likeness "which by like way,/Kindled of yours, your likenesse doth display." Here again, in utterly conventional fashion, the poetry of praise, by means of its ostention, implicitly prepares an ostentatious praise of poetry itself. What is worth remarking, however, because it is characteristic of the especially self-conscious way in which Spenser responds to the formal exigencies of epideixis, is how the concluding two lines of the stanza work pointedly and nonthematically, by means of their manner, to reflect these themes and topoi back upon their own expression. For the two mirrors which are meant to exemplify the circular operations of Love's "likenesse" are also figurations of the "like as" with which they are introduced. Almost heavy-handedly, the thematic similitude of indicative resemblance—"which by like way . . . your likenesse doth display"—is associated, by the repetition of "like," with the metaphoric likeness of "like as." As a result, the "opposd reflexion" of the two mirrors is presented as the illustration of the *trope* of likeness, as an illustration of "like as." This is very much a limit case of praise or of "Ideas Mirrour." Mirroring and self-displaying each other's mirroring, reflecting within themselves only the smooth, silver, homogeneous, glassy surface of a reciprocally reflexive showing of showing itself, the two mirrors become the finally imageless image of an idealized sameness. In a very literal way, that is to say, the two mirrors exemplify, on the one hand, the imitation of metaphor, and, on the other, the metaphor of mimesis itself.[24]

Again, the significance of such motifs and tropes derives from the fact that they are utterly conventional. Spenser's two mirrors are commonplaces in laudatory literature, and so too are the other topoi and conceits to which I am referring. However, it is because they are common that they are important. If I have so far labored a series of correspondences, thematic and material, the perenniality of which is well known and the logic of which seems obvious, it was in order to emphasize both the consistency and the coherence with which it is specifically these themes, motifs, and things that regularly appear in the poetry of praise. These are the items that flesh out an idealist erotics and an idealist metaphysics. They are so, however, because they are the objectification of the rhetoricity of idealization. The point is simple, but it is also precise. If one is going to speak the language of praise, then, by rhetorical necessity, it is about just such themes, motifs, things, that one will speak. It is not in a figurative but in a literal way that the manner of praise prescribes its matter. For, as a practical consequence, since this manner is conceived and conceited in terms of a particular kind of double likeness—the resemblance of mimesis and the similitude of metaphor—so too is the matter, with the result that epideictic literature consistently portrays a world composed of things, mimetic and metaphoric both at once, which work materially to instantiate this twofold likeness. As a result, such poetry regularly depicts a particular kind of literary world, one wherein everything functions as idealizing mirror image of everything else, a universe the very phenomenology of which makes of it a poem of praise, a phenomenology, moreover, that makes of every particular element within this world an epideictic uni-verse.

If this is the case, however, it also makes clear just what it is that praise, as such, can never speak about. As a medium of idealizing likeness—as a language of *species, simulacra, eidola,* and the like—the epideictic cannot indicate, display, or show forth either the idea or the operation of whatever would be at odds with its essential and essentializing likeness. Because it "see[s] the same," it cannot see what is not the same. Precisely because it "imagines," it cannot imagine what is other than itself. Shakespeare has a formula for this that occurs in a sonnet to which I will return in the next chapter. Speaking of the young man, whom he imagines as a "wondrous scope" (105), and speaking also of the way "all alike my songs and praises be" (105), the poet observes that "one thing expressing, leaves out difference" (105). This omission, specifically the omission of "difference," defines the limits of even the limit case of praise, for it points to that which is, *in principle,* beyond praise, to that which necessarily passes praise because it is beyond, on the one hand, the mimetic resemblance of imitation, and beyond, on the other, the figurative likeness of metaphoric comparison. The practical consequences of this are also considerable. As a homogeneous discourse, as a language of "one thing expressing," the epideictic, by virtue of its own rhetorical propriety, cannot express the heterogeneous. It cannot entertain thematic heterogeneities, it cannot speak about things that are materially heterogeneous, and finally—and this is what regularly presents a difficulty for a poetry of erotic admiration—it cannot speak about sexual heterogeneity. Putting this last point more bluntly, the language of praise cannot imagine sexual difference without being false to its own rhetorical nature, without, that is to say, on its own terms, being false to the rhetoricity of "one thing expressing."

We are close here, obviously, to the duplicity, specifically the *duplicity*, of Shakespeare's dark lady, and to the way she is an image, specifically an *image*, of what has "no correspondence with true sight" (148). However, before turning to Shakespeare's sonnets and to the way, by virtue of their paradox of praise, they manage to "express" the "difference" that an orthodox poetics necessarily "leaves out," I want first briefly to consider the place or, rather, the "no place" of this excised "difference" in traditional and commonplace representations of the language of Idea. I will do so by looking quickly at two famous pictures by Robert Fludd which are pictures, so to speak, of the "speaking picture." In part this will be a useful way to review what I have already said about the visual imagery of praise. More important, however, it will also make clear how this visionary tradition of praise, despite or through its blind spots, anticipates in specific ways what is novel in Shakespeare's sonnets.

The first picture, figure 1, is Fludd's illustration of the seventh verse of Psalm 63 (misnumbered in the picture as verse 8).[25] *In alarum tuarum umbra canam*, says or sings King David, and the picture shows precisely this. King David kneels in prayer beneath an eyeball sun while from out of David's mouth, in line with the rays of theophanic light that stream down on him, a verse of psalm ascends up to a brightness that is supported, shaded, and revealed by its extended wings. Because King David is the master psalmist, and because the picture employs familiar and perennial iconographic motifs, it would be fair to say that Fludd's picture is an illustration of psalmic speech per se. In the picture we see traditional figurations of the way a special kind of anagogic language does homage to its elevated referent. This referent, moreover, is itself a figure of a special kind of speech, as is indicated by the Hebrew letters inscribed upon its iris. These letters—*yod, he, vau, he*—spell out the name of God, "Jehova," which is the "Name" in which, according to the fourth verse of the psalm, King David lifts up his hands: "Thus wil I magnifie thee all my life, and lift up mine hands in thy Name."[26] These letters spell out this holy name, but, in principle, they do not

Figure 1. Robert Fludd, illustration of the seventh verse of Psalm 63 (mis-numbered in the picture as verse 8). First published in 1621. Courtesy of Library of Congress.

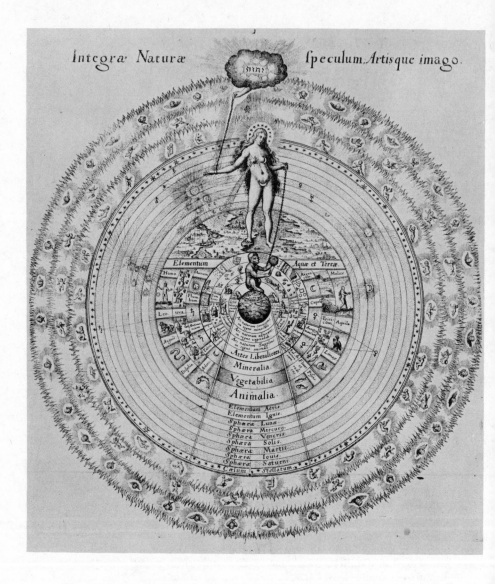

Figure 2. Robert Fludd, *Integrae Naturae Speculum, Artisque Imago*. First published in 1617. Courtesy of Library of Congress.

sound it out, for these are letters whose literality, when combined in this sacred Tetragrammaton, must never be pronounced. Instead, in accord with both orthodox and heterodox mystical prohibitions, this written name of God, which is the only proper name of God, will be properly articulated only through attributive periphrasis, with the letters vocalized either as *Adonai*, the Lord, or as *Ha Shem*, the Name or, even, the Word.

In Fludd's picture, where the verse of psalm and *Jehova* lie at oblique angles to each other (just as the Latin stands in translational relation to the Hebrew), it is clearly the case that King David does not literally voice the name of God. It is possible, however, reading either up or down, to take inscribed *Jehova* as a syntactic part of David's speech, either as its apostrophized addressee or as the direct object of its *canam*. This syntactic, but still silent, link between the Latin and the Hebrew is significant, for unspeakable *Jehova* thus becomes the predicated precondition through which or across which what the psalmist says is translated into what the psalmist sees. The picture is concerned to illustrate the operative effect of this translation, showing David's verse to be the medium of his immediate vision of the sun, drawing David's verse as though it were itself a beam of holy light. In this way, because the verse is pictured as the very brightness that it promises to speak or sing about, Fludd's picture manages to motivate its portrait of a genuinely visionary speech. We can take this as an illustration of the way that epideictic speech turns back upon its own ostensive indication. In the psalm the reason why the psalmist praises is the very substance of his praise: "For thy loving kindnes is better then life: therefore my lippes shal praise thee" (verse 3). The same thing happens in the picture where we see the future tense of *canam* rendered present, and where the promise praise amounts to the performative fulfilment of the promise.

In several respects, therefore, Fludd's picture is a portrait of the kind of ideal language that I have been describing, a portrait of language that is ideal *because* it is idealizing. As the picture shows it, King David speaks a visual speech, a language *of* vision that promotes a vision *of* language, a language which is of the mouth only insofar as it is for the eye. Again, this visual and visionary logos, speech which is ideally circular in this straightforward way, is so for specifically epideictic reasons. Aquinas offers the standard theological logic for such recursive reflexivity when he explains:

> We need to praise God with our lips, not indeed for His sake, but for our own sake, since by praising Him our devotion is arroused towards Him,

according to *Ps.* xlix, 23: "The sacrifice of praise shall glorify Me, and there is the way by which I will show him the salvation of God."[27]

As I have suggested, this theology of praise regularly becomes in the poetry of admiration an equally standard psychology of praise. To take what is surely the most magnificent literary example, we can think of Dante's vision of eternal light, *O luce etterna*, at the end of the *Paradiso*, where Dante finally receives the "beatitude" (*beatitudine*) that twenty years earlier, in *La Vita nuova*, he had identified with "those words that praise my lady." Here too God is figured as a self-sufficient luminosity, as self-absorbed and even narcissistic light. Here again, however, in the same way that Fludd's David is illuminated by the brightness that he praises, this light centrifugally exceeds its own centripetal completeness and offers to the praising poet a salvific mirror image of the "likeness," the *effige*, of himself:

> O Light Eternal, that alone abidest in Thyself, alone knowest Thyself, and known to Thyself and knowing, lovest and smilest on Thyself! That circling [*circulazion*] which, thus begotten, appeared in Thee as reflected light [*lume reflesso*] seemed to me, within it and in its own color [*colore*], painted with our likeness [*pinta della nostra effige*], for which my sight [*mio viso*] was wholly given to it.[28]

In the second picture, figure 2, which is by no means a strictly Elizabethan world picture (since it derives from Macrobius' *Commentary on* The Dream of Scipio), we see yet more clearly the aesthetics and cosmology traditionally attaching to this idealism of the "Word", of *Ha Shem*.[29] As is indicated by the title—*Integrae Naturae Speculum, Artisque Imago*—all arts are images of the specularity of integrated Nature because both Art and Nature reciprocally will simulate the *eidolon* or likeness of beatific light. This commonplace eidetic reduction, which, by commutation, enables representation iconically to replicate whatever it presents, is what makes both Art and Nature into psalmic panegyric. Art becomes an Art of Nature just as Nature is itself a kind or Art, because they both reflect the Holy Name and shaded brightness which is the signified, because it is the signifier, of Art and Nature both.

From this phenomenologically mutual admiration, which makes of Art and Nature each other's *special* likeness, derive the onto-theological imperatives that inform the visionary, elemental, and panegyric aesthetics of *ut pictura poesis* and "speaking picture." Suspended from the hand of God, which pokes itself out from the penumbral *Ha Shem*, the great chain of mimetic being (which Macrobius imagines as a series of successive and declensive mirrors) reaches down to Nature (the "Nature" that Chaucer, for example, translates as "kynde"), and through her to Man, the Ape of Nature, whose artful calibration of a represented little world produces a *mise en abyme* that in no way disturbs, indeed confirms, the solidity and the centrality of the material world on which the Ape of Nature squats.[30]

This is the same pietistic, demiurgic poetics, multiplying kind after kind, that Sidney presupposes when he urges his readers to "give right honor to the heavenly Maker of that maker, who, having made man to his owne likenes, set him beyond and over all the workes of that second nature, which in nothing he sheweth so much as in Poetrie." So too this is the materially "phantastic" "phai-nomenology" that makes the cosmos a system of hierarchically graded, luminous "kinds," *elementum* upon *elementum*, all of them mimetically and metaphorically significant of the larger macrocosmic order in which they take their microcosmic place. It is for this reason that, for example, "the heavens declare the glory of God, and the Firmament [*Ha Rakia*] sheweth forth the workes of his handes." And it is for *this* reason that, as John Dee says, when he comments on that "kingly Psalme":

> The whole frame of gods creatures, (which is the whole world) is to us, a bright glasse: from which, by reflexion, reboundeth to our knowledge and perceiverance, Beames, and Radiations: representing the image of his Infinite goodnes, Omnipotency, and wisedome.[31]

In all of these ways Fludd's picture shows the structure of the world, the rhetoricity of the world, and the material specularity of the world to be of the same epideictic piece, for it is thus, and only thus, that order, meaning, and actuality join reflectively and reflexively together in a poetics as well as in a universe of praise.

We see here, therefore, how it is that the physics (the *phusis*, the "nature"), the metaphysics, and the poetics of idealist Nature all participate in the same ideal Sameness. On the one hand, a particular ontology, theology, phenomenology, anthropology, psychology is embedded in the language consistently used to express the nature of this Nature. On the other hand, these various theorizations of the nature of Nature in turn determine, or are determined by, a particular expression or conceptualization of the visual language, the transparently luminous and the darksomely iridescent, logos or "logy," the *Ha Shem*, that links these theorizations each to each. At a certain level of generality—the level, precisely, of genus and species, the level of "kind"—the visual motifs informing both this Nature and this Language, as well as the epideictic import accorded these motifs, define the consistency of the history of ideas as it begins in the cinematic theater of Plato's cave (which is why the only poetry Plato allows into the Republic is the praise of "gods and virtuous men") through the Neo-Platonism of Fludd's diagrams, through to, at the very least, the revelatory play of *a-lethetic* light and shadow in Heideggerean metaphysics, or, say, the early Wittgenstein's "picture theory of language" (where, however, it is sentences, rather than individual words, that deictically "bring to light," like Cratylitic magic wands, the logical structure of the world of which they speak). For all these philosophers, for all the differences between them, language plays the same praiseworthy part. It is at this level of generality that we can speak intelligibly, albeit broadly, of a structure of thought that is, to use Heidegger's word, "logocentric," in the sense that this is a structure of thought that consistently sees its own logic reflected and repeated in the way that it sees language work. At the same level of generality, recognizing the perenniality of these visual motifs, we can speak intelligibly of a structure of "photocentric" thought, for this is how, from an iconographic point of view, the idea or the ideal of language is understood to *look*.[32]

Having said all this, however, it is important also to notice that at the very same level of generality this tradition—at least as Fludd represents it (but Fludd's representation is in fact traditional; indeed, by Fludd's time such a picture of the integrated, specular world would have seemed old-fashioned, even antiquated)—is not exactly photo- or logocentric, as can be seen by the position, in figure 2, of the founding Word, *Jehova*, at a tangential, supplementary, clouded point upon the lucid universe of which it is at once the telos and the source. In the same way, in figure 1, even the all-seeing eye of God cannot read the writing that is written on its iris, a writing that appears there, therefore, as a darkness even more eternal than what Dante calls "eternal light." To the extent that the Name from whence all other names derive cannot itself be spoken, or to the extent that the source of light cannot itself be seen, we approach here a realm of paradox. The point to be emphasized about such paradoxes, however, is that, *as paradoxes, they are profoundly orthodox.* Such photo-logo-ec-centricity is a *commonplace* topos in an epideictic poetics, just as the ineffability of the universal signifier-signified goes without saying when the height of praise regularly amounts to saying "We . . . have eyes to wonder, but lack tongues to praise" (106).

The holy Name that a traditional piety euphemistically pronounces as *Ha Shem* corresponds, perhaps, to that whereof, as the Tractarian Wittgenstein might put it, we cannot logically speak, but this interdiction is itself a panegyric formula, just as visionary poets often eloquently speak about their dumbstruck muteness: "O, learn to read what silent love hath writ:/To hear with eyes belongs to love's fine wit" (23).

It is important to insist upon the fact that such themes of circumspection are standard in the language of Idea, for the regularity with which an epideictic poet speaks about "my dumb thoughts, speaking in effect" (85) or about the way that "I impair not beauty being mute" (83) forces a significant revision with regard to what, until now, I have heretofore characterized as the homogeneous complexion of the poetry of praise. Such "inexpressability" topoi (the technical term is *adynata*, "words cannot express . . ."; this is what Auerbach calls "the Outdoer") are not only common in but also seem required by the poetry of praise. Moreover, to the extent that this is the case, to the extent that panegyric makes a point of its own limits, to precisely this extent does such poetry rather pointedly give expression to the existence of something fundamentally outside the system of its likeness. What is significant about this is the emphatic way in which the height of praise is placed *beyond* the logic of comparison, beyond the self-remarking, self-confirming indication of an epideictic logos—displaced, that is to say, by means of circumlocutory light, to a peculiar place, outside of sight, that visionary words cannot express. There is, for example, a clear-cut difference between *Jehova* and *Ha Shem*, between the proper name of God and the "Word" that it is called. So too it is precisely to this difference that successive *eidola* implicitly and tacitly refer as they ascend up to a point of asymptotic liminality whose shrouded light defines the boundary of likeness. This place *between* the edges is neither here nor there, and yet, as such and for this very reason, it serves to mark the difference between the world of Nature and the world of Super-Nature.

For so long as this constitutive difference remains in this way *systemically* unspeakable by a language of light, for so long as it is pictured as a scotomized occlusion at the borderlines of brightness, it is effectively projected, specifically as a border, to a place outside likeness where it can function as the transcendental Other to the Nature of the Same. This defines the *positive* necessity associated with the literally unspeakable graphesis—the *yod, he, vau, he*—of the proper name of God. More generally, this explains why the language of praise regularly adverts back through its "Word" to a more secret word beyond its visionary speech. The name whose literality is logically excessive to a visionary mouth defines by its exclusion the proper limits of an epideictic light. Straddling the inside and the outside of the Mirror of the World, unspeakable *Jehova*, whose first significant creative action is to distinguish light from darkness, is himself the principle of an implicit, because structurally extrinsic, "difference" that "one thing expressing" explicitly and happily "leaves out" for so long as language is understood to work by means of likeness or is conceived in terms of light. Thus projected to the edge or to the edging of the universe and uni-verse of likeness, this difference, which is the difference *between* likeness and difference, in this way both establishes and secures, just as it is established and secured by, the difference between Nature and Super-Nature. Precisely because He is thus excluded and "left out," because He is in this way outspokenly unspoken, God remains a complementary Otherness to a complimentary Sameness, an ineffable "beyondness" whose expulsion thus confirms the natural and present logic of the panegyric logos of *Ha Shem*.

It is not exactly the case, therefore, as I said earlier, that because the epideictic "see[s] the same" it cannot see what is not the same, that because it "imagines" it cannot imagine what is other than itself. Quite the contrary, the epideictic can imagine—indeed it *must* and regularly does imagine—this alternative to itself, but it does so precisely as that which it *cannot* imagine, as precisely that which visionary language cannot speak. For this reason, however, there is a very thin line separating the good faith of the epideictic from its bad faith, literally a matter of saying and not saying, of speaking and not speaking, the difference between likeness and difference. The Idea of sameness cannot manifest its likeness without calling on, and therefore up, a difference that the Nature of its likeness must in principle exclude. To the extent that this exclusion is respected, to that extent will this "unnatural" difference be effectively remaindered or projected out beyond the world of "special" Nature to a "no place" where as sacred Other it can function as the *arche* and the *telos* of a hierarchic cosmos. With difference thus excreted, metaphors can logically proceed to theorize a sameness, just as mimetic representations can logically reduplicate the referents they present.

On the other hand, if this deliberately ostracized difference comes explicitly to enter the world of Nature, if such expulsed difference is literally *put into* words, and is thereby seen to enter into the luminous likeness of *Ha Shem*, then the very logic of a visionary logos will force *Ha Shem* to speak against itself. This is the danger derived from the *articulation* of *Jehova:* the "Word" that *speaks* of difference will then become the paradoxical likeness of its difference from itself. By the same logic, the universe of natural fullness will thereupon be filled with an originary lack. The Signifier of all signifiers, which was formerly, because it was unspeakable, in a class apart from all of its sub-classes, will now appear explicitly as empty hole within, instead of as a supplement without, the cosmic whole. Accordingly, if *Ha Shem* continues to speak logically, it will thereupon speak, again paradoxically, *against* the fullness of its Logos; it will speak a contra-diction that registers the way in which the universal quantifier is extrinsic to the total that it fathers, or the way in which the Logos as a comprehensive name or title is, *because* it is explicitly a part of, inherently apart from whatever wholeness it entitles. In either case, whether taken as a signifier or as a signified, the "Word" or "Name" will manifest a Oneness that is more and less than one, a sameness that is different not only from its likeness but also from itself. *Ha Shem* will thus become a signifier at one remove both from itself and from what it signifies.

Elaborated in this abstract way, these are paradoxes that possess very little literary interest. What Fludd's pictures bring out, however, is that such paradoxes are implicitly embedded and virtually incorporated within the figurative logic of the language of Idea, and that *as* paradoxes they are potentially available for literary exploitation on condition that the prohibition with regard to speaking difference is explicitly transgressed. It is in this way, I want to suggest, that the very same epideictic logic that determines the specific themes, images, motifs, with which the language of praise will idealize itself also predicates, in advance, the specific themes, images, motifs, with which, as happens in Shakespeare's sonnets, such language will speak against itself. If idealizing language articulates the difference that the likeness of its Nature would normally excise, it will find itself specifically subverted by the difference that it speaks.

To see one concrete example of this, we can look at the erotic logic represented in Fludd's picture of the integrated world, the way in which figure 2 illustrates generic Man or *Homo* with his arms unfolded toward the Sun (at the left of the circle of animals) in complementary contrast to the way that Woman or *Mulier* looks instead up at the Moon which is the pale reflection of the sun that shines above it (to the right of the circle of animals). On the one hand Man, and on the other Woman. Pictured in this way, we see the horizontal axis on which the hierarchy of the vertical universe perpendicularly depends, and it is easy enough to derive from this familiar opposition the patriarchal order that makes of Woman the subordinate subspecies or reflection of a universal Man. The point to notice, however, is that as Fludd's picture shows it this is not a simple or a simply polar opposition. Man is figured by a sun that is always the same as itself, whereas Woman is figured by a waxing-waning changing Moon that is always other than itself because its light of simulation illuminates its difference from the sameness of the Sun. Perhaps this constitutes a paradox, this lunar light which folds up likeness into difference. But again the point is that, so long as this is kept a secret, the paradox implicitly depicted will stand in service of an orthodox erotics for which woman is the Other to man, the *hetero* to *homo*, precisely because her essence is *to be* this lunatic difference between sameness and difference. In the same classical way that the difference between the Sun and the Moon *is* the Moon (and the iconography associated with this irrational ratio remains powerful at least through Milton), so too, and equally traditionally, is the difference between Man and Woman, Woman herself, a piety we see fleshed out in the ornaments of Nature, who sports a Sun on one breast, a Moon on the other, and, as the castrated and castrating difference between them, a second, fetishistic Moon upon her beatific crotch.[33]

Such is the erotics that is called for by traditional metaphysics. The Word (at the tangential top of the Universe) whose solar brightness is revealed by that which clouds it bespeaks a female darkness (at the ec-centric center of the Universe) that is veiled by lunar brightness. And we could put this point more strongly by asserting that Fludd's picture manifests the way in which a universe of sameness is built *around* the secret, private parts of difference, as though it were the very lunacy of Nature that returns both Man and Woman to the solar order of the "Word."[34] All this follows, however, only for so long as this erotic point of difference is maintained as an official and emphatic secret, as an internalized beyondness in between the legs of Nature that is kept discreetly covered by a light whose euphemistic function is itself a kind of teasing leer. The sickle-crescent Moon of Nature, which is cut and cutting both at once, highlights *by* concealing a salacious darkness deep within the recesses of Nature, a darkness that appears there, therefore, as an arcane darkness just as foreign to her lucent, even haloed, nature as is unspeakable *Je-*

hova from the periphrastic attribution of *Ha Shem*. In either case, however, whether we consider the erotic shame of Nature or the ontological pudendum of the universal cosmos, whether we look at Sub-Nature or at Super-Nature, a scandal is avoided by virtue of the tacit and respectful modesty of circumlocutory light.

There is more that might be said about the deliberately esoteric and anachronistic hermeticism of Fludd's cosmological drawings, especially about what might be called, to use Lear's phrase, their "darker purpose." Even this cursory consideration, however, makes it very evident that an epideictic poetics cannot overlook or be indifferent to the difference that defines the limits of its visionary praise. A Cratylitic semiotics that wants to see words as truthful simulacra of that which they bespeak, an idealist taxonomy that wants to see in individual particulars the logical sub-species of a universal genus or Idea, an erotic psychology of admiration that wants to identify loving subject with beloved object, a visionary poetics of effective idealization that wants its metaphor and mimesis to "see the same"— these are all perspectives that are obliged explicitly to banish heterogeneity to an elsewhere clearly marked and coded as somewhere *out of view*. With regard to the literary history of the Renaissance sonnet, where this idealist tradition of *artisque imago* and *speculum mundi* is regularly expounded, it is important to recognize the consistent operation of this principle of exclusion, to see it as a strict and rather self-consciously apprehended necessity. For when we do so, we can acknowledge, but acknowledge without overemphasizing, the various resistances to such a homogeneous discourse that are present in the poetry of admiration from the very beginning, and which, in fact, grow increasingly more palpable in the Renaissance sonnet as it develops from Dante, through Petrarch, to Sidney, to and through the general phenomenon of the Elizabethan sonnet-sequence vogue.

As we will see, such resistances are very powerful in the pre-Shakespearean sonnet. Indeed, it would be fair to say that the poetry of praise regularly chafes against the limits of the integrated world and that, to a considerable degree, this is responsible for the complexity and the self-conscious difficulty of a poetry that is somewhat oversimply called "golden" or "ideal." Until Shakespeare's sonnets, however, these resistances are always left *thematically* unspoken; though they are regularly manifest, they are so in an implicit and evocatory way, as suspicions that are sounded only indirectly in between the lines. Petrarch, for example, in his sonnets to

Laura seems always on the verge of remarking and regretting an insistent and intractable discrepancy between his laudatory signifiers and his praiseworthy signifieds. In various ways, some of which I will mention later, Petrarch's poetry suggests to the reader that the poet feels his verse to be inadequate to his high poetic purpose, and, associated with this, it often seems that Petrarch wants to disavow the puns he makes on "Laura," as though a confession of false Cratylism were always on the tip of the poet's laudatory tongue. Even so, though this is something very forceful in Petrarch's sonnets, it remains in them something that is insinuated and latent. It is only in the *Secretum*, the confessional dialogue Petrarch imagines to take place between himself and St. Augustine—a confidential dialogue that was intended only for Petrarch's eyes, and which was never supposed to be published—that Petrarch gives explicit voice to a set of suspicions that are powerfully but, again, only tacitly suggested by the verse (in the *Secretum*, for example, St. Augustine accuses Petrarch of having fallen in love with Laura *only* on account of her suggestive name).[35]

This reticence on the part of Petrarch in his sonnets—a reticence that is operative in the public poetry but not in the private, literally "secret" prose—is sufficiently resonant and pregnant as to evidence the fact that Petrarch worries over much the same kind of issues that later become the thematic center of Shakespeare's sonnets. For what follows it is important to recognize that this is the case, first, because it suggests, though only in a very general way, a continuity of concern that informs the historical development of Petrachan poetry, second, because it eliminates whatever temptation there might be to characterize Petrarch's poetry in terms of a naive idealism, as though a sophisticated Shakespearean lyric somehow comes to know something about ontological, linguistic, or sexual difference that a less knowing Petrarchan lyric does not.

At the same time, however, this reticence also helps to identify, specifically and particularly, just what it is that distinguishes Shakespeare's sonnets from the sonnets they succeed. For what is distinctively peculiar about Shakespeare's sonnets is the way in which, taken as a whole, they work to render *explicit*, to put directly and expressly into the very words they speak, a sense and sensibility of difference that is structurally inherent within, but for this very reason thematically unspeakable within, an orthodox poetry of praise. In the traditional laudatory sonnet that Shakespeare inherits, this difference, treated as a kind of ultimate Otherness, will either be piously and ostentatiously occulted, as is unspeakable *Jehova*, or it will be felt as an intrusively abeyant presence held at bay by an oblique and a conflicted speech, as in the troubled tonalities of Petrarch's vaguely guilty praise of Laura. In either case, however, the topic of difference, which, as difference, is necessarily *u-topic* in an epideictic poetics of likeness, will not be vocally elaborated in the sonnet until Shakespeare. It might be said, therefore, that what Shakespeare introduces into the sonnet is a *merely* thematic novelty, i.e., the theme of difference. But the explicit appearance of this particular theme in poetry is more consequentially significant for literary history than might otherwise be imagined. For when "difference" is no longer thematically "left out," when it happens that the dormant paradoxes built into the poetics of praise are activated in an explicit, not implicit, way, the result for the literary genre of the sonnet is a difference in poetic *kind*—a difference generated by a transgression of traditional poetic decorum equivalent to the blasphemy accomplished by the voicing or the speaking of unspeakable *Jehova*.

There is of course another literary genre and tradition, both like and unlike the poetry of praise, where the kind of logically illogical difference to which I am referring is regularly put into explicit words. This is, precisely, the tradition of the paradox of praise. In this comic literature it is possible to see very clearly what happens when it is no longer the case that "one thing expressing, leaves out difference." To take an example relevant not only to the venereal Nature of Fludd's diagram but also to the "mourning" morning and evening light of Shakespeare's sonnet 132, consider Donne's ninth paradox, where the question at issue is, "Why is Venus-Star multinominous, called both *Hesper* and *Vesper*?" Donne's answer reads, in part, as follows:

> Venus is *multinominous* to give example of her *prostitute disciples*, who so often, either to renew or refresh them selves towards *lovers*, or to *disguise* themselves from *Magistrates*, are to take new names.[36]

The example is interesting because it illustrates how very specific are the motifs and conceits through which paradoxical difference will find itself imagined. In order to accomplish a comic praise of Venus, Donne parodically develops standard images from the poetry of praise. More precisely, he re-presents commonplace images of epideictic likeness but does so in a way that makes them into images of difference. Thus Venus is a peculiar star because she shines both in the growing brightness of the morning and in the growing darkness of the night. This visible duplicity calls up an equivalent linguistic equivocality since Venus is both "Hesper" and "Vesper," an example of a polysemic reference and referent, "multinominous," therefore, both as signifier and as signified. In turn, this verbal duplicity—a word whose plural indication is untrue to any single referent—calls up a corresponding erotic duplicity when linguistic infidelity becomes the alibi of prostitutes who are not singly related to any single lover.

These are all familiar conceits in the comic repertoire of paradox. The dissimulation of all appearance, the dishonesty of all speech, the nymphomania of all women—all this is as commonplace in mock encomium as is eternal light, or Cratylitic language, or true love, in the poetry of praise. This is the case, however, because paradoxical epideixis such as Donne's arrives at itself by means of a structurally consistent transformation of the epideictic homogeneities it intends to mock. Paradoxical praise works by developing the very same themes and conceits as are developed by orthodox praise, the only difference being that paradox develops this traditional imagery of likeness as imagery of difference, thereby importing *into* epideictic likeness a difference that would otherwise remain unspoken in the language of praise. The sexy, polysemic, twofold light of Venus exemplifies what happens to beatific light when poetic admiration discovers by uncovering the deception of what Donne here calls "disguise." More explicitly, this is what happens when "one thing expressing" puts "difference" into its own expression—as happens here when the language of homogeneous and univocal praise expressly and paradoxically speaks about the "multinominous."

As I have already recalled, there is in the Renaissance a considerable vogue for such comic panegyric. Even so, despite the popularity of the genre, this is a literary mode that is never taken very seriously. Paradoxical exercises such as Donne's are characteristically treated by Renaissance literary theory as something minor and unimportant, as instances of the literary that are as marginal to proper literary discourse as straightforward praise is central. In this way, like the difference that straightforward praise keeps secret and unspoken, the paradox of praise is a literary genre placed at the outside border of traditional and epideictic literariness. Either paradox is banished explicitly and altogether for being too trivial for words (which is why Sidney, in the *Apology*, speaks against the genre; *AP*, 181–82) or it is accepted to the extent that, and on the condition that, it is treated as something light and comic.

As something comic, it is surely the case that praise paradox figures frequently and prominently in Elizabethan and Jacobean drama. Again, however, it is important to realize that it does so only as an index of the ridiculous, the marginal, and the excessive. In drama, praise paradox of the kind to which I have been referring is typically associated either with zany misanthropes who stand at one onlooking remove from the central action of the play, or with characters who, though they are central to the action, are significantly alienated from the norms of social life. In either case, when characters articulate paradoxical praises, they are treated as examples of perversion or inversion that the plays in which they appear are designed to refute. Moreover, because what these characters say is always undercut by the way in which they say it, neither the inevitability nor the success of this eventual refutation is ever really left in doubt. For this reason, because praise paradox is a rhetorical form that disavows its own seriousness, because it invites its own rebuke, the mode is especially common in comedy. Because it belies itself, the device allows the dramatist to introduce and to invoke transgressions and peculiarities that, from the very beginning, are coded as provisional, as something the force and consequence of which need not be taken seriously. The moment praise paradox is sounded, an audience will anticipate its subsequent silencing. This is why praise paradox serves so regularly as an unthreatening example of comic madness, of a madness, that is to say, into which sanity may sometimes lapse but from which, at least in comedy, it always recovers.

Shakespeare is very alert to this conservative, reassuring dramatic function of praise paradox, and many of his comedies are designed so as first to exploit and then to show up the abnormality of mock encomiastic postures. To take an example that provides a useful contrast to what happens in the sonnets, consider Petruchio's deliberately false Petrarchan praise of Kate in *The Taming of the Shrew*:

> Say that she rail, why then I'll tell her plain
> She sings as sweetly as a nightingale;
> Say that she frown, I'll say she looks as clear
> As morning roses newly wash'd with dew;
> Say she be mute, and will not speak a word,
> Then I'll commend her volubility,
> And say she uttereth piercing eloquence
> (2.1.170–76)

The humor here derives from the bravado with which Petruchio systematically gainsays familiar panegyric conceits, indiscriminately applying cliché compliments each against the other so that the only thing they have in common is that, all together, they are equally untrue. In the play as a whole this becomes the model for all Petruchio's odd behavior, the consistent inconsistency of which is made to seem the example and extension of such laudatory contradiction. More elaborately, this provides the logic of Petruchio's taming strategy, where Petruchio acts out a flamboyant paradox of praise—directly so, as, for example, in 2.1, more generally so insofar as Petruchio's mad wooing is a recognizably crazy version of the way Petrarchan lovers, such as Lucentio in the subplot, conventionally express their admiration. All this the play presents as the action of straightforward madness. But again, to the extent that Petruchio's behavior is understood as something comic, the audience is at all times certain that the paradox he enacts eventually will come to stand in service of a customary praise:

> Hearing thy mildness prais'd in every town,
> Thy virtues spoke of, and thy beauty sounded,
> Yet not so deeply as to thee belongs,
> Myself am mov'd to woo thee for my wife
> (2.1.191–94)

The Taming of the Shrew is a clear example—many others could be cited—of the way, specifically through the medium of praise paradox, Shakespeare rather regularly conceives both the psychology of his comic characters and the large dramatic rhythms of his comic plays. It is also an example, however, of the way, yet more specifically, Shakespeare associates the genre of praise paradox, at the level of theme, with the *speaking* of a particular kind of problematic "difference," a difference that, as Shakespeare imagines it, is intimately connected to, or is generated by, a particular kind of language whose articulation entails the undoing of pious homogeneities such as those that are represented in Fludd's pictures of an integrated, epideictic world.

To appreciate the pointed specificity of this we need only briefly recall that what is wrong with Kate, what makes her something monstrous and unnatural, is that she is a shrew. Kate *speaks*, and it is the motivating assumption of *The Taming of the Shrew* that such speaking is, by virtue of its very sounding, essentially disruptive of a patriarchal, hierarchic order based upon the logos and the logic of uncomplicated likeness. What the scandalous example of Kate is supposed to demonstrate is that if there exists a language *of* woman, this means either that the woman who speaks it is really a man (which raises a question as to what man is) or that language is no longer something that is uniformly homogeneous (which raises a question as to whether language is something to be trusted). These and other paradoxes are unfolded in several registers throughout the play, for *The Taming of the Shrew* works consistently to associate the confusion of the sexes, the displacement of fathers, the reversal of master and servant, with a general craziness of language that derives from and is illustrated by the shrewishness of Kate.

Large archetypes loom behind all this. Quite apart from the proverbial shrew of folklore, the play makes reference to the garrulous Xantippe and to the loquacious Wife of Bath, these being famous personifications of the way the cursing, chattering babble of a specifically female language is perennially at odds with the voices of orthodox male philosophy and patristic "auctoritee."[37] As are her precursors, however, Kate is presented as a *comic* figure. Whatever challenge she and her speaking might seem to pose to official patriarchal culture, it is a challenge whose danger and urgency are deflated to the extent that Kate is turned into or treated as a laughing matter. Hence Petruchio's taming strategy, which holds a satiric mirror up to Kate's unnatural nature, which presents itself as mimic contradiction both to her contra-diction and to her "cuntra-diction." On the principle of an eye for an eye, Petruchio matches unkind with unkind, madness with madness, all of this "mad mating" (3.2.244)—from the "mad attire" (3.2.124) of his patchwork marriage costume, which is "a very monster in apparel" (3.2.70), to the way "Petruchio is Kated" (3.2.245), to the way Petruchio almost "kill[s] a wife with kindness" (4.1.208)—presented as the objectification of, but also as an object lesson defensively responding to, the fact that woman speaks: "he is more shrew than she" (4.1.85). Finally, at a moment of maximum lunacy, and by means of the very same onto-theological confusion of the sun and moon as is represented in Fludd's picture of naked Nature, Kate capitulates:

> Then God be blest, it is the blessed sun,
> But sun it is not, when you say it is not;
> And the moon changes even as your mind.
> What you will have it nam'd, even that it is.
>   (4.5.18–21)

Taken seriously, this "changing" of "names"—this rupture of the
sameness of *Ha Shem*—like Donne's "multinomynity," would spell
the end to any univocal patriarchal orthodoxy; its logic leads immediately, for example, to the mad transformation of the play's father
into a woman: "'A will make the man mad, to make a woman of him"
(4.5.36). Taken instead, however, as it is here, as a *reductio ad absur-
dum* of linguistic "change," it serves to resecure the logic, the language, and the erotics of Petruchio's Petrarchan world; the tamed
Kate acknowledges this when, in Petrarchan accents, she addresses
the transformed father as "young budding virgin, fair, and fresh,
and sweet" (4.5.37).

As with the iconography of Fludd's diagrams, there is much more
that might be said about the particular motifs Shakespeare in *The
Taming of the Shrew* associates with the language of woman. It would
be possible to show, for example, that what is particularly offensive
about Kate's speech is that from the very beginning it speaks against
vision: "A pretty peat! it is best/Put finger in the eye, and she knew
why" (1.1.78–79). So too it would be possible to show how this anti-
visual language of woman is associated in the play as a whole with
the instability and peculiarity of figurative language in general, for
example, the "ropetricks" played by "rhetoric":

> Why, that's nothing; and he begin once, he'll rail in his rope-tricks. I'll tell
> you what, sir, and she stand him but a little, he will throw a figure in her
> face, and so disfigure her with it, that she shall have no more eyes to see
> withal than a cat.[38]
>
> (1.2.111–15)

So too it would be possible to show how Shakespeare relates all this
to a more general principle of linguistic "translation" that he understands to enrich the "Word" at the cost of the "world," as in the opening lines of the Sly frame: "Therefore *paucas pallabris*, let the world
slide" (Ind. 1.1.5–6).[39]

Leaving all this to the side, the generic point I wish to emphasize
is that in *The Taming of the Shrew* all the confusions and catastrophes
that Shakespeare expressly associates with the speaking of a particular kind of language are readily defused and deferred to the extent
that they are rendered comic. This is the case not only in the main
plot but also in the subplot, where the mixup of fathers is definitively resolved when Lucentio, until then disguised as Cambio,
kneels down before his father and reveals his proper self. "Cambio is
chang'd into Lucentio" (5.1.123) is the line with which this final

revelation is theatrically announced, and it can serve as an economical example of the way in which, in Shakespearean comedy, it is possible for the principle of linguistic "change" itself to change into "light" on condition that "change" itself is treated as something merely witty or absurd. Translation, transformation, disguise, metamorphosis, all such instances and operations of difference serve, when developed in this comic way, to reestablish the serious hierarchy governed by a patriarchal sun. This is why *The Taming of the Shrew,* or why Donne in his praise of prostitute Venus, or why the paradox of praise in general, can speak so volubly and explicitly of difference: because difference, thus comically bespoken, is really guarantee and warrant for the truth it seems to mock.

In another rhetorical mode, however, one that is not purely comic, it is not so easy for difference to be so comfortably or so conservatively put into explicit words. In this other mode, which is the mode that Shakespeare employs in his sonnets, Lucentio can change into Cambio but the corresponding re-turn to ex-changed light is not so readily effected. In Shakespeare's sonnets translation is *unilaterally* directed, from a language of the Same to a Language of the Other, and for this reason Disguise, though it can be put on, cannot be put off. This identifies what is new in Shakespeare's sonnets. The difference that is serious but implicit in a poet such as Petrarch, and the difference that is explicit but trivial in praise paradoxes such as Donne's, turn out to be the same difference in Shakespeare's sonnets, serious *and* spoken both at once. For reasons I want now to consider, this makes a real and permanent difference in the tradition of lyric praise.

HAMLET:	Ha, ha! are you honest?
OPHELIA:	My lord?
HAMLET:	Are you fair?
OPHELIA:	What means your lordship?
HAMLET:	That if you be honest and fair, your honesty should admit no discourse to your beauty.
OPHELIA:	Could beauty, my lord, have better commerce than with honesty?
HAMLET:	Ay, truly, for the power of beauty will sooner transform honesty from what it is to a bawd than the force of honesty can translate beauty into his likeness. This was sometime a paradox, but now the time gives it proof. I did love you once.
OPHELIA:	Indeed, my lord, you made me believe so.
HAMLET:	You should not have believ'd me, for virtue cannot so inoculate our old stock but we shall relish of it. I lov'd you not.
OPHELIA:	I was the more deceiv'd.

(*Hamlet*, 3.1.102–19)

Visionary images of the sort to which I have been referring pervade the sonnets addressed to the young man. So too, in the ways I have suggested are conventional, the young man sonnets explicitly associate these images with the poetics and the poetry of praise. The young man is the poet's ideal and the poet addresses him with a language of idealization. Accordingly, the young man sonnets repeatedly employ a vocabulary of visionary, epideictic likeness that in a reciprocal and mutually corroboratory way reflects well upon the praised young man and reflexively upon the praising poet: "your praise shall still find room, / Even in the eyes of all posterity" (55). On the other hand, in pointed contrast to this visual imagery that governs the sonnets addressed to the young man—imagery that makes the young man into an *imago* of ideal visibility, "Their images I lov'd I view in thee" (31), and that leads the poet to wish that "I could write the beauty of your eyes" (17)—the sonnets addressed to the dark lady consistently speak against such ideal specularity. Moreover, it is not only that the "eyes" of the dark lady's poet "have no correspondence with true sight" (148), but, in addition, the dark lady's poet consistently speaks a language that "censures falsely what they see aright" (148). It is not only that the dark lady is dark, not "fair," but, in addition, the sonnets addressed to her substitute for the imagery of true vision that runs through the sonnets addressed to the young man an alternative imagery, if that is the right word for it, of false language, language that, as the poet imagines it, speaks against the poet's vision: "mine eyes seeing this, say this is not" (137).

This is a *dramatic* fact about Shakespeare's sonnet sequence. As the sequence unfolds, an initial, traditional, and familiar language of vision, a language of admiration, is faced off against a novel, because blind, language with which the poet expresses a desire for something he does not admire. At least at the level of imagery, this amounts to a clear-cut difference between the two sub-sequences. Associated with this, however, the sequence as a whole seems generically to progress from a poetry of praise to a poetry of praise paradox, a movement that, speaking somewhat more abstractly, manifests itself as a progress from a poetry of likeness to a poetry of difference. Moreover, the sequence as a whole remarks this progress it enacts, remarks it in a thematic way such that these contrasts between the two sub-sequences come to function as dynamic interrelationships rather than as static oppositions. Because the sonnets to the dark lady explicitly rethink the themes and motifs first presented in the sonnets to the young man, because the two sub-sequences are engaged with each other in this self-consciously thematic way, the progress of the sequence as a whole seems directed from the start. It is as though the sequence were designed to motivate this movement of motifs, as though the sequence were determined to make something consequential of its own sequentiality. But then—and this is the practical critical question that concerns us—if it is the pointed difference between these two sub-sequences that links them each to each, how is it that these two different poetic points of view also seem the expression of a single poet's voice?

However we characterize either the young man sonnets or the dark lady sonnets, they cannot be related to each other by a simple opposition. Taken separately, and then compared one with the other, the two sub-sequences of the sequence—with their different tonalities, stories, metaphoric constellations, not to mention their two different loves—might appear to constitute a moralizing tableau. Taken separately, that is, and then compared one with the other, we might want to say the two sub-sequences compose a kind of allegorical psychomachia, with idealized virtues displayed on the one side and with vicious vices contrapuntally displayed on the other. There are, of course, many precedents for such an abstract and dichotomizing literary form. Yet the sequence as a whole refuses to be thus discriminated into two distinct and isolated parts. Assuming we read them both, the two parts of the sequence cannot be kept separate from each other, for when we begin to compare them each with each the second sub-sequence retroactively undoes the first, with the latter "forswearing" the former in a definitive revisionary way. For this reason, if the young man sonnets and the dark lady sonnets together form a homiletic diptych, it is one the two sides of which fold over upon each other in a mutually refractory collation, closing over upon each other in so conflicted and displacing an articulation that it is the very opposition between the two sub-sequences that turns out to complicate their opposition.

This is obviously the case at the level of the sonnets' narrative, where the double cuckolding of the poet links the ideal young man to the corrupt and corrupting dark lady, and where the coupling of the poet's two separated loves coherently divides the poet from himself. But the same is also true at the level of the sonnets' themes and images, for here again what connects the two sub-sequences is their disjunctively sequential, their specifically *gainsaying*, juxtaposition. It is not, therefore, as a metacritic that a reader is led to wonder on what hinge the apparently positive valuation of visionary language in the first sub-sequence subsequently turns into the neither purely positive nor the purely negative valuation of lying, nonvisual language in the second. Again, in the most straightforward way, this defines a practical, not a metacritical, question raised by Shakespeare's sonnets, for it is the poet himself to whom the pressing question is:

> O, from what pow'r hast thou this pow'rful might
> With insufficiency my heart to sway,
> To make me give the lie to my true sight,
> And swear that brightness doth not grace the day?
> (150)

To begin to understand the sonnets' answer to this question we must first recognize something very obvious; namely, that the visionary motifs of the young man sonnets are not really developed in the simple, uncomplicated way I have so far described. This complexity is not altogether unusual. Many of the visionary complications evidenced by Shakespeare's sonnets are quite common in the sophisticated literary atmosphere of the pre-Shakespearean sonnet, and Shakespeare's concern with such complications is in many respects nothing but traditional. It is certainly the case, for example, that the sonnets addressed to the young man emphatically, even exaggeratedly, portray their own illumination, highlighting their own panegyric light in a perceptibly self-conscious way. However, such visual and almost exhibitionist self-consciousness is not, in itself, particularly peculiar. The poetry of praise will regularly display itself in just this stylizing way as something to be *seen,* and just such self-display will often seem its most especial virtue, as, for example, in Petrarch's or in Dante's reflective and reflexive poetries of laudatory, beatific light. Moreover, it is neither especially novel nor disturbing that the young man sonnets will sometimes paint themselves as pictures that show off the highest form of praise—"Mine eye hath play'd the painter and hath stell'd/Thy beauty's form in table of my heart" (24)—but will just as often, indeed, more often, see in such pictoriality a flattery which is the lowest form of imitation:

> So is it not with me as with that Muse
> Stirr'd by a painted beauty to his verse,
> Who heaven itself for ornament doth use,
> And every fair with his fair doth rehearse.
>
> (21)

Here again, however, from the perspective of the poetry of praise, such suspicions of a visual poetics as are voiced in sonnet 21—the poet's distaste for a "Muse" of "painted beauty" (cf. "their gross painting" in sonnet 82, or "I never saw that you did painting need" in sonnet 83)—are nothing but conventional. This too is characteristic of a self-conscious poetry of praise, for this is the way a poetry that is perennially a poetry of "speaking picture," of *ut pictura poesis,* of illustrative example, of admiring blazon, of idealizing *effictio,* will regularly revive the tired topoi of a visual poetics whose literary *enargia* would otherwise be dim.

It is important not to underestimate either the irony or the subtlety of the poetic tradition that Shakespeare inherits when he sits to sonnets. If it is the case that Shakespeare's young man sonnets regularly make negative as well as positive reference to the tradition of the poetry of praise, and to the imagery of vision historically endemic to this tradition of poetic idealization, it remains the case that such positive and negative reference is itself traditional *in* the poetry of praise. So too the resemblance of praise to flattery is itself a matter of epideictic convention (e.g., Spenser's "The world that cannot deem of worthy things,/When I doe praise her, say I doe but flatter"), calling up a familiar worry and uneasiness about specifically pictorial and visual mimesis that goes back to Plato, and that, *as* a worry, forms the basis of innumerable exercises of sonneteering wit.[1] The poetry of praise, that is to say, especially in the sonneteering tradition that begins with Dante, is neither stupid nor sentimental, and so it rarely imagines itself a "Mirrour" of "Idea" without at the same time registering the possibility that the ornaments of its copiousness might be infected by the problematic aesthetics of the copy.[2] Petrarch, for example, is no naif when he speaks of Laura as "My idol [*idolo*] carved [*scolpito*] in living laurel."[3] And neither is Spenser indifferent to the complications he establishes in the *Amoretti* when, for example, he describes his beloved as an ideal idol— "The glorious image of the maker's beauty,/My souerayne saynt, the Idoll of my thought"—at the same time as he tells us that she is the "idle" "Spectator" of her loving poet's theatrical admiration: "Of this worlds theatre in which we stay,/My love lyke the Spectator ydly sits/beholding me that all the pageants play."[4]

In these and other ways, and with such conceits of self-consciously intromissive and extromissive visuality, the poetry of praise, long before Shakespeare, evidences its own specular sophistication. At least in part, such poetry is remarkable *because* it thus conventionally remarks itself and its theatricality, and one of the special pleasures such poetry provides is the variety of ways it lets us notice this. For this reason, however, it is equally important to realize that, however elaborately or playfully the poetry of praise displays the glass of its literary fashion or the mold of its epideictic form, it nevertheless consistently and confidently idealizes its "ideas." That is to say, it is not by ignoring, but by embracing and emphasizing its own specular sophistication that the poetry of praise will come to see a difference between an idol which is false and an icon which is true. This is why, for all the often bitter insights of their self-suspicions, the self-conscious "visions" of such epideictic poetry will always seem ideal. Looking on itself, such epideictic poetry will unambiguously distinguish the specious shadows and mirages of its flattery from the lucid substance of its praise, as when Constable writes "To His Mistresse": "Thy image should be sunge for thow that goddese art/Which onlye we withoute idolatry adore."[5]

It is just this distinction, however, or the confidence with which it is traditionally maintained, whose absence can be sensed in Shakespeare's young man sonnets. In the ideal poems addressed to the young man, the difference between an Una and Duessa (according to Spenser, it is Una, not Duessa, who is "th'Image of Idolatryes") is not so obviously clear, and if the fallible young man, as "observ'd of all observers"—"The lovely gaze where every eye doth dwell" (5)—does not straightforwardly deserve the poet's admiration, neither does the poet's observation transparently illuminate itself.[6] On the one hand, "all things turns to fair that eyes can see" (95), but, on the other, "'tis flatt'ry in my seeing" (114). One the one hand, "Full many a glorious morning have I seen" (33), but, on the other, what the poet sees in the morning is the way the sun "flatter[s] the mountain tops with sovereign eye" (33), the way it "gild[s] pale streams with heavenly alcumy" (33). Despite the apparent familiarity of these tropes and themes, they point to a genuinely novel ambiguity with which the young man's poet regularly colors all the young man's visionary praise. And it is just this thoroughly peculiar epideictic point of view that regularly leads the young man's poet to suspect that there is more to praise than meets his panegyric "eye" and "I."

Sonnet 24, whose first two lines I have just cited as an example of the young man's poet's visionary mode, offers a good example. The poet begins by explaining how:

> Mine eye hath play'd the painter and hath stell'd
> Thy beauty's form in table of my heart;
> My body is the frame wherein 'tis held,
> And perspective it is best painter's art.

The conceit is familiar, and the poet proceeds to develop it in what seem to be familiar ways. Thus, in the first quatrain, the poet paints a picture—with his eye and on his heart—of his ideal so that, in the second quatrain, the ideal might see the truest picture of himself.

> For through the painter must you see his skill,
> To find where your true image pictur'd lies,
> Which in my bosom's shop is hanging still,
> That hath his windows glazed with thine eyes.

In turn, in the third quatrain, the poet sees himself in that which he portrays:

> Now see what good turns eyes for eyes hath done:
> Mine eyes have drawn thy shape, and thine for me

Are windows to my breast, wherethrough the sun
Delights to peep, to gaze therein on thee.

There are several reasons why all this seems familiar. First of all, the sonnet recalls many Petrarchist conceits in which the lover sees himself in the eyes of his beloved (the poet's "stelling," for example, is an amplification of the way Astrophil finds Stella's image engraved upon his heart). Second, the poet's painting recalls the poetics of "speaking picture" and of *ut pictura poesis*. Even more important, however, the visual conceit of sonnet 24 is one the main outlines of which the poet develops throughout the opening procreation sonnets addressed to the young man. In sonnet 3, for example, the poet tells the young man that because he is "thy mother's glass" the young man ought to reproduce himself, for in this way the young man, in future time, "through windows of thine age shalt see,/Despite of wrinkles, this thy golden time." In sonnet 3 the young man is quite literally a self-regarding "image," but one whose solipsistic prospects are uncertain, for, unless reduplicated, this "image" will "die single, and thine image dies with thee." Later I will discuss the various difficulties that result from the way the poet thus assimilates to himself at the end of the procreation series the imagery of visual identification and multiplication that he at first associates with the young man's reproduction. Thinking specifically of sonnet 24, I will be concerned with the ways in which the young man's "windows of thine age" in sonnet 3 problematically anticipate, as projected and projecting surface, as mirror and as lamp, what in sonnet 24 are the "windows" in the poet's "bosom," which are "glazed with thine eyes," and also the young man's eyes, which "are windows to my breast, wherethrough the sun/Delights to peep, to gaze therein on thee," and also the "perspective" of sonnet 24's line 4, one of whose Elizabethan meanings—based upon the etymology of *perspicere*—is "window."

For the moment, however, it is enough simply to realize that the poet's pictorial creation in sonnet 24, the picture he paints upon his heart, is intended in a fairly obvious fashion to be a thematic recreation of the young man's self-repeating procreation, and that we therefore take the point that just as the ideal image of the young man is initially identified with his visual issue ("through windows of thine age" in sonnet 3), so too does the general conceit in sonnet 24 ("windows to my breast") suggest an amatory visual identification, a kind of specular reciprocity or replicating symmetry, between the poet's "I" and "thou." At the very least, this seems to be what the poet wants the young man to see when he tells him: "Now see what good turns eyes for eyes have done." And again, even if we were to bracket from our consideration all the other themes of visual or pictorial correspondence in the young man sonnets, there would still be nothing particularly astonishing about the intromissive-extromissive terms of sonnet 24's conceit, for it is precisely this that defines what is conventional in the reflexive reflections of the sonnet's visual motifs: namely, the mutual identification of painter with painted, of seer with seen, of eye with eyed.

Having said so much, however, we immediately realize that we have not said enough, for the couplet to the sonnet, which I have so far left unmentioned, interferes with and rebuts the logic of this familiar Petrarchist conceit: "Yet eyes this cunning want to grace their art,/They draw but what they see, know not the heart." Again, in some respects there is nothing at all unusual about the couplet. It is just as much a commonplace of the sonnet tradition for the poet to insist upon the superficiality of visual appearance as it is for him to insist upon the profound correspondence of his eye and heart. Even if we did not know this, the sententious proverbiality of the couplet, along with its repetition of the first quatrain's rhyme of "art" and "heart," would be enough to make a reader register its deliberately commonplace effect. It is not, therefore, the sonnet's explicitly stated ideas that are the basis of the sonnet's peculiarity. Rather, the only thing that strikes a reader as uncommon about sonnet 24— what makes it seem at least a little peculiar—is the rapidity or abruptness with which these two familiar commonplaces are deployed against each other, so that the suddenly announced "yet" of the couplet is given as both the inexorable, but also as the inexplicable, conclusion to the idealizing lines that it succeeds.

Accordingly, in the light of this "yet," and of the sentiments it introduces, the sonnet obliges the reader to rethink the large visual conceit to which the couplet so peremptorily, but irresolutely, puts an end. The couplet reacts back upon the body of the sonnet, with the result that as a reader concludes the poem he ceases to overlook the way the visual conceit has all along resisted the familiar pictorial imagination it professes. Thus, performing the rereading that the sonnet seems itself to ask for—a second reading not entirely unlike the retroactive rereading of the young man sub-sequence that is enjoined by even a first reading of the dark lady sub-sequence—a reader will wonder more precisely just what the poet means by "stell'd," or how the poet's material "body" is the formal "frame" to a very Neo-Platonic, yet material, "beauty's form." It is not necessary really to answer such questions, or even to formulate them precisely, in order to realize that the sonnet does in fact raise them. The vexed critical commentary regarding "stell'd" in sonnet 24—"portrayed," "carved," "styled," "mirrored," "steeled" (I will here add "stolen")—is itself a measure of, and a response to, the sonnet's own uncertainties regarding its idea of its ideal.[7]

So too, the distinctively twisted syntax of the sonnet, the way the referents of its pronouns and demonstratives are consistently uncertain, works effectively to obscure what are the sonnet's most transparent visual claims, as though the actual deictics of the sonnet were at odds with the sonnet's ideal epideixis. This can be seen in the stressed diffuseness of the "that" in line 8—"That hath his windows glazed with thine eyes"—or in the "'tis" of line 3 (coherently referring back at once to "mine eye," to "thy beauty's form," and to the "table of my heart"), or, more striking yet, in the grammatically indeterminate "it" of line 4—"And perspective it is best painter's art"—which leaves a reader, as Stephen Booth points out, undecided as to whether "perspective" functions here as adverb or as noun, and which calls up the semantic overdetermination whereby, in addition to "window," "perspective" refers both to the realistic art of monocular three-dimensional painting and to the equally Shakespearean, but bifocal, art of anamorphic *tromperie* (cf. Orsino's "A natural perspective, that is and is not!" *TN,*5.1.217).[8]

Finally, responding to the eruption of the couplet out of what has come before it, the temporalities of the sonnet will impress a reader with a hitherto unnoticed affective resonance. The sudden appearance of a perennially present tense in the couplet, the urgent, yet ongoing, currency with which "eyes this cunning want to grace their art," resituates the tenor and the time of the past participles of the first three quatrains in a remote, yet recent past. From the temporal point of view of the abruptly interpolated present tenses of the couplet, such actions as "hath play'd," "hath stell'd," "have drawn," all become the kind of gestures that have only just now been completed and yet, at the same time, are removed to a historic and habitual past of long ago. At the end of the sonnet the visual conceit of the first twelve lines exists in a poetic past that has been *made such* by a decision of the poetic present: it exists in a retrospect that is produced by a contemporary suspicion. And these same temporalities are what make the "want" attaching to the couplet's "eyes" persuasively express a sense of *present* lack that, as the poem develops it, supplies the motive of the poem's desire. The way in which the poet's eyes fall short defines a "want" which for the eyes is equal to a lack of "heart" as well as "art." In the couplet to the sonnet, therefore, the "wanting" of the eyes becomes the eyes' desire *for* the heart, which is to say the eyes' desire for desire: "Yet eyes this cunning want to grace their art,/They draw but what they see, know not the heart."

If we were to look more carefully at other sonneteering commonplaces in the sonnets addressed to the young man, we would find a good many thematic, temporal, and tonal peculiarities similar to those we sense in sonnet 24, all these peculiarities, moreover, introduced in the same quiet yet effectively insistent fashion. The hesitant uncertainties surrounding "stell'd" in sonnet 24 characteristically circumscribe almost all the young man sonnets' metaphors of indelible "marking," and, further, such hesitations are characteristically related to these sonnets' curious ambivalent sense of amatory praise, for example, the way in sonnet 112: "Your love and pity doth th' impression fill/Which vulgar scandal stamp'd upon my brow," for which reason, as the poet somewhat irritatedly explains: "You are my all the world, and I must strive/To know my shames and praises from your tongue;/None else to me, nor I to none alive,/That my steel'd sense or changes right or wrong." So too the attentuations and disjunctive temporalities conveyed by the way the poet develops the conceit of visual mutuality in sonnet 24 is also something that is characteristic of the young man sub-sequence. For example, it is precisely this disjunctive temporality that regularly makes a problem of the correspondence between the poet's eye and eyed, or between the poet's "I" and "thou," as in, for shortest example, the pathos and the pastness of "for as you were when first your eye I ey'd" (104).

Nevertheless, even if it is agreed, at least provisionally, that this is the case—if it is agreed that just such problematic nuances distinguish Shakespeare's young man sonnets from the poetic tradition they repeat, giving them a density or quality quite unlike anything we are accustomed to in Elizabethan lyric—it would still be a great mistake to see in this a rupture or a break with the tradition of idealizing praise, a tradition the young man sub-sequence manages in this way both sadly to remember and only partially to regret. The young man sonnets neither naively reiterate the poetry of praise nor cynically reject it. More poignantly, they both repeatedly see *through* their own poetic visuality, and, at the same time, they insist on seeing *in* this gilded vision an image worthy of a retrospect respect. Hence, for example, the disjunct timing *and* "per-spective" of sonnet 24, "*Now* see what good turns eyes for eyes *have done*," as though "perspective" only used to be "best painter's art."

I want to argue, first, that this characteristic "re-vision" is responsible for the special melancholy of the poems addressed to the young man; second, speaking more generally, that this marks a moment in literary history when poetic vision, by virtue of its own self-regard, implicitly admits itself and the "scene" of all its admiration to be explicitly imaginary, praiseworthy only as something literary and, for this reason, fictive and unreal. This is already the beginning, that is to say, prepared for by the specular self-consciousness of a Sidney or a Spenser, of a poetry that only sees its visionary ideality in rueful retrospect—"Thus have I had thee as a dream doth flatter" (87)—and that therefore makes its own literariness, which it recognizes as something *merely* literary, the basis of its praise: "That in black ink my love may still shine bright" (65). Further, I want to argue that it is in the split that thus emerges, both spatially and temporally, within the poet's "eye" and "I" that the novelty of the subject or subjectivity of Shakespeare's sonnets is initially revealed.

This is to speak to the tones and textures of the poems addressed to the young man. For this reason, because a matter of tone and texture, the point cannot readily be made by citing individual lines or by identifying separate themes, even when these golden-gilded lines and themes explicitly announce the poems' conception of themselves. Characteristically, the young man sonnets silently inflect the praise they speak, and so it is only obliquely that what these poems directly say can count as evidence of their peculiar, but unspoken, epideictic intention. Thus, to take another illustration, sonnet 105 explicitly presents itself, *in laudis laudem*, as a praise of its own praise:

> Let not my love be call'd idolatry,
> Nor my beloved as an idol show,
> Since all alike my songs and praises be
> To one, of one, still such, and ever so.
> Kind is my love to-day, to-morrow kind,
> Still constant in a wondrous excellence,
> Therefore my verse, to constancy confin'd,
> One thing expressing, leaves out difference.
> "Fair," "kind," and "true" is all my argument,
> "Fair," "kind," and "true" varying to other words,
> And in this change is my invention spent,

Three themes in one, which wondrous scope affords.
"Fair," "kind," and "true" have often liv'd alone,
Which three till now never kept seat in one.

Here, summarizing standard epideictic formulas, there is an ideal
commutation between the poet's desire ("my love" in the first line),
the object of his desire ("my beloved," in the second line) and the
language of his desire ("my songs and praises" in the third line).
What these three share is a common "ideality." In accord with a conventional epideictic literary self-consciousness, the young man is
"'fair,' 'kind,' and 'true'" precisely *because* "'fair,' 'kind,' and 'true' is
all my argument," where "argument" refers both to what the poet
speaks and to what he speaks about. That is to say, according to at
least one logic of the poem, the young man is an ideal idol *because* the
poetry of praise—here capturing the etymological resonance built
into "admiration" itself—displays him in its "wondrous scope."

On the face of it, therefore, sonnet 105 seems to offer nothing but
the most straightforward language of idealizing praise, developing
not just a two-term but a three-term correspondence between the
speaker, the spoken, and the speech of praise. Yet for all its familiar
brightness the poem never really seems to recover from, or to forget, the withdrawn ambiguity of its explanatory "since"—"Since all
alike my songs and praises be"—since this concessive particle indifferently introduces the "all alikeness" of the poet's "songs and
praises" as both the reason why the young man is an idol as well as
the reason why he is not. As a result, as we read through it, the
deliberate abstraction of the poem—the blandness of its diction, its
isotopic syntax, its invariant repetitions—becomes itself a comment
on the claustrophobia of a verse and also of a desire that are both
equally monotheistically, monogamously, monosyllabically, and mo-
notonously "to constancy confin'd": "To one, of one, still such, and
ever so." By the end of the poem, therefore, the poem's declarative
admission of the "difference" that it says that it "leaves out"—"One
thing expressing, leaves out difference"—becomes a kind of unexpressed confession of an "invention" which is "spent."

Sonnet 105 is not an isolated moment in the young man sequence
as a whole. In several poems the poet complicatedly complains that:

I always write of you,
And you and love are still my argument;
So all my best is dressing old words new,
Spending again what is already spent.
(76)

And the poet also repeatedly wonders:

> Why is my verse so barren of new pride?
> So far from variation or quick change?
> Why with the time do I not glance aside
> To new-found methods and to compounds strange?
>
> (76)

Thus, in sonnet 108, the poet quite explicitly regrets that there is nothing "new to speak" and that, therefore:

> I must each day say o'er the very same,
> Counting no old thing old, thou mine, I thine,
> Even as when first I hallowed your fair name.

Here, because the poet of "eternal love" must "make antiquity for aye his page," the poet is obliged to "find the first conceit of love there bred,/Where time and outward form would show it dead" (108). So too the young man's poet seems very sensitive to the fact that he invents a poetry that endlessly repeats preceding repetitions, and this is an insight that appears to color even the poet's imagery of self-replicating procreation: "If there be nothing new, but that which is/Hath been before, how are our brains beguil'd,/Which laboring for invention bear amiss/The second burthen of a former child" (59).

Alternatively, because the poet is in this way distanced from his sense of his poetic past, so too does he uneasily anticipate the nature of his own poetic future, as when the poet worries that the young man, "finding thy worth a limit past my praise," will be "enforc'd to seek anew/Some fresher stamp of the time-bettering days" (82). Even more pointedly, when the poet thinks about his own posterity, his thoughts invite prospective retrospection, as in:

> If thou survive my well-contented day,
> When that churl Death my bones with dust shall cover,
> And shalt by fortune once more re-survey
> These poor rude lines of thy deceased lover,
> Compare them with the bett'ring of the time.
>
> (32)

In the depressing future that he here envisages for himself, the poet's sole excuse will be the one he puts into the young man's "re-survey[ing]" eye and elegiac mouth: " 'Had my friend's Muse grown with this growing age,/A dearer birth than this his love had brought/To march in ranks of better equipage' " (32).

Simply to quote such lines is surely insufficient. It is certainly the case that all this fond poetic regret and anxious poetic expectation requires far more commentary than I give it now (and I will return to these sonnets later), if only because such thematic evocations of past and future literariness are common in the poetry of praise. Such passages are important, however, because they illustrate the delicate and reserved way in which the poet refers to the fact that he is writing something metaleptic and proleptic, the way in which the poet understands his poetry as somehow oddly poised between the old and new. This is why it would be a great mistake to say that the vaguely or potentially blasphemous conceit of sonnet 105, with the complicated logic of its mutually inclusive "since," is really an unspoken invective of the young man or his praise. For the same reason, it would be a gross reduction of the poet's tone to say that sonnet 105 unimaginatively quotes itself (it repeats three times its "three themes in one") so as thus to announce its own exhaustion: "To one, of one, still such, and ever so." Rather, the poem's inconoclast iconophilia works to reveal its "excellence" *as* "wondrous" at the same time as it brings out the poet's exasperated sense of the copy in his copiousness, the sense that as a poet he can do no more than once again repeat another version of the same. This is certainly not the same thing as a simple reassertion of traditional visionary themes, but neither is it altogether a rejection of them. Instead, and far more complicatedly than perhaps the phrase suggests, this sense of unhappy repetition and "secondariness" that runs through sonnet 105—as it does through many of the sonnets addressed to the young man: "I must each day say o'er the very same" (108)—seems the expression of a *divided* epideictic point of view.

It should be clear that I am here assuming that there is more at stake in the syntactic ambiguities and conflicted tonalities of sonnet 105 than the worth of the young man (ideal or idol?), or even the worth of the poet's admiration for him. Explicitly, sonnet 105 rehearses what from Aristotle on is the conventional understanding of the rhetoricity of praise, a rhetoric that, as all the rhetoricians uniformly say, *enargically* "heightens its effect," and copiously extends itself, by means of visual figures of comparison and amplification: "Shall I compare thee to a summer's day?" (18), "Describe Adonis, and the counterfeit/Is poorly imitated after you" (53). The sonnet thus explicitly describes—more, in fact, than with its abstractions it exemplifies—a traditional conception of poetically vivid and vivifying figure that "sees the same," thematically embracing a particular kind of idealizing vision—

the "wondrous scope"—as complement to the idealizing ways in which "all alike my songs and praises be." Like Juliet, when she is told to give her heart to Paris (and with the same kinds of unspoken doubts about the outcome), the sonnet "look[s] to like, if looking liking move" (*RJ*, 1.3.97), and in sonnet 105 both "looking" and "liking" are understood to carry an explicitly poetic as well as an erotic force. This, at any rate, is what the sonnet seems to mean when it puts its focused "scope" together with its various, yet changeless, "invention" and announces, "one thing expressing, leaves out difference." This is also why there seems nothing shameful about the way "all alike my songs and praises be." And this is a conception of epideictic figure on which all the young man sonnets, not only sonnet 105, seem continually to insist, seeing and saying, over and over, that the yoked terms of its various panegyric tropes—"Two households, both alike in dignity" (*RJ*, Prologue, 1); "making a couplement of proud compare" (21)— are two of a single, visible kind.

Recognizing this—their expressed commitment to inventive similitude, to analogizing likeness, to imaginary, specular resemblance, in short, to the tropic, epideictic "truth" of "fair" and "kind"—I earlier called the figurality of the young man sonnets univocal and homogeneous, and I also made the point that the vision and desire of the young man's poet also regularly "look" to "leave out difference," as in sonnets 46 and 47, where eye and heart were literally made to *see* the image of identity subtending their initial opposition: again, it was "thy *picture* in my sight" that "awakes my heart to heart's and eye's delight." To be sure, in sonnets 46 and 47 the playful development of this conventional conceit in some way speaks against the convention; even so, in sonnets 46 and 47 the play is both so genial and urbane that it seems reasonable to take the sonnets at their specious word: "With my love's picture then my eye doth feast,/And to the painted banquet bids my heart" (47). In sonnet 105, however, which is the sonnet in the young man sequence that most clearly speaks about its praise, the play is not so playful, and so the sonnet's hesitations seem considerably more serious. If, as Murray Krieger has suggested, there is an ideal "one" in the sonnet's "*won*drous scope," then so too is there a "two" in its univocating "one"—"T[w]o one, of one, still such, and ever so"—and this divided multiple of unity therefore functions in a more insistent and more urgent way to undercut the sonnet's monomanic panegyric.[9] The sonnet phlegmatically advances the ambiguity of its "since," but does so only so as to worry over the laudatory "likeness" of its "all alikeness." And by thus implicitly resisting the epideictic conventions they explicitly assert, by making the univocal itself equivocal, the sonnet's "songs and praises" make a question of the single "truth" of "fair" and "kind" that they repeatedly repeat.

It is in this surplus or overly repetitive fashion that the young man sonnets "moan th' expense of many a vanish'd sight" (30). This is how they convey their vision of "beauties" which "are vanishing, or vanish'd out of sight" (63). And it is in this way also, assimilating this excess repetition to themselves, that the poems addressed to the young man consistently will make themselves eccentric versions of a traditionally heliocentric poetry of praise. Conventionally, as we have seen, epideictic tropes are imagined as heliotropes in the gardens of dainty poetic devices; they are "figures of delight" (98), turning toward and with the sun that they look like so as to do respectful homage to a brightness they mimetically and metaphorically repeat: "Great princes' favorites their fair leaves spread/But as the marigold at the sun's eye" (25). As a poetry of praise, Shakespeare's young man sonnets regularly seem to model themselves upon such epideictic tropes, and they therefore regularly speak about their vision of an ideal light and likeness. At the same time, however, this visual image of unity that the young man sonnets idealize, and to which they liken themselves, seems itself, to some extent, divided. In ways that are genuinely surprising, the sun toward which the young man sonnets and the young man's poet turn—"that sun, thine eye" (49)—turns out to be an image of difference, not of likeness, or, more precisely, an image of an eternal sameness that no longer seems the same *because* of its too frequent literary repetition. In the young man sonnets it seems that all of praise is written by Time's "antique pen" (19), as though the old gold of poetic admiration has lost its glister from being rubbed too often by the tradition of Petrarchan praise. One consequence of this is that even the purest and clearest expressions of the "'fair,' 'kind,' and 'true'" somehow convey, if they do not express, a novel kind of optic disillusion. Another consequence, however, one that is sometimes quite directly thematized, is that what the poet sees in the present is its difference from the visionary past.

Thus in sonnet 59 the poet draws a new conclusion from the fact that even ideal repetition now will bear no further repetition:

> If there be nothing new, but that which is
> Hath been before, how are our brains beguil'd,
> Which laboring for invention bear amiss
> The second burthen of a former child!

This is different from the way that Astrophil, at the beginning of his sonnet sequence, after "studying inventions fine" and "oft turning other's leaves," looks "to see if thence would flow/Some fresh and fruitful showers upon my sun-burned brain." This is also different from the way that Astrophil's "Invention, nature's child, fled step-dame Study's blows." When Astrophil is "great with child to speak," he manages to look into his heart to write and he therefore also manages, however archly and self-consciously, "in verse my love to show" (*AS*, 1). In contrast, the young man's poet in sonnet 59, realizing that he comes after the poetry of praise, sees the object of his admiration only very indirectly, by looking backward to and through a literary image of what is retrospect and past.

> O that record could with a backward look,
> Even of five hundreth courses of the sun,
> Show me your image in some antique book,
> Since mind at first in character was done.

This is more than a casual comparison of the present to the past, more than a minor skirmish in the battle of the ancients and the moderns. When the poet imagines the young man's "image in some ancient book," it is in order

> That I might see what the old world could say
> To this composed wonder of your frame,
> Whether we are mended, or whe'er better they,
> Or whether revolution be the same.

But for the poet to wonder "whether revolution be the same" is for the poet to wonder whether what Perdita, for example, calls "the self-same sun that . . . looks on alike" (*WT*, 4.4.444–46) remains itself the same despite its countless revolutions. Insofar as the poet directly addresses this question in sonnet 59, his answer in the couplet is curiously restrained: "O, sure I am the wits of former days/To subjects worse have given admiring praise." But the question of the *sameness* of the turning sun extends beyond this final, qualified contention, as does the catachretic force of the sonnet's opening conceit: the abortive "labor" of an "invention" that will "bear amiss/The second burthen of a former child."

There is more to say about this sonnet, especially about its imagery of birth and bearing. I will return to this sonnet and its "sun" in later chapters. The point to notice now, however, is that when the poet wonders "what the old world could say/To this composed wonder of your frame," the possibility dawns upon him that the sun whose "*won*drous" revolution traditionally returns it to itself has now, *because* of repetition—"five hundreth courses of the sun"—been re-turned into something other than itself. When sonnet 59 balances off its present to its past, when it wonders "whether revolution be the same," it therefore shows the same disjunctive visual and temporal discrepancies that disturb the turning, troping mutuality of "now see what good turns eyes for eyes have done" (24), or the visual confidence that supposes "all things turns to fair that eyes can see" (95).[10] This link between the poet's fractured time and sight is, therefore, not an isolated or unusual correlation in the young man sub-sequence as a whole, nor is it accidentally that the poet brings this linkage out by reference to the ancient history of praise. It regularly happens in the young man sonnets that the poet thematically "makes antiquity for aye [eye] his page" (108) and, therefore, "find[s] the first conceit of love there bred,/Where time and outward form would show it dead" (108). Correspondingly, it regularly happens in the young man sonnets that the traditionally rejuvenating revolution of the shining sun turns into something that the poet thinks is aged by its poetic past, as in:

> O, know, sweet love, I always write of you,
> And you and love are still my argument;
> So all my best is dressing old words new,
> Spending again what is already spent:
> > For as the sun is daily new and old,
> > So is my love still telling what is told.
> > > (76)

This is a consistent aspect of the young man sonnets' imagery of the visual and the visible, imagery that is characteristically presented in the young man sonnets as though it were so tarnished with age that its very reiteration is what interferes with the poet's scopic or specular identification of his poetic "I" with the ideal "eye" of the young man: "For as you *were* when first your eye I *ey'd*" (104). In general, the young man's poet, *as* a visionary poet, but one whose "invention" bears the burden of "the second burthen of a former child!" (59), seems capable of expressing only a love at second sight, his identification of his ego with his ego ideal—"thou mine, I thine" (108)—seems worn out by repetition, as though it were the very practice by the poet of an old-fashioned poetry of visionary praise that effectively differentiates the poet as a panegyricizing subject from what he takes to be his ideal and his praiseworthy object. This

is why I referred earlier to the mixed-up deictic and epideictic compact of the couplet to sonnet 62—"'Tis thee (myself) that for myself I
praise,/Painting my age with beauty of thy days." Initially I said that
this confused identification of the poet's "I" and "thou" identifies the
first person of the poet with the difference that obtains between the
youth and age of visionary praise. The point can now be put more
precisely: writing a poetry of re-turn rather than of "turn," the
young man's poet regularly inverts the conventional dual unities,
the traditional reflexive reflections, of ideal epideixis.

It is important, therefore, to register the way in which the young
man's poet insists upon the fact that he writes nothing but a passé
poetry of praise. This is not only the historical literary context
within which the sonnets addressed to the young man are conceived; it is also the way these sonnets work practically to make a
personal issue out of their self-remarked literary belatedness, regularly associating what they themselves characterize as their old-
fashioned literary matter and manner with their poet's sense of his
senescence. In sonnet 76, for example, whose opening quatrain I
have already cited, the poet asks:

> Why is my verse so barren of new pride?
> So far from variation or quick change?
> Why with the time do I not glance aside
> To new-found methods and to compounds strange?

As the poet first poses them, these are rhetorical questions, questions specifically about his own rhetoric. But these questions then
will press themselves upon the poet's person; they define for him
his sense of superannuated self: "Why write I still all one, ever the
same,/And keep invention in a noted weed,/That every word doth
almost tell my name,/Showing their birth, and where they did proceed?" (76) A good many young man sonnets are concerned with
just this kind of rhetorical question, but, as in sonnet 76, in these
sonnets it appears as though the very asking of such questions turns
out to empty out the poet's praising self. The poet "shows" his own
"birth" as "the second burthen of a former child" (59), or as "the first
conceit of love there bred,/Where time and outward form would
show it dead" (108). And, as a result, *because* he is committed to an
ancient poetry of praise, the poet, as a person, is himself entropi-
cally exhausted by the tired tropes with which, according to the old
poetic custom, he ornaments himself:

> So all my best is dressing old words new,
> Spending again what is already spent:
>> For as the sun is daily new and old,
>> So is my love still telling what is told.
>> (76)

This is significant because it introduces a new kind of literary self-consciousness into the already highly self-conscious tradition of the Renaissance sonnet. In familiar ways, the poet in sonnet 76 identifies himself with his own literariness. At the same time, however, it is in an unfamiliar way that the poet's subjectivity here seems worn out by the heavy burden—"the second burthen of a former child"—of the literary history that his literariness both examples and extends. For what is novel in a sonnet such as 76 is not so much the way the poet takes the ever-renewed sameness of the sun, its perennially revivified vivacity, as a dead metaphor for the animating *energeia* and *enargia* of an ideal metaphoricity. Rather, what is striking, and what is genuinely novel, is the way the visionary poet takes this faded brightness *personally*, the way he identifies his own poetic person, his own poetic identity, with the afterlight and aftermath of this dead metaphoric sun. Identifying himself with an aged eternality, which is itself the standard image of an ideal and an unchanging identity, the young man's poet is like a bleached Dante: he is a visionary poet, but he is so, as it were, after the visionary fact, a Seer who now sees in a too frequently *luce etterna* a vivid image, an *effige* or an *eidolon*, the visionary *likeness*, of the death of both his light and life, as, for example, in sonnet 73:

> In me thou seest the twilight of such day
> As after sunset fadeth in the west,
> Which by and by black night doth take away,
> Death's second self, that seals up all in rest.

This is the peculiarly inflected imagery of light with which the young man's poet assimilates to his own poetic psychology the self-consuming logic of "spending again what is already spent," for it is with this imagery of afterlight that the poet makes his own poetic introspection into something retrospective:

> In me thou seest the glowing of such fire
> That on the ashes of his youth doth lie,
> As the death-bed whereon it must expire,
> Consum'd with that which it was nourish'd by.
> (73)

In terms of what we can think of as the conventional imagery of the poetry of praise, it is as though, in Shakespeare's sonnets to the young man, "Ideas Mirrour" had now become the "glass" of sonnet 62. But, as I have already said, this is an old-fashioned "glass of fashion" that "shows me myself indeed,/Beated and chopp'd with tann'd antiquity," the subjective consequence of this for the poet being that, as sonnet 62 goes on to say, "Mine own self-love quite contrary I read."

There is more to say about the way this imagery of tired light, or tired imagery of light, functions in the sonnets addressed to the young man. I will want later to argue that such imagery determines not only the poet's sense of space and time but also his erotic sensibility as well. As it is, however, it seems clear that a reader should not overlook—as sentimental readings often do—the novel coloring that Shakespeare's young man sonnets give to their visual imagery, to their imagery *of* the visual, for this is responsible, to a considerable degree, for the pathos of poetic persona that these sonnets regularly exhibit. In the same way, the retrospection that attaches to the poet's imagery of the visual also gives a novel tenor to the poet's praise of the young man. The poet, for example, regularly insists upon the ways in which the visual tradition of ancient praise "prefigures" the young man. The result of this, however, is that the present glory of the young man is made into a kind of souvenir "remembrance of things past" (30), an image in the present of "th' expense of many a vanish'd sight" (30). Sonnet 68 is a characteristic example:

> Thus is his cheek the map of days outworn,
> When beauty liv'd and died as flowers do now,
> Before these bastard signs of fair were born,
> Or durst inhabit on a living brow;
> Before the golden tresses of the dead,
> The right of sepulchres, were shorn away,
> To live a second life on second head;
> Ere beauty's dead fleece made another gay.

It is, of course, a commonplace within the poetry of praise to make the past, as here in sonnet 68, a promissory token of the present, or to see the present as a glorious fulfillment or surpassing of the past. This is the standard epideictic topos with which sonnet 68 begins. But what regularly happens in the young man sonnets, as it does in sonnet 68, is that the young man is presented as the visible and temporal disruption of such typological and chronological succession. What the poet characteristically sees in the young man, as here in sonnet 68, is the difference that obtains between the present and the past:

> In him those holy antique hours are seen,
> Without all ornament, itself and true,
> Making no summer of another's green,
> Robbing no old to dress his beauty new.

If this is the case, however, it is a way of pointing to a *different* difference that the young man of Shakespeare's sonnets represents within the poetry of praise and in the tradition of the "all alike." It is easy enough, that is, to note the way in which "to live a second life on second head" in sonnet 68 is but a version of "the second burthen of a former child" in sonnet 59, and to note in turn how both of these are versions of "Death's second self, that seals up all in rest" in sonnet 73. but this thematic repetition, a repetition of the theme of "second," also seems to make a kind of anticlimax of the young man's panegyric second coming—of the apocalyptic way that "all their praises are but prophecies/Of this our time, all you prefiguring" (106). For at his best the young man is an image of the past *within* the present, as sonnet 68 explains: "Thus is his cheek the map of days outworn." But, for just this reason, as he is presented in the sonnets he inspires, the young man is an epideictic image that is neither in the past nor in the present. Instead, as his poet seems to see it, because the young man in the present merely represents the past, the young man is an image that, however perfect in himself, is but the "map" of beauty rather than the thing itself "and him as for a map doth Nature store,/To show false Art what beauty was of yore" (68).

This is a small but characteristic example of the way the young man sonnets typically redeploy traditional epideictic images and conceits so as to give a novel twist to what are standard panegyric themes. It is certainly possible, for example, for a reader to take a couplet such as that of sonnet 68—"And him as for a map doth Nature store,/To show false Art what beauty was of yore"—as a conventional expression of the young man's consummate perfection. But a reader can only do this if he ignores not only the sonnet's elegiac tone, but also the way the sonnet is an elegy not for what is gone, but, instead, for what is present. To think of sonnet 68 as a conventional extension or reiteration of the poetry of praise would be to ignore the way the sonnet as a whole elaborately cross-couples a conventional conceit: the peculiar and *new*-fashioned way the sonnet says that ancient and eternal "beauty liv'd and died as flowers do now," in contrast to the way that through "false Art" the beauty of today ephemerally lives forever.

This kind of introverting reduplication of the conventional is a distinctive formal feature of the young man sonnets, a consequence of the way these sonnets characteristically "cross-couple" what are traditional conceits of dual unity in the poetry of praise. This explains, at least in part, both how and why these sonnets carry and convey their own distinction from the tradition they invoke. The young man sonnets thematically remark the way they are "pre-figured" by their epideictic past, but, at the same time, they consistently re-figure, by redoubling, that which they repeat. Admittedly, this identifies in only a very formal way the novelty inhering in the young man sequence as a whole. But this formal feature helps explain why the young man sonnets characteristically add a covert and foreboding reservation to what are their overt sentiments of clairvoyant, visionary praise:

> When in the chronicle of wasted time
> I see descriptions of the fairest wights,
> And beauty making beautiful old rhyme
> In praise of ladies dead and lovely knights . . .
> I see their antique pen would have express'd
> Even such a beauty as you master now.
>
> (106)

It is not, therefore, the explicit themes of the young man sonnets that make these sonnets so peculiar. For the most part—with exceptions I will speak of later, such as the procreation theme—the themes and conceits of the young man sonnets are thoroughly and insistently familiar. Rather, what specializes the young man sonnets is the way they first stress the fact that they are repetitions, and the way they then proceed to make this very repetition into something novel. In sonnet 17, for example, where we are given the temporal alternative to a sonnet such as sonnet 68, the poet explains how even newly fashioned praise will inevitably become in the future just as funereal and just as fantastic as old-fashioned praise now seems in the present:

> Who will believe my verse in time to come
> If it were fill'd with your most high deserts?
> Though yet heaven knows it is but as a tomb
> Which hides your life, and shows not half your parts.

> If I could write the beauty of your eyes,
> And in fresh numbers number all your graces,
> The age to come would say, "This poet lies,
> Such heavenly touches ne'er touch'd earthly faces."

By itself the sentiment is both admiring and admirable. Certainly it is in many ways familiar. But—and this is what is characteristic of the young man sub-sequence as a whole—its expression does not leave it by itself. For what counts in the sonnet, and it is made to count *against* the young man's praise, is the way the poet numbers his numbers and touches his touches: "And in fresh numbers number all your graces . . . Such heavenly touches ne'er touch'd earthly faces."

These are the same euphuistic cognate accusatives with which the poet in sonnet 106 sees ancient "beauty making beautiful old rhyme," or the way in which in sonnet 76 the poet is restricted to "still telling what is told." Sonnet 17 invokes, that is to say, *in* its own dictional reduplications a system of noted and coded literary doublings whose accumulations the sonnet then unsentimentally adds up:

> So should my papers (yellowed with their age)
> Be scorn'd, like old men of less truth than tongue,
> And your true rights be term'd a poet's rage,
> And stretched metre of an antique song.

The troubling or implicitly qualifying point here is not exactly that in the poet's own imagination his "papers" are already "yellowed with their age"; neither is it that in his imagination the poet sees himself "like old men of less truth than tongue." Rather, if the poet's future praise will always be an "ancient song," what kind of afterlife will the young man lead in the double revival promised to him by the sonnet's couplet: "But were some child of yours alive that time,/You should live twice, in it and in my rhyme."

To the extent, therefore, that Shakespeare's sonnets to the young man amount to something new in the tradition of the poetry of praise, this is because they present their praise of the young man, as well as the young man himself, as this tradition's literary repetition: "Thus is his cheek the map of days outworn," "the golden tresses of the dead," "the dressings of a former sight." The young man sonnets are indeed a "Mirrour" of "Idea," but the mirror is now as old as the "Idea," and so it follows that "thy glass will show thee how thy beauties wear" (77). This is why the young man sonnets amount to the representation of praise rather than its presentation. Because the young man bears the burden of his literary history, it is only as a *question*, again as a specifically *rhetorical* question, that the young man is the "subject" of the poet's praise, as in sonnet 38:

> How can my Muse want subject to invent
> While thou dost breathe, that pour'st into my verse
> Thine own sweet argument, too excellent
> For every vulgar paper to rehearse?

But, for just this reason, the young man is a "subject" whose own "sweet argument" is instantly belied because it is belate:

> O, give thyself the thanks if aught in me
> Worthy perusal stand against thy sight,
> For who's so dumb that cannot write to thee,
> When thou thyself dost give invention light?
> Be thou the tenth Muse, ten times more in worth
> Than those old nine which rhymers invocate,
> And he that calls on thee, let him bring forth
> Eternal numbers to outlive long date.

Again the sentiment of sonnet 38 at first seems altogether admirable. The young man is the "tenth Muse" because he surpasses the nine that came before. In this sense, as is the epideictic custom, the young man passes praise. And yet, finally, how is it that the "tenth Muse," whose number is beyond all ancient laudatory number, re-numbers "eternal numbers to outlive long date"? Does the young man lead his poet to add something novel to the poetry of praise or does the young man instead invite his poet's multiple reiterations of it? Just what kind of epideictic "increase" does the young man here amount to? The mock arithmetic of the sonnet is comically evasive on this point, being serially and multiply expansive and excessive in one calculating breath: "Be thou the tenth Muse, ten times more in worth/Than those old nine which rhymers invocate." But it is more than arithmetically that "eternal numbers to outlive long date" refers the poet to a panegyric future that deprecates its past. In the end, which is the present ("these curious days" of the sonnet's couplet), the young man is only unlike his precursors to the extent that he is merely like them; his poet can add only a regretting repetition to that which he repeats. And if this seems an overcomplicated reading of sonnet 38, how else does one explain the way the "tenth Muse" of the body of the sonnet is suddenly and painfully reduced in the couplet to something which is "slight": "If my slight Muse do please these curious days,/The pain be mine, but thine shall be the praise." Commenting on the singular "pain" of sonnet 38's conclusion (and thinking, presumably, of the way the sonnet begins with "thine own sweet argument"), Stephen Booth remarks that "Shakespeare gives the line a bitter undertaste."[11] It would be better to say, however, that by thus "slighting" his "tenth Muse" the poet gives the young man back in kind the "light" that "thou thyself dost give invention." In this change, that is to say, from "light" to "slight" (an example of the way the poet is "defeated" "by adding one thing to my purpose nothing" [20]), we see another way in which, as in sonnet 105's "wondrous scope," "is my invention spent." And in this way, too, "thine own sweet argument" is once again "confin'd" to the same confining "constancy" of "'fair,' 'kind,' and 'true' is all my argument."

In such indirect and oblique, yet effective, ways, the young man sonnets, which Shakespeare begins to write in those "curious days" during which the sonnet vogue begins to end, reflect the situation of a poetic tradition that, having repeated itself so frequently, can no longer innocently reinvocate "those old nine which rhymers invocate." To paraphrase Gertrude Stein, when the flowers of fancy faded, fancy faded, and so, in his sonnets to the young man, Shakespeare substitutes for the familiar incarnational poetics of epideictic poetry a poetics of re-incarnation where the "re-" registers the tired literariness of what now is seen to be a *merely* epideictic gesture. This is a point that could be developed further by looking to literary allusions and citations scattered throughout Shakespeare's sonnets, and this would lead to a much larger moment in Renaissance literature when a poetics of simple, golden ornament, already "yellowed" with its age, begins to pass over into a poetics of brashly difficult conceit, when the physical "Elizabethan" prepares for what is called the metaphysical "Baroque," when the literal "glorious morning" of English poetry becomes a literary "School of Night." If this were to be pursued in any kind of detail, it would be possible to see that Shakespeare's is not the only literary sensibility for which the figures of a dead poetic vivacity will be revived by being shrouded and opaque, for which the traditional showy light of poetic representation will come to be obscured by the penumbral "re-" of representation itself:

> That, *Enargia,* or cleerenes of representation, requird in absolute Poems is not the perspicuous delivery of a lowe invention; but high, and harty invention exprest in most significant, and unaffected phrase; it serves not a skilfull Painters turne, to draw the figure of a face only to make knowne who it represents; but hee must lymn, give luster, shaddow, and heightening; which though ignorants will esteeme spic'd, and too curi-

ous, yet such as have the judiciall perspective, will see it hath, motion, spirit and life . . .

Obscuritie in affection of words, & indigested concets, is pedanticall and childish; but where it shroudeth it selfe in the hart of his subject, uttered with fitnes of figure, and expressive Epethites; with that darknes wil I still labour to be shaddowed . . .

I know, that empty and dark spirits, wil complaine of palpable night: but those that before-hand, have a radiant, and light-bearing intellect, will say they can passe through *Corynnas* Garden without the helpe of a Lanterne.[12]

Chapman, from whose 1595 prefatory letter to *Ovids Banquet of Sence* I take this quotation, provides an especially convenient, because so strident, example of this new "judiciall perspective." However, there are many other poets who might be cited to evidence the way, toward the turn of the century, brightness begins to fall from the literary air. Drayton's revisions of "Idea," the career of Greville, the development of Donne, even, earlier and in parts, Spenser's "darke conceit"—all these would testify to that historical darkening of epideictic *enargia* whose shadows Shakespeare's sonnets both instantiate and interpret.[13] This larger literary development, much larger than the tradition of the sonnet cycle, is of course something that deserves a study of its own, for its interest in the poetically imperspicuous quite obviously defines the relevant literary context within which Shakespeare's sonnets, which regularly look to see the darkness in the glass of literary fashion, are imagined and conceived. In chapter 4 I will refer to some of the poetic background to this negative development. For the present, however, with regard to what I have called the Shakespearean "subject," what is more immediately relevant is the way Shakespeare incorporates such general literary trends into the particular thematic configurations and literary practices of his sonnets, for this is something—"where it shroudeth it selfe in the hart of his subject"—with a historical specificity and consequence of its own, and it is also something, as will be seen, at some considerable remove from its contemporary context.

It is sufficient, therefore, for the moment, to note that for the young man's poet "the ornament of beauty is suspect" (70)—where "suspect" carries a powerful visionary resonance—that the poet's visionary praise does not entirely delight him, and that, for this reason, picking up an ancient topos, the young man's poet regularly remarks the floridity of praise so as in this way to occlude its customary brightness. Thus the courtier favorites of great princes do indeed spread their fair leaves like marigolds; they do so, however,

"*but* as the marigold at the sun's eye,/And in themselves their pride
lies buried,/For at a frown they in their glory die" (25). More telling,
it is with just this dead epideictic glory that the poet then will regularly associate—"making a couplement of proud compare"—his
own memorializing verse:

> Not marble nor the gilded monuments
> Of princes shall outlive this pow'rful rhyme,
> But you shall shine more bright in these contents
> Than unswept stone, besmear'd with sluttish time.
>   (55)

Again, such eternizing claims are extremely common in the poetry of praise, just as the elegy is a central epideictic form. So too the
many sonnets Shakespeare devotes to this theme have generally
been valued as amongst the strongest in the sequence as a whole. It
is not my purpose, therefore, to suggest that there is something nec-
rophiliac in the way the young man's poet regularly looks forward to
the time in which "your monument shall be my gentle verse,/Which
eyes not yet created shall o'er read" (81). Yet, once we have said this,
it becomes possible also to recognize that the young man's poet's
epitaphic praise is something the poet characteristically seems in
this quite complicated way to *see* as marking something dead. It "lies
in thee," says the poet to his muse: "To make him much outlive a
gilded tomb,/And to be prais'd of ages yet to be" (101). But the life
that "lies" in the poet's praise is equally the death of "When you
entombed in men's eyes shall lie" (81). As in sonnet 55, the poet's
praise is surely and litotically "more bright" "than unswept stone,
besmear'd with sluttish time." But even if it is a golden, rather than
a "gilded," monument, the poet's eternizing lines are something the
poet will peculiarly describe as "satire to decay" (100). There is, that
is to say, a kind of mimic, generally visual, correspondence between
the poet's elegiac praise and that which it commemorates, a specular
resemblance that is oddly morbid in its iconicity, as in sonnet 55,
where the poet's "living record of your memory" gloomily memori-
alizes a kind of living death:

> your praise shall still find room,
> Even in the eyes of all posterity
> That wear this world out to the ending doom.
> So till the judgment that yourself arise,
> You live in this, and dwell in lovers' eyes.

We broach here what is a general economy of self-canceling visuality that runs through the young man sequence as a whole and that is regularly counterposed to the apparently ideal compact of "fair" and "kind" and "true." From the beginning of the sequence, the young man is "contracted to thine own bright eyes" (1), and so, by virtue of this self-contraction, he "feed'st thy light's flame with self-substantial fuel" (1). In this thematic way—where visual circles become vicious circles, where visual reflections become *exhaustingly* reflexive—even the most traditionally vivifying images of vision in the young man sub-sequence—"There lives more life in one of your fair eyes" (83)—somehow manage to project a mirror image of their own funereality: a kind of "autopsy." Eyes are images of life but also of their own demise; the narcissistic mirror somehow veils the exhibitionist lamp that it reflects, and in a strange, insistent way the poet's golden verse begins itself to seem a species of "the golden tresses of the dead" (68).

Just why this should be so remains something that must be accounted for. The very frequency with which this happens, however, establishes in the young man sonnets an ensemble or constellation of epideictic themes and images that make the visual and the visible into a medium or instrument of loss. This is something quite emphatic in the young man sub-sequence, and the peculiarities that result would surely have been registered by an audience accustomed to the standard evocations of presence in the poetry of praise. In *Troilus and Cressida*, for example, Ulysses, speaking in accents that are intended to sound proverbial, remarks the way "the present eye praises the present object" (3.3.180). In Shakespeare's sonnets, however, something quite different regularly occurs. In the young man sonnets the poet's praising eye consistently looks at a brightness that reveals either an incipient absence or a kind of bygone visionary presence. Though the young man regularly manifests an ideal luminosity, he just as regularly appears, to use Shakespeare's phrase, a kind of omnipresent image of the "present-absent" (45). Consider, for example, the ideal vitality of the young man as it is developed in sonnet 31. The young man's "bosom is endeared with all hearts/Which I by lacking have supposed dead" (31). The effect of this, however, is not that the young man brings the dead to life, but, rather, that what the poet sees in the young man is a kind of death *in* life: "all those friends which I thought buried . . . now appear/But things remov'd that hidden in thee lie!" (31). And it is because "thou art the grave where buried love doth live" (31) that a reader notes the loss inhering in what seems to be

familiar visionary brightness: "Their images I lov'd I view in thee,/
And thou (all they) hast all the all of me" (31).

For several reasons it is important to stress, and I do not think
that I have so far overstressed, the way Shakespeare's young man
sonnets in this consistently oblique and indirect way constitute
themselves a retrospective re-vision of a poetry of epideictic vision—the way that "all my best is dressing old words new" (76) is
associated with the "dressings of a former sight" (123). First of all,
this indirection speaks to the complexity of a collection of poems
which seem uneasily and at times astringently at odds with the tradition they explicitly recall. As almost every reader would agree, the
praise of the young man sonnets is rarely so simple as at first it
seems, not only because the young man is less than ideal, but also
because the poet's panegyric vision seems always ruefully to see a
"vanish'd sight" (30): "Since I left you, mine eye is in my mind,/And
that which governs me to go about/Doth part his function, and is
partly blind,/Seems seeing, but effectually is out" (113). So too it is
important to recognize this in order to appreciate the way in which it
affects the young man's poet's sense of himself: "Incapable of more,
replete with you,/My most true mind thus maketh mine untrue"
(113). All this helps to account for, or at least to recall, what is too
often forgotten: namely, the peculiar pathos attaching both to the
young man sonnets and to the young man's poet. At the same time,
however, if we recognize the implicit reservations with which the
young man sonnets develop and express a conventional poetics of
true vision, this also helps to distinguish them from the yet more
peculiar sonnets addressed to the dark lady. And this is important
because it prevents any oversimplified characterization of the relationship obtaining between Shakespeare's poetry of praise and the
poetry he makes out of the paradox of praise.

For much of what I have said so far about the young man sonnets
would apply directly and immediately to the dark lady sonnets, especially to the dark lady sonnets as I described them in chapter 1.
Thus the young man sonnets question their praise because they
note—and as or when they note—that they repeat it, in the same
way that the paradox of praise is the duplication of praise that renders praise passé. So too the young man's poet colors his praise by
observing his observation—"Their images I lov'd I view in thee"
(31)—in the same way that the dark lady's poet, seeing that his eyes
"have no correspondence with true sight" (148), admits to having
"put fair truth upon so foul a face" (137). So too the sonnets ad-

dressed to the young man "suspect" the ornamental vision of their "wondrous scope" in the same way that in the sonnets to the dark lady the poet's eyes "behold and see not what they see" (137). In short, much of what the young man sonnets do implicitly is preparation for what the dark lady sonnets subsequently say explicitly, the latter thus articulating directly in their matter what is indirectly present in the manner of the former.

But if this identifies a similarity linking the two sub-sequences, a similarity that leads us from the one sub-sequence to the other, so too does it distinguish the salient point of difference separating the two sub-sequences, a difference both of matter *and* of manner. For the dark lady sonnets actually say what the young man sonnets only intimate, or what the young man sonnets only say *between* their panegyric and "eternal lines to time" (18). And if the dark lady sonnets literally "express" the ambiguous "difference" that the young man sonnets—loyal, however ruefully and conflictedly, to the visionary ideality of the poetry of praise—literally say that they leave out— "One thing expressing, leaves out difference" (105)—it is because in thus naming the special insight of the young man's poet Shakespeare's sonnet sequence as a whole for the first time finds a *voice*.

This may seem an overstatement, but it is only in the second sub-sequence that the poet's language comes to be thematized as something to be spoken rather than as something to be seen, as though it is only when the poet speaks against his vision that he can speak about his speech as speech. Moreover, this thematic counterpoint, a progress from eye to tongue, seems also to determine how the poet represents the difference that obtains between his loves of comfort and despair. Where the first sub-sequence consistently presents the young man as the mirror image of his poet's ideal praise, the second sub-sequence instead develops the dark lady as the speaking figure of her poet's speech, not the visual but the verbal instantiation of what her poet says about her. Where the young man is the *picture* of his poet's admiration—one that leaves the poet at a loss for words: "my dumb thoughts, speaking in effect" (85)—the dark lady is instead the *discourse* of her poet's lust, as though it were language itself that is responsible for lasciviously fleshing out the poet's first suspicions of poetic ornament, as in sonnet 147:

> My thoughts and my discourse as madmen's are,
> At randon from the truth vainly express'd;
>> For I have sworn thee fair, and thought thee bright,
>> Who art as black as hell, as dark as night.

This progress, from an uncertainly ascetic poetry of picture to a definitively erotic poetry of word, from a vestigially ideal poetics of *ut pictura poesis* to, as it were, a sexy and unhappy poetics of *ut poesis poesis*, represents in very obvious ways a fundamental rewriting of the assumptions of the poetry of praise, not least of those assumptions that such poetry makes about itself. Acting out what seems to be a preordained conclusion, the poet's praise becomes its own rebuke when it is distanced from its ideal image of itself, just as all the poet's old poetic gold loses its currency when it is reassessed and seen to be a counterfeit. Moreover, according to the poet, it is these specifically epideictic disappointments that make of admiration an "expense of spirit in a waste of shame" (129). Again we come upon the fact that the relationship of the first sub-sequence to the second is neither one of simple repetition nor of simple contrast. As Romeo says:

> These happy masks that kiss fair ladies' brows,
> Being black, puts us in mind they hide the fair,
> He that is strooken blind cannot forget
> The precious treasure of his eyesight lost.[14]
> (*RJ*, 1.1.230–33)

The darkness of the second sub-sequence is just such a reminding and memorializing mask, a masquerading blackness that, "being black," explicitly recalls the fairness that it hides. Built up on and as the ruin of the first, the second sub-sequence is both cause and consequence of visionary blindness. Even so, it still presents itself as the true record of the way that it is blind.

This seems the most striking aspect of the dark lady sonnets, the way they both mask and unmask a fairness they in this way both cover and discover, the way they come, like Antony, to bury and to praise a Caesar over whose dead body they mournfully, duplicitously, and yet, like Antony, still honestly discourse. For if the dark lady sonnets speak against the visionary truth of a traditional poetic speech, this loss of an ideal veracity, both poetic and erotic, is at the same time the one regret, again poetic and erotic, that the paradox of praise can say it speaks with perfect truth. As we will see, it is in a very coherent way that the paradox of praise, which is traditionally a device of comic and rhetorical play, a way of not really saying what one really means, becomes in the dark lady sub-sequence something that takes itself, and thereby forces its readers to take it, both more seriously and more literally than the ironic young man sonnets take the idealizing tradition of the poetry of praise. The dark lady sonnets articulate directly what the young man sonnets only gesture at obliquely. But this explication of the young man sonnets' implications enforces a poetic consequence that the young man sonnets do not, and this because, activating the poetics of the paradox of praise, *performing* the belying that they also talk about, the dark lady sonnets actually and literally *speak* a double truth that, no longer "constant" to "one thing expressing," admits itself to be a "lie":

> Thou blind fool, Love, what dost thou to mine eyes,
> That they behold and see not what they see?
> They know what beauty is, see where it lies,
> Yet what the best is take the worst to be.
>
> (137)

I stress the performative function of language in the dark lady sonnets because the poet himself, in various ways, makes this into a thematic issue. It is not simply that the dark lady's beauty is dishonest or that the lover's eyes are blind. These are, after all, possibilities that the young man's poet often entertains only so as then to overlook them by skewered reference to his disavowing self, for example: "But what's so blessed-fair that fears no blot?/Thou mayst be false, and yet I know it not" (92); or,

> So shall I live, supposing thou art true,
> Like a deceived husband, so love's face
> May still seem love to me, though alter'd new:
> Thy looks with me, thy heart in other place.
> For there can live no hatred in thine eye,
> Therefore in that I cannot know thy change.
>
> (93)

Neither is it that the young man's poet cannot envisage "false adulterate eyes" (though in sonnet 121 these are the eyes of "others' seeing") nor is it that the young man's poet cannot imagine the paradox of praise, for he does this several times, as in sonnets 28 or 68, or as, more obviously, in sonnet 100, where the young man's poet expressly prepares for what is soon to come (though only by describing it as something alien to his current purpose):

> Where art thou, Muse, that thou forget'st so long
> To speak of that which gives thee all thy might?
> Spend'st thou thy fury on some worthless song,
> Dark'ning thy pow'r to lend base subjects light?
> Return, forgetful Muse, and straight redeem
> In gentle numbers time so idly spent.

In all these ways the young man's poet, numbering his "gentle numbers," touching his "touches," with "beauty making beautiful old rhyme" (106), is fully the match of the dark lady's poet; both poets are equally aware that eyes might "have no correspondence with true sight" (148), both poets are thoroughly attuned to the precarious position of both truth and beauty when "both truth and beauty on my love depends" (101). But if both poets clearly "know what beauty is" (137), it is only the dark lady's poet who claims to "see where it lies" (137). And with this pun, which subtends almost all the sonnets addressed to the dark lady, with this *seen lie* which, on the one hand, says that vision is false, and, on the other, collates that vision with false language—a pun which is not a pun if by that is meant a word play that does not mean its double meaning—the sequence moves away from a poetry that wants to show us what "your own glass shows you, when you look in it" (103) to a poetry of "perjur'd eye" that truly "swear[s] against the truth so foul a lie!" (152)

Again, to appreciate the effective force of the way the dark lady sonnets speak against themselves it is necessary first to contrast them with the strained and suggestive reticence of the young man sonnets. In the first sub-sequence the poet's optic admiration is often lightly touched with "lie." In sonnet 17, for example, whose prospective retrospection I have already mentioned, because the poet wants to "write the beauty of your eyes" he imagines how "the age to come would say, 'This poet lies.'" In sonnet 115, to take an example where the poet looks backward instead of forward, the poet speaks about the way "those lines that I before have writ do lie,/Even those that said I could not love you dearer." Such sonnets are quite clearly poems of praise; even so, their eternizing claims are noticeably inflected and attenuated by their poet's sense of temporal mutation. As I said earlier, there is something overly harsh and bitter about the vivid way the poet in sonnet 17 imagines how "my papers (yellowed with their age)/[will] Be scorn'd, like old men of less truth than tongue,/And your true rights be term'd a poet's rage,/And stretched metre of an antique song." So too, in sonnet 115, to which I will later return, the poet, "fearing of Time's tyranny," the "Time" whose "million'd accidents/Creep in 'twixt vows, and change decrees of kings," rather poignantly divides himself in two: into a wise "I" of the present who remembers in a fond but chastened way a more naively idealizing "I" of the past: "Might I not then say, 'Now I love you best,'/When I was certain o'er incertainty,/Crowning the present, doubting of the rest?"

In such sonnets, where the evocation of an ideal but bygone long ago is very powerful, it is difficult to ignore the darker and potentially subversive resonance of "lie." Even so, in these sonnets the young man's poet manages to maintain, at least for the present and however precariously, a real distinction between the true and false: "crowning the present, doubting of the rest." On the one hand, because he is "certain o'er incertainty," there is a strong sense that the young man's poet feels himself situated somewhat indeterminately between truth and falsehood. On the other hand, precisely because these ambiguities are so powerful, the reader also notices that the young man's poet does not bring himself to curse. Instead, as a "fair appearance," as in sonnet 72, the poet's praise (in sonnet 72 a praise of the poet's own self) becomes a species of:

> some virtuous lie,
> To do more for me than mine own desert,
> And hang more praise upon deceased I
> Than niggard truth would willingly impart.

With whatever reservations, therefore, and however wryly or indecisively, it is poetically important that the young man's poet always looks "to find where your true image pictur'd lies" (24). And if it is the case that the young man's poet consistently suspects that "picture" "lies," he nevertheless retains a clarifying "image" of the "truth."

In contrast, the dark lady's poet, speaking with and of his "perjur'd eye" (152), unambiguously, literally, and explicitly "give[s] the lie to my true sight" (150). To begin with, the second sub-sequence does this by giving over the visionary ideality of the first, substituting for a poetry of fair a poetry of foul. But, in addition, the dark lady's poet talks about the way that what he says is false, and as the dark lady sonnets develop them, these two claims are consequentially related to each other. For the dark lady sub-sequence does not simply blind itself. There is a movement in the sequence as a whole from the initial brightness of the young man sub-sequence to the subsequent darkness of the dark lady sub-sequence. But this large-scale movement makes it seem as though the blindness toward which the sonnets move is itself enabling of speech, though of a speech whose only theme is that it "censures falsely what they [eyes] see aright" (148). Again this may seem an overstatement, but where the young man sonnets consistently develop a mute poetic anxiety out of their perception of the way true vision might be false, the dark lady sonnets instead develop, and very explicitly *say* that they develop, an account of a discursive speech that, speaking against vision, says both more and less "than niggard truth would willingly impart" (72):

> When my love swears that she is made of truth,
> I do believe her, though I know she lies,
> That she might think me some untutor'd youth,
> Unlearned in the world's false subtilties.
> Thus vainly thinking that she thinks me young,
> Although she knows my days are past the best,
> Simply I credit her false-speaking tongue;
> On both sides thus is simple truth suppress'd.
> But wherefore says she not she is unjust?
> And wherefore say not I that I am old?
> O, love's best habit is in seeming trust,
> And age in love loves not t' have years told.
> > Therefore I lie with her, and she with me,
> > And in our faults by lies we flattered be.
>
> (138)

This is a properly famous sonnet, already an anthology piece in *The Passionate Pilgrim*. It economically summarizes the May-December topos that informs the cuckoldry plots of Shakespearean comedy, tragedy, and romance, at the same time as it manages to give both to the dirty old man and to the licentious wench of fabliau a dignity that, at least for the moment of the poem, passes for worldly wisdom. For all the attending elements of farce, however, this is not a wisdom that the poem means to undo with unspoken literary ridicule. Quite the contrary, if there is thematic paradox in the poem, it is a paradox that the poem presents as a straightforward statement of the truth. If the sonnet evidences the same kind of rhetorical and syntactic doublings that are characteristic of the young man sonnets, they are deployed here so as to support and to confirm the poem's explicit theme rather than, as in the young man sonnets, to undermine it. Thus the hard rhyme of "truth" and "youth" is explicated rather than ironically duplicated by the homophonic innuendo of "lies" and "subtilties." The enjambed assonance of "old" and "O" is the instantiation rather than the belying of an authentic sigh. The questioning iterations of "But wherefore says she not she is unjust?/ And wherefore say not I that I am old?" are answered rather than problematized by the emphatic, "plain-style" "therefore" of the couplet, where the sonnet marshals its doubled pronouns of indirect, reported speech ("says she not she is," "say not I that I") into what for each of them would be their properly discursive and erotic place: "Therefore I lie with her, and she with me."

What is striking about all this is the way the poem's technique works to support its theme. The poem's sound, diction, rhythms underwrite and ratify the falsehoods that, speaking paradoxically, the sonnet speaks about. This is what gives the poem, despite the obvious humor of its Liar's paradox, its peculiar sincerity, a sincerity that seems peculiar only because the earnest tonality of the poem is at odds with and frustrates the comic expectations the theme of the poem invites. In sonnet 138 the poet first announces how and why he approves the lies his lady tells him, and he then announces how and why he approves the lies that he tells her. The reason for this is that these "lies" enable the poet, in verbal word and erotic deed, to "lie" with the lady: "Therefore I lie with her, and she with me." According to traditional formulas and conventions, this kind of paradoxical praise—licentious praise of that which does not deserve praise—should make a point of sounding as though it does not really mean the things it says. Indeed, if the poem managed in this way to undercut its approbation, its wit and humor would be nothing but familiar. And yet, though this is precisely the sonnet's comic and sophistic theme—i.e., that the poet does not really mean the things he says—the sonnet seems to mean precisely what it says. The difference between this and the young man sonnets is clear enough. Where it regularly happens in the young man sonnets that the ideal matter of the poet's praise is belied by the poet's manner, in sonnet 138 it is the poet's manner that turns his paradoxical matter into something that, at least so far as the poet is concerned, is really very serious.

Several different points follow from this, but what I want now especially to emphasize is the way sonnet 138, supporting rather than belying the comic claim that it is lying, associates this paradoxical conflation of use and mention with a literary as well as an erotic complaint. Taking the poem at its word, which is how it asks its readers to take it, and remembering the assumptions of the poetry of praise, the poet's sexual regret is equally poetic retrospection. By the conventions of the sonneteering mode, the dark lady is as much the poet's Muse as she is his love, and so the old lover who admits he feigns his youth is equally the voice of an old poetics that "knows my days are past the best." In both cases, as poet and as lover, the speaker of the poem will purchase the revival of desire with the outspoken travesty of praise, his perjured admiration presented as the literal embodiment of his lust: "And in our faults by lies we flattered be." But with this "suppres[sion]," both poetic and erotic, of a "simple truth," with the poet-lover "simply" "credit[ing] her false-speaking tongue," the sonnet adduces a poetry as well as a desire whose "best habit" is in "seeming trust," which is to say a novelly poetical desire of—and here I use the gloss provided by *The Passionate Pilgrim's* intelligent emendation—"a soothing tongue."

This is part of what it means to "give the lie to my true sight." The imagery of vision that dominates the sequence of sonnets addressed to the young man is consistently "forsworn" in the sequence of sonnets addressed to the dark lady. There is a transition from a poetry of praise to a poetry of epideictic paradox, and this is accomplished, at the level of theme, by translating the poet's true vision into truly false language, a move from "that sun, thine eye" (49) to a "false-speaking tongue." Thus, even in the relatively benign first sonnet that he addresses to the dark lady, the poet announces a poetic present defined as the verbal "succession" to what has come before, a present in which "black" becomes the antinomian "name" of ideal beauty precisely because true beauty now has lost its proper visual "name":

> In the old age black was not counted fair,
> Or if it were it bore not beauty's name;
> But now is black beauty's successive heir,
> And beauty slander'd with a bastard shame,
> For since each hand hath put on nature's power,
> Fairing the foul with art's false borrow'd face,
> Sweet beauty hath no name, no holy bow'r,
> But is profan'd, if not lives in disgrace.
>
> (127)

I said earlier that this reiteration and reversal of the poetry of praise also introduces its perversion. By a double logic, the dark lady, whose foul is fair, is at once the perfect opposite to beauty and its best example. As with the punning "mourning"-"morning" eyes of sonnet 132, the lady's eyes in sonnet 127 are dressed in mourning for the morning after which they grieve. Her eyes call up the "morning," but they do so from a distance, in such a way that they both are and are not that which they recall. On the one hand, therefore, the lady's eyes will be alternative to the way false beauty now is "sland'ring creation with a false esteem." On the other, because their beauty follows beauty, the lady's eyes are also witness to the fact that beauty now is dead:

> Therefore my mistress' eyes are raven black,
> Her eyes so suited, and they mourners seem
> At such who, not born fair, no beauty lack,
> Sland'ring creation with a false esteem.
>
> (127)

From the very beginning of the sonnets addressed to her, therefore, the lady's eyes are oddly linked to that which they are not.
Their "black" contains the "lack" to which they are supposed to be
an answer, and they are image of true beauty only as the truthful
afterimage of that which they lament. In a peculiar way, but one that
comes to be distinctive, the lady's eyes are thus the recantation of
the very thing that they recall, just as they are happy opposite to that
which they unhappily reflect. To put it very simply, the lady's eyes
both are and are not what they seem. And in sonnet 127, which is the
beginning of the dark lady sub-sequence, the poet sees this as the
motive for the paradox of praise. Specifically, the lady's eyes are inspiration to his novel and revisionary speech: "Yet so they mourn,
becoming of their woe,/That every tongue says beauty should look
so" (127).

The difference between poetic visuality here and in the young
man sub-sequence is considerable. In the young man sonnets praise
was something solely visible, a rhetoric of purely visible display and
self-display. As a medium of admiration, praise in the young man
sonnets is both the mirror and the lamp of both its object and itself,
and this is why to "write the beauty of your eyes" (17) reciprocally
defines the poet's object and his subject. In the young man sonnets
there is a general assumption, however much it is implicitly problematized, that, at least ideally, everything is fair, kind, and true, and
that, as a consequence, lover, beloved, and the language with which
they are connected are generically the same. Characteristically,
therefore, in the young man sonnets seer and seen are panegyric
illustrations of each other. The poet's deixis constitutes an epideixis
such that when the young man is a "star" to which the poet points
with praise, so too is he a "star" whose ideal light returns the poet's
compliments:

> [a] star that guides my moving
> Points on me graciously with fair aspect,
> And puts apparel on my tottered loving,
> To show me worthy of thy sweet respect.
>   (26)

It was with reference to the general circularity of these laudatory
assumptions, and to the specular materiality with which this circularity is consistently conveyed—none of this being in any way idiosyncratic to Shakespeare—that I spoke of the reflexive reflections of
the young man's poet's praise. This was why I said the young man's

poet "looks to like." In the young man sub-sequence, to point to "there" is equally to point to "here," and this is a complementarity that is characteristically developed through elaborate imagery of visual concurrence. What the young man's poet is as agent corresponds to what the young man's poet is as patient, and this because in either case the poet is a "Mirrour" of "Idea." As in sonnet 26, therefore, "aspect" and "respect" ideally indicate each other in accord with the perfect reciprocity of an ideally mutual admiration. With regard to what he speaks, the poet can assume a kind of stellar astrophilia such that even though he might be "wanting words to show it," "some good conceit of thine/In thy soul's thought (all naked) will bestow it" (26). In turn, the praising poet, locating his own self within the ideally reciprocal tradition of "speaking picture"—"Now see what good turns eyes for eyes have done" (24)—identifies his own "I" with his visual admiration. "Wanting words to show it," the poet becomes himself a speaking *eye*, a poet whose first-person voice, because ideally visionary, because composed of sight, is literally *mute:* "For we which now behold these present days/Have eyes to wonder, but lack tongues to praise" (106); or "O, learn to read what silent love hath writ:/To hear with eyes belongs to love's fine wit" (23); or "This silence for my sin you did impute,/Which shall be most my glory being dumb,/For I impair not beauty being mute" (83).

All this, however, remains nothing but familiar. To the extent that the young man's poet is a speaking eye, a mutely visionary mouth, he repeats and assimilates to himself what are commonplace topoi in the tradition of sonneteering praise: he is like King David in Fludd's drawing. What distinguishes the young man sonnets and their poet, what makes both them and he seem novel and peculiar, is that while these sonnets frequently employ such patently specular conventions—the sort of conventions that in other sonnet sequences regularly lead to thematizations of the beloved as silent picture or statue (e.g., Petrarch, *RS*, 78)—these conceits are characteristically complicated by the differentiating "re-" implicit in the young man's poet's fond "respect." In sonnet 26, for example, the identification of "fair aspect" and "sweet respect" is sufficiently deferred so as to oblige the poet, at least for the present, to hide his self-display: "Then may I dare to boast how I do love thee,/Till then, not show my head where thou mayst prove me." More generally, we read these poems and discover that what qualifies their visionary themes is the way the poet is regularly left speechless before a sight that brings into his mind an absent, ancient, epideictic sight: "When in the chronicle of wasted time/I see descriptions of the fairest wights,/And beauty making beautiful old rhyme/In praise of ladies dead and lovely knights" (106).

In contrast, therefore, but also as a *consequence*, the dark lady's poet explicitly draws the moral, the emblematic "motto," of such love at second sight. It is this *special*, retrospective "sorrow" that "lend[s] me words" (140) to "give the lie to my true sight" (150). "Wound me not with thine eye but with thy tongue" (139), says the dark lady's poet, as though desire, along with its hurt, were now something verbal rather than visual, something to be sadly spoken rather than *enargically* to be seen. In the young man sonnets "it is my love that keeps mine eye awake" (61) (though in sonnet 61 it is especially suspiciously that the poet "play[s] the watchman ever for thy sake"), but in the sonnets addressed to the dark lady desire is, instead, explicitly disdainful of such vision:

> In faith, I do not love thee with mine eyes,
> For they in thee a thousand errors note,
> But 'tis my heart that loves what they despise,
> Who in despite of view is pleas'd to dote.
>
> (141)

It is "in despite of view" that the dark lady's poet consistently finds himself lost, as in "me from myself thy cruel eye hath taken" (133), whereas the young man's poet regularly strives to see himself in "spite" of this "despite": "In our two loves there is but one respect,/Though in our lives a separable spite" (36). It is not the mistress's eyes, but "those lips that Love's own hand did make/Breath'd forth the sound that said 'I hate'" (145). And it is only because her heart, "chiding that tongue" (145) insists upon retraction that "'hate,'" within thematized quotation marks, is "alter'd with an end": "'I hate' from hate away she threw,/And sav'd my life, saying 'not you.'" (145). So too, the mistress "swears that she is made of truth" (138), though what she swears is false, and her poet says "I call/Her 'love'" (151), though he does so against his "conscience." And if all of this bespeaks a "discourse as madmen's are,/At randon from the truth vainly express'd," (147), or if "now this ill-wresting world is grown so bad,/Mad slanderers by mad ears believed be" (140), it is because the lady maddeningly ignores the poet's plea that she not "press/My tongue-tied patience with too much disdain,/Lest sorrow lend me words, and words express/The manner of my pity-wanting pain" (140). And even here the most the poet asks for is: "If I might teach thee wit, better it were,/Though not to love, yet, love, to tell me so" (140).

In short, and these examples could be multiplied, there runs through the dark lady sonnets a language of and about language which is opposed to the language of and about vision that runs through the sonnets addressed to the young man. And it is the poet himself who says that this discursive language of language—a language of words as opposed to a language of images, a language which is characterized as something linguistic, of the tongue, rather than as mirror or as lamp—is opposed to the ideal language of vision it replaces and succeeds. It is for this reason, referring to large themes and images, that I speak of a progress from eye to tongue. Taken together, the young man sub-sequence and the dark lady sub-sequence act this progress out as a succession of opposites: from man to woman, from true to false, from fair to foul. It is a downward movement, from good to bad, from love to lust, from kind to unkind, which is developed as a progress from vision to speech. In the second sub-sequence this progress becomes explicitly the story that the poet tells about his desire, about his poetry, and about himself. According to the poet, it is because "every tongue says beauty should look so" (127) that eyes will "swear against the thing they see" (152). According to the poet, it is because he speaks against his eyes that his speech must henceforth speak against itself. And it is because vision is translated into language that the poet ceases to admire either his lady or himself. In the dark lady sub-sequence this is a consistent logic, a logic that not only informs individual poems, but one that organizes the relationship of individual poems in the sub-sequence to each other. To begin with, the poet's eyes "behold and see not what they see" (137). Then this doubleness of vision will teach the poet's eyes about the world of verbal puns: "They know what beauty is, see where it lies" (137). Then the poet's eyes will learn to speak: "mine eyes seeing this, say this is not" (137). And then this punning lie of vision becomes a bitter truth: "In things right true my heart and eyes have erred,/And to this false plague are they now transferred" (137).

I say a progress from eye to tongue, as though the two of these were utterly distinct. But in the dark lady sonnets language and vision are disjunctively collated in the compact of a "perjur'd eye" (152). They are opposed to each other, but they are so by being superimposed upon each other such that the poet's language lies against the poet's sight, propped up on the vision it belies. It is not only that "I mistake my view" (148), but that, as correlative or corollary, the poet "*give*[s] the lie to my true sight" (150). This is the odd relationship or interrelationship that the dark lady sonnets develop between vision and language: the latter "forswears" the former, but it is only when the two are joined together that they disclose the difference between them, only when they are next to each other that they are far apart:

> If that be fair whereon my false eyes dote,
> What means the world to say it is not so?
> If it be not, then love doth well denote
> Love's eye is not so true as all men's: no,
> How can it?
>
> (148)

A succession of opposites, therefore, but not a polar system of antithesis that moves from white to black or from fair to foul. For the lady's foul, at least initially, is fair, and, moreover, it is fair, the poet says, *because* thus foul. Between the two sub-sequences, therefore, there is certainly a progress, but not from white to black or from fair to foul, but, instead, from white to white *and* black, or from fair to fair *and* foul. This is why there is no clear-cut line of succession with which to link the second sub-sequence to the first. The latter sub-sequence differs from the former, but this difference is discovered and determined by and as the way the second sub-sequence doubly reiterates the visual unities given to it by the first. Thus, for example, the young man sonnets begin by telling us how the young man is supposed to live forever in his procreated repetition, "proving his beauty by succession thine" (2). So too, therefore, do the dark lady sonnets begin by telling us how "black" is now "beauty's successive heir" (127). In this redoubling way the lady does indeed succeed the young man's beauty, but she does so as a morbid repetition of beauty's eternal repetition, as a re-visionary repetition whose blackness both extends and puts an end to beauty's endless repetition. In a perfectly comprehensible way, the lady's "black" has now become the legitimate issue of true beauty now that beauty has been "slander'd with a bastard shame" (127). So too "black" has now become the name of beauty now that "sweet beauty hath no name" (127). But in this way "beauty's successive heir" will continue only by concluding, will invoke by thus revoking, the succession she succeeds.

This is the complicated logic with which the poet conducts his progress from eye to tongue, the way the sequence as a whole moves from an initial image of fair beauty to the expressive blackness of its genuinely improper "name." It is a logic of juxtaposed disjunction whereby the lady is the same as beauty *because* she is different from it, its repetition *because* its variation, its replacement *because* its displacement. Alternatively, she is different *because* the same, a variation *because* a repetition, a displacement *because* a replacement. In accord with this logic the poet generates the wit of the benign dark lady sonnets, where example equals opposite such that "every tongue says beauty should look so" (127). But out of the same logic comes the complaint of the more bitter dark lady sonnets, whose regret is always that the lady is unlike what she seems like: "For I have sworn thee fair, and thought thee bright,/Who art as black as hell, as dark as night" (147).

Whether developed benignly or malignly (mostly malignly), this is a profoundly unsettling logic to which the poet gives expression in his sonnets to the lady. The lady is similar to that with which she is contrasted, she is opposed to that on which she is superimposed. It is something like the primal scene of the dark lady sequence, as it is presented in sonnet 144, where the poet sees "a man right fair," and "a woman color'd ill" lie differentially together as "one angel in another's hell." Or it is like the way the poet is *in contact* with a fracture such that "thy unkindness lays upon my heart" (139). Or it is like the way the lady's "larges and spacious" "Will" will most display its difference from the poet's when the two are joined together: "Wilt thou, whose will is large and spacious,/Not once vouchsafe to hide my will in thine?" (135).

In general, the dark lady's poet commits himself to this peculiar logic of a "different sameness," and this is what leads him, in a fairly obvious way, to a set of themes strikingly unlike those associated with "all alike my songs and praises be" (105). More particularly, however, the poet gives explicit *voice* to this logic in his portrait of a lady whose essence is to be unlike what she is like. Looking at the lady, the poet sees an image of an anamorphic, "unkind" kind. Her black is fair, or her novel fair is foul, but this darkness always *is* for the poet something that is not as it seems. In herself the lady therefore shows the poet how a difference is compacted into sameness or how disjunction is embedded in conjunction. For this reason, however, as a picture of the way that things are far apart when they are closest together, the dark lady becomes for the poet something more and less than an image. If the lady is an illustration, she illustrates the very thing that "make[s] me give the lie to my true sight" (150). If she is an image, she is the kind that leads her poet to forswear his vision. And thus the final consequence of this peculiar logic seems to be that what the poet sees in the lady is precisely an insistent "difference" that will force the poet into speaking what he *hears* as speech.

> Thy black is fairest in my judgment's place.
> In nothing art thou black save in thy deeds,
> And thence this slander as I think proceeds.
>
> (131)

The lady is not an image because, unlike the young man, she is not fair and kind and true. Despite the ambiguities and the reservations with which they make the point, the young man sonnets continually remind us, both when they describe the young man and when they describe themselves, of the way an image is supposed to correspond, as a generic copy, to that of which it is an image, of the way an image is iconic replication of whatever it reflects. This is the optics of *eidola, simulacra, species*, that the young man's poet presupposes when "my soul's imaginary sight/Presents thy shadow to my sightless view" (27), or that the young man's poet adapts to his procreation theme when he tells the young man to repeat himself as issue lest the young man "die single, and thine image dies with thee" (3). So too it is this kind of *special* image to which the young man's poet characteristically compares his epideictic speech, as when "so long as men can breathe or eyes can see,/So long lives this, and this gives life to thee" (18). This defines the tautological "truth" intrinsic to the poetry of praise. As the "Mirrour" of an "Idea," which is itself a mirror, the poet's epideixis is generically the same as that of which it speaks. Its laudatory signifiers simulate its signifieds because, following out the visual analogy, its being is the likeness or the *simulacrum* of its meaning—a peculiarly self-validating, self-confirming language, therefore, whose reference is self-referentially secured by the special and the specular correspondence of word with thing. Hence, as I have said, the common circularity of the poetry of admiration, the recursive way, as in the young man sonnets, the poet's praise will turn itself back on itself, or the way, by reference to such visionary praise, the poet will reflexively identify his "I" and "thou."

However, though the young man sonnets regularly advance such commonplaces, they do so only so as then to cloud them with profound qualifications. In more ways than I have so far discussed, the young man sonnets inflect and attenuate this traditional epideictic immanence of vision to speech, and, as a consequence, the young man sonnets also regularly complicate the various conceits of dual or reflexive unity traditionally attaching to these visionary themes. Yet, if this kind of complicating reservation is characteristic of the young man sub-sequence, it remains the case that the young man sonnets only manifest such complications obliquely, through a style of implicit reservation. Explicitly—either in the portrait that he gives of his beloved, or in the account he offers of his admiration— the poet in the young man sub-sequence continues to develop and to elaborate a logic of visual presentation and self-presentation that stands in the sequence as ideal model of idealizing speech. It is only tonally that we sense regret in the way "'tis thee (myself) that for myself I praise,/Painting my age with beauty of thy days" (62), or in "their images I lov'd I view in thee,/And thou (all they) hast all the all of me" (31). It is only by a stylized extravagance that we are distanced from the way "either by thy picture or my love,/Thyself away are present still with me" (47). At least ideally, it remains the visionary case in the young man sonnets that the young man might be brilliant origin of legitimate succession, the special father of a re- petition of the same, as when he is a "seal" that "Nature" "carv'd" as imitation of herself, "and meant thereby,/Thou shouldst print more, not let that copy die" (11). So too, and correspondingly, in the young man sonnets it remains at least ideally possible that the poet's praise will be the ideal duplication of the young man's special brightness, as when: "So till the judgment that yourself arise,/You live in this, and dwell in lovers' eyes" (55). In short, the young man sonnets do not *talk* about what they suspect.

In contrast, but as something more subversive than a contrast, the dark lady is explicitly presented in terms of the enigma whereby she is that which is not as it seems. As an image, the lady is the *simulacrum* of an incompatible similitude: she is like what is unlike what it is like. There is an essential, and an articulated, heteroge- neity about or in the lady, a contradiction of an elementary nature, that makes her disconcertingly discrepant to the homogeneous sim- plicity of what is fair and kind and true. For this reason, however, when the poet looks at the lady he cannot "look to like." There is an irreducible distinction interposed between the lady as a signifier and the lady as a signified, and this interval of difference, a syncope intruded in between the lady's being and her meaning, forecloses any correspondence of the lady to iconic correspondence. Funda- mentally, in her essence, the lady is an image of what cannot be imagined by an optics based on likeness. She is *essentially* alternative to sight, beyond the specular, because she is a "species" of the non-species, an "idea" that is intrinsically excessive to true vision because it is a visual "kind" of that which is, what Hamlet calls, "a little more than kin and less than kind" (just as the lady's "common place" is what Hamlet would call "common").

This is why in the young man sonnets, where the young man is "'fair,' 'kind,' and 'true,'" "my soul's imaginary sight/Presents thy shadow to my sightless view" (27), whereas in the dark lady sonnets, where "thy unkindness lays upon my heart" (139), the poet's eyes "behold and see not what they see" (137). The doubleness of the lady's darkness is at odds with the oneness of such visionary presence, and it is so in a more explicit way than is a suspect praise whose only claim is that it is exhaustingly "t[w]o one, of one, still such, and ever so" (105). Where the young man is the "seal" of "Nature" who "shouldst print more, not let that copy die" (11), the lady is instead the "heir" of beauty whose black "succession" spells the end to any endless repetition of the specularly same. Where the young man is "this shadow" that "doth such substance give," "that I in thy abundance am suffic'd,/And by a part of all thy glory live" (37), the lady is a countervailing "power" that has "this pow'rful might," "With insufficiency my heart to sway,/To make me give the lie to my true sight,/And swear that brightness doth not grace the day" (150). The contrast serves to measure the power of the lady: the lady is an "insufficiency" whose doubleness disrupts the poet's visual imagery of the homogeneously self-sufficient, just as with her heterosexual duplicity the lady will disrupt the singularity of the poet's homosexual ideal.

This is what the lady stands for, for a doubleness that both includes and yet divides the poet's image of a oneness, a doubleness that somehow leads the poet into a speech that as a "lie" or as a "perjur'd eye" will speak against the poet's sight. "I mistake my view" (148), says the dark lady's poet, punning also, as we will later see, on the way that "I mistake my . . . you." But if vision can mistake itself, this raises the possibility that presentation can misrepresent itself, as when "mine eyes seeing this, say this is not" (137). Correspondingly, if the poet identifies his "I" with a "you" that is unlike itself, this raises the possibility of a poetic first person cut off from itself, as when "me from myself thy cruel eye hath taken" (133). It is this difference introduced *into* the poet's vision, a corrupting interruption of a visual ideal, that the lady both presents and represents by virtue of the echo in her "mourning"-"morning" eyes. It is a difference *between* vision and language that *only* language can express, as when "every tongue says beauty should look so" (127), or as when the lady with "her false-speaking tongue" (138) "swears that she is made of truth" (138). And it is precisely this "difference" that "one thing expressing" necessarily "leaves out" because it is a "wondrous scope" whose being is restricted to reflecting and repeating what is fair and kind and true. But it is precisely this difference that the poet can put into paradoxical words when "words express" not only "the manner of my pity-wanting pain" (140), but also the way their very verbal being is what makes them different from a visionary truth:

> My thoughts and my discourse as madmen's are,
> At randon from the truth vainly express'd;
>> For I have sworn thee fair, and thought thee bright,
>> Who art as black as hell, as dark as night.
>
> (147)

Because they explicitly talk about this difference, at the same time as what they say performs the difference that they talk about, the sonnets addressed to the dark lady can be more effectively suspicious of true vision than even the most ironic of the sonnets addressed to the young man. In the first sub-sequence—forgetting, for the moment, the way the young man sonnets covertly resist these themes—language is visual and therefore it is true. This is why the young man's poet says that he is mute, and this is also why what he admires is an ideal "figure of delight" (98). In the second sub-sequence, however, where language is spoken rather than seen, language is no longer like the things of which it speaks. And because it cannot be compared to the simulating vision that it was, the poet's language, because it is a language not a mirror, is what gives the lie to the poet's true sight. In the first sub-sequence language literally is the thing it speaks about because it is itself the visual similitude, the epideictic "image," the picture, the *imago*, of its referent. Thus the young man's poet's golden praise presents itself *as* that which it admires, and this remains the ideal visionary case however ironically the poet says "that in black ink my love may still shine bright" (65), however much the sub-sequence silently subverts its praise by imaging its self-redeeming presentation of itself, its epideictic self-presentation, as but "the map of days outworn" (68). In contrast, in the second sub-sequence, the poet's praise paradoxically presents itself as distanced from the things of which it speaks. As but a verbal representation, rather than a visual presentation, of whatever it bespeaks, the speaking of this praise in this way opens up a space between its referent and itself. As a result, no longer the mirroring example of what it speaks about, the poet's speech becomes instead the mournful witness of the difference between the vision that it used to be and what it now can merely say that it is not.

In the second sub-sequence, therefore, it is language itself, *heard* as such, that is presented, like the lady, as a species of dissimulation rather than of likeness. Like all the "eyes" in the dark lady sub-sequence, this linguistic language "ha[s] no correspondence with true sight" (148). Hence the paradox of praise, or what we can call the praise *of* representation, "that censures falsely what they [the poet's eyes] see aright" (148), and which can be defined as the kind of praise a poet speaks when speech is thematized as verbal word and not as visual thing. In the dark lady sonnets the poet thus passes *into* language, as though through the defile of the lady's unimaginably double eyes. But the cost for the poet is that he thereby gives over a visionary poetics and a visionary self. Correspondingly, speaking for the first time of a speech that *speaks*, the poet's subject then becomes the loss of "I" and "eye" occasioned by this heterological speech that puts an end to epideictic tautology. In the dark lady sequence, to "swear" is already to "forswear," to say is to gain-say. And because speech, *as* speech, is always one remove from ideal truth, always a "perjur'd eye," the relationship between language and desire is determined as the structural discrepancy between what the poet verbally says and what the poet visually wants: "In loving thee thou know'st I am forsworn,/But thou art twice forsworn, to me love swearing" (152). Poetically and erotically, therefore, the poet's "truth" in turn becomes the way a visionary language that is "'fair,' 'kind,' and 'true'" turns out to be belied by speech:

> And all my honest faith in thee is lost;
> For I have sworn deep oaths of thy deep kindness,
> Oaths of thy love, thy truth, thy constancy,
> And to enlighten thee gave eyes to blindness,
> Or made them swear against the thing they see;
>> For I have sworn thee fair: more perjur'd eye,
>> To swear against the truth so foul a lie!
>
> (152)

Recognizing this intimate and thematized relationship in the dark lady sonnets between false language and erotic desire—which takes over and substitutes for the equally intimate and thematic relationship of true vision and ideal desire in the young man sonnets ("O, let me, true in love, but truly write" [21])—the question arises as to why it is specifically the lady's "common place" (137), at once erotic and linguistic, that the poet looks at when "mine eyes seeing this, say this is not" (137). Later, I will suggest that this space (which is also a temporal interval between a continual present and its duration) between vision and language, or between presentation and representation, is necessarily the "large and spacious" (135) space of nominal "Will" in which the dark lady's poet comes "to hide my will in thine" (135). (This is the "space" that Edgar calls the "indistinguish'd space of woman's will," *KL*, 4.6.271.) For the moment, however, it is enough simply to recognize how forcefully, explicitly, and *personally* the dark lady's poet speaks against a traditional visual ideal. When the poet says "My mistress' eyes are nothing like the sun" (130), he is not only giving over Petrarchan epithets like "that sun, thine eye" (49). To rewrite in this way, without entirely erasing, a traditional idealizing language of laudatory admiration is to reconstitute what is traditionally understood to be the poet-lover's proper self. So explicitly to revise the visual language of poetry and desire is to come upon and actually to express a novel desire *of* language that is utterly at odds with what has come before. If we think only about the tradition of praise, we can say that with this kind of conceit, which breaks, like Richard II, the "brittle glory" of the mirror of language, the dark lady sub-sequence gives over a poetics and erotics of vision because it gives over a poetics and erotics of iconic likeness. Mimetically and metaphorically, the dark lady sonnets pervert their praise by turning all such heliotropic verses back upon themselves, re-versing these familiar tropes, so that, quite literally, "my mistress' eyes are nothing like the sun" (130) because the lady's eyes *are nothing*—like the sun. But the lyric force and novelty of this rhetorical inversion derives from the way the dark lady sonnets, advancing a poetics of "false compare," invent a new and different sonneteering self:

> My mistress' eyes are nothing like the sun;
> Coral is far more red than her lips' red;
> If snow be white, why then her breasts are dun;
> If hairs be wires, black wires grow on her head.
> I have seen roses damask'd, red and white,
> But no such roses see I in her cheeks,
> And in some perfumes is there more delight

Than in the breath that from my mistress reeks.
I love to hear her speak, yet well I know
That music hath a far more pleasing sound;
I grant I never saw a goddess go,
My mistress when she walks treads on the ground.
    And yet, by heaven, I think my love as rare
    As any she belied with false compare.

Again, for all the analogues and precursors that exist for sonnet 130, the poem strikes a reader as more than conventionally anti-Petrarchan for the simple reason that it takes its anti-Petrarchanism more seriously than is the custom either in orthodox or in paradoxical praise. The young man's poet, for example, also speaks against elaborate ornamental praise, seeing in such epideictic excess a concealed defect. Yet the way in which the lady is excessive to true vision is very different from the way in which the young man is beyond poetic compliment:

Who is it that says most, which can say more
Than this rich praise, that you alone are you,
In whose confine immured is the store
Which should example where your equal grew?
Lean penury within that pen doth dwell
That to his subject lends not some small glory,
But he that writes of you, if he can tell
That you are you, so dignifies his story.
                               (84)

For the young man's poet, the young man passes praise because the young man is himself the best example of himself: "that you alone are you." It is because he is like only himself that the young man is the measure of all other metaphoric likeness, just as elemental gold, measured only by itself, is the value to which every other value is compared. Following the young man's example, therefore, the poet, in order to "dignify" his own story, contrasts his "true plain words" with the florid hyperbolic rhetoric of his rival praising poet:

                yet whey they have devis'd
What strained touches rhetoric can lend,
Thou, truly fair, wert truly sympathiz'd
In true plain words by thy true-telling friend;
    And their gross painting might be better us'd
    Where cheeks need blood, in thee it is abus'd.
                               (82)

Here again the self-surpassing height of praise consists of turning praise against itself so as thus to describe a paragon beyond compare. "You alone are you" is intended as extravagant hyperbole, a statement about ineffable, incomparable majesty no more modest than Yahweh's "I am that I am," and a statement which is literal only insofar as that which it refers to is divine. In the same way, sonnet 121 will explicitly propose "I am that I am" as the tautologically magnificent alternative to being "vile[ly] esteemed." There is, therefore, nothing at all "plain" about "you alone are you," for the epideictic claim of the sonnet is that such a self-example is the only adequate comparison with which to amplify or "truly sympathize" a *nonpareil*. Accordingly, because the poet's praise can only asymptotically or "adynatonically" approach the young man's worth, the poet's "true plain words" become the limit case of praise because as ideal praise they mutely speak, or they illiterately write, the truth:

> My tongue-tied Muse in manners holds her still,
> While comments of your praise, richly compil'd,
> Reserve their character with golden quill
> And precious phrase by all the Muses fil'd.
> I think good thoughts whilst other write good words,
> And like unlettered clerk still cry "Amen"
> To every hymn that able spirit affords
> In polish'd form of well-refined pen.
>
> (85)

For the moment we can leave aside the irony with which these poems about the young man's poet's and the rival poets' praise are touched—the poet's writing of illiteracy, which is like his eyes that "wonder" but "lack tongues to praise" (106), the hollowness reverberating in the very *sound* of repetition: "Making their tomb the womb wherein they grew" (86), "Lean *penury within* that *pen* doth dwell" (84)—in order to stress the thematic difference between this mutely breathless panegyric and the "wordiness" of epideictic paradox. For the young man's poet does not criticize his rivals' praise for being false, but only says that such laudation is not nearly true enough:

> Hearing you prais'd, I say, "'Tis so, 'tis true,"
> And to the most of praise add something more,
> But that is in my thought, whose love to you
> (Though words come hindmost) holds his rank before.

Then others for the breath of words respect,
Me for my dumb thoughts, speaking in effect.
(85)

What the young man's poet adds as surplus to praise is the silence
that a visionary poetics by tradition reverently speaks:

This silence for my sin you did impute,
Which shall be most my glory being dumb,
For I impair not beauty being mute,
When others would give life and bring a tomb.
(83)

For this reason, "speaking in effect," the young man's poet advances
as the height of praise "that you alone are you," because this is the
self-exampling comparison that is the epideictic equivalent to visionary silence. As the ultimate similitude this expresses the ultimate compliment, for this tautology is the only genuinely laudable
way mimetically to "copy what in you is writ" (84) or metaphorically
to make "a couplement of proud compare" (21).

But it is precisely this kind of amplifying and silent identity, this
ideal imitation and metaphor, that the dark lady sub-sequence explicitly speaks against, developing a poetics in which even to say
"you alone are you" is to "belie" with "false compare:" "If thou dost
seek to have what thou dost hide,/By self-example mayst thou be denied" (142). Instead, what the dark lady's poet says is that "my mistress' eyes are nothing like the sun" (130), introducing in this way a
blazon whose praise develops from the way it doubly negates itself
and its comparisons. According to sonnet 130 "if snow be white,
why then her breasts are dun." But snow is not so white as poets say,
and neither are the lady's breasts "dun." "If hairs be wires, black
wires grow on her head." But hairs are not wires, certainly not the
golden tresses of a dead Petrarchan praise, and neither does the lady
have black wires growing on her head. The poet has indeed "seen
roses damask'd, red and white," but flowers are not like women, and
what the poet therefore sees in the lady is precisely that "no such
roses see I in her cheeks."

Logically the poem makes its point by counterfactual implication:
modus ponens, the mood of affirmation, is first negated by *modus pollens*, the mood of negation, and then *modus pollens* next negates itself. This is the formal logic of chiasmic cross-coupling as I described
it earlier, and it is in accord with such a logic that the dark lady—an

argument against her own metaphoricity, denying in her own self her own self-example—can only be characterized as that which is unlike what it is like. Again, therefore, the poet compares the lady to that which she is not, or, speaking more precisely, he compares her to the way comparison has failed—"I think my love *as rare/ As* any she belied with false compare"—where, given the grammatical ambiguity of "she," the lady is at once alternative to and example of the way generic woman is "belied with false compare." Rhetorically and tonally the poem supports this logical and grammatical chiasmus by joining a catachretically pejorative diction—"dun," "wires," "reeks," "treads"—with a vocabulary of the material ideal—"sun," "coral," "roses"—so as to divide *in* speech the referent that these different words all share, the lady being neither white nor dun, neither one visual thing nor another, but, instead, the verbal difference, stressed as such, that stands between these famous oppositions. Thematically, the sonnet writes *against* a poetics of visual comparison and *for* a poetics of verbal disjunction that foregrounds the diacritical difference built into familiar similarities. Thus the vision that is traditionally understood to be the sense *of* comparison ("I have seen roses . . . ") is forsworn by a dissimulating poetics whose eyes, like those of the mistress herself, "are nothing like the sun." And so too does the poet come to "love" what is specifically discordant speech: "I love to hear her speak, yet well I know/That music hath a far more pleasing sound."

This logic, along with this rhetoric and these themes, organizes other sonnets in the sub-sequence addressed to the dark lady. The poems to the lady characteristically displace a poetics of silent, visual similitude with a poetics of verbal disjunction (for example, sonnet 128, usually much maligned for "mixing its metaphors," where, again, the "living lips" of the dark lady's poet are cross-coupled with the musical "deadwood" of the lady's virginal, and where the "wiry concord" of music—which, as in "my mistress' eyes," is the auditory opposite of speech—is disjunctively collated with the poet's "poor lips"). This verbal disjunction is both like and unlike what happens in the young man sonnets, and for this reason we must once again ask how the two different voices sounded in the sequence as a whole can be related to each other. More specifically, it is important to explain how two quite different thematizations of poetic discourse— one that characterizes poetry as something visual, another that characterizes poetry as something verbal—together determine the persona of the poetic first person who gives expression to them both. It is important to understand this, for I will be arguing that these two voices together define a specifically "Shakespearean" subject, one who is, because half visual and half verbal, the very first "person" of our literary tradition.

In order to make this argument, it will be necessary to take up the way Shakespeare's large figurations of a visual and a discursive poetics in turn determine more particular characterological qualities, if only because Shakespeare's sonneteering self does far more than simply see and speak. Yet, as the argument grows more detailed and precise, we should continue to bear in mind how very central the themes and associated metaphorics of vision and language are to Shakespeare's imagination, not only in the sonnets but also in the plays. In the comedies, which regularly stage a confrontation between vision and language, there is characteristically a concluding and reassuring transformation or translation of language into sight, as in *The Taming of the Shrew,* where "Cambio is chang'd into Lucentio." Later, in the tragedies, in quite a different fashion and to quite different dramatic effect, this staged relation of vision to language grows increasingly more complicated. In the tragedies the difference between language and vision grows both more powerful and less reconcilable, and this is responsible both for the more individuated texture of Shakespeare's tragic heroes and for specific narrative developments, as when Othello demands "ocular proof" (3.3.360) for that which "it is impossible you should see" (3.3.402) and receives instead what "speaks against her with the other proofs" (3.3.441), or as at the end of *King Lear,* when the king holds a mirror up to Cordelia's ever-silent mouth and calls on all to see the "nothing" in her speech: "Do you see this? Look on her! Look her lips,/ Look there, look there!" (5.3.311–12)

It was with this tragic development in mind that I took Hamlet's cruel words to Ophelia as epigraph to these still preliminary remarks on Shakespearean "forswearing." "Your honesty," says Hamlet, "should admit no discourse to your beauty," as though it were "discourse," not "beauty," that leads "honesty" astray. As with the dark lady, the question raised is whether beauty is here a figure of speech or, instead, whether speech is a figure of beauty. There can be no easy answer to this question because it is through a particular kind of "translating" and "transforming" figure that beauty and honesty speak, and thus cross-couple, with each other. Like the young man, who is "'fair,' 'kind,' and 'true,'" Ophelia is "honest" and she is "fair"—"Ha, ha! are you honest?" "Are you fair?"—but "the power of beauty," says Hamlet, "will sooner transform honesty from what it is to a bawd than the force of honesty can translate beauty into his likeness." This is the asymmetrical "paradox" (the tragic version of "Cambio is chang'd into Lucentio"), to which "the time gives proof," that governs Shakespeare's sonnet sequence. The likeness of beauty is beautiful, whereas, according to Hamlet, the likeness of honesty is false. When "beauty" ornaments itself even with false beauty it shows itself more beautiful, whereas the "likeness" of "honesty," however exact, at best turns into "beauty" which is false. This is what happens in Shakespeare's sonnets, where the poetry of what is "honest" and "fair" comes to have "discourse" with "the power of beauty," where the likeness of fair honesty is "translated" to a "bawd," leaving over as remainder what sonnet 141 will call "the likeness of a man." In Shakespeare's sonnets the poetics of epideictic similitude, of an Aristotelian *translatio* whose virtue is "to see the same," the poetics of "'fair,' 'kind,' and 'true,'" is itself transformed into something that now explicitly admits, "the better to beguile," the power of discursive beauty over the force of visual honesty.

In the context of Elizabethan poetics, Hamlet's conflation of discourse with bawdy beauty reflects what is a larger and more general eroticization and suspicion of the rhetorical that begins to manifest itself in literary self-consciousness toward the turn of the century, for example, in the way the rhetoric handbooks come more and more to remark the seductive dissimulations of courtly manner, or, more directly, in the lurid nicknames—*belles lettres*—that Puttenham gives to rhetorical tropes, names that Hamlet soon will echo when he speaks about the ambling, jigging, nicknaming, lisping, false painting of women, and when he recalls the way these sexy ornaments, metaphors of metaphor, have now made him "mad." In this sense, Hamlet here discourses on a decisive moment in literary history. In the particular context of Shakespeare's career, however, we should remember that this passage from *Hamlet* comes in the middle of the tragedy, and in the middle of the tragic period, which is itself poised midway between Shakespearean comedy and Shakespearean romance, in the middle of Shakespeare's middle, as it were, as though the power of beauty's verbal translation of the visual were itself the hinge on which these different, specifically Shakespearean genres turn. Written in 1600, which is the *terminus ad quem* of the dark lady sonnets, it is perhaps appropriate that *Hamlet*, which is the play of "words, words, words," is also the play of universal mourning, of just that mourning-morning developed in the dark lady sonnets whose paradox of reduplicated lucidity "make[s] the night joint-laborer with the day." Later, I want briefly to discuss the relationship of Shakespeare's sonnets to questions of dramatic genre. For now, however, it is still necessary to address the question posed by a desire whose "constancy" is summarized by Hamlet as "I did love you once" and "I lov'd you not," and whose serious truth amounts to the Liar's paradox of "you should not have believ'd me." This is the problem the dark lady's poet confronts when he realizes that "in things right true my heart and eyes have erred,/And to this false plague are they now transferred" (137).

· 4 ·

And that thou teachest how to make one twain,
By praising him here who doth hence remain.
(Sonnet 39)

I have so far argued that the Renaissance sonnet develops specific themes and motifs with which it not only expresses but also objectifies the praise it speaks. These themes—primarily themes of reflexive reflection, of simulating identity and correspondence—and these motifs—frequently visual, characteristically conceived in terms of a materiality or a phenomenality that both "shows" and is "self-showing"—are rhetorically convenient to the poetry of praise because they enable the poet variously to elaborate the ways in which his language of idealization is adequate to, indeed the same as, the ideal of which he speaks. The epideictic poet has at his command, as a kind of thesaurus of praise, a metaphysics of genus and species that allows him to identify his own particularity with categorical universals, an erotics of admiration that joins him as a lover to his beloved, a Cratylitic semiotics that makes words into the *eidola* of things. I have argued that such themes and motifs are called forth by the literary logic of epideictic rhetoricity, that they are a response to the ways in which the language of idealization circularly and self-consciously invites, if it does not entail, an idealization of the language that it speaks. Very generally, all this is evidenced in the poetics and the poetry of praise from antiquity up through the Renaissance; however, all this is yet more particularly and emphatically observable in the Renaissance sonnet, which is a poetic form or genre that especially foregrounds and thematizes its panegyric purpose and intention.

I have also argued that Shakespeare's sonnets—both the sonnets to the young man and the sonnets to the dark lady—markedly distance themselves from the tradition of idealizing poetry and poetic idealization that they inherit and to which they regularly refer. Shakespeare's young man sonnets characteristically imply that the poetics of praise they explicitly employ is somehow old-fashioned

187

and exhausted. For this reason, the young man sonnets implicitly resist and problematize, by accentuating the fact that they repeat, the idealizing themes and motifs they reemploy. The dark lady sonnets do something similar, but the dark lady sonnets write the epilogue of epideixis in a far more explicit way than do the young man sonnets, and this because they use the literary genre of praise paradox to speak directly, not obliquely, against the commonplace themes and motifs of epideictic idealization. As a result, the dark lady sonnets additionally develop and elaborate what in the literary history of the sonnet are new themes and motifs. These new themes and motifs give voice to and exemplify what is the real literary novelty of the dark lady sonnets. I have spoken, for example, though so far only very generally, of the way a language of false words substitutes in the dark lady sonnets for a language of true vision, of the way a poetics of difference displaces a poetics of likeness, of the way the essence or essentiality of a Nature based on "kind" is subverted by an unnatural Nature that displays an "unkind" "kind," of the way a homosexual erotics of ideal admiration is replaced by a heterosexual, and therefore misogynous, desire for what is not admired, of the way a poetics of presentation turns into a poetics of re-presentation, thereby performatively transforming a familiar *image* of the present into a far less familiar *echo* of the past. I have further suggested that the most important literary consequence of all this is, first, that it produces, in both the young man sonnets and in the dark lady sonnets, a poetic first person altogether novel in Renaissance lyric, second, that this Shakespearean subjectivity subsequently becomes in post-Renaissance literature the dominant model of subjectivity per se.

In general, therefore, my argument derives both the novelty and the power of Shakespeare's sonneteering persona from the way Shakespeare's sonnet sequence, taken as a whole, registers and responds to the normative tradition of praise poetry; specifically, from the way it situates itself posterior to an ideal epideixis that it presupposes and alludes to in a retrospective way. To appreciate the novelty and force of either this situation or of this poetic persona, however, it is important that we once again recall the literary sophistication of the sonneteering tradition that precedes Shakespeare. For it happens that the orthodox tradition of praise poetry also frequently makes poetic and personally *individuating* capital out of the way it feels itself to be belated, and, moreover, this tradition regularly stresses and regrets the way it is constrained to do no more than quote and echo a prior epideixis. So too, this orthodox and pre-Shakespearean poetic tradition is in many ways just as claustrophobic in its response to the fact that it is "to constancy confin'd" as are Shakespeare's sonnets, just as this tradition—especially in England, where Petrarchism begins by introducing itself as an already achieved and foreign novelty, a poetic mode already done and over-done elsewhere—is fully aware of the fact that epideictic "likeness" is translated into something different when subjected to excessive repetition.

I have already mentioned, for example, the "re-turning" way in which *Astrophil and Stella* begins with Astrophil "oft turning others' leaves," or the wittily mimetic way in which Astrophil apes "*Pindare's* Apes" when he cries out against those "daintie wits" who "crie on the Sisters nine." Sidney deliberately makes Astrophil's complaint in sonnet 3 about "ennobling new found Tropes with problemes old" seem itself antique, for in this way his sonnet can archly define its own literary originality in terms of a strictly literary repetition: "in *Stella's* face I reed/What Love and Beauty be, then all my deed/But Copying is, what in her Nature writes."

Such themes readily lend themselves to a kind of personalized literary history, with the poet using them to distinguish his poetic past from his poetic present. The fifth "Song" of *Astrophil and Stella*, for example, begins with Astrophil's remembering back to when "favour fed my hope, delight with hope was brought,/Thought waited on delight, and speech did follow thought." As Astrophil describes it, this was an epideictic time when "grew my tongue and pen records unto they glory," a bygone panegyric time when "I said, thine eyes were starres thy breasts the milk'n way,/Thy fingers *Cupid's* shafts, thy voyce the Angels's lay:/And all I said so well, as no man it denied."

Astrophil recalls all this bygone Petrarchan praise, however, only so as the better to contrast it in the rest of the "Song" to the way "now that hope is lost, unkindnesse kils delight,/Yet thought and speech do live, though metamorphosd quite." According to Astrophil, what is new about his present verse is that he now gives blame where credit formerly was due: "I thinke now of thy faults, who late thought of thy praise,/That speech falles now to blame, which did thy honour raise." The rest of Astrophil's "Song" demonstrates this "metamorphosis" by amplifying, in an increasingly horrific series, the lady's vices. Thus Astrophil explains to his lady why she is, to begin with, a thief, then a murderer, a tyrant, a rebel, a witch, and,

190 · Chapter 4

finally, because this is the height of blame, the way she is a devil. In several respects these curses that Astrophil directs toward Stella—an invective pointedly developed as the direct antithesis of the preceding praise—can remind a reader of the terms in which Shakespeare's poet will revile the dark lady after praising the young man. Yet, despite the similarity, there is an effective difference between the way Astrophil straightforwardly reverses a remembered poetry of compliment and the way that the dark lady's poet instead inverts it. On the one hand, Astrophil here simply negates Petrarchanism, retracting the oxymoronic conceits and material comparisons that he assumes are familiar from the poetry of praise: "Thinke now no more to heare of warme fine odourd snow,/Nor blushing Lillies, nor pearles' ruby-hidden row." On the other, Astrophil adapts such commonplaces for the purposes of blame, using them now to speak an epideictic invective instead of epideictic praise:

> A witch I say thou art, though thou so faire appeare;
> For I protest, my sight never thy face enjoyeth,
> But I in me am chang'd, I am alive and dead:
> My feete are turn'd to rootes, my hart becommeth lead;
> No witchcraft is so evill, as which man's mind destroyeth.

Astrophil thus translates, in a systematic way, the positive assertions of the past into the negative curses and complaints of the present, his golden heart translated into "lead." Yet, though "I in me am chang'd," this is a change that occurs here only at the level of matter, not of manner. Speaking rhetorically, Astrophil's "metamorphosis," as he calls it, from praise to blame, takes place *within* the literary register of a generic epideixis, and so, though there is surely a thematic difference between his praise and blame—for Astrophil now disapproves what he had formerly approved—this is not a difference of *rhetorical* kind. Speaking rhetorically, Astrophil's negative blame is but the mirror image of the positive praise that it withdraws, and it is therefore developed by and in the "Song" as a rhetorical opposite which is really generically the same as that which it opposes. Like the difference between eye and heart in sonnets 46 and 47, this is a difference that does not really make much difference. Like the "change" at the end of *The Taming of the Shrew,* this is a linguistic "change" that leads inevitably to light. Because it is Astrophil's purpose in his "Song" to show off his skill with curses in the same way that a praising poet characteristically displays his skill with praise, the reader, responding to the displayed epideixis, to the poetic showing and self-showing, knows very well from the very beginning of Astrophil's complaint that the poet can, and that the poet very likely will, convert his artful and his artificial blame back into the equally artful and equally artificial praise from which the blame initially derives. And, indeed, this is how Astrophil's "Song" explicitly concludes:

> You witch, you divill, (alas) you still of me beloved,
> You see what I can say; mend yet your froward mind,
> And such skill in my Muse you reconcil'd shall find
> That all these cruel words your praises shall be proved.

This kind of playful and wry rhetorical reversal is characteristic of high Elizabethan lyric; it is especially typical of the strong pre-Shakespearean sonnet, which is a poetic form that commonly deploys its own literary sophistication against itself so as to retrieve in literature—perhaps it would be better to say *as* literature—the theological and amorous assumptions with which it is concerned: a poetry that tries literarily to mean the epideictic things it can no longer say literally. Hence, for example, the deliberately "sunburned" archaisms of Spenser, not only in the *Amoretti*, but also in *The Faerie Queene* and in pastoral eclogue such as *The Shepheardes Calender*. Hence the exuberance, the formal inventiveness, the ostentatiously poetical self-display of *Astrophil and Stella*, where what is imitated is Petrarchan literature itself, but in a way that is quite different from the more delicately shaded *contrapposto* sadness underlying Shakespeare's praising sonnets to his bright young man—"So all my best is dressing old words new" (76)—and, of course, in a way that is utterly unlike the vocal paradox Shakespeare makes of the dark lady. Hence "Stella" herself, whose name literally, but at the same time only playfully, denotes the energetic and *enargic* brightness that comes when mimesis and metaphor meet. Sidney's "Stella" manifests a Cratylism different from the authentic beatitude we find in "Beatrice," closer to the *belle lettristic* laud that we sense in "Laura." But again this amounts to a difference of degree, not of kind, for the same reflexively reflective epideictic structure is confidently, even when it is ridiculously, maintained, as in sonnet 35 of *Astrophil and Stella*: "Not thou by praise, but praise in thee is raisde:/ It is a praise to praise, when thou art praisde."

Taking Sidney's "Astrophilia" as an example, I want to suggest that two general tendencies effect and condition the historical literary situation when Shakespeare turns to sonnets. First, from Dante, through Petrarch, through to the high or "golden" moment of the Elizabethan sonnet tradition, poets continue to employ the theory and the topoi of praise—either directly when they write poems of praise, or indirectly when they take praise as a particular metonymy for poetry as a whole. As the sonnet develops, however, this employment grows increasingly artificial and self-conscious: poetry becomes more deliberately poetical, praise becomes explicitly a praise of its own praise. Second, and correspondingly, at the level of theme, the sonnet, as it develops, more and more concerns itself with the way it praises rather than with what it praises, no longer foregrounding the object of its praise, but, more pointedly, its epideictic subject, both the subject it speaks thematically about—i.e., its praise—and also the subject who speaks—i.e., the praising poet. As a result, as the sonnet develops, it more and more emphasizes the literariness of both its epideictic manner and, correspondingly, the literariness of its epideictic persona.

This is why, for example, a poet such as Sidney not only directs the reader's attention more toward Astrophil than to Stella, but toward an Astrophil whose principal interest is in his own poeticality, as in the first sonnet, where the problem of the poet is explicitly poetical, i.e., how to make his lady act according to Petrarchan formulas when those formulas are already registered as formulaic: "Loving in truth, and faine in verse my love to show,/That the dear She, might take some pleasure of my paine:/Pleasure might cause her reade, reading might make her know,/Knowledge might pitie winne, and pitie grace obtaine,/I sought fit words to paint the blackest face of woe." The thematic concern with the "fit" word, a word that "shows" itself to be at once appropriate and fashioned—the concern, if only thematic, with the way that one might give a "turn" to "others' leaves"—correlatively affects the dramatized persona of the speaking poet, a persona that, or who, is in this way also rendered "fit." In this way, because increasingly self-conscious, poetry becomes increasingly more conscious of its poet's self, a self that is itself increasingly more artificial as it becomes increasingly more literary. This is why, for example, the opening sonnet of *Astrophil and Stella* concludes with the poet looking, as I have said, very archly, to himself: "Biting my trewand pen, beating my selfe for spite,/'Foole,' said my Muse to me, 'looke in thy heart and write.'"

This is an important point because it allows us to distinguish between the person and the persona of the epideictic poet, a distinction that becomes gradually more important as the sonnet form his-

torically develops toward Shakespeare. Quite clearly, in Dante and
in Petrarch, and in Dante more so than in Petrarch, a reader hears a
more authentic or a more individuated and personal voice than in
Sidney. This is the case, however, precisely because these earlier
poets manage unself-consciously to elaborate and speak their
praise. This is not to say that either Dante or Petrarch fail to take
advantage of the simultaneously objective and subjective registers
of praise, its epi-*deixis* and its *epi*-deixis. But in Petrarch and in Dante
it is assumed that praise, by pointing to itself, will also point beyond
itself, just as the things of this world are epideictic indices of things
beyond and higher than themselves. Dante is closest to this theological and ontological universe in which an epideictic thing is metaphysically incarnate in its epideictic word, and so the Dantean poetic personality, if that is what it should be called, will, with all its
singularity and its specificity, orient itself toward, because it subjects itself to, the praiseworthy phenomena about which it epideictically discourses. Dante's poetic subject is, *in truth*, beatified by its
poetic object, because Dante writes his poetry on the model of Aquinas' psalm or prayer, where the penitent's praise of God redeems his
penitential self.

So too, to some considerable extent, in Petrarch, but here the epideictic universe that Dante presupposes has already begun to lose,
at least in part, its metaphysical force, and, complementing this
loss, we sense a corresponding shift to a more obviously psychological, rather than an ontological or a theological, register. Thus—and
in this case we deal with what we know to be deliberate decisions
with regard to sequential arrangement—Petrarch begins the *Rime
Sparse* with a sonnet about his own poetic past: "You who hear in
scattered rhymes [*rime sparse*] the/sound of those sighs with which I
nourished my/heart during my first youthful error, when I was/in
part another man from what I am now." For Petrarch, this is an initia-
tory and foundational retrospection, and if we take it seriously, as Petrarch clearly does, it appears that Petrarch himself begins, literally
begins, as an anti-Petrarchan, as a poet painfully divided by the fact
that he lives after what he can now recall as epideictic youth. In this
way, Petrarch's *present* looking backward is what leads Petrarch to an
intensely personal sense of self, but, and this is the point to notice, it
is a self that originates out of the failure of a bygone poetical ideal:
"But now I see [*Mal ben veggio*] how for a long time I was the talk of the
crowd, for which often I am ashamed of myself within; and of my rav-
ing, shame [*vergogna*] is the fruit, and repentance [*pentersi*], and the

clear knowledge [*conoscer chiaramente*] that whatever pleases in the world is a brief dream."[1] We can say, therefore, that the poetry of praise, as it progresses toward Shakespeare, grows increasingly thematically concerned with epideictic psychology, in the sense that the poet's own personality, thematized as such within his poems, becomes more and more the central focus of the poetry of praise. But it is a somewhat conflicted literary self that is thus acquired. This is one way the poetry of praise, through its reflexive self-consciousness, will revive epideictic themes. Turning its attention to itself and to its own authorial production, the poet's own poetry, rather than his divinity, now will sanctify, as best it can, the poet's self. In the same way, poetic fame (the laud and laurel) will come thematically to substitute for soteriological beatitude (Beatrice).

Such an account oversimplifies Dante and Petrarch both, ignoring Dante's poeticality as much as Petrarch's piety. The generalization is useful, however, because it allows us not only to recognize the developing self-centeredness of the poetry of praise, but also to identify the anxiety accompanying this anthropomorphizing, "Humanistic," progress. For if poetry becomes more "personal" as admiration becomes less metaphysically ideal, so too does poetic personality become, as a result, increasingly and guiltily poetical. If, as poetry develops toward Shakespeare, we hear more about the poetic status of the poet's self, his persona, this is in direct proportion to an increasing doubt about the ontological grounding of the literary self.

Again, this oversimplifies the way Petrarch's "I" is "in part another man from what I am now." However, even as early as Petrarch, there is a characteristic nervousness about the way, throughout the *Rime Sparse*, Petrarch's praise expresses what seems a kind of carnal desire for its ideal. This distinctively Petrarchan dialectic (prepared for by troubador and Provençal erotic idealization) makes the physical and the metaphysical figure each other in very traditional ways. But Petrarch often ashamedly reminds his reader, in a way that Dante rarely does, that the elevation of the former is accomplished, in part, by a deflation of the latter. To be sure, Petrarch is very certain that *in* poetry the real and the ideal will join idealistically together. But the fact that poetry must mediate between the two points up the fact that, *except* in poetry, reality and ideality are for Petrarch, as are person and persona, definitively disjunct. So too, in the same self-conscious way, Petrarch takes his love for Laura, at least in part, as but an imitation and a metaphor of Dante's love for Beatrice. Thus it is true that Petrarch regularly valorizes Laura's name—"my nights are made sad and my days dark by her who carried off my thoughts and left me nothing of herself but her name" (*RS*, 291); "and if my rhymes have any power among noble intellects your name will be consecrated to eternal memory" (*RS*, 327). But, as mentioned earlier, Augustine objects in the *Secretum* to this literary commitment to the "name" on the grounds that Petrarch is obsessed with the signifier and not the signified:

> Infatuated as much by the beauty of her name as of her person, you have with incredible silliness paid honor to anything that has the remotest connection with that name itself. Had you any liking for the laurel of empire or of poetry, it was forsooth because the name they bore was hers; and from this time onwards there is hardly a verse from your pen but in it you have made mention of the laurel.[2]

In Sidney, however, taking Sidney as exemplary of a poetic development larger than himself, it is possible to see how this "personalizing" epideictic evolution or devolution reaches a kind of logical limit or conclusion. If Beatrice is a type of higher things, and if Laura is a type of Beatrice, then Stella is, instead, a type of Laura, and, as such, as poetical imitation of Neo-Platonic imitation, her poet is more than doubly cut off from the ideality to which his praise continues to refer. As a figure of the strictly literary, Stella will confer on Astrophil a self whose features are restricted to the strictly literary. In Sidney, therefore, a debilitated epideictic phenomenology is quite forcefully rewritten in terms that stress an epideictic psychology, but the poetic self thus generated is, as many critics have remarked, a *merely* literary figure of a self. Moreover, this is often Sidney's theme, not only when Astrophil looks into his heart to see there what to write. It is fair to say that this theme completes the introspective, psychologistic evolution or devolution of epideictic poetics. If Stella's image is, as *eidolon*, already printed on her lover's heart, it is because her lover is, as he admits, himself already written: "then all my deed,/But Copying is, what in her Nature writes" (*AS*, 3).

We broach here only one aspect, but a particularly important one, of what Stephen Greenblatt has called "Renaissance self-fashioning," by which he means to refer to the characteristically troubled way in which strong writers of the period dramatize their own personalities, at once assuming and resisting the different roles with which they both underwrite and overwrite their selves.[3] This is

surely a much larger phenomenon than the representation of self in
the poetry of praise. But in English literature of the sixteenth century this relatively new literary problematic—the relation of an authentic self to its deliberate theatricalization, where the notion of an
authentic self is, in large part, a reaction to, or consequence of, self-
dramatization—finds itself very quickly associated with, and most
readily developed in terms of, the influence of Italian models in general and of the epideictic traditions of the Renaissance sonnet in particular. As early as Ascham the cry goes out against:

> the inchantementes of *Circes*, brought out of *Italie*, to marre mens maners
> in England; much by example of ill life, but more by preceptes of fonde
> bookes, of late translated out of *Italian* into English, sold in every shop in
> London, commended by honest title the soner to corrupt honest maners,
> dedicated over boldlie to vertuous and honorable personages the
> easielier to begile simple and innocent wittes.[4]

As time goes by, this kind of critical complaint becomes an increasingly established and prominent literary theme, no longer discussed,
as in Ascham, in terms of the moral corruption or "Circean" transformation of "honest maners," but, rather, in terms of the artificiality
attaching to a pointedly literary epideictic self, as when Sidney objects to poets who, forgetting their mistresses altogether, "had rather
re[a]d lovers writings" than be in love themselves, (*AP*, 201) or as
when Mercutio mocks Romeo's romantic panegyric postures:

> O flesh, flesh, how art thou fishified! Now is he for the numbers that
> Petrarch flow'd in. Laura to his lady was a kitchen wench (marry, she had
> a better love to berhyme her), Dido a dowdy, Cleopatra a gipsy, Helen
> and Hero hildings and harlots, Thisby a grey eye or so, but not to the
> purpose. Signior Romeo, *bon jour!* there's a French salutation to your
> French slop.
>
> (2.4.37–45)

Such, it can be suggested, is an inevitable development of a literary
tradition that takes seriously the claim that poetry can be justified
because its praises offer epideictic literary models for the self. Spenser can imagine that his praise of Arthur will work mimetically and
metaphorically to "fashion a gentleman or noble person in vertuous
and gentle discipline," just as Puttenham (more cynically) assumes
that his guide to rhetoric, modeled on the rhetoric of praise, will also
be a guide to proper or successful conduct.[5] But as Humanism develops, from Castiglione's *Courtier* to *Hamlet*'s Osric, this epideictic
literary ideal serves only to establish the psychological authority of

the figure of the fop. The literary representation of the self turns out, at least in literature, to falsify or "counterfet" the self, just as litera- ture, when it becomes increasingly a thematic concern of literature, is characteristically represented in literature as mere imitation and mere metaphor, which is to say as *mere* literature.

In a poet such as Sidney, the production of a literature and of a literary personality both of which are in this way *authentically* artificial provides the basis for a genuinely moving poetry in which the poet negotiates and worries over the distance between his person and his stylized persona. I am thinking here not only of the set pieces in which Astrophil explicitly deprecates the literary tradition he em- ploys—as in "You that with allegorie's curious frame/Of other's chil- dren changelings use to make" (*AS,* 28) or "I never dranke of *Aganippe* well" (*AS,* 74)—but also of the urgent and powerfully questioning at- titude that the sequence characteristically adopts toward writing it- self, as in "Come let me write, 'And to what end?' To ease/A burthned hart. 'How can words ease, which are/The glasses of thy dayly vexing care?'" (*AS,* 34), and, also, of the attenuated answers that such ques- tions characteristically receive, as in the conclusion to this sonnet, with its "wit" which is at once disturbing and disturbed: "Peace, fool- ish wit, with wit my wit is mard. /Thus write I while I doubt to write, and wreake/My harmes on Inks' poore losse, perhaps some find/*Stel- la's* great powers, that so confuse my mind." In such ways Astrophil characteristically aspires to make himself into a literary *fiction:* "Then think, my dear, that you in me do read/Of lovers' ruin some sad trag- edy. /I am not I, pitie the tale of me" (*AS,* 45).

Sidney's various developments of this problematic are, however, as his poems repeatedly insist, prefigured and determined by the assumptions and the topoi of the epideictic tradition within which and through which Sidney conceives poetic admiration. Though it is in a very wry way, Sidney's Astrophil is concerned precisely with what he calls "a praise to praise," and this is one reason why *Astrophil and Stella,* for all its novelty, is so accessible to, and immediately ap- pealing to, Sidney's literary contemporaries, for whom, of course, the epideictic poetic tradition that Sidney plays with and within in *Astrophil and Stella* is equally authoritative and to whom the waning of an epideictic metaphysics is equally apparent. This is also why Sidney's stagey theatricalization of Petrarchan conceits, his deliber- ate overstylizing of Petrarchan themes and diction, so rapidly be- comes a cliché manner of the Elizabethan sonneteering vogue, a vogue whose self-conscious future *Astrophil and Stella* in this way both inaugurates and conditions (though in some respects this kind of resistance, if not to Petrarch, then to Petrarchism, distinguishes the way the English lyric responds to continental sonnet models from the first—as we see, for example, in Wyatt).

When Shakespeare turns to sonnets, however—only a few years but effectively a literary generation after Sidney—this poetic future is already past. For Shakespeare, Sidney's almost campy revival of "poor Petrarch's long deceased woes" (*AS*, 15) is already stale, and even Sidney's archly literary strategies for representing poetic personality are already, to a considerable extent, exhausted. Yet the same pressure to psychologize poetics, the same impulse to focus on an epideictic poetic self, an impulse that arises in response to the declining authority of an epideictic metaphysics, continues to exert itself, with the result that Shakespeare is obliged to develop a poetic personality that is at once within and without the literary tradition he inherits. This is the central problem and the reiterated theme of Shakespeare's sonnets, and it is in registering and responding to this "persona-lizing" exigency imposed by the unfolding development of a now old-fashioned epideictic poetics that Shakespeare newly fashions, in very particular ways, a "fit" literary subject which is heretofore unknown to poetry but which subsequently becomes in our literary tradition, in ways that I want now to begin to discuss, the authoritative model of literary subjectivity per se.

I would less confidently emphasize the significance of a specifically epideictic subjectivity in Shakespeare's sonnets were it not for the fact that the sequence itself regularly talks about the way poetic subjectivity derives from what the sequence characterizes as the traditional topics and procedures of the poetry of praise. We see this very clearly in the young man sub-sequence. The young man's poet takes rhetorical questions such as "What can mine own praise to mine own self bring?" (39) in a very literal way, and for this reason the question of an epideictic subject becomes in the young man sonnets a straightforward thematic issue. As in the problematic formula of "'Tis thee (myself) that for myself I praise" (62), the young man's poet stakes his being on the identification of his epideictic object and his epideictic subject, "thou mine, I thine" (108). As a result, the poet seems to assume, in a familiar way, that he will come to *be* through praise. And yet, though the poet proceeds conventionally to transpose the praiseworthy attributes of the young man first to his poetry and then to himself, the epideictic *being* that the poet thereby acquires presents itself to the poet as a difficult and pressing question, as a specifically *rhetorical* question, possessing more urgent and more intimate consequence for the poet than is the epideictic custom: "What's in the brain that ink may character/Which hath not figur'd to thee my true spirit?" (108)

One way to appreciate both the urgency and the peculiarity of the poet's epideictic self in Shakespeare's sonnets is to remark the relatively anomalous anonymity of the poet at the opening of the sequence, the fact that there is no poet at all in the first few sonnets, no first-person speaker, thematized as such, with reference to whom we locate what we hear. This is unusual and would have been felt as such. The sonnet sequences of Dante, Petrarch, Sidney, Spenser all begin with their poet introducing himself by commenting on the words he is about to speak. In the opening sonnet of *La Vita nuova* Dante addresses himself

> To every captive soul and gentle lover
> Into whose sight this present rhyme may chance,
> That, writing back, each may expound its sense,
> Greetings in Love, who is their Lord, I offer.[6]

Petrarch begins by apostrophizing "you who hear in scattered rhymes the sound of those sighs with which I nourished my heart during my first youthful error." Astrophil, having considered the alternatives—"I sought fit words"—is told to "look in thy heart and write," and Spenser, reversing Astrophil, imagines instead how his beloved will come to read what he is now about to write and thus see into his poetic heart: "Those lamping eyes will deigne sometimes to look/And read the sorrowes of my dying spright,/Written with tears in harts close bleeding book."

In all these cases, both by conceit and by a stress on first-person verbs and pronouns, the sonneteering poet is, from the very beginning, noticeably present to and in his poetry. Moreover, in all these cases the poet is prompted to speak about himself by that which he has *seen*. In the prose that prefaces his first sonnet Dante explains how "I decided to write a sonnet in which . . . I described what I had seen in my sleep" (*nel mio sonno veduto*), and it is this poetic vision that controls the "sight" (*cospetto*) into which, according to the sonnet, "this present rhyme may chance."[7] Similarly, Petrarch explains how in the past "I was in part another man from what I am now" so as in this way to foreground, at the very beginning, the nature of his retrospective present: "now I see [*veggio*] well how for a long time I was the talk of the crowd, for which I often am ashamed of myself within." So too with Sidney who "look[s]" into his heart, and so too with Spenser for whom "that Angels blessed looke" reflects "my soules long lacked food, my heavens bliss." In each case the reader is immediately confronted, at the very beginning of the sequence, with the situation of a specifically visionary poet. And because each poet in this introspective way talks about himself, the poet's visionary or specular self becomes the central focus of the poem.

In contrast, though the same visionary motif is surely very present in them, Shakespeare's opening sonnets say nothing at all about their poet. Instead, the sequence opens in a pointedly apostrophizing and self-effacing mode, with the poet perceptibly anonymous within and absent to his hortatory speech. This is a stylistic or a rhetorical peculiarity that complements the poet's odd absorption in the young man's solipsistic self-regard, but it also tightly links the poet's own vacuity to the young man's narcissistic fullness. In Shakespeare's opening sonnets the poet addresses the young man in a voice whose half-imploratory, half-imperative tonalities establish the young man as a focused addressee, but, as a seeming consequence, the poet himself, as an addresser, is himself left correspondingly and noticeably indistinct. To take the very first example, it is a neutral, plural, almost public "we" who announces in abstractly sententious, "plain style" manner that: "From fairest creatures we desire increase,/That thereby beauty's rose might never die" (1). But it is a vivid and an individual, if not an individuated, "thou" to whom the poet pleads: "But thou, contracted to thine own bright eyes,/Feed'st thy light's flame with self-substantial fuel" (1).

Such a stance is a complicated variation on a traditional lyric mode. It simulates the kind of dramatic apostrophizing that is common in the conventional sonnet, as when Petrarch addresses his lady or his song, but it is also strikingly and unusually impersonal in the way it leaves the poet, thematically and tonally, with an unidentified and disembodied voice. A similar peculiarity attaches to the first sonnet's imagery of vision, which is employed in such a way as to be both reminiscent of, yet different from, familiar epideictic conceits. I mentioned earlier the way in which, at the end of the *Paradiso*, Dante sees his "likeness" or *effige* in the blinding brightness of eternal light. As a kind of epideictic *cogito*—"I praise, therefore I am"— Dante's vision concludes when he himself becomes a troping marigold, his "desire and will" (*dissio e 'l velle*) "turning" (*volgeva*) in unison with the turning universe, "like a wheel that spins with even motion . . . revolved by the Love that moves the sun and the other stars." It is the same mutually reflexive and reflective visuality that Spenser presupposes when "yet since your light hath once enlumin'd me,/ With my reflex yours shall encreased be." In contrast, as though beginning where Dante concludes, what the poet in Shakespeare's opening sonnet sees in the young man's seeing is the way the young man is "contracted to thine own bright eyes." Very pointedly, what the young man's poet sees in the young man's seeing is that the young man does not see the poet. This has its poetic effect. The reader puts the young man's narcissism together with the poet's self-effacement as if the one were explanation of the other. It is as though the young man's poet does not talk about himself precisely because he sees the young man looking at himself.

This thematic focus on the young man, complemented by a rhetorical absence of poetic first person, is characteristic of the opening sonnets. On the one hand, these opening sonnets place an emphasis on the young man as a person *in* himself, a person who becomes a dominating "you" or "thee" toward whom the poet, himself unspoken, turns to speak. On the other hand, because there is no vocal "I" or "me" (none at all until we arrive at the tenth sonnet) to balance the young man's reiterated "yous" and "thees", these opening sonnets also introduce a strange rhetorical all-or-nothing personal economy in which the young man visually *is* precisely to the extent that the young man's poet vocally *is not*.

Later in the sub-sequence this I-thou economy, which erases rather than foregrounds the poet's "I," is associated with familiar terms of praise, as in "you alone are you" of sonnet 84: "Who is it that says most, which can say more/Than this rich praise, that you alone are you," or, for another example, the ontological "art" of sonnet 78: "thou art all my art." But from the very beginning of the young man sonnets we are grammatically or rhetorically accustomed to a poetic posture from which, or to a psychological space in which, such "self-substantial" being is something that happens in the locus of a second person rather than a first:

> But thou, contracted to thine own bright eyes,
> Feed'st thy light's flame with self-substantial fuel,
> Making a famine where abundance lies,
> Thyself thy foe, to thy sweet self too cruel.
>
> (1)

This is a point that is enhanced by rhyme as well as syntax, as in the couplets to three of the first four sonnets, where the "be"/"thee" rhyme makes it seem as though to "to be" were necessarily to be a "thee," and where, as though this were a gloss on "self-substantiation," such second-person "being" is identified with death: "Pity the world, or else this glutton *be,*/To eat the world's due, by the grave and *thee*" (1); "But if thou live rememb'red not to *be,*/Die single, and thine image dies with *thee*" (3); "Thy unus'd beauty must be tomb'd with *thee,*/Which used lives th' executor to *be*" (4).

It is thematically significant that the "being" of the poet's "thee" is in this way grounded in a death that might be thought to be its opposite. This is the point the poet means to make when he unpacks the self-consuming logic of "making a famine where abundance lies." It is equally significant, however, that the poet's second-person characterization of the young man seems negatively to rebound back upon the poet's first-person self, so that for the poet to highlight the former is also for him to erase the latter. Again, this is both familiar and strange. The first few sonnets seem deliberately to deploy grammatical markers of personality—personal pronouns, demonstrative adjectives, i.e., deictics—in such a way as, on the one hand, to point up the famished absence of the poet's self, and, on the other, to explain this by referring to the abundant yet self-consuming presence of the young man's self. It is true that Shakespeare often exploits the linguistic possibilities of direct and reflexive personal reference, sometimes to indicate characterological complexity, sometimes merely to add an extra syllable to a line. In the opening "procreation" sonnets, however, such pronomial references, along with demonstrative, possessive, and reflexive modifiers, are given an especial emphasis and stress, as though intended to intensify, even to reify, the generic selfness of a self—"But *thou,* contracted to *thine own* bright eyes . . . *Thyself thy* foe, to *thy* sweet *self* too cruel." And yet, precisely because the indicators of personality are in this way stressed in the opening sonnets, these sonnets work to emphasize the way the poet is himself *without* an indicated self.

Thus, for example, there are indeed first-person markers in sonnet 2. However, these are not the poet's "mys" and "mine," but, rather, the young man's:

> Then being ask'd, where all thy beauty lies,
> Where all the treasure of thy lusty days,
> To say within thine own deep-sunken eyes
> Were an all-eating shame, and thriftless praise.
> How much more praise deserv'd thy beauty's use,
> If thou couldst answer, "This fair child of mine

Shall sum my count, and make my old excuse,"
Proving his beauty by succession thine.

This introduces the consistently confusing logic of subjectivity that
governs the young man sub-sequence as a whole, and introduces it,
moreover, specifically in terms of "thriftless praise." At the beginning of the young man sonnets, the poet, as a merely virtual "I,"
cannot be a person *in himself* because first-person personality, at
least as it is here initially conceived, is made to seem the exclusive
personal possession of a second person, literally his "my" and
"mine." The rhetorical self-presence of a self to itself, which is the
poet's image of identity per se, is something that only exists for the
poet, or for the reader reading sonnet 2, when the poet represents
the discourse of a "thee," with the poet placed exterior to his image
of a speaking "I"—"'This fair child of mine/Shall sum my count, and
make my old excuse'"—by means of address to a spoken "thee":
"Proving his beauty by succession thine."

The force of this pointing to the first person of a second person is
to make subjectivity into something that occurs in the objective
case, something to be indicated from a point outside itself precisely
because it is the object of an epideictic gesture. For the same reason,
and yet more distancing, in sonnet 2 even the poet's young man can
only "sum" *his* epideictic "count" by pointing to "this fair child of
mine," as though the young man's child were the self-confirming
"thee" whose being will redeem the *young man's* pointing "I." And,
again, the same peculiarly anonymous indication, the same self-effacing deictic self-promotion, will eventually govern the poet's self
itself, so that the poet will later be obliged to point ostensively and
ostentatiously to the young man, as does the young man to "this fair
child," in order thus to demonstrate the "goodness" of his own "report": "I love thee in such sort,/As thou being mine, mine is thy good
report" (36).

Shakespeare's sonnets thus open with their poet at a kind of rhetorically—following the lead of the second sonnet's "thriftless
praise," it is fair to say an epideictically—enforced zero degree of
personality, his personal presence systemically remarkable only in
and for its absence. The selfishness of the young man is tied to the
selflessness of the poet. By means of a diffusion or slippage of deictic
and epideictic indication, the poet gives all being over to a demonstrated "thee," but in a way that makes identity into a way of being
that is in essence foreign to the poet's self. Initially there is an im-

plicit, but charged, contrast drawn between the poet who rhetorically is nothing and the young man who thematically is everything.
And this is made to seem a causally reciprocal interrelationship because the grammatical markers of personality in these poems—
deictics or pointers, which by rhyme and repetition draw attention
to themselves—situate the poet as somehow structurally extrinsic
to the enclosed circle of narcissistic plentitude figured by the young
man's "self-consuming" "self-substantiation."

This is not to say that as the sub-sequence develops the young
man's poet will be unable to assume an "I" that he can call explicitly
his own. Indeed, it will be with an increasing personal emphasis
that the poet announces how "I do count the clock that tells the time"
(12), or how "Not from the stars do I my judgment pluck" (14), or how
"I consider every thing that grows" (15). Yet this increasingly more
vocal "I" to which the poet often *looks*—"Sin of self-love possesseth
all mine eye" (62), "For as you were when first your eye I ey'd" (104)—
bears striking similarity to the visually self-contracted "thee" in
terms of which the young man is initially imagined—"But thou, contracted to thine own bright eyes" (1). Moreover, this is a similarity
that seems both to clarify and to limit the scope of all the poet's later
introspection.

For there is a modulated, yet insistent, change in personal focus—of specifically visual focus—that occurs as the procreation
sonnets repeat and develop their argument that the young man
"breed another thee" (6), and this modulation seems in turn to condition the way in which the poet later represents himself. Thus, for
example, at the start of the series, the poet will tell the young man to
"look in thy glass and tell the face thou viewest,/Now is the time that
face should form another" (3), whereas, by the end of the series, it is
the poet, rather than the young man, who looks into the mirror to
behold his own self-admiration: "My glass shall not persuade me I
am old,/So long as youth and thou are of one date" (22). Similarly, as
I have already mentioned, at the beginning of the procreation series
it is the young man who sees himself reflected in his progeny—"So
thou through windows of thine age shalt see,/Despite of wrinkles,
this thy golden time" (3)—whereas, by the end of the procreation
series, it is the poet who remarks the introspective way in which:
"Mine eyes have drawn thy shape, and thine for me/Are windows to
my breast, wherethrough the sun/Delights to peep, to gaze therein
on thee" (24).[8]

It may be that such homologies between first and second person, such thematic affinities between, and repetitions of, the imagery applied to the poet and to the young man, are intentionally over-stressed in these opening sonnets. Perhaps they are deliberately made to strike a reader as both precious and amusing so that it will thereby come to seem a merely witty regulation that limits the poet's vision of himself to his initial vision of the self-regarding young man. Whatever the reason, it would certainly be too much to say that the poet becomes the other "thee," the "sun-son" (7) that the young man is supposed to "breed"—if only because what the poet "beholds" in sonnet 22 is the vision of his own extinction ("Then look I death my days should expiate") just as the poet's eyes in sonnet 24 "draw but what they see, know not the heart." Even so, however ironically conducted the progression, there is surely an increasing thematic egoism associated with the way the poet first watches the young man watching himself, and then later watches himself watching the young man. So too the poetic self which is in this way increasingly more present to these poems of procreation seems to be explicitly an epideictic self, one that draws the energy with which to motivate itself, and the conceits with which to ornament itself, from an equally emphasized thematic shift in the procreation sequence whereby it is the poet's visionary praise, rather than the young man's visionary progeny, that comes to function as the young man's eternizing mirror—for example, the move from "So thou, thyself outgoing in thy noon,/Unlook'd on diest unless thou get a son" (7) to "So long as men can breathe or eyes can see,/So long lives this, and this gives life to thee" (18).

To a degree, this seems nothing but conventional. These sonnets develop a familiar transition whereby the poet's praise becomes the poet's subject. The young man's poet points to the young man so as then to point in turn back to himself, the deictic circle being closed with a traditional panegyric, epideictic flourish. This is how these opening young man sonnets are often read, with the elision they effect between progeny and poetry understood as preparation for all the poetic self-inflation that occurs in the later young man sonnets. Thus the young man's young man is identified with the poet's verse—"But were some child of yours alive that time,/You should live twice, in it and in my rhyme" (17)—so that, soon after, the poet's rhyme will "leav[e] thee living in posterity" (6): "Yet do thy worst, old Time: despite thy wrong,/My love shall in my verse ever live young"

(19). As a result, where initially only the young man's young man "can make you live yourself in eyes of men" (16), later, in the larger context of the young man sonnets, "your praise shall still find room,/ Even in the eyes of all posterity" (55). So too, by means of these opening thematic identifications—i.e., because both the poet's praise and the young man's progeny are both equally the same vivid and vivifying "images" of the young man—the poet eventually can transfer the young man's promised immortality to himself: "and Death to me subscribes,/Since spite of him I'll live in this poor rhyme,/While he insults o'er dull and speechless tribes" (107).

Yet if we accept this self-promoting commutation by means of which the "I" of the poet comes to be identified with the "thee" of the young man, does this mean that we identify the poet with the young man or do we instead identify him with "this fair child"? Is the poet properly identified with the young man's original narcissism or with his endless repetition, with his "decease" (1) or with his "increase" (1), with his "unus'd beauty" (4) or with his "beauty's use" (2), with his "thriftless praise" (2) or with his procreated epideictic profit? Where precisely, that is to say, is the "I" in "Ideas Mirrour," and where is the eye in "the lovely gaze where every eye doth dwell" (5)?

This is an important question precisely because the sonnets make it one that is difficult to answer. We can agree that at the beginning of the young man sonnets the young man, because he is so thoroughly absorbed within his solipsistic self-absorption, is presented as the (somewhat disturbing) image of identity per se. We can further agree, perhaps, that, for this reason, the young man functions for the young man's poet as an ego ideal—an ideal, that is, of what it is to be an ego or an "I." To some extent, this is the force of the poet's rhyming "thee," not "me," with "be." Yet if the young man, as a "thee," is thus the poet's image of an ideal self—indeed, the poet's image of what it is for "me" "to be"—it is a self that is ideal only because, and on condition that, it is itself ideally duplicated, only because it is a "seal" that "shouldst print more, not let that copy die" (11), only because it is a "semblance" that ideally will initiate its own re-semblance: "And your sweet semblance to some other give" (13).

This is the logic on which all the procreation arguments depend: that the young man is a copy that ideally should be copied, that his beauty is a "gift"—"Which bounteous gift thou shouldst in bounty cherish" (11)—that for his own sake he should give away—"To give away yourself keeps yourself still" (16). If this is the case, however, does the poet therefore identify himself with the self-centered gift or with the selfless giving? Does the "I" of the poet identify itself with the original "I" of the young man (which is itself already a "copy"), or with the young man's second "I," a second "I" (the young man's young man) who to the young man is a "thee" to whom the young man epideictically points, as does the poet to the young man, in order to confirm an oddly oblate narcissistic self or "I" that "prov[es] his beauty by succession thine" (2)? Alternatively, if "to give away yourself keeps yourself still" (16), what does the poet possess, specifically what kind of "character" does he possess, when "thy gift, thy tables, are within my brain/Full character'd with lasting memory" (122)? And if the young man is himself "that copy" (11), what precisely does the poet copy if he is to "copy what in you is writ" (84)?

The infinitely recursive regressions of these questions—a spiraling, rather than a closed and circular, recursiveness—develop the traditional reflexive reflections of epideictic indication in a novel way, showing what is a very personal problem attaching to the way in which in the young man sonnets an epideictic subject is supposed to see himself or his *effige* in his epideictic object. It is true that the procreation sonnets, taken in order, plausibly progress from the initially impersonal imperative of "look in thy glass and tell the face thou viewest,/Now is the time that face should form another" (3) to the very personal first-person introspection of "my glass shall not persuade me I am old,/So long as youth and thou are of one date" (22). And it is also true that the young man's poet stands, or wants to stand, as a poet, in the same rejuvenating relation to the young man as does the young man stand in relation to "this fair child." Both of them, both poet and young man, by virtue of their relation to the youthful object with which they identify, will "be new made when thou art old" (2). But if this is the case, if the poet with his praise repeats the young man's repetition, then, to the extent that the poet stresses the homology, it cannot be said that the poet identifies himself with the young man. Rather, what the poet reproduces is the young man's reproduction. And this repetition of repetition adds a wrinkle to the poet's project. Developing his praise through the theme of procreation, identifying his praise with the young man's "succession," the poet does not epideictically point to the young man: instead, he points to the young man's epideictic pointing. Accordingly, we do not see the

poet identify himself with the young man, and this because, in a peculiar and self-conscious fashion, we see him instead identify himself
with the young man's identification.

This is a very formal and abstract way to account for the literary
self-consciousness that informs the young man sonnets from the
very beginning, from "from fairest creatures we desire increase." Yet
the sonnets themselves make just this kind of formal play upon the
theme of visual identification and repetition when they develop the
epideictic resonance of "die single and thine image dies with thee"
(3). By means of the procreation argument—a theme which is itself
unprecedented in the genre of the sonnet sequence (though familiar
enough, of course, in other literary contexts)—the poet projects the
traditional visionary poetics of epideictic identification, the poetics
of "'fair,' 'kind,' and 'true,'" onto the young man's iteration in his
progeny, onto "this fair child," who is such because he is multiplied
after the young man's "kind":

> Be as thy presence is gracious and kind,
> Or to thyself at least kind-hearted prove:
>   Make thee another self for love of me,
>   That beauty may still live in thine or thee.
> (10)

By virtue of this genealogical metaphor and mimesis the young
man's young man can then be characterized as the young man's perfect panegyric. This is why, for example, as the poet himself explains, "this fair child" is "much liker than your painted counterfeit"
(16). As floral metaphor—"your living flowers" (16)—and as mimetic
copy—"your sweet semblance" (13)—the young man's "print" (11)
best "write[s] the beauty of your eyes" (17). By the same token, however, the literary "presence" of this "gracious and kind" second
young man continually brings home the fact that the ideal self or
"thee" whom the poet praises is praiseworthy only insofar as he will
be thus duplicated. The young man's self will prove itself "kind-
hearted," as the poet puts it in sonnet 10, only to the extent that yet
"another self" repeats him: "Make thee another self for love of me."
And the "presence" that the young man is supposed to "be as"—"Be
as thy presence is gracious and kind"—is "gracious and kind," therefore, only insofar as in this way it will be a "presence" re-presented.

This doubling of the young man, a duplication that the poet then
reduplicates with praise—"you should live twice, in it and in my
rhyme" (17)—is again something conventional and unconventional

both at once. On the one hand, to the extent that the young man is "thy mother's glass" who "through windows of thine age shalt see,/ Despite of wrinkles, this thy golden time" (3), the procreation sonnets develop familiar images in the tradition of sonneteering admiration. Indeed, it is only because these visual images, images *of* vision, carry with them all the traditional identificatory assumptions of the poetry of praise that the poet can so readily assimilate his peculiar concern with the young man's replication in his progeny to what are the rather more conventional concerns of a sonneteering poet. This is the starting point of the progeny-praise collation, for it is only because both praise and progeny are equally "mirrors" of "Idea" that both "can make you live yourself in eyes of men" (16). On the other hand, there is something more than thematically novel in the way the poet thus makes a point of *showing* what he sees, in the estranging way in which the poet presents a vision of his epideictic vision. In a very obvious way, because the poet's images of visual identification are introduced with the example of the young man *and* his duplicated mirror image—an image which is the *same* whether it is selfishly narcissistic or selflessly procreated—these images become something to look at just as much as they are something with which or through which to see. Thus, for example, from the very beginning of the sequence, we are spectators of the way the young man is "contracted to thine own bright eyes" (1), or we watch the way the young man is urged to "look in thy glass and tell the face thou viewest,/Now is the time that face should form another" (3), or we regard "the lovely gaze where every eye doth dwell" (5), or we imagine how "thyself outgoing in thy noon,/Unlook'd on diest unless thou get a son" (7).

This is conventional because there is nothing at all new in the knowledge that "from thine eyes my knowledge I derive" (14). As in sonnet 78, "thine eyes, that taught the dumb on high to sing,/And heavy ignorance aloft to fly,/Have added feathers to the learned's wing." It is unconventional, however, because the tenor and consequence of this visual imagery is profoundly altered when we see it thus reduplicated. As sonnet 78 goes on to say, "thine eyes" have "given grace a double majesty." Because the poet develops his visual imagery through the theme of procreation, he is situated at least at one remove from what he sees. Presupposing the conventions, the poet's portrait of the young man's procreation ekphrastically portrays the poetics of the poet's own admiration. It is something like the way in which Lucrece, for example, sees her plight depicted in the tapestry that illustrates her rape, or the way that Claudius' crime is represented in the dumb show. But, for this reason, unlike the case with Lucrece or Claudius, there is no place for the poet in his epideictic picture, just as, taking the peculiarity of the procreation theme seriously, there is no place for the poet in the young man's marriage other than that of enthusiastic voyeur. By illustrating praise with procreation the poet therefore makes a traditional spectacle of praise. At the same time, however, he puts himself outside the unitary point, or pointing, of an epideictic point of view.

As we have seen, the historical preparation for this is considerable. From Aristotle on, the audience of praise is the "observer" (*theoron*) of epideictic speech. So too in the poetic tradition Shakespeare inherits this visual motif is glossed both by theory and by practice so as to function as summary image of the poetical per se. From the very beginning of the young man sub-sequence, however, by means of the procreation argument, the young man's poet is one degree above and beyond such ideal observation: he is already the observer of the way in which the young man is "th' observ'd of all observers," he is already the "glass" to the young man's "glass of fashion." This provides a genuinely new perspective on the conventions of visionary poetics. With the tradition of idealizing representation thus presented through the "image" of the young man *and* his young man, the reader is given what is literally a per-spective on the poet's idealizing admiration. It is the same kind of anamorphic "perspective" that Orsino speaks about at the end of *Twelfth Night* when he is confronted and confounded by the double image of his love: "One face, one voice, one habit, and two persons,/A natural perspective, that is and is not!" (5.1.216 –17) But it is also the same kind of mixed-up vision that sonnet 24 hints at with its ambiguous "perspective it is best painter's art" (24). This *doubled* imagery of vision suggests at least one way in which the procreation theme interferes with the dual unities of "now see what good turns eyes for eyes have done" (24). By illustrating the antique, established, official imagery of visual identification with the example of the young man *and* his duplicated mirror image, the poet is, in effect, placed outside what he envisages. He is extrinsic to that which he depicts with the procedures of *specchio exemplare, pictura, idea, imago, imaginem, eidolon*, and, for this reason, he is beyond the young man's visual replication. Because he is the observer of the young man's observation, especially of the young man's self-observation, the poet cannot simply identify himself with the young man, and this because, to the extent that the poet is "glass" to the young man's "glass of fashion," the poet can only identify himself with the young man's identification, which is to say with the young man *and* with the young man's young man, which is to say with the young man *and* with his "succession," or, to be yet more precise, with the young man's ego *and* with that ego's duplicate ego ideal.

The *and* here is intended to specify a connection that, because it is stressed and noted in the young man sequence, also registers itself as a disjunction. To identify the representation of identity in this way, to hold even a monocular mirror up to the tradition of "the mirror of nature," is effectively to double it, and to double it is, it turns out, to divide it. As with the poet's simultaneously conventional and unconventional praise—"What can mine own praise to mine own self bring" (39)—or as with sonnet 24's "perspective," this betrays a literary self-consciousness that serves inevitably to complicate the poet's own self-introspection. To use an involuted formula, the poet is himself divided by his identification with the young man's identification, just as the tradition of visionary reflection is refracted when it is itself reflected. Admittedly, this is only a formula, but such refraction of reflection is for Shakespeare not only a particularly favored principle of formal design but is also one with specific thematic consequences. A straightforward example would be *Richard II*, where a structure of foiled characterological doubles—Richard and Bolingbroke—and the character of a king whose identity is defined by the way he breaks the "flatt'ring glass" (4.1.279) in which he sees the image of himself— "The shadow of your sorrow hath destroy'd/The shadow of your face" (4.1.292 –93)—receive their fullest gloss when

> sorrow's eyes, glazed with blinding tears,
> Divides one thing entire to many objects,
> Like perspectives, which rightly gaz'd upon
> Show nothing but confusion; ey'd awry
> Distinguish form.
>
> (2.1.16 –20)

In the sonnets to the young man, however, this kind of divided and bifocal visuality (of which the art of perspectival anamorphosis is only one example) is operative from the very beginning, consistently affecting the way the sonnets address and characterize "the lovely gaze where every eye doth dwell" (5). Moreover, in the young man sonnets this con-fusion of vision is directly assimilated to sonneteering conventions of visionary speech. And one consequence of this is that from the very beginning of the sequence the identity of the visionary poet itself becomes something "that is and is not" what it is.

At the very least, it is possible to notice that it is just this peculiar kind of divided subjectivity that seems to be the initial consequence of the way the young man's poet insinuates or inserts himself into the "issue" of the young man's procreation. For the sonnet in which the poet makes his first explicit reference to himself, the sonnet which presents the poet's *first* grammatical first person, tells the young man to "make thee another self for love of me" (10). But for the poet thus to commit himself to the young man's procreated "thee" is for the poet to predicate his "I," from its first articulation, on the young man's duplication: "O, change thy thought, that I may change my mind" (10). The poet's identification with the young man's reproduction in this way defines his "I" as a metamorphosizing transformation, as, precisely, an exchange of "change." As a result, insofar as the poet has an "I," or "eye," or "mind" that he can call his own, they all exist for him as something *in between* the young man's duplication:

> Shall hate be fairer lodg'd than gentle love?
> Be as thy presence is gracious and kind,
> Or to thyself at least kind-hearted prove:
> Make thee another self for love of me,
> That beauty still may live in thine or thee.
> (10)

The point is both simple and chilling. In this sonnet whose verbal anticipations of the poetics of "'fair,' 'kind,' and 'true'" are fairly straightforward, and in this sonnet where the poet for the first time speaks *in* and *of* his own first person, the claim is not that the poet's "I" is equal to the young man's "thee." Rather, the poet's "I" is one that lives disjunctively and anamorphically "in thine *or* thee."

This may seem an overly precise distinction to insist on, but it is one that the sequence comes progressively to emphasize in many ways, and it is one that speaks to the fact that the young man always is to the poet something structurally and affectively double: he is always originally a "copy," his beauty always a gift that he receives in order to transmit. And it is in this same double sense that the young man is both agent and patient of the poet's vision, or a moment in between a father and a son: "You had a father, let your son say so" (13). It is this essential and specifically *binary* indeterminacy of the young man—which marks him as an instance of transition between the transitive and the intransitive, which makes his transient narcissistic beauty into the figure of an eternity of repetition, as in "so should that beauty which you hold in lease/Find no determination" (13)—that explains why the poet cannot identify himself with the young man even though the young man is explicitly presented as the poet's second self. The poet is a divided "I" to match the young man's duplicated "thee," a reduplicated eye and "I" caught up in his vision of a colored, doubled "you": "A man in hue [you] all hues [yous] in his controlling,/Which steals men's eyes and women's souls amazeth" (20). And this is the case whether the poet looks to the young man or to the young man's subsequent "succession." For when the poet looks at the young man looking at himself, the poet does not see a self per se, and this because, per se, the young man's is a self abstracted from itself: "O that you were yourself! but, love, you are/No longer yours than you yourself here live" (13). Correspondingly, when the poet looks at the young man looking at his procreated reproduction, what the poet sees is the mirror image of the young man's solipsistic, yet divided, "self-substantiation": "Thou art thy mother's glass, and she in thee/Calls back the lovely April of her prime,/So thou through windows of thine age shalt see,/Despite of wrinkles, this thy golden time" (3). To this extent, whether we begin with the young man or with "this fair child," identity in the young man sequence is always defined *as* its own duplication; it is something that can be itself only insofar as it is something other, just as the young man's narcissism is literally repeated in the young man's ideal repetition, or just as the "profitless usurer" (4) operates within the same economy as "that use is not forbidden usury" (6), or just as the young man remains "contracted to thine own bright eyes" (1) when he "breed[s] another thee" (6).

It is true, therefore, but only in a very complicated way, that the poet assimilates to himself the reproductive wisdom of "look in thy glass and tell the face thou viewest,/Now is the time that face should form another" (3). And there is indeed a visionary subjective truth, but again a very complicated one, attaching to "my glass shall not persuade me I am old,/So long as youth and thou are of one date" (22). But the wisdom and the truth consists in this: that the poet *cannot* identify his subject with his object because both subject and object are themselves already doubled and divided by the identification that would join them. The young man is twice himself, and so the poet is himself reduplicated. The poet of sonnet 22 looks into his mirror—and it is a mirror that goes back to Macrobius' Mirror of

Nature—but in order to associate the "old" of his "I" with the "youth" of the young man, the poet will more subtly collate the young man's "thou" with the "you" of "youth": "My glass shall not persuade me I am old,/So long as *you-th-and-thou* are of one date." The elision that makes "one date" of "you-th-and-thou" both resists and sutures the double identification it asserts, dividing the poet into two parts of himself, just as it identifies the young man with his binary multiplication.[9]

Again, this is a small moment in the sequence as a whole—though it is an important one because it concludes the opening pro-creation series—but it shows the way in which the young man's poet is characteristically dispossessed of his first person, temporally divided between his *now* and *then*, spatially located in between his *here* and *there*. For it is with this troubled, iterate identification, with this implicit structure of disjuncted and alienating sameness, with this unspoken vision of a double other—the mirrored "you-th-and-thou," the colored "man in hue [you] all hues [yous] in his controlling" (20)—that the poet regularly identifies his own poetic self. This is what prepares a reader for the "heart" of the dark lady's poet which "in despite of view [you] is pleas'd to dote" (141), or the way that "I mistake my view [you]" (148). And this is why, as the poet himself explains when he develops the logic of sonnet 22, the poet consistently envisages in the young man the alienating question of his own—that is, the poet's own—identity:

> My glass shall not persuade me I am old,
> So long as youth and thou are of one date,
> But when in thee time's furrows I behold,
> Then look I death my days should expiate.
> For all that beauty that doth cover thee
> Is but the seemly raiment of my heart,
> Which in thy breast doth live, as thine in me:
> How can I then be elder than thou art?

This is partial explanation of how the young man's poet, taking the sonnet's conventions of amatory and visionary identification very seriously, draws out of them something more personally or subjectively complex than does Sidney, for example, when he looks into his heart to see the stellar image of himself imprinted on it, or than does Spenser when he tells his lady to leave her "glasse of christall clene . . . and in myselfe, my inwarde selfe I meane/Most lively lyke behold your semblant trew." The young man's poet beholds "time's furrows," rather than truth, when he looks at his "semblant," and in his "inwarde selfe" he sees a "death my days should expiate," rather than his metaphoric or mimetic "lively lyke." Both tonally and thematically this asserts a distance from the eternizing tradition of the Mirror of Idea and from the self-confirming poetic self-reflections associated with such specular identity. For the young man's poet both the logic and the psychologic of reciprocal exchange—of the gift that is received in order to be given away, of the "use" that is and is not usury—involves a considerably more personal "alteration" than anything the tradition heretofore develops. And if this is already a striking variation on the normative tradition, so too is there something yet more novel in the way the young man's poet repeatedly sketches out the familiar Petrarchist quid pro quo of "thou mine, I thine" (108), the "mutual render" of "only me for thee" (125), only so as then to make it seem that such identification contains a substituting reciprocity to which the poet wants to put an end, as in the couplet to "my glass shall not persuade me I am old": "Presume not on thy heart when mine is slain,/Thou gav'st me thine not to give back again" (22).

What I am suggesting here, therefore, is that it is primarily poetic subjectivity, the presentation of poetic self, that is most immediately affected by the way the procreation sonnets reduplicate traditional epideictic themes and motifs. The doubleness that is formally inherent in the procreation sonnet's imagery of vision (it is still necessary to speak about this doubleness in a less formal way) registers the difference between the idealizing tradition of the sonnet and the way that this tradition of the "'fair,' 'kind,' and 'true'" is effectively troped in the sonnets addressed to the young man. This doubleness obliges the poet, "making a couplement of proud compare" (21), to identify himself with something double, most pointedly, with the "I" of the young man which only is such because it is itself displaced, at least ideally, onto a second "thee." What the poet therefore sees in the young man, either in the young man's narcissism or in the young man's procreated iteration, is precisely the traditional image of epideictic identity. But the identity of this identity has an edge put on it, or is brought into question, because and when it is confronted with its epideictic duplication, the copy thus undone by its copying, the poet both seeing and seeing into his own ideal imagination of what is "'fair,' 'kind,' and 'true.'"

Very traditionally, therefore, the young man sonnets begin by showing the subjectivity immanent in the poetry of praise, "demonstrating" the personality that is intrinsic to, or the embodiment of, an epideictic rhetoricity whose objective showing is equally subjective showing off. Hence the initial familiarity of so many conceits in the young man sonnets, conceits by means of which the poet stakes his being on the young man whom he praises, pointing, I have said, panegyrically toward the young man in order thus to point in turn back to himself. Yet, very untraditionally, it is the poet himself who notices that there is something missing in the mutuality of this panegyric self-reflection, and that there is therefore something empty in the self discovered through such praise. In the young man sonnets the poet sees that there is something fundamentally old-fashioned in the self he fashions with his praise, or that a kind of entropy has eaten away at the tropes of epideictic identification. As a result, because he is committed to an aged poetics of sameness, the poet is left with nothing "new to speak," "but yet like prayers divine,/I must each day say o'er the very same,/Counting no old thing old, thou mine, I thine,/Even as when first I hallowed thy fair name" (108). And, as a further result, the very imagery of procreated renewal, the imagery of mimetic and metaphoric "revival," becomes the image of the poet's age, as in the conclusion to sonnet 108, where the poet "makes antiquity for aye his page,/Finding the first conceit of love there bred,/Where time and outward form would show it dead," or as in sonnet 59, where the poet, figuring forth the young man's duplication, is clearly "laboring for invention" so as to "bear amiss/The second burthen of a former child!"

In the young man sonnets such "secondariness" opens up or introduces a difference between the epideictic pointer and the epideictic pointed. The poetic subject who was formerly composed by the continuity informing what he is and what he praises—the subject of a "star that guides my moving/Points on me graciously with fair aspect,/And puts apparel on my tottered loving,/To show me worthy of thy sweet respect" (26)—is now, instead, decomposed by the reciprocal separation of his epideictic object and his epideictic subject, both of these separate, *by* their duplication, both from each other and both from themselves. This is a "couplement of proud compare" (21) that produces something different from the ideal unity of the real and the ideal that is developed in Dante. So too this is not the witty copy of a copy that we see in Sidney. Rather, what the young man sonnets seem repeatedly to dwell on is the *difference* between a subject and his object, between the real and the ideal, or between the original and its copy. And what I want now to suggest is that it is by emphasizing this difference, by identifying poetic identity or subjectivity *with* this difference—the difference between the poet and his young man, or the difference between the young man and his young man, or the difference between the poet and himself—that the young man sonnets inaugurate a literature of subjective introspection which is both the consequence of and the epitaph of the death of the epideictic. Specifically, my claim is that the way the young man's poet points to the difference between his first and second person initiates (though it does not in itself complete, for that requires the introduction of a "third person," as will happen in the triangular cuckoldry story of the dark lady sonnets) what soon becomes the poetics of the person in the aftermath of praise.

I have already suggested why the failure or exhaustion of traditional literary epideixis might be developed by Shakespeare in specifically subjective or psychologistic terms. I said earlier that as the sonnet evolves from Dante to Shakespeare there is a transition from an epideictic ontology to an epideictic psychology, and that, complementing this historical development, there is a corresponding shift from poetic person to poetic persona, so that the representation of self in the poetry of admiration becomes increasingly self-conscious, increasingly artificial and *merely* literary, in palliating response to, and as measure of, the waning of an epideictic cosmological and theological universe. I am now suggesting that Shakespeare takes this metaphysical decline to heart, to what Chapman called "the hart of his subject," showing us in the young man sonnets the divided subjectivity that motivates all panegyric gesture in the epilogue of epideixis, giving us the psychological correlative of the ontological being of a Beatrice who no longer metaphysically is the ideal thing she also indicates. Both literally and literarily, in metaphysics and in poetry, the pointing, indicative, laudatory links in the great chain of epideictic being have now grown thin, have worn away, to a point where they are now discretely disconnected, like jewels in a circle, in the shape of a necklace, but lacking the string, mimetic and metaphoric, that would join or bind each to each. This is why "thy glass will show thee how thy beauties wear" (77). In the young man sonnets, "the world's fresh ornament" (1) is no longer "fresh," praise has become "a satire to decay" (100), and the result is that the poet is left with only the husk of praise with which to decorate himself.

Reading the sonnets as a narrative of an epideictic self, therefore—and, again, it is the sonnets themselves that self-consciously refer to the formation of an epideictic self—I am suggesting that, as the sequence proceeds, the poet assumes in his person, that he *becomes*, his panegyric relation to the young man, but that this is precisely what makes the poet into a panegyric ghost of himself—"Thus have I had thee as a dream doth flatter" (87). The poet becomes a human being who is in this way cut off from Humanist Being, and this in accord with a poetic psychology that emerges as, and is experienced as, the failure of an epideictic ontology. It is in this sense that the young man sonnets are the memory of praise, its unhappy, ineffective simulacrum. But it is in this sense also that the young man's poet is more than artificial imitation of an ideal literary self. In the young man sonnets Shakespeare continues to explore the literary possibilities for the representation of self within an epideictic poetics; he continues to employ the literary techniques, themes, motifs, imagery, of admiration with which a poet will traditionally come upon, "invent," himself. But, at the same time, this exploration is both motivated and conditioned by the fact that epideixis no longer instantiates, either mimetically or metaphorically, the things toward which it gestures. And for this reason, because praise no longer corresponds to that to which it points, neither does the praising poet that Shakespeare portrays in his sonnet sequence correspond to or instantiate the self that he mimetically and metaphorically invents. In the young man sonnets, even before we meet the dark lady, neither the poet's eyes nor his "Is" have "correspondence with true sight" (148).

It is, therefore, only provisionally and initially true that the young man, as an object of praise, functions for the young man's poet as an ego ideal, as an object with which the poet, as a subject, might identify himself: "thou art all the better part of me" (39). For, as the sequence proceeds, the identification thus initially promoted opens up, when it is seen to be repeated, a space of rupture between the poet's ego and what is that ego's duplicate ideal, between the poet and his object, or between the poet and himself. The poet does not express a traditional Petrarchan regret that there is a difference between himself and his ideal, but, more particularly, that he *is* the difference between them. Rather then leading him to "invent" or even to "reinvent" himself, the poet's repetition of the tradition of praise leads him to the intervention of an epideictic self. This is why if there is a difference in Shakespeare's sonnets between the pointer and the pointed, the poet cannot be indifferent to it, or why when the poet's "showing" fails the poet cannot help but show it. The experience of this rupture—between panegyric signifier and panegyricized signified, between ideal sign and idealized referent, between the praising "image of art" and the praised "mirror of nature"—is what defines the poet's self as *being* this division, and is what makes the poet's present a "remembrance of things past" (30). This rupture both constitutes and circumscribes the poet's "I," is what it is as well as what contains it, so that the young man's poet *to* himself becomes an "I" who is, for just this reason, dispossessed of his first person, just as the young man to whom the poet points will point in turn to his young man. The poet of the young man sonnets—and for now I postpone a discussion of the poet of the dark lady sonnets—becomes this pointed and pointing self, but he does so *as* their difference; he becomes the missing connection between them, existing only as the intervening indication of the difference between the "I" he is not and the "thou" "I" is.

This is the posthumous personality that defines the legacy of the poetry of praise, the "after-loss" (90) of "thou art all my art" (78). Having given all his being to a duplicated "thee," the poet will himself be broken when he identifies himself with duplication. To be in the young man sonnets is thus to be positioned in a space where one is not. To be, we must not hesitate to say, is also, therefore, not to be. And this familiar Shakespearean space of ontological indeterminacy, a space of *deictic* questioning—for, indeed, "that" *is* the question, not only in *Hamlet*, but also, for example, in Othello's "that's he that was Othello, here I am," or, for that matter, in Orsino's "that is and is not"—is developed in the young man sonnets as a specifically psychological space of *persons*, a space occurring in between a second-person-pointed "I," fully present to itself but absent to the poet, and a first-person "thou," whose absence to the poet is palpably present to the poet's pointing person. This is where we can locate the "eye" in Shakespeare's "Ideas Mirrour," and this is where we can see the "I" in "the lovely gaze where every eye doth dwell" (5). Caught up in his vision of his antique vision, the poet's "I" is located at the vanishing point of epideictic indication, in between his twofold vision of his past and present self: "For as you were when first your eye I ey'd" (104), "*Now* see what good turns eyes for eyes *have done*" (24). And the poet is placed in this eutopic place that is no place by his deployment of the dead epideictic conventions of the poetry of praise. For the poet who, in the aftermath of praise, epideictically commits his person to "*that* sun, *thine* eye" (49) will discover, equally personally and equally deictically, that he, as "I," is neither here nor there, neither now nor then, neither "eye" nor "eyed."

It will be said that this is to overread the young man sonnets, to import into them a double dialectic at odds with their idealism and with their ideas. The reading I am developing places the poet in between a divided subject and a divided object, it bifocally situates him in between his seeing and his seen, and it will surely be objected that this is to make of Shakespeare's sonnets something far more complicated than in fact they are. Alternatively, it will be said that the reading I develop here underreads the young man sonnets, reductively imposing on them a grid of binary bifurcations that constrains within a finite frame the infinite ironies of their multivalent, polysemic resonation. My reading of the sonnets says that the sonnets do this and not that, whereas a certain kind of literary criticism would sooner say that Shakespeare's sonnets do everything or nothing rather than that they do any one particular thing at all. No doubt such objections to the argument I am presenting might be developed in fuller and more persuasive terms. But, really, is it my argument that overreads, or is it instead a sentimental tradition of idealizing literary criticism that underestimates, indeed ignores, the way the young man sonnets earn the subjective pathos of a text in which in almost every line "mine own self-love quite contrary I read" (62)? So too, is it my reading that reduces, or is it instead an oversophisticated literary criticism that dissolves and diffuses the specificity of the young man's poet's variously phrased, variously connotated, but nevertheless "still constant" system of quadrilateral complaint? Take, for a comparatively obvious example, sonnets 44 and 45, both of which express equivalently ideal themes, and both of which depend upon the same elaborate and difficult conceit, but both of which, for all their ideality and for all their difficulty, position the poet within the space of chiasmic separation opened up between what I have characterized as the poet's doubly divided panegyric "I" and "thou," a personal space that the poet here develops by dividing into two chiastic parts the four substantial elements of which he is composed: "My life being made of four, with two alone/Sinks down to death, oppress'd with melancholy" (45). It is best, perhaps, to quote the two sonnets in their entirety:

> If the dull substance of my flesh were thought,
> Injurious distance should not stop my way,
> For then despite of space I would be brought,
> From limits far remote, where thou dost stay.
> No matter then although my foot did stand
> Upon the farthest earth remov'd from thee,

For nimble thought can jump both sea and land
As soon as think the place where he would be.
But ah, thought kills me that I am not thought,
To leap large lengths of miles when thou art gone,
But that, so much of earth and water wrought,
I must attend time's leisure with my moan,
    Receiving nought by elements so slow
    But heavy tears, badges of either's woe.

                                         (44)

The other two, slight air and purging fire,
Are both with thee, where ever I abide;
The first my thought, the other my desire,
These present-absent with swift motion slide.
For when these quicker elements are gone
In tender embassy of love to thee,
My life being made of four, with two alone
Sinks down to death, oppress'd with melancholy;
Until live's composition be recured
By those swift messengers return'd from thee,
Who even but now come back again, assured
Of thy fair health, recounting it to me.
    This told, I joy, but then no longer glad,
    I send them back again and straight grow sad.

                                         (45)

That these two sonnets are a pair goes, presumably, without saying, and not simply because they develop in complementary tandem the physics of four elements and a corresponding humoral psychology. In the first sonnet the poet plays on a syntactic and semantic ambiguity that is built into his "thought," for "thought" is what the poet wants both actively and passively to be. In the second sonnet, where "thought" is further subdivided into itself and its desire, this ambiguity becomes yet more ambiguous. But even this doubling of an ambiguity, though it may make a problem of and for the unity of the ideal, does not lead to utter indeterminacy, or if it does, it is an indeterminacy that seems in turn to lead to a determinate effect. In both sonnets, the poet is "forc'd," like his young man or his dark lady, "to break a twofold truth" (41), but in both sonnets such chiasmic fracture is what puts the poet in the same subjective, intersected place that we see broached in "change thy thought, that I may change my mind" (10). We see this if we see the way these sonnets reiterately complement each other, if we see, that is, the way the poet of sonnet 44 first defines himself as the ontological alternative between being "thought" and being "not thought," so as then to locate himself in sonnet 45 *at* and *as* the affective disjunction between his being "glad" and being "sad."

Thus, in the first sonnet, sonnet 44, the poet wishes, on the one hand, that his dull and heavy, viscous flesh, which he associates with earth and water, were instead a light and airy, "thoughtful" incorporeality—anticipating here, though only loosely, the air and fire of the second sonnet—for "if the dull substance of my flesh were thought," then the poet would be free to transport himself, "despite of space," to the young man: "from limits far remote, where thou dost stay." We can call this first "thought" that he would be the ideal, first-person, subjective "I" of the poet; this "I" is ideal if it is connected to an ideal, second-person, objective "thee." On the other hand, the poet in the first sonnet also wishes that he were himself the object of the young man's thinking, for if he were in this way an "idea" of the young man, he would thus avoid the death that comes from being out of mind and unregarded—this but one of several meanings attaching to "but ah, thought kills me that I am not thought." We can call this second "thought" that he would be the ideal, first-person, objective "me" of the poet; this "I" is ideal if it is connected to an ideal second-person, now subjective "thou."

The wit of the first sonnet, then, if that is what it amounts to, consists of thus collating, by means of the general elemental conceit, these two senses of "being-thought"; on the one hand, a subjective substance, an "I," i.e., something one might *actively* be, the energy of whose being is directed toward its absent, complementary object, a "thee"; on the other, an objective substance, a "me," i.e., something one might *passively* be, the energy of whose being is quite obviously dependent on its absent, complementary subject, a "thou." It is because "nimble thought can jump both sea and land/As soon as think the place where he would be," that these two senses of *being* "thought"—active and passive, transitive and intransitive, subjective and objective—will not only join together but in such a way that the expression of the one will necessarily reciprocally express the other, as in the syntactic enjambment appended onto "but ah, thought kills me that I am not thought," where the poet's initial regret that he is not mobile "thought" also contains and conveys the poet's fear that the young man will not think the poet thinks about the young man: specifically, that the young man will not think the poet wants "to leap large lengths of miles when thou art gone." (We can also mention, without pursuing, the dizzying permutations that open up when the poet thinks about the young man thinking about the poet thinking about the young man thinking about the poet, and so on.)

All this is complicated, no doubt, but only in the most mechanical and readily comprehensible way. These various and different, yet mutual and complementary, meanings and persons all coherently make sense by reference to the literal level of the physical conceit—namely, that because the poet is not "nimble thought" he cannot "leap large lengths of miles when thou art gone"—and this literal level very readily lends itself to an equally coherent elaboration of what are relatively familiar sonneteering themes. Indeed, it is because these familiar themes are so neatly—almost superficially—developed through the showy apparatus of the humoral psychology and the four-term elemental physics that the sonnet acquires its peculiar tonality, a tonality that leaves us somewhat puzzled as to just how seriously or playfully the poet means for us to take his glibly interlocked abstractions. Thus, underlying all the poet's thinking about "being-thought" is the poet's initial desire for a perfect identification or complementarity, ontological and psychological, with the object of his desire. This is what the opening octave describes: a world in which there would be a total correspondence between the poet's double subject and the poet's double object, a world of consummated reciprocity in which to think is also to be bethought, in which to love is also to be beloved. And it is with reference to this ideal situation, wherein there would be no difference whatsoever between the poet's "I" and "thou" or between his "me" and "thee," that the poet measures his actual physical separation from the object of his desire and, therefore, from his twofold self. This is what leads the poet to imagine the metaphysical means with which to heal or bridge the gap of "injurious distance." So too this is what generates the poet's desire to translate his physical being into metaphysical being, his wish that "the dull substance of my flesh were thought."

The sonnet seems, therefore, to call out for an orthodox interpretation. The poet's separation from the young man develops at a personal level, at the level of Petrarchist amatory psychology, a traditional and immediately recognizable opposition or dialectic between the fleshly and the spiritual, between a gross materiality (earth and water) and an incorporeal ideal (air and fire). In this sense, a sense that is prepared for by innumerable sonneteering conventions, the reader is invited to read the sonnet as a rather ingenious, somewhat brittle, but nevertheless familiar meditation on the way, as Brent Cohen puts it, "we are made of the same stuff that separates us from

what we desire."[10] Thus the poet, being "of earth and water wrought,"
cannot "jump both sea and land," and, as a result, because he cannot
jump beyond his physical self, the poet is reduced to the affective
essence of his substantial being. At the end of the sonnet, therefore,
the poet simply becomes what he already is, receiving from his two
"slow" elements nothing, "nought"—or "naughts," to take the Quarto's plural printing—"but heavy tears, badges of either's woe," and
this in accord with a humoral psychology whereby the poet's mental-
ity literally embodies his physical body.

This would be a very sophisticated version of an idealist reading,
solemnly deriving the melancholy of the poet's desire out of the poet's distance from his ideal, and then situating the poet's morose
admiration in the tradition of Petrarchan complaint. The poet is
here, the ideal is there, and the poet's project or desire, here frustrated, is to bring the two together. Yet however familiar and summary such a reading might seem, it is only a partial response to the
sonnet, a half-response that divides its four dimensions into two,
and then, yet more reductively, these two dimensions into one. For
it is also the poet's theme here, as well as his condition, that his two
physical elements only join together as oxymoronic "heavy tears"
because the poet's ideal "thought" is correspondingly divided or
striated into two disjuncted parts. This is to recognize—presumably
no overreading—that the poet *thinks* paradoxical thoughts about
not being "thought" just as much as he cries "heavy tears" about
being earth and water, and that these conflicted thoughts are supposed to match the "naughts" which are the poet's "heavy tears":
"But ah, thought kills me that I am not thought."

This is to say more than that the poetic value of the poet's
"thought" is derived from its distinction to the poet's flesh, for by
the Neo-Platonic premises through which the sonnet thinks itself
we are supposed to recognize that the poet's being is deeply implicated in this diacritical distinction. It is only because the poet thinks
about the "thought" that he is not that the poet is more than the dull
flesh that he is, for it is only because the poet wants metaphysically
to be what he is not—"If the dull substance of my flesh were
thought"—that the poet is filled to physical overflowing both with
the "thought" that he is not *and* with the "heavy tears" he is. It is in
this contradictory, but coherent, sense that the poet's desire stands
as bridge as well as bar between the poet's flesh and thought. And it
is in this strong, mutually canceling and reinforcing sense that
"thought kills *me* that *I* am not thought." For it is only insofar as a

reader appreciates and registers the irony of the negative existential,
only insofar as a reader observes the way in which the poet, as counterbalanced objective "me" and subjective "I" thinks he is not
thought at the very moment that he is the thought he thinks, that the
poet's chiastically divided personality effectively intrudes upon,
and thereby vivifies, and otherwise uninteresting, impersonal conceit. Hence the strong affective force of the "but ah," with which the
"thought," the line, and the sestet each achingly begin.

Paraphrasing in this heavy-handed way—with the poet made to
announce explicitly that "I think, therefore I am and I am not what I
want to be," or, "being here, I am there where I am not"—we arrive at
what Desdemona calls, when she asks Iago for some praise, "old fond
paradoxes to make fools laugh i' th' alehouse" (2.1.138–39). The sonnet itself is somewhat more delicate, more muted and reserved, than
my commentary here suggests. But it is important to go to the trouble
of thus spelling out the implications of the "but ah," on which the
sonnet turns (the opening "but" of the sestet characteristically arguing with the "if/then" reasoning of the octave) so as to make it clear
that it is neither under- nor overreading to say that if the poem works
to show its reader that the poet is made of the same "dull" stuff as that
which separates him from his ideal desire, so too does it work to show
its reader that the poet's desire is what separates the poet from the
merely fleshly being that he is. And the poet as a whole must be understood as the concatenated effect of such conjoined and sundered
parts because the entirety of his being is defined by the way in which
these two divided oppositions are superimposed upon each other.
The poet is more than the earth and water to which he is oxymoroni-
cally reduced, but the more that he is is precisely the intelligible ambiguity of the ideal "thought" that he is not.

Again, if this is complicated, it is so only in the most mechanical
of ways, and it is only because I here unpack with clumsy paraphrase the succinct and efficient formulations of the sonnet that the
movement of the poem is made to seem at all opaque. Given the
terms of the conceit, every reader (assuming he neither over- nor
underreads), registers the fact that though the poet is physically but
earth and water, though he is but dull and heavy flesh, he is nevertheless metaphysically more than this because his earth and water
join together as "heavy tears" to lament that they are not air and fire.
So too, if it is a trivial, still it is by no means an unfathomable, exploitation of the negative existential that leads a reader to recognize
that the poet is thought-full to the extent that "thought" in him *is*

"nought[s]," or that the ideality of air and fire really does effectively
inhabit the poet because it is operatively present in him as the poet's
real experience of its absence. In the most straightforward way, this
is how the poet seems to a reader: conflicted, because weighed
down and uplifted, by the thoughts he thinks. And it is precisely
because we register this difference *in* the poet, the difference between what he is and what he is not, the difference between an oxymoronic physicality and an ambiguous metaphysicality, that we
have no conceptual difficulty locating the poet above his sodden
flesh and below his high ideal. And again, whether we take this as
something playful or as something serious—and it is typical of the
young man sonnets that the poem itself will leave us undecided as to
just how we should take it—this is what constitutes the poet's desire
just as this is what defines for us the totality of what the poet is. For it
is only when the poet becomes the systematic difference compre-
hended by "But ah, *thought* kills *me* that *I* am not *thought*" that the
objective "me" of the poet and the subjective "I" of the poet will join
together at the point of their disjunction so as to produce a psychological *want* of being which corresponds in an intelligible way to the
poet's ontological lack.

My purpose here is not to develop a series of banal and precious
double double binds—though, to some extent, the sonnet, doubly
identifying "thought" with "nought[s]" does indeed depend on and
begin with such—but to stress again that the sonnet works, in the
most natural and unforced way, assuming we recognize the elementary logic of the general conceit, to present the poet to us as a personality or a subjectivity who is in fact doubly bisected when his real
and his ideal paradoxically intersect. The poet is neither one thing
nor another, neither fully "thought" nor "nought," because he is precisely half and twice the one unified thing he is. The poet is no
Mirandellian mediator in between the angels and the beasts. He is
instead himself the living witness of, or the embodiment of, or the
occasion of, a structural discrepancy between an ambiguous ideal
and an oxymoronic real, both of which here join together at and as
the poet's twofold self-division.

This too, of course, is not entirely unprecedented in the tradition
of the sonnet. Petrarchan oxymoron regularly generates such elementary paradoxes—especially paradoxes of atomic mix-up, as in
"icy-fire"—and Petrarch regularly uses these in order to remark his
own self-alienation, referring, for example, either to "what steals
me away from myself" (*RS*, 71), or to the way "I steal myself away

from myself" (*RS*, 169; compare *RS*, 23, "I felt myself drawn from my own image" [*i' senti' trarmi, de la propria imago*]). But in Petrarch, as in the sonnet tradition as a whole, if the lover is divided by his love, or if the poet is sundered by his poetry, this is but one temporary moment in the course of a potentially complete—even if it is a currently postponed—progress toward total self-fulfillment. Either the grace of the lady will eventually bring the poet to herself, and therefore bring the poet to himself, or, when the sonnet grows more self-consciously literary, it will be the poet's poetry that resolves the difference between his real and his ideal. In sonnet 44, however, where the poet's fracture consists not of one but of two disjuncted combinations, there are no such intimations of synthesizing immortality. The poet receives neither soteriological nor literary salvation; neither does he receive the deferred promise of such. Rather, he remains beside himself, there where he is not, with both his double subject and his double object in between the subjective and objective "thought" that "I am not."

Here it might be said, as though this were an objection to what has just been said, that if the poet of sonnet 44 is in this way dislocated, this is because sonnet 44 is only the first of a deliberately coupled pair of sonnets. If the poet of sonnet 44 regrets that he is only half himself, this is, perhaps, in part, because we have as yet received but half the poet's story. Certainly the first sonnet seems to anticipate, or to call out for, a more extended narrative with respect to which its melancholy would stand as invocation and as introduction. For this reason, a reader might very well say or feel that the very inconclusiveness of sonnet 44, its unhappy irresolution, prepares for a complementary and a reconciliatory conclusion in sonnet 45—a conclusion that is in this way virtually present in sonnet 44, like "thought" *is* in the poet, by virtue of its marked and noticed absence. This is to say more than is perhaps really necessary, but it is certainly the case, given the elemental conceit, given the tradition of the sonnet, and given the conventions presupposed by sonnet 44, that a reader has every reason to expect that the succeeding sonnet will present just such a harmonious resolution or, perhaps, a dissolution, of the poet's "heavy tears." At any rate, a reader can certainly imagine, even before he gets to sonnet 45, a good many conventional ways in which the poet might effectively translate his person across "both sea and land" when, subsequently, he transfers his direct attention from the earth and water that he is to the air and fire he is not.

Yet, when we in fact turn to sonnet 45, where the poet does in-

deed "think the place where he would be," we do not find the poet
thus transported either to or by the other side of his initial story.
Instead, though sonnet 45 begins as though it were about to heal the
breach disclosed by sonnet 44, the sonnet nevertheless proceeds to
develop the very same disruption of the poet's being as was developed in the sonnet it succeeds. Rather than repairing or unifying the
poet's introductory self-division, sonnet 45 instead repeats and
even doubles it, drawing and, as it were, quartering the poet by reduplicating his division. And again, whether we take this failed "re-
pairing" of the poet as something comic or tragic—for the second
sonnet again employs the same combination of playful seriousness
that the first sonnet used to formulate its "heavy tears"—it requires
neither an under- nor an overreading to discern the four-term structure of the poet's double split. Thus the second sonnet begins as
though "the other two" with which it sets out were a kind of balm to
be applied to the first poem's concluding "either's woe," as though
the poet, because he now will place his "I" with the young man's
"thee," were now about to be alchemically transported to his better
self: "The other two, slight air and purging fire,/Are both with thee,
where ever I abide." Yet we no sooner register the abiding ideal unity
of the poet's "I" and "thee" (already somewhat dislocated by the
paratactic syntax with which it is expressed—the caesural comma is
the Quarto's, not an editor's, punctuation), then we discover that the
poet's air and fire are no more stably located than was the poet's
thoughtful flesh: "The first my thought, the other my desire,/These
present-absent with swift motion slide."

This is not what sonnet 44 leads us to expect, either insofar as it
allows us to think its "heavy tears" are only temporary, or insofar as
it defines the nature of its "thought." In the first sonnet, "nimble
thought can jump both sea and land/As soon as think the place
where he would be," and it is for this reason that "thought" is what
the poet in the first sonnet wants both actively and passively to be.
In the second sonnet, "thought" remains equally "nimble," but what
this "swift motion" means for the poet who identifies himself with
it is that there is nowhere he abides, either as an "I" or as a "thou" or
as a "me" or as a "thee," or as the four conjoined together. It is not
simply that the subjective and objective genitives implicit in "my
thought" and "my desire" inherit the same subjective and objective
double correspondences and reciprocal complementarities of the
poet's antecedent active and passive "thought." Rather, what strikes
a reader is that the "slight air and purging fire" into which the poet

now breaks down the "thought" of the first sonnet are literally interposed between himself and the young man, as though it were
"thought" and "desire" that are themselves opposed, both actively
and passively, to what the poet wants to think, or as though it were
"swift motion" itself that both motivates and frustrates the poet's
most ideal emotions.

This is the point of the epistolic conceit, latent in the first sonnet,
manifest in the second, which tells us that we are to identify the
"thought" that formerly "can jump both sea and land" with letters
that the poet exchanges back and forth with his young man. These
letters both express and figure, they present and represent—as
though there were a unitary correspondence between presentation
and representation—both the poet's "thought" and his "desire." But
where formerly the "nimble" mobility of "thought" would bring the
poet "from limits far remote, where thou dost stay," or help him to
span the distance of "the farthest earth remov'd from thee," now it is
the "swift motion" of "thought" itself, the double back and forth
movement of correspondence itself, that places the poet at one "remote" "re-move" from himself. Thus the poet, identifying himself,
or at least one half of himself, with the letters he dispatches and
receives, is mortally subdivided when he writes to the young man:

> For when these quicker elements are gone
> In tender embassy of love to thee,
> My life being made of four, with two alone
> Sinks down to death, oppress'd with melancholy.

Correspondingly, the poet is rendered whole, is literally "re-paired,"
when:

> live's composition be recured
> By those swift messengers return'd from thee,
> Who even but now come back again, assured
> Of thy fair health, recounting it to me.

But the poet is no sooner resurrected and recomposed by being "recured" than he re-returns "those swift messengers return'd from
thee," recounting their "recounting," so that the "joy" of correspondence is present to the poet only for the instant that it takes for him
to make a record of, and repetition of, its loss: "This told, I joy, but
then no longer glad,/I send them back again and straight grow sad."

These accumulating "re-"s (44: "remote," "remov'd"; 45: "recured," "return'd," "recounting") that the poet recites only so as

then to turn them around upon themselves, are a good example of the way, as I put it earlier, reflection is refracted when it is itself reflected, or the way that identity is divided by its own identification. Even if we do not associate these letters about which the poet writes with the sonnets that we read (though it is really rather difficult not to do so), we cannot help but notice that it is the expression, or the re-expression, of thought and desire that frustrates as well as satisfies thought and desire. The letters rush back and forth between the poet and the young man, and so the poet, identifying himself with an equivocal medium, becomes the intermediate conjunction between his moiety and whole. The poet and the young man exchange the same letter (assurances "of thy fair health"), but, for just this reason, the poet is a sender who receives a message opposite in import to the message he transmits. The poet counts himself both "two" and "four"—as though "summing," as in sonnet 2, his epideictic "count," or as in sonnet 108, "counting no old thing old, thou mine, I thine"—but he therefore once again becomes both half and twice himself, broken into two disjointed counter-parts who are themselves divided by their own "recounting."

In this way we are once again returned to a too easily acquired or a too quickly stipulated double double bind, and this perhaps explains why sonnets 44 and 45 are not really very powerful poems. Writing self-consciously about writing (which, perhaps, is always overwriting), as in the first sonnet of the pair he self-consciously thought about his thought, the poet of sonnet 44 repeats himself in sonnet 45. But what he repeats with this repetition is the initial duplication, now reduplicated, that originally both multiplies and divides him. For most readers this is no doubt a bit too neat and a bit too much, even from a poet who does not hesitate to say he wants to "suffer" "th' imprison'd absence of your liberty" (58). Speaking formally, however, the two poems—in themselves and in their relation to each other— are highly characteristic of the young man sub-sequence as a whole, and their very schematism helps identify the metamorphosing and emphasized literary "re-" that I spoke of earlier: the "re-" that markedly reiterates Petrarchan conceits and thus rewrites them, the "re-" that, because stressed, separates representation from that which it presents, the "re-" whose noticed repetition is what registers the merely literary status of a too frequently asserted literary claim.

For it is in accord with a convention reaching back at least to Dante's beatific praise of Beatrice that the poet initially identifies his ideal self with his writing, that "live's composition" is for him literally liter-

ary composition, that the letters he exchanges back and forth between himself and the young man are supposed to join him to that
which he desires and therefore join him to himself. (The epistolic conceit is a special but conventional subset of the larger convention, e.g.,
Donne's "more than kisses, letters mingle Soules;/For thus friends absent speake.")[11] But the poet deploys the convention only so as then
to redeploy it, calling it up only so as then to show that, here at least,
in sonnets 44 and 45, the identification, via poetic medium, of poetic
subject with poetic object produces no poetic closure but instead poetic fracture of the poet's self. Instead of "thou art all my art" (78),
writing itself stands—not subtly, but explicitly—between the poet's
first and second persons. Writing itself (the *same* writing written by
the "I" of the poet and by the "thou" of the young man) gives the poet
an ontological and poetic "art" of interference whose transference
both is and is not what it is supposed to be. Rather than bridging the
external distance between himself and his young man, the exchange
of thoughtful letters instead creates such open, gaping space *within*
the poet, spelling out for him the very same continuing exchange of
change that we first hear about in "change thy thought, that I may
change my mind" (10), or the same "withinness" that is sounded out in
"lean penury within that pen doth dwell" (84). And again, whether
this seems a trivial or a significant conceit—whether a reader takes as
something playful or as something serious the fact that the epideictic
poetics of "correspondence" is here literally disrupted by the literature, by the letters, of epistolic correspondence—it is on just this conceit that the sonnet, again in the most natural and unforced way, must
be understood to turn. Only in this way do we understand why
"thought" and "desire" are never permanently at the place either of
the poet's double subject or of his double object, but instead are always "slid[ing]" "with swift motion" back and forth between the poet's here and there. Only thus can we explain why the "thought" and
"desire" with which the poet identifies himself are always "present-
absent" to a poet whose profoundly personal complaint (which,
apart from the personal inflection given to it by sonnet 45, is otherwise conventional) is that he is, for just this reason, always "present-
absent" to himself.[12]

Once again I am here merely paraphrasing, clumsily, the explicit
conceit of the poem, saying what for a competent reader goes, presumably, without saying. But it is important to recognize, even at
the risk of laboring the obvious, first, that the ideal air and fire of
sonnet 45 do to the poet what his real earth and water did to him in

sonnet 44, second, that they do so in the same chiastic way, third, that because the second sonnet repeats the first, the two sonnets together rescind whatever promise of reunification might have been implied by the initial sonnet's introductory unhappiness. In the first sonnet the "sea and land" that the poet physically is separates the poet from his ideal thought-full being, but this also leads the poet incompatibly to be in part the "thought" that he is not. In the second sonnet, "thought" itself, composed of air and fire, of itself and its desire, divides the poet into two divided parts. In the second sonnet we are therefore once again placed in a field of conventional poetic associations whose turns and returns we might be tempted to control and to comprehend with a familiar reading. A reader might assume or expect, for example, that the poet's physical desire separates the poet from the ideal thought that he would be. But sonnet 45 seems not at all concerned to elaborate this kind of traditional opposition between the physical and the metaphysical or between the real and the ideal. The poet's fiery desire is just as ideal as is the poet's airy thought, and the two of them together are equally opposed to the poet's heavy earth and sluggish water. Rather, as a rejoinder to the poem that it succeeds, sonnet 45 seems deliberately to select against such anticipated and framing resolutions, choosing instead to intensify and to deepen, to fix *by* duplicating, the structural discrepancy inherent in "thought kills me that I am not thought." In this sense the logic of "the other two" in sonnet 45 *conclusively* repeats the doubly disjunctive logic that is developed through or to the first poem's "either's woe." And, as a result, putting the one sonnet next to the other, whether we look to the real or to the ideal, to earth and water or to air and fire, "but, ah," remains in both sonnets the most exact expression of the poet's self. Indeed, the "but" of this "ah" is perhaps more expressively suited to the ideal realm of the second sonnet, where, because "thought" is now divided into itself and its "desire," there is twice as much at issue for the poet to regret.

My own point here remains, for the moment, a purely formal one: that for the young man's poet neither the reality nor the ideality of unity serves him as anything but a placeholder or a coefficient with which to multiply and to divide himself by two. The poet is neither the "four" of which his "life" is "made" nor the "two alone" with which he "sinks down to death." Instead, he is the criss-crossed alternation, the dihescent oscillation between the two of these together, between, to use the themes of the poem, total presence and total absence, between the full and the empty, between the healthy and the sick, between the glad and the sad. In very obvious ways such a form will lend itself to the enumeration and narration of such binary oppositions; it requires stark dichotomization, and it therefore exploits all the rhetorical devices of counterpoised antithesis and balanced isocolon that it inherits from a Petrarchist poetics of oxymoronic juncture and distributive contrariety. So too such a form readily gathers to itself all the images, motifs, themes with which the sonneteering tradition historically unfolds either the opposition or the correspondence between the real and the ideal. But, again, the point to be emphasized is that in the young man subsequence such coupled or antithetical pairs are characteristically (not always, but often enough) invoked only so that *both* their coupling and their contrariety, their marriage and their psychomachia, might be systematically subverted by binary inversion. Even more important, it is by means of this system of cruciform interrelationship that the sub-sequence characteristically (again not always, but often enough) characterizes the person of its poet.

So frequently and so casually does it happen that the young man's poet is placed at the "interventive" center of his "bifold" identifications that it seems an almost natural extension of familiar Petrarchist procedure, a simple repetition of oxymoron, or of Petrarch's "I steal myself away from myself," or of Sidney's "I am not I." But the device, along with its personalizing deployment, is specifically Shakespearean. The young man sonnets regularly halve and double what are taken to be traditional dual unities, and they do so in order then to place the poet at the intersection of the four terms thus produced, between both the two halves of the four *and* between the division of each half. No doubt this represents a peculiarly double and divided place for the poet to be located, and a peculiarly limited place as well. But this is precisely the point: it is this peculiarity, recognized and felt as such, that individuates the young man's poet and distinguishes him from traditional sonneteering personae. For all its peculiarity, and for all its limitations, this system of four-term chiasmic disjunction defines and determines a specific and particular place of subjectivity in the young man sonnets, one whose psychological and poetic exigencies are strictly coordinated and constrained by the form, themes, images, with which it is repeatedly introduced. And this criss-crossed psychological space is no more complicatedly permuted, no more beyond a reader's literary ken, than is the dramatic space traced out, for example, by the doubled pairs of twins in *The Comedy of Errors,* or the mixed up pairs of paired lovers in *Two Gentlemen of Verona* or in *A Midsummer Night's Dream,* or the four pairs of lovers in *Love's Labor's Lost* (itself perhaps counter-balanced by the lost *Love's Labor's Won*)—to refer in passing only to a few plays, but plays that are roughly contemporaneous with the composition of Shakespeare's sonnets, and plays whose considerably less obvious affinities with the sonnets have often been remarked. So too in these plays we also find, as central theme, the paradox of sonneteering praise.

It is no accident, therefore, that other coupled "present-absent" sonnets in the series addressed to the young man are structurally as well as thematically related to sonnets 44 and 45. In sonnet 50, for example, the poet makes a painfully slow and "heavy" "journey" away from the young man and toward his "weary travel's end." In the next sonnet, backtracking, repairing himself to his beginning, the poet imagines how, "mounted on the wind," or on his "desire," he will sometime return to the young man with such a swift and paradoxically "winged speed [that] no motion shall I know." More than the repetition of key words sounded by sonnets 44 and 45 ("heavy," "woe," "slow," "dull," "return," "swift," "fire-y," "desire"), what strikes a reader in sonnets 50 and 51, again taking the poems either individually or together, is the way the poet, whether he is quick or slow, is neither fully present to nor fully absent from the young man. Instead, the poet is caught up or arrested in the middle of a more intermediary and interminable journey back and forth between a whence and thence, a structurally incessant journey within whose compass the poet neither departs nor arrives but only comes and goes to no beginning and no end. Thus the irresolute conclusion of the first sonnet— "My grief lies onward and my joy behind"—is unpacked and confirmed by the pun on "going" in the couplet of the second, where "desire" and "will," "doubly seconded," to use Ulysses's phrases, "meet in mere oppugnancy" (*TC*, 1.3.122, 110–11): "Since from thee going he went willful-slow,/Towards thee I'll run, and give him leave to go" (51). In both poems, too, affective personal climax is signaled by chiasmic inversions, syntactic and semantic, whose self-denials repeat the logically reciprocal disjunctions of "But ah, thought kills me that I am not thought," as in sonnet 50, where the poet reflexively "spurs" his "mind" by spurring his "dull" and "heavy" horse, or as in the well-known editorial puzzle of sonnet 51: "Therefore desire (of perfect'st love being made)/Shall neigh (no dull flesh) in his fiery race,/But love, for love, thus shall excuse my jade."

Taking another paired example, in sonnets 97 and 98 the four elements of sonnets 44 and 45 reappear as the four seasons of the year. Once again, however, this fourfold scheme serves only to place the poet in the middle of a rectilinear confusion. Thus, on the one hand, "How like a winter hath my absence been" (97), and yet, "And yet this time remov'd was summer's time,/The teeming autumn, big with rich increase" (97). On the other, "From you I have been absent in the spring," and yet, "Yet seem'd it winter still, and, you away,/As with your shadow I with these did play" (98). Much the same occurs in another matching pair of sonnets, 27 and 28. Here the poet's sleepless dreaming anticipates the motionless "journey" of sonnets 50 and 51. In the first sonnet, the poet travels wearily by day away from the young man, and so, at night "begins a journey in my head/ To work my mind, when body's work's expired" (27). As a result, "by day my limbs, by night my mind,/For thee, and for myself, no quiet find" (27). In the second sonnet, night and day again "meet in mere oppugnancy," agreeing only on or in their "mutual render" (125) of the poet:

> When day's oppression is not eas'd by night,
> But day by night and night by day oppress'd;
> And each (though enemies to either's reign)
> Do in consent shake hands to torture me,
> The one by toil, the other to complain
> How far I toil, still farther off from thee.
>
> (28)

It is not only in such coupled pairs of sonnets, however, that we can sense the operation and subjective consequence of Shakespearean cross-coupling, though it is perhaps in these yoked pairs of sonnets that the cross of a chiastic scheme is most emphatically pointed up. In very obvious ways these sonnets that are paired together turn upon the re-turn of their binary conceits, as when the opening of sonnet 28—"How can I then return in happy plight/That am debarr'd the benefit of rest?"—makes a question of the conclusion to sonnet 27: "Lo thus by day my limbs, by night my mind,/For thee, and for myself, no quiet find." To this extent these sonnets are, perhaps, a little heavy-handed (some more so, of course, than others). But if they strike us so, this is not so much because they are anomalous Shakespearean sonnets, but, rather, because these sonnets, with their pairing and re-pairing, *too* graphically display or elaborate what is a more subtly manifest, yet nevertheless distinctive, formal feature of the young man sub-sequence as a whole. This is not to say that in all the poems addressed to the young man it always happens that unifying continuities become doubly discontinuous, or that traditional mediations are always rendered ambiguous and then opposed to, or interposed between, the two terms they conjoin. I have already spoken, for example, of the coupling of sonnets 46 and 47 where only a tonal playfulness complicates the sympathetic war and peace between the poet's eye and heart. It would certainly be possible to cite a good many other sonnets where the young man's poet develops familiar Petrarchist antitheses and syntheses in an apparently straightforward and complementary way—for example, sonnet 43, to take another "absence" sonnet, where the traditional association of imagination and dreaming leads to a traditional conclusion:

> When most I wink, then do mine eyes best see,
> For all the day they view things unrespected,
> But when I sleep, in dreams they look on thee,
> And darkly bright, are bright in dark directed.

For which ideal reason, the poet explains, "All days are nights to see till I see thee,/And nights bright days when dreams do show thee me."

Yet, though we can recognize the frequent appearance in the young man sonnets of such normatively intricate conceits, almost invariably even the most conventionally closed of Shakespeare's oxymoronic formulations are coded, both by their context and in themselves, with a formal reduplication that puts an edge on their most balanced resolutions. In sonnet 43, for example, it is not the use, but the overuse, of rhetorical devices of repetition—anadiplosis, antimetathesis, antistasis, epizeuxis, diacope, polyptoton—that "make[s] the language of the poem," as Stephen Booth puts it, "suggest mirror images," as in the first quatrain, which I have already quoted, or as in the second quatrain where all the Neo-Platonic resonances of "shadow" are put into play:

> Then thou, whose shadow shadows doth make bright,
> How would thy shadow's form happy show
> To the clear day with thy much clearer light,
> When to unseeing eyes thy shade shines so![13]

Booth is surely right to speak in this context about mirrors, as he does elsewhere when describing similar displays of euphuistic rhetoricity. So too Booth relevantly refers here to Renaissance theories of vision—where beams of light go in one eye and out the other—when he teases out of sonnet 43 its series of paradoxical ideas: "a poem that is a succession of paradoxes and reversals of the norm." Perhaps he is also right, at least to some extent, to say that the reader's confused responses to these reiterated reciprocities "make him a genuinely (though casually) engaged participant in the speaker's sudden desire for certainty, solidity, and a precise distinction between image and actual object."[14] The point to realize, however, is that this excess of rhetorical duplication, such as is developed in sonnet 43, not only clouds and obscures whatever mirroring or reciprocity it stylistically and thematically suggests, but, in addition, that this excess also becomes—that it presents itself *as*—the not at all confusing explanation of whatever confusions it concurrently provokes.

For it is not "reversals of the norm" that are unusual or confusing in a sonnet such as 43. Such reversals are the normative custom of Petrarchan wit, and the particular conceit developed in sonnet 43 is, in fact, a commonplace. Rather, what is striking and novel in sonnet 43, and what is characteristically Shakespearean about the effect of the poem, is the way these reversals are parodically foregrounded so that our appreciation of their exaggeration controls and also clarifies our reading of the poem's antitheses and complementarities. It is because "Then thou, whose shadow shadows doth make bright" ostentatiously invites a double reading that we, in fact, read the poem one way and not another. On the one hand, such displayed duplicity is what protects us from overreading the poem, for it is because sonnet 43 thus deliberately overstylizes its Petrarchist style and overthematizes its conventionally oxymoronic themes that we do not really read the poem as a solemn inquiry into optical epistemology. This is why sonnet 43, *as* we read through it, does not really raise for a reader, at least not in any serious way, a question about the "precise distinction between image and actual object." On the other hand, this is also what prevents us from underreading the poem, for it is only because we, in fact, register this unexpressed rhetorical excess that we are prepared to see the poem undo, if only very delicately, its own explicitly articulated black and white assumptions. This is why, for example, we do not overlook the shading on the young man's double shadow, or the way it is a "fair imperfect shade" that mediates in an ambiguously novel fashion between the poet's more familiarly antithetical "living day" and "dead night":

How would (I say) mine eyes be blessed made
By looking on thee in the living day,
When in dead night thy fair imperfect shade
Through heavy sleep on sightless eyes doth stay!
(43)

There is no need to make the wit of sonnet 43 be anything more than witty. I do not mean to suggest that with its "imperfect" sonnet 43 either intends or accomplishes a strong subversion of its visionary themes. There are, after all, a good many perfectly orthodox, Neo-Platonic ways to explain "imperfect" besides purely pejorative ones. So too both the movement and the conclusion of the poem make fairly clear just what the poet wants. Yet, in the context, precisely because the poem predicates itself on a strategy of neat and comprehensive reversal, there is in the final line of the sonnet a noticeably troubling and irreducible uncertainty, an unambiguous ambiguity, as to just whose dreams are showing whom to whom, "me" to "thee" or "thee" to "me": "All days are nights to see till I see thee,/ And nights bright days when dreams do *show thee me.*"[15] And it is precisely this kind of invidious ambiguity, an ambiguity that is somehow more tellingly and disturbingly effective than any produced by more obvious Petrarchist structures of sympathetic and antipathetic complementarity, that characteristically inflects even those young man sonnets that seem most deliberately determined to see the similarity between comparative dissimilars.

The device that I have called cross-coupling in part explains, though only in a very formal way, why and how it happens in the young man sub-sequence that we so often come upon this kind of distortion nestled within what are on the face of it apparently straightforward comparisons. By means of a chiastic doubling of unified doubles, the young man's poet regularly insinuates a problematic difference into his most ideal identifications. We grow accustomed to a kind of rhetorical mirroring of traditional visual imagery of unity, a mirroring that pervades the poems in the sequence, and that establishes a distinctive and discriminating screen or film or lens through which both the poet's compliments and his complements are regularly filtered. This is something we also assimilate to the relationship the poet develops between himself and his young man, and, as a result, we tend always to see the poet—or at least we are always prepared to see the poet—somewhere between himself and his ideal image of himself, doubly projected to or onto a place between a subject who is joined to, and disjoined from, his corresponding object.

This is why the concluding ambiguity of sonnet 39, which I took as epigraph for this chapter, comes as no surprise or, rather, this is why we are not totally puzzled by a "him" that refers either to the poet or to the young man, or by a "here" that refers indifferently to "there." These are specifically deictic and epideictic confusions in the tradition of the sonnet; these confusions, however, are novel not because they render opposites coincidental, but, instead, because they do *not* presuppose the unity of two: "And that thou teachest how to make one twain,/By praising him here who doth hence remain" (39). In this way, with this specifically double perspective, the young man sonnets locate for their poet a determinate place of first-person indeterminacy. This is how and where the poet "hence remains," almost as arithmetic "remainder," after he subtracts from praise its paradoxical reduplication.

To specify this place is not to ignore the variety of the poet's epideictic postures and rhetorical devices. Instead, it is a way of recognizing, as does the poet himself, how they derive from the general situation of divisively reflective visual duality within which, either as poet or as lover, the poet consistently finds himself. Like the elusive "purblind hare" in *Venus and Adonis*—to take another Shakespearean example, one that is contemporary with the sonnets, but one that Shakespeare seems purposefully to develop in a comic and absurd mode—the young man's poet "cranks and crosses with a thousand doubles" (682). As it does for the rabbit, this cranking and crossing determines for the poet a specific zig-zag path between "the many musits through the which he goes" (683). Repeatedly, therefore, though with a higher dictional decorum than that accorded the rabbit, we "see the dew-bedabbled wretch/Turn, and return, indenting with the way" (703–4). But it is precisely this poised and frozen back-and-forth movement—"like a labyrinth to amaze his foes" (684), says the narrator of *Venus and Adonis*—that formally organizes the relationship of the poet to the young man, and that links the young man sonnets each to each. This is what makes the sonnets in the young man sub-sequence, for all the local differences of tone and theme between them, seem the expression of a single, albeit a doubled and divided, epideictic point of view.

A formal organization certainly, but it should be recognized that, at least in the terms I have so far developed, this organization is only and merely formal. The deictic features to which I have referred throughout this chapter, the slippage between "I" and "you," or the disjunctive elision between pointer and pointed, or the fractured identification of identification, or the unconventional refraction that the young man sonnets derive from otherwise conventionally reflexive reflection—all this does not speak to the *stuff,* the content, the phenomenal experience, of the poet's subjective predicament even if it outlines its shape. We are still left, therefore, with what are obvious questions. Why should such a cross-coupling poetic form possess literary force? More precisely, why should a chiastic personality such as has been formally described possess, as the historical response to Shakespeare's sonnets suggests that it does to an extreme degree, a particularly powerful literary authority? It was to answer just these questions that I spoke earlier of the phenomenology of praise, i.e., of the particular materiality, as well as of the rhetoricity, that is traditionally embedded, described, and developed in epideictic poetics. What I want to consider in the next chapter is the way this traditional materiality is itself cross-coupled in both the young man sonnets and the dark lady sonnets. It is because cross-coupling is *phenomenally* assimilated to the poet's self that the paradoxical subject of Shakespeare's sonnets has behind it, or in it, as an "after-loss" (90), not only the logic but also the very physicality of the poetry of praise. It is by cross-coupling this traditional epideictic phenomenality *in himself* that the poet psychologically *materializes* the self that speaks the paradox of praise.

Again, it is only in a very formal way that sonnets 44 and 45 show how their poet might simultaneously be composed of and decomposed by the chiasmic interrelationship of his four constitutive elements. And for this reason—because it is only very indirectly that the young man's poet might be properly described as the concatenated mix-up of earth, air, fire, and water—sonnets 44 and 45 do not really seem profound or powerful exercises in poetic introspection. It is quite a different matter, however, when the poet fleshes out chiasmic form by cross-coupling the great and master images and imagery of epideictic poetics, for then his poetic subjectivity acquires a density that seems authentic because backed up not only by the entire tradition of the sonnet, but, to the extent that poetry is traditionally identified with the poetry of praise, by the entire tradition of poetry itself. Certainly the poet is no chiastic compost of earth, air, fire, and water. But the poet who "suffer[s]" "th' imprison'd absence of your liberty" (58) will properly see himself reflected in "a liquid prisoner pent in walls of glass" (5). This, I want to argue, is how it *feels* to be the subject of chiasmus, to be subjected *to* chiasmus, and this feeling extends both to the spatial and to the temporal existence of a poet whose admiration is articulated in and by the paradox of praise. This feeling is what I want now to discuss, for it will lead in a more pointed and textured way than do sonnets 44 and 45 both to the "substance" of the poet's "flesh" and to the incarnate object and subject not only of "my thought" but also of "my desire."

·5·

Think all but one, and me in that one Will
(Sonnet 135)

I have so far argued that Shakespeare's sonnets reduplicate, in various ways, the dual unities of traditional epideictic poetry. Taken as a whole, Shakespeare's sonnets repeat, but with a distancing difference, the sameness that is regularly featured and foregrounded by the themes, the imagery, and the poetic devices of the poetry of praise. The young man sonnets do it implicitly and the dark lady sonnets do it explicitly, and this alternately implicit and explicit differential repetition accounts, on the one hand, for the way the two sub-sequences differ from the orthodox and conventional Renaissance sonnet as it develops from Dante to and through the Elizabethan sonnet-sequence vogue, and, on the other hand, for the way in which the two sub-sequences differ from each other.

To summarize what I have said so far, the young man sonnets seem estranged from the laudatory sentiments they assert primarily because they code these sentiments with formal and conceptual duplications that add an equivocating disjunction to the conventional univocities and complementarities of Petrarchan admiration. Thus, for example, though the young man sonnets say that "one thing expressing, leaves out difference" (105), they say this in an ambiguous way, with the result that "one thing expressing," even as it is spoken, seems, to some extent, duplicitous, just as "difference," even left unspoken, does not seem entirely "left out." In turn, in consequence, but also, to a considerable degree, in contrast, the dark lady sonnets are also estranged from the poetry of praise, but they are so in a more definitive and less ambiguous way. The dark lady sonnets share many of the features of the young man sonnets—they employ, for example, similar cross-coupling conceits and similarly stress chiasmic diction—but, in addition, the dark lady sonnets put directly into words a set of suspicions that are only suggested by the tonal and formal reservations of the young man sonnets.

242

"Suspicion" is the right word here, for what is put into question in Shakespeare's sonnets is, truly *sub-spicere*, the ideality of a perennially visual language of admiration, i.e., the traditional language of epideictic display and self-display, a language that "shows" and "shows forth." The young man sonnets frequently raise and insinuate such suspicions, but they do so only obliquely, as when "the age to come would say, 'This poet lies' " (17), "if I could write the beauty of your eyes" (17). It is, however, in a quite different, because more positive, way that the dark lady sonnets speak against any idealization of the language that they speak. The dark lady sonnets differ from the young man sonnets because they articulate thematically the paradoxical duplicity of a language that is verbal, not visual, as when "when my love swears that she is made of truth,/I do believe her, though I know she lies" (138) or "mine eyes seeing this, say this is not" (137). I have argued, and in this chapter I want further to argue, that these explicit formulations amount to a significant and more than merely thematic innovation on the part of the dark lady sonnets. By voicing this theme, the dark lady sonnets manage *practically* to substitute for a language of true vision a language of true-false word. In the dark lady sonnets we hear the "languageness" of language, as I have called it, belie the ideality of language, and it does this *as* the poet speaks about his speech. As a result, as the consequence of a kind of mimic or second-degree Cratylism, the very speaking of the dark lady sonnets becomes performative "proof" of what they speak against. This is a claim that refers more to the rhetorical effect of the dark lady sonnets than to their logical argument, though rhetorical effect and logical argument are of course related to each other. Moreover, I have also argued, though so far only very generally, that this heterodox language that the dark lady sonnets literally "invoke" is more broadly assimilated in the dark lady sub-sequence both to the heterogeneity of the lady—as a person in herself, that she is simultaneously fair and unfair, that she is simultaneously true and false—and to the poet's disjunctive, heterogeneous, heterosexual relation to the lady—the way "that thy unkindness lays upon my heart" (139). The large claim that all of these subordinate claims lead to is that this produces an unusual, but, in the literature successive to Shakespeare's sonnets, a subsequently governing, poetic first person.

Recognizing both the connection and the difference between the young man sonnets' suspicious implications and the dark lady sonnets' more straightforward, and, as I will want to show, more *realized* explications, it becomes possible to understand how the conflicted tonalities of the young man sonnets prepare for, even though the young man sonnets do not enunciate, the novel sonneteering themes that are developed in the sonnets addressed to the lady, the lady who is presented in the sonnets to and about her as a species of the nonspecies, as a "kind" that is "unkind." Where the young man sonnets circumspectly hint that the young man is more than simply less than ideal—"So are those errors that in thee are seen/To truths translated, and for true things deem'd" (96)—the dark lady's poet instead expressly speaks about the way the lady "make[s] me give the lie to my true sight" (150). Where the young man's poet finds it difficult uncomplicatedly to admire that which he desires—"Some say thy fault is youth" (96)—the dark lady's poet directly says, though with dismay, that he desires something he does not admire: "If thy unworthiness rais'd love in me,/More worthy I to be belov'd of thee" (150).

In both sub-sequences such revisionary recapitulations, formal and thematic, implicit and explicit, of an idealizing poetics are directly related by the poet to literary history, to the poet's sense that he now writes his sonnets in the aftermath of praise. Thus the young man's poet wonders "what the old world could say/To this composed wonder of your frame" (59), and thus the dark lady's poet introduces the novelty of his "now" by remembering how "in the old age black was not counted fair" (127). In this way, in both sub-sequences, the poet's reservations with regard to the poetry of praise, as also the reduplications through which he develops them, are associated with the poet's feeling that he both can and cannot do much more than once again repeat the praise that comes before him. This sense of literary belatedness, of poetic secondariness, of literary repetition—all these qualities being somewhat different but connected by the poet to one another—becomes the poet's explanation of why his laboring "invention" bears, in a novel way, "the second burthen of a former child" (59). Moreover, even when Shakespeare's sonnets do not expressly refer to their literary antecedents and precursors, they nevertheless presuppose and play themselves off against sonneteering conventions of such massive familiarity that they invite their reader to situate them within the context of specifically literary, laudatory commonplaces. Again, however, this invitation is no sooner tendered by Shakespeare's sonnets than it is revoked, and this because these sonnets characteristically give an unexpected turn to the literary expectations they provoke.

Such refiguring of what is epideictically prefigured affects Shakespeare's sonnet sequence from the very beginning, from "From fairest creatures we desire increase" (1). At the epiphanic, epideictic end
of the *Paradiso*, Dante, turning with the turning universe, sees himself
or his *effige* in his vision of "eternal light." As I have argued, this
amounts to a kind of paradigm of the central images, motifs, conceits,
and lyric postures of the laudatory sonnet as it develops toward
Shakespeare. In this way, I said, the end of the *Paradiso* not only objectifies but also "subjectifies" the phenomeno-logy of epideictic rhetoricity, fleshing out with the being of poetic person the kind of language that a praising poet speaks. In contrast, as though beginning
where the *Commedia* ends, Shakespeare's sonnet sequence opens
with its peculiarly anonymous blazon of a young man who:

> contracted to thine own bright eyes,
> Feed'st thy light's flame with self-substantial fuel,
> Making a famine where abundance lies,
> Thyself thy foe, to thy sweet self too cruel.
>
> (1)

In a sense, at first sight, this self-contracted, self-substantial "light"
of the young man repeats Dante's vision of the "light eternal, that
alone knowest Thyself, and, known to Thyself and knowing, lovest,
and smilest on Thyself!" But where for Dante this displays the solipsistic yet expansive plenitude of God, the young man's poet sees
instead in this the self-depleting, narcissistic mechanism of "making
a famine where abundance lies." Where for Dante the circularity of
light offers itself as the only adequate image with which to imagine
(through the poet's "high fantasy," *alta fantasia*) the way God's immanent reflection returns fully back upon Himself, the young man's
poet instead employs this image to show a self disrupted and disjointed *in* itself: "Thyself thy foe, to thy sweet self too cruel." Where
Dante's light is centrifugally replete, the young man is instead claus-
trophobically "contracted to thine own bright eyes."

This difference—the difference between, on the one hand, the
image of divine self-containment as it is figured by traditional poetics, and, on the other, the image of narcissistic self-absorbtion as it
is figured by the young man—determines in the opening sonnet the
self-expending economy that "mak'st waste in niggarding" as well as
the self-consuming appetite of a "glutton" who, and this is a common Shakespearean motif, eats himself up. As the first sonnet develops them, such paradoxes of self-contradiction and compacted

division are no more strained or bewildering than are the corresponding orthodox paradoxes of Christian and Neo-Platonic self-
fulfillment and unity to which the first sonnet in this way implicitly
refers. Indeed, it is only because we are so familiar with, and accustomed to, a poetic tradition in which the ideal reflexively reflects
upon itself that, even before we read the opening sonnet, we are
prepared for the logic of what amounts to that tradition's daemonic
parody. And yet, though this opening sonnet is not purely praise,
neither is it purely blame. Instead, because the young man first
emerges as the simulacrum of the ideal, because he is introduced as
a kind of perverse citation or askew quotation of the tradition of the
ideal, it is difficult easily to distinguish the young man from the ideality that his narcissism both mimics and displaces rather than
straightforwardly opposes.

This difficulty is built into the diction of the poem. Thus the first
sonnet begins by describing how the young man's "tender heir," the
procreated repetition of himself, "might bear his memory." It concludes with a description of the way the young man, as a "tender
chorl," will fruitlessly dilate upon himself. The relationship of "tender heir" to "tender chorl" is not a simple relationship of antithetical
alterity. "Tender chorl," the oxymoron to which the sonnet builds,
continues to bear the memory of the ideal "tender heir" that it sub-
lates, just as the sonnet as a whole remembers from a distance the
tradition of ideal poetics it succeeds. We might say that as "tender
chorl" is to "tender heir," so is the opening of Shakespeare's sonnet
sequence to Dante's conclusion, and to all that such a Dantesque
vision might imagine that it sees. This would account for the ambiguous tonality that colors the entirety of the sonnet. For the young
man is not presented as an altogether disappointing contrast to the
ideal he is not. Contracted to his own self-image, the young man
seems a clear-cut instance of the selfishness of self. Even so, his eyes
are nevertheless described as "bright." Though he is cruel foe to his
sweet self, the young man nevertheless remains one of those "fairest
creatures" from whom "we desire increase." Putting the point perhaps too simply, it seems clear that, whatever his flaws, and critics
have rushed to list them, the young man is in fact a perfect beauty
and to this extent deserves a real respect.

This is the complexity that both the young man and the sonnets
addressed to him share. As oxymoronic "tender chorl," but in the
connotative field of "tender heir," the young man is just as much a
version of the ideal as he is its equally clear-cut subversion. Tender

and churlish, the young man is the very image of the ideal at the same time as he is its invidious, self-canceling example. Only by appreciating this double articulation is it possible to see how the young man, *as* a repetition, bears and yet inflects the burden of his literary history, the way in which, on the one hand, with his narcissism the young man duplicates the appearance of an ideal that is always the same as itself, and yet, on the other, precisely because he thus perfectly duplicates eternal unity, the young man therefore seems to his poet something which, or someone who, is ephemeral, divided, and imperfect. In the sonnets that immediately follow the first sonnet this excess of likeness, this unhappy replication of the young man's repetition, will be the blight in Shakespeare's sonneteering garden that makes the flowers of an ideal poetics into "a totter'd weed" (2), or into "lusty leaves quite gone" (5), or into "the violet past prime" (12). But even here, at the very opening of the sequence, there is a sense that, finally, there is *too much* of a likeness between, on the one hand, the eternally self-perpetuating, memorial multiplications of "beauty's rose" and, on the other, the suicidal self-division of a flower that, not even fully born, "within thine own bud buriest thy content" (1).

I want to insist upon the young man's initial and vestigial filiation with the ideal—upon the way the "tender chorl" bears the memory of the "tender heir" who is supposed to "bear his memory"— because this is how the first sonnet insinuates a principle of self-difference into the most orthodox conception of ideal and homogeneous self-adequation. Because the young man "within thine own bud buriest thy content" (1), he appears both to repeat and to revise, but to revise *because* he repeats, the autocircularity with which divine fullness perennially unfolds itself back on itself. Turning himself upon himself, the young man describes a vicious introspective circle within whose circumference he is fixed and enclosed, making him, as the first sonnet puts it, "thyself thy foe, to thy sweet self too cruel." In this way the circuitous fracture or self-division of the young man, the very self-regard that makes him foe to himself, opens up by implosion a heterogeneous internality in the heart of the ideal, an unlocalizable *inside* that resides within the very "desire" for "increase," an inside that disrupts the smooth internal complexion of homogeneous interiority, a wrinkle, literally a "crease," *within* the sonnet's logic of "increase." In the diction of the poem, this heterogeneity, this kernel of difference that comes to inhabit the self-substantiality of the sonnet's image of perpetual self-sameness, may be as small as, as delicately nuanced as, the indecorous discrepancy we register when the first sonnet tells us that "the world's fresh ornament" is now the "only herald to the gaudy spring." But this difference that the first sonnet thus articulates within the idea of the ideal is sufficient to set in circulation the economy of self-expense that "mak'st waste in niggarding," or to generate the self-mortifying appetite with which the young man both eats and owes a debt which is both himself and "the world's due."

I am concerned with the place of this difference *within* the commonplace of reflexive reflection. Turning upon himself, looking himself in his own eye and I, the young man discovers the death that "within thine own bud buriest thy content" (1). This "within" describes the same recessed and invert site and sight wherein, in sonnet 2, the young man's "beauty" and his "treasure" "lies": there "within thine own deep-sunken eyes," there as an "all-eating shame" and "thriftless praise." It is no exaggeration to say that this "within," this circumscribed bisection of the self-contained, traces out the "depths" of all the sonnets addressed to the young man, spreading itself out as a kind of striated, interior hollowness that is composed of liquid depths of sunken eyes. It is, for example, this same back and forth "within" that is introduced *into* the poet when "thy gifts, thy tables, are within my brain" (122). So too it is this same chiasmicized "withinness" that governs the poet's present-absent, hither-thither relationship to the young man, as in:

> Thee have I not lock'd up in any chest,
> Save where thou art not, though I feel thou art,
> Within the gentle closure of my breast,
> From whence at pleasure thou mayst come and part.
> (48)

So too it is this same "within" that fractures the poet and makes him foe to his own sweet introspective self, as in:

> Against that time do I insconce me here
> Within the knowledge of mine own desert,
> And this my hand against myself uprear,
> To guard the lawful reasons on thy part.
> (49)

Finally, it is with this "within" that the young man's poet problematizes the exemplary tradition of the poetry of praise, so that the merely epideictic poet—the poet whose comparisons would say

more than "you alone are you" (84), or who seeks to find "example
where your equal grew" (84)—will only write the hollow, repetitious
writing of "Lean *penury within* that *pen* doth dwell" (84). So too it is
this same "within" that the poet sees *in* the young man when he
looks at "the lovely gaze where every eye doth dwell" (5). The poet
identifies himself, spatially, temporally, but also, as will be seen,
sexually, with the material feel of this divided "withinness," with "a
liquid prisoner pent in walls of glass" (5). This is what the poet now
sees when he looks into "Ideas Mirrour": a dissolved liquidity
within a brittle hardness, this hourglass being, again, the very image of the passing of an ideal time.[1]

As I have said, the device that Puttenham calls "cross-coupling"
characterizes, but only formally, the way in which throughout the
sonnet sequence—obliquely in the young man sonnets, more
straightforwardly in the dark lady sonnets—traditional epideictic
tropes and conceits of identificatory comparison are distorted and
displaced when they are mirrored by their own likeness. This is most
obviously the case in those explicitly coupled pairs of sonnets I discussed in the preceding chapter (such as 27 and 28, 44 and 45, 50 and
51, 97 and 98), where large-scale binary conceits combine in accord
with a logic of double complementarity that is neither purely sympathetic nor purely antipathetic. Much the same happens, however,
in individual sonnets as well. Sometimes, for example, a sonnet will
question a preconceived dual unity by drawing its premises out to a
stressedly equivocal conclusion, as in sonnet 39, where the poet
learns "how to make one twain,/By praising him here who doth
hence remain!" Elsewhere, a sonnet's sestet will turn by inverting
the assumptions of its octave's opening conceit, as in sonnet 43,
where the poet's "days are nights" "and nights bright days," and yet,
for all this familiar oxymoronic yoking, it is only ambiguously that
the poet's "dreams do show thee me." Much the same thing also
occurs at the microlevel of the single line, or phrase, or word, as in
the vitiating, punning identity proposed by "thou art all my art"
(78), or as in sonnet 111, where the poet, "like a willing patient,"
"drink[s]/Potions of eisel 'gainst my strong infection," and where
this poison-remedy pharmacology prescribes the cognate accusa-
tive syntax of: "No bitterness that I will bitter think,/Nor double
penance, to correct correction."

As I have argued, this formal or stylistic doubling of unified doubles, this extra twist or fold applied to a traditional analogizing poetics of identificatory trope and conceit—this heteropathic homeop-

athy, to use the medicinal imagery of sonnet 111—is sufficiently habitual and frequent in the sonnets as to allow us to call it a distinctively Shakespearean feature. To a considerable extent, it is this formal feature that helps give to Shakespeare's sonnets, to the young man sonnets especially, their peculiarly nostalgic and elegaic atmosphere or mood, with the poems, both individually and collectively, continually calling up and deploying a poetics of ideal unity only so as to distance themselves from that ideal at the very moment and in the very way that they repeat it. So too this is how, from the very beginning of the sequence, we see the poet yearningly situated with respect to an ideal that is placed beyond his reach precisely because it is put before his eyes. Perhaps the best example of all is the fragility of the claim that "love is not love/Which alters when it alteration finds,/Or bends with the remover to remove" (116), the tremulous tonality of the "ever-fixed mark/That looks on tempests and is never shaken" (116).[2] What the example of "withinness" suggests, however, is that it is not only through their themes and through their formal stylistic devices that these poems present themselves as untraditionally traditional. In addition, there is a specific *materiality* that complements the way the young man sonnets break the poetics of ideal complementarity. On the one hand, from the very beginning of the sequence, the poet's diction and his broadest concerns recall traditional epideictic assumptions, themes, motifs, but, on the other, they do so in a noticeably odd and an eccentric way. In a similar fashion, the images employed in these sonnets recall traditional epideictic things, but they do so in such an odd and eccentric way that these apparently familiar images become themselves, in their very phenomenality, examples of the way the artifacts of praise no longer are the same.

This is most clearly apparent in the imagery used to develop the initial procreation argument, an argument that is thematically unprecedented in the genre of the sonnet sequence, but that is nevertheless both like and unlike all that comes before. Thus the poet's young man is supposed to be the model of the ideal, with all the force and resonance that "model" carries in an idealist metaphysics. The young man is the exemplar, the form, the type, the *eidos*, the "kind," of all subsidiary virtues. Rather, he is the exemplar of all exemplifications, the Form of forms, the Type of types, the very Idea of the ideal. The Neo-Platonic presuppositions at stake in such a conception are clear enough, and it would be possible to cite innumerable sonneteering parallels to the way the young man, as beloved, is "the pattern of all those" "figures of delight" (98) or to the way he is "beauty's pattern to succeeding men" (19).[3] Despite the peculiarity of his gender, therefore, the young man is presented in an immediately recognizable literary context. Like a Beatrice or a Laura or a Stella, the young man stands, or is supposed to stand, both for a singularly perfect nature and for the yet more total perfection of the Nature of nature. As "beauty's rose" (1) he represents not only the particular token and the general type of ideality, but, also, at the same time, the harmoniously organic way these are related to each other. The eternizing themes of the procreation argument—which, outside the conventions of the amatory sonnet, are old themes, going back at least to Cicero—translate this familiar ontology into the terms of what is an equally familiar biology, fleshing out a half-Platonic and half-Aristotelian categorial logic of genera and species by referring it to, or exampling it with, the reproductive generations of replicating human kind, each generation repeating the generation it succeeds. In a straightforward way, therefore, the opening young man sonnets stress the familial likeness of "like father, like son" by reapplying well-known conceits of ideal likeness, of "Ideas Mirrour." And it is easy for them to do so, for it is a metaphysical as well as a physical imperative that "your sweet issue your sweet form should bear" (13).

Perhaps this was the only way that Shakespeare could have so readily adapted the heterosexual tradition of the Petrarchist sonnet to the exigencies of poetic address to a man. Or perhaps, as has been suggested by several critics, Shakespeare really was commissioned to exhort a patron's son to marriage, and he therefore seized upon the procreation theme as a uniquely appropriate sonneteering means with which to accomplish such a serviceable end. Whatever the reason, it remains the case that it is only because there is so perfect a fit between the metaphysics of resemblance, as developed by traditional poetics, and the physiology of resemblance, as developed by traditional biology, that the poet's arguments for procreation carry any literary weight at all. Only in such an idealist context can we understand how the young man's young man initiates what is to be the eternal repetition of the young man's sameness. Only in the context of the kind of idealism for which time is "the moving image of eternity," as Plato describes it in the *Timaeus*, does the young man's progeny become the temporal unfolding of the young man's timeless permanence. Only if we grant the unitary arithmetic of idealism does it make sense that the young man, multiplying himself after his own kind, will father the "many" that will prove him "One." And only if we accept the tidy categoriality of genus and species will we understand how the young man spawns a series of particulars whose lineal succession embodies the young man's universality: "Proving his beauty by succession thine" (2).

And, as I have said, as with the characterization of progeny, so with the characterization of poetry. By comparing his own epideictic verse to the young man's procreated issue the poet is able to modulate in the opening sonnets from advising the young man "to breed another thee" (6), who will "leave thee living in posterity," to boasting instead about the way "my love shall in my verse ever live young" (19). To be sure, the explicit relationship developed between poetry and progeny varies in the course of the series, so that sometimes poetry and progeny are opposed to each other, as in sonnet 16, where "my barren rhyme" is unflatteringly compared to "your living flowers," whereas elsewhere—this is the more frequent case—the two are instead identified with each other, as in sonnet 17: "But were some child of yours alive that time, / You should live twice, in it and in my rhyme." Quite apart from these explicit comments, however, there is from the beginning of the procreation series, which is the beginning of the sequence as a whole, a consistent and an insistent figural equating of the poet's verse with the young man's "succession," the effect of which is that we readily think of the one as the example of the other. Thus the young man's young man is an immortalizing flower, as, for example, the issue of the ever-renewable "beauty's rose" of sonnet 1, or he is the alternative to the "totter'd weed" of sonnet 2, or he is "flowers distill'd" in sonnet 5, and all of this floral imagery prepares us for the way the gardening poet, speaking about his poetry, will subsequently say: "And all in war with Time for love of you, / As he takes from you, I ingraft you new" (15). Similarly, to take the visual image which I have most discussed, the young man's young man is his father's vivifying image, as in "die single, and thine image dies with thee" (3), so that later poetry itself can become the young man's animating mirror, as in: "So long as men can breathe or eyes can see, / So long lives this, and this gives life to thee" (18).

It is this kind of reiterated figural sympathy between poetry and progeny that enables the poet progressively to substitute the latter for the former. Indeed, as I have said, if it is too much to say that in the course of the series the poet becomes a version of "'this fair child of mine'" (2), it is certainly the case that the poet's "I" grows increasingly more present to the poems of procreation in direct proportion to the way the series is less and less thematically concerned with progeny and more and more self-consciously concerned with its own literariness. By the end of the procreation sequence, progeny, as a theme, is forgotten almost entirely, and it is in an almost aggressively resentful way that the poet replaces the childish immortality of the young man's issue with his own more adult, literary memorial—for example, the way "thy mother's glass" in sonnet 3, who "through windows of thine age shalt see,/Despite of wrinkles, this thy golden time," becomes instead:

> O, let me, true in love, but truly write,
> And then believe me, my love is as fair
> As any mother's child, though not so bright
> As those gold candles fix'd in heaven's air.
> (21)

To the extent that a reader registers it, this tension between poetry and progeny is significant, for it leads the reader to rethink the poet's originally disinterested interest in the young man's "succession." Visual images appear to generate the emulating "envy" of *invidere*, and there is something stagily and vexingly premeditated in the way the sequence announces that poetry eventually does better what fathering initially did best. Yet even such *ressentiment* bespeaks the fundamental likeness of progeny and poetry. In both cases, poetical and genealogical, we are given an *imitating* similitude that is true to what it copies—"your sweet semblance to some other give" (13)—and, at the same time, a figural *simile* that truly multiplies that which it repeats:

> That's for thyself to breed another thee,
> Or ten times happier be it ten for one;
> Ten times thyself were happier than thou art,
> If ten of thine ten times refigur'd thee.
> (6)

In the context the point, perhaps, is obvious. But if the procreation series repeatedly insists upon the fact that "'this fair child'" (2) is the profitable alternative to "thriftless praise" (2), this is because the poet sees in the conventional biology of "like father, like son" the unitary, twofold likeness that informs both the conventional laudatory mimesis that will "copy what in you is writ" (84) and the conventional laudatory metaphoricity that will "make a couplement of proud compare" (21).

From the very beginning, therefore, the unity or reciprocity or, as I have characterized it, the likeness of these two kinds of likenesses, mimetic and metaphoric, defines the poet's most directly stated concern, and defines it, moreover, as something epideictic. Both figuratively and literally this is the developed meaning of the "increase" that the very first line of the very first sonnet tells us "from fairest creatures we desire." The young man's "increase" is precisely the young man's "amplification," where amplification is understood to be the panegyric "heightening" of the mimetic by the metaphoric, of the similitude by the simile, of the mere imitation by the ornamental comparison. All the imagery of the procreation series carries with it this familiar epideictic assumption that there is a mutually confirming complementarity between, or a vivifying sympathy subtending, these two quite different likenesses. Thus the perennial flowers of the procreation series are all a species of the courtly, heliotropic marigold whose twofold miming of the eye of the sun—"as the marigold at the sun's eye" (25)—joins verisimilar imitation to animated troping. Similarly, the imagery of vision in the series—"Look in thy glass and tell the face thou viewest,/Now is the time that face should form another" (3)—advances a conventional logic of simulating admiration whose reflexive reflections make the young man's "image" (3) the figurative equivalent both of the biology and of the poetics of "fresh repair" (3). So too the usury imagery—"that use is not forbidden usury" (6)— along with the accompanying imagery of remunerative investment— to "sum my count" (2), "a sum of sums" (4), "acceptable audit" (4), to "pay the willing loan" (6)—assumes the same profitable replication of kind by kind, the same surplus poetic value, that makes financial minting into a version of augmenting "printing": "She carv'd thee for her seal, and meant thereby,/Thou shouldst print more, not let that copy die" (11).

It is, therefore, in a very obvious way that the poet's argument for procreation employs the same kind of conceptual reasoning presupposed by "'fair,' 'kind,' and 'true' is all my argument." In addition, it is in a very emphatic way that the poet in these opening sonnets applies the imagery of "increase" to progeny and poetry alike. Over and over, we are shown how a poetics of generic and homogeneous resemblance perfectly matches the young man's genealogical family of resemblance. Visually, florally, financially, to mention just a few of the major motifs, we see how the young man's young man copiously repeats and increases his father in the same epideictic way that the poet's copious verses are "to constancy confin'd" (105). It is, we should note, a specifically unified and unifying poetics, "to one, of one, still such, and ever so" (105), that is thus anticipated by the way the poet imagines the young man's "succession." The potentially infinite and transcendental sequence of descent that the young man is supposed to sire gives us in advance a living example of a panegyric poetics in which a series of multiple and multiplying similitudes all amount to, and mount up to, the same initial and originary unit, a poetics in which all variation is invariably, yet resplendently, an endless laudatory repetition of the same. Thus, speaking biologically: "Ten times thyself were happier than thou art,/If ten of thine ten times refigur'd thee" (6). But, speaking poetically, this is also the model for the multiple and serial literary way in which the young man is "the tenth Muse, ten times more in worth/Than those old nine which rhymers invocate" (38).

And yet, if the young man's procreation is in this way presented as a living version of the orthodox poetics of augmenting, unifying, eternizing praise, still this identification, between poetry and progeny, is at the same time thoroughly peculiar, both within the tradition of the sonnet and as it is developed by the young man's poet. Initially the procreation theme seems odd simply because it is unusual. "What man," as C. S. Lewis once wondered, "except a father or a potential father-in-law, cares whether any other man gets married?"[4] The answer to this question is that many kinds of men have done so, as we know from the fact that there is an enormous literature reaching back to antiquity in which they do so in serious and quite reasonable ways.[5] Lewis's otherwise ridiculous remark makes sense, however, to the extent that this kind of man and this kind of issue are not regular features of the Renaissance sonnet. The question Lewis asks points up the *generic* novelty attaching to Shakespeare's introduction of the theme.

But it is not simply because the procreation theme is generically unusual that it presents itself in these opening sonnets as something odd. Rather, what is peculiar about the procreation theme, as it is developed at the beginning of Shakespeare's sonnet sequence, is that, even though it is unprecedented in the sonnet tradition as a whole, it nevertheless turns out to lend itself to, and with a surprising and remarkable convenience, the elaboration and exemplification of familiar sonneteering conceits and motifs. As these opening sonnets handle it, the procreation theme seems so perfectly to instantiate and to accommodate itself to traditional sonneteering ideals that it is as though, without knowing it, this is what the sonnet form had been concerned with from the very beginning. This bizarre familiarity identifies what is odd about the procreation theme as it appears in Shakespeare's sonnets. Despite the fact that it is uncommon in Petrarchan poetry, the procreation theme is developed by Shakespeare as though it were a Petrarchan commonplace. It is presented as, so to speak, an unfamiliar poetic cliché, as but another, though an as yet unformulated, sonneteering banality, as, for example, the deliberately proverbial-sounding "From fairest creatures we desire increase,/ That thereby beauty's rose might never die" (1).

For the same reason, and in the same way, this is why it seems so weirdly appropriate that the poet in these opening sonnets addresses himself to a man, not to a woman. Developing conventional themes and imagery of ideal identification, the procreation sonnets give a strangely homosexual inflection to the traditional homogeneities of Petrarchan admiration (as in "That use is not forbidden usury" [6]—Dante puts usurers and homosexuals in the same circle of hell, on the grounds that they both attempt to generate an unproductive profit—"thriftless praise"—by coupling kind with kind).[6] Presented in this phlegmatic and unembarrassed way, it is as though homosexuality were the secret truth of all ideal and idealizing desire from Dante onwards. As a result, stripped in this defamiliarizing fashion to their bare essences and essentials, the familiar and kindly ideals of Petrarchan erotics, metaphysics, poetics end up displaying and praising a kind of lurid, even perverse, "sameness," as though this is what ideal *beatitudine* inevitably amounts to.

In itself, this uncanny propriety works to place these familiar ideals in a novel and somewhat alienating light. Correspondingly, however, because the poet's identificatory relation to the object of his desire is developed in terms of the young man and his procreated repetition, because the poet's identification with the young man is projected onto the young man's relation to his young man, the poet himself is effectively placed at one mediated remove from the idealized relation of dual unity that he says that he admires. On the one hand, therefore, with the procreation theme the poet develops a familiar and familial logic and imagery of ideal likeness and identification: "your sweet semblance to some other give" (13). At the same time, however, this is something from which the poet-lover, by the very logic of reproduction, is in principle excluded: "Make thee another self for love of me" (10). As a result, because the poet is neither the young man nor the young man's young man, the poet's procreation imagery manages to describe an Ideal and an *Ideas Mir-*

rour in which the poet does not see himself. Instead, what the poet sees in his traditionally visual imagery of the Same is nothing but the Other: "Look in thy glass and tell the face thou viewest,/Now is the time that face should form another" (3).

This is not an isolated example. In the young man sonnets, imagery of unity, sameness, likeness characteristically shows itself to the poet as an estranging dissonance, as an identity with which the poet cannot identify, as a sterile difference built into an otherwise fecund resemblance. Consider, for another example, the lute of sonnet 8, the lute in whose "true concord of well-tuned sounds,/By unions married," the young man is supposed to:

> Mark how one string, sweet husband to another,
> Strikes each in each by mutual ordering;
> Resembling sire, and child, and happy mother,
> Who all in one, one pleasing note do sing.

The first thing that is striking here is the uniformly homosexual, the oddly homogeneous and purely patriarchal, composition of a family in which "one string [is] sweet husband to another." On the one hand, the "mutual ordering" of the fruitful lute "resembles" the concordantly nuclear triangle of "sire, and child, and happy mother." On the other hand, however, this is a marriage of true minds that makes each one of these three—"sire, and child, and happy mother"—too much "resemble" one another. Because each string is "sweet husband to another," there is an excess of likeness in the "all in one" of the lute's "true concord." The result is a music whose harmonious "oneness" sounds like the doubled and claustrophobic "three themes in one, which wondrous scope affords" in sonnet 105. For just this reason, however, it is the very unity of the lute, precisely that which makes it "'fair,' 'kind,' and 'true,'" that leaves the reader wondering just what the poet means "by unions married."

Corresponding to the problematic "resemblance" of the lute in sonnet 8 is the refractory relation of the young man to the lute's "speechless song." For all the chordal reverberations of the sonnet's "mutual ordering," and with the entire tradition of Renaissance philosophy urging the young man to marry so as thereby to reiterate himself forever, the young man nevertheless maintains in sonnet 8, as he does throughout the procreation series, his obstinate and discordant singularity. This is a singularity that is both like and unlike the single, but still sympathetic, strings which "all in one, one pleasing note do sing." Married to his own oneness, yet divorced from

himself thereby—"die single, and thine image dies with thee" (3)—
the young man not only seems a counterexample to Renaissance
harmonics, but also manages to make its resonating musical vibra-
tions into something less than sympathetic.

For the young man is supposed to live in a world of proverbially
and perfectly complementary similitude, a world in which, as sonnet 8 puts it, "sweets with sweets war not, joy delights in joy." In
such a world it is supposed to go without saying that likeness goes
with likeness. And yet, in a way which is finally inexplicable in a
world of concord:

> the true concord of well-tuned sounds,
> By unions married, do offend thine ear,
> They do but sweetly chide thee, who confounds
> In singleness the parts that thou shouldst bear.

Given the empathetic assumptions of Renaissance aesthetics—
assumptions on which depends the privileged literary status of the
exemplifying, hortatory poetry of praise—how is it that "unions
married" also "sweetly chide thee," as though they were the auditory equivalent of an oxymoronic "tender chorl"? Alternatively, how
do they "offend thine ear"? Whence derives the young man's disso-
nant response to what is, after all, the music of the spheres? If
"sweets with sweets war not," and "joy delights in joy," how is it that
the young man both likes *and* dislikes that which is his likeness and
thus "confounds in singleness" the parts that he should bear?

Sonnet 8 begins with the poet himself raising just these questions, and in just these on-the-one-hand, on-the-other terms:

> Music to hear, why hear'st thou music sadly?
> Sweets with sweets war not, joy delights in joy.
> Why lov'st thou that which thou receiv'st not gladly,
> Or else receiv'st with pleasure thine annoy?

Phrased in this witty way, these are no doubt rhetorical questions to
which perhaps there is no need to give an answer. But if gladness
here can join with sadness (as they do in sonnet 45: "no longer glad
. . . and straight grow sad"), what happens to the logic, either poetical or biological, of resemblance and "mutual ordering"? The confusion here derives not from a simple but from a *double* oxymoron. The
young man "loves" the music of the lute because he receives it "not
gladly" and, at the same time, the music "annoys" him because he
receives it "with pleasure." Developed in this way, the lute, which is

a traditional image of poetry itself, becomes the instrument of a chi-asmic music which is the objective equivalent to the way the young man "confounds/In singleness the parts that thou shouldst bear."

No doubt it is *only* and uniquely the young man who can thus indifferently "receive with pleasure thine annoy" and "love . . . that which thou receiv'st not gladly," for it is only the young man who is "to thy sweet self too cruel" (1) and who can therefore argue with the force of "sweets with sweets war not" by attending to a music that works to "sweetly chide thee." But it is just this problem of unique "in-difference" that the young man and the lute pose to an epideictic poetics that resolutely resolves to "leave out difference" for the sake of copious amplification. The young man embodies a discordant unity that is not a *concordia discors*; he is a "one" whose singularity "confounds/In singleness" the harmonious collation of the "many" and the "one." And so too does the lute itself, whose sounding and whose moral both belie each other, "whose speechless song," as the couplet to sonnet 8 has it, "being many, seeming one,/Sings this to thee, 'Thou single wilt prove none.'"

This is the logic, as well as the arithmetic, of what I have called a different sameness. The excess of likeness—such that "sire," "child," and "happy mother" are "sweet husband to another," each one of them one and the same—generates a difference in such a way that the "one" plus the "many" adds up to "none." It is a logic that is regularly corroborated in these opening sonnets by the poet's imag-ery of epideictic procreation, imagery that is developed so as to in-troduce a kind of material disturbance or disruption into the homo-geneous complexion of conventional poetic phenomena. Such imagery gives a distinctive body or physicality, a specific feel, to the way the procreation sonnets characteristically add a wrinkle to tra-ditional poetic forms and themes. Like the lute in sonnet 8, which cross-couples the complementarities of an ideal poetic music, such imagery objectifies the young man's poet's own poetic practice.

To take one more example, but one that develops the master im-age of visual admiration to which all the procreation sonnets regu-larly refer, consider the immediately preceding sonnet, sonnet 7, where the poet identifies the young man's sun and son. Here again the sonnet works by redoubling "likeness" in such a way that topoi and motifs which are familiar images of poetic ideals (sonnet 7 is based on several famous Ovidian passages) are translated into something recognizably peculiar.[7] In the first quatrain the sonnet gives a description of the rising of the sun:

Lo in the orient when the gracious light
Lifts up his burning head, each under eye
Doth homage to his new-appearing sight,
Serving with looks his sacred majesty.

In the second quatrain, the sun advances to its brightness and its height:

And having climb'd the steep-up heavenly hill,
Resembling strong youth in his middle age,
Yet mortal looks adore his beauty still,
Attending on his golden pilgrimage.

In the third quatrain, the poet then turns to the sun's decline, answering the first two quatrains with a sestet introduced by a characteristic "but":

But when from highmost pitch, with weary car,
Like feeble age he reeleth from the day,
The eyes ('fore duteous) now converted are
From his low tract and look another way.

From all of which the sonnet's couplet then concludes:

So thou, thyself outgoing in thy noon,
Unlook'd on diest unless thou get a son.

In general terms the sonnet's point could not be clearer. The third quatrain follows on the octave like the night the day, but only so the couplet can in turn assure us that the young man's son revives the young man's sun. As in all the other procreation sonnets, therefore, we are invited to identify the young man with his issue, for this will make the young once again a "new-appearing sight" whose reappearance reconverts "the eyes ('fore duteous) [that] now converted are." It is the same logic of visual identification, of *special* succession, that we are given, for example, in sonnet 3, where the young man, as "thy mother's glass," will see through procreated "windows of thine age" "despite of wrinkles, this thy golden time," or the way in sonnet 9 (where sonnet 3's "window" turns to "widow") "every private widow well may keep,/By children's eyes, her husband's shape in mind." And it is this reasoning, as much as the implicit, though significantly never explicit, rhyme of "sun" with "son," that governs a reader's first responses to the poem.

And yet, in accord with a more complicated logic of succession that we have now seen several times developed, the young man in the sonnet is the sun *before* he is the son, and the effective force of the progression—after sun, then son—is to identify the latter with both the rising and the setting of the former. The son is like the sun that he repeats, but the initial circuit of the sun itself describes a double likeness—"resembling strong youth in his middle age," "like feeble age he reeleth from the day"—that describes a difference in the sun itself, a doubleness that puts a creasing furrow in the image of the sun *before* it is repeated. This crease or rift is what the sonnet's couplet and the young man's son inherit: the contrast between the height of the sun's "highmost pitch" and the depressing fall of "his low tract." Moreover, this difference in the sun itself, the way the sun burns up its "burning head," is discovered in the very movement of identification and succession—after "resembling," then "like"—when the "highmost pitch" of the sun is literally re-tracted by the "reeling" of "his low tract," when the visionary turning of the sun and the reaction thereto—"the eyes ('fore duteous)"—are literally "con-verted."

It is this intractable difference *in* the imagery of originary likeness—in the conventional poetic image of the way "the sun is daily new and old" (76)—a difference that effectively emerges out of the conjoining of "resembling" and "like," that the young man's subsequential son repeats. And it is by stressing this initial difference of re-semblance, by likening son to both a positive and a negative sun, to both a youthful and an aged brightness, that sonnet 7 interferes with, even as it argues for, the sameness of the young man's repetition. This is what disturbs an otherwise familiar and familial circle of reiterate succession. The young man's son repeats the young man's sun's original division, the difference between the epideictic way "each under eye/Doth homage to his new-appearing sight," and the way "the eyes ('fore duteous) now converted are/From his low tract and look another way." Taking the force of the reduplication, we therefore register the truth that the young man's sun and son are only like each other if they are like each other's difference, if they are each of them the likeness of the way each one of them is different from itself.

This is also why the two together—sun and son—trace out a double circle whose return upon itself anticipates the young man's death, as happens when the sonnet's couplet, looking backward at the sonnet's double sun, looks forward to the way: "thyself outgoing in thy noon,/Unlook'd on diest unless thou get a son." What I have called the identification of likeness with difference is here instantiated by the way the sonnet moves from "sun" to "son." The young man's sun and son are perfect simulations of each other in the same way that the father's sameness to his son is equal to the father's difference from himself. This is the same disjunctive way in which the young man and the lute go together in sonnet 8, and it is worth noting that sonnet 7 concludes with the same cross-coupling arithmetic as was sounded by the lute, i.e., the way the couplet to sonnet 8 rhymes the young man's "son" with punning "noon" and "none" so as in this way to compact in a chiasmic frame of "sun" and "son" and "noon" and "none" the way the young man's procreated reappearance is what makes the young man disappear.[8]

Several points that I have already discussed here come together, but in a way that makes it possible to see that the cross-coupling relationship of difference to likeness, a relationship that works to register a difference *of* and *in* likeness, informs Shakespeare's sonnets in more than the merely formal and abstract ways that I have so far considered. I spoke earlier of the poet's sense of literary retrospection, his sense that he can only copy a preceding copiousness, his sense that his verse is "barren of new pride" (76) and that he writes "all one, ever the same,/And keep[s] invention in a noted weed" (76), his complaint that he lives in a literary present in which there is nothing "new to speak . . . but yet like prayers divine,/I must each day say o'er the very same,/Counting no old thing old, thou mine, I thine" (108). The sonnets in which such themes appear characteristically carry, I said, an elegiac pathos, a kind of subsistent plangency, that remains even after these sonnets attempt to turn their recapitulation of a past poetics toward familiar epideictic ends. In part, this is the consequence of formal and stylistic features whose repetitions implicitly qualify the poet's praise. In part, this is the consequence of verbal and syntactic ambiguities whose double significations add a reservation to the poet's panegyric. In part, too, this is the consequence of the way these sonnets thematize repetition, as when they speak about "the golden tresses of the dead,/[that] live a second life on second head" (68), or "Death's second self, that seals up all in rest" (73), or the "dressings of a former sight" (123). I spoke also of the way the young man sonnets will often problematize their praise by means of repetitious afterthoughts which attenuate and revise, rather than reinforce and confirm, an opening conceit: either in the move from sonnet to sonnet, as when the young man's animating repetition is confused by its poetic reduplication—"You should live twice, in it and in my rhyme" (17)—or in the internal movement of individual sonnets, as when the "tender heir" of sonnet 1 becomes a "tender chorl," or as in sonnet 24, which begins with "eyes" that in the past "hath play'd the painter and hath stell'd/Thy beauty's form in table of my heart," but which ends with "eyes" that in the present "draw but what they see, know not the heart."

In addition to these thematic and formal features, however, the young man sonnets also develop a specific materiality or phenomenality that embodies the differentiating repetition that these sonnets sometimes speak about and sometimes formally enact. In the young man sonnets we are given a set of *things*, like the lute in sonnet 8 or the sun-son in sonnet 7, the physical substantiality of which incarnates the way these sonnets are cross-coupledly related to an epideictic poetics. In large part these perversely epideictic things are what give the young man sonnets their affective precision. These things are objective correlatives to the novel literariness of Shakespeare's sonnets: they hypostasize the corporeality of a chiasmicized praise. With the example of these peculiar poetical things, peculiar because they reduplicate with a difference conventional "artifacts" of praise, the young man sonnets manage tangibly to demonstrate their own peculiar poeticality. The major images of the young man sonnets—imagery of vision, of flowers, of printing, painting, minting, and the like—images which are conventional images *of* conventional poetry, are developed in the sequence so as to display a kind of disjunctive physicality that essentializes, realizes, materializes, the rhetoricity of a novel poetics whose novelty consists of the way it conceives itself to be the differentiating repetition of the poetry of praise.

This explains why, for example, in sonnet 59, when the poet complains about the fact that "there be nothing new, but that which is/Hath been before," he employs an imagery of noticeably eccentric likeness to exemplify the way he looks "with a backward look" to see "your image in some antique book." Specifically, this explains the sonnet's concern with the grotesque "second burthen of a former child" and the revolutionary sun whose "revolution" is no longer "the same." Such images derive their literary value and signification from the way they materially reduplicate familiar imagery of poetic likeness. The afterlight of this mutating sun and the monstrous afterbirth of this "former child" are images whose own mixed-up physicality objectifies the way that repetition ruptures likeness, and in this way they portray the doubleness that now intrudes upon a singular ideal. This is the case whether we think of the metaphoric likeness conventionally figured by a sun whose turning should return it to its customary brightness or of the mimetic likeness of a procreated child whose generation ought to "breed another thee" (6). The sun and son of sonnet 59 instead are illustrations of the way that repetition makes a difference out of sameness: specifically, the variant succession of "five hundreth courses of the sun," the fruitless, reinventing duplication of a "second burthen." It is the particularized peculiarity of these images that effectively distinguishes sonnet 59 from the tradition of the ideal and the idealizing sonnet. With the example of a novel, broken sun, with the example of the re-birth—indeed, with the "Re-naissance"— of a ghostly child, sonnet 59 palpably imagines its difference from the sonnets it thematically remembers or whose "image" it sees "in some antique book." These images substantiate the mode and mood of Shakespeare's paradox of praise. This different kind of solar brightness, which eclipses its poetic past, this different kind of "special" procreation, which generates its own abortion, is what poetic complements will look like when ideal poetic vision no longer "sees the same." Because they are developed as a difference bred by ideal repetition and by epideictic likeness, the afterlight of the sun and the afterbirth of the son of sonnet 59 become the *matter* that is called for by the aftermath of praise.

In this way the literary retrospection of Shakespeare's young man sub-sequence obliges these sonnets to think and to imagine themselves through a novel, but still specific and predetermined, phenomenology of furrowed likeness the physical details of which are both the record of and the response to the breaking of the "Mirrour" of "Idea." A *particular* materiality informs and interferes with the sonnets' invocations of traditional poetic likeness, the likeness, on the one hand, of mimetic resemblance, and the likeness, on the other, of metaphoric figurality. As a result, because the young man sonnets' examples of poetic likeness are no longer "all alike," the amplifying, animating "increase" that traditionally is generated when metaphor and mimesis meet emerges in these sonnets, instead, as a kind of remnant surplus whose animation is the vivid replica of death. Where before the ideal correspondence of verisimilar similitude and analogizing trope spoke to the laudatory correspondence of admiring "I" and admired "thou," this correspondence now is coded, by the imagery with which it is developed, with a residue of difference that serves to break the unity of poetic subject and poetic object. The young man sonnets present images *of* difference that by themselves effectively disturb the complementarity of poetic compliment. The very being of these images manifests an interrupted mutuality; the way they *are* is demonstration of the way that the familiarity of homogeneity, the identity of unity, the circularity of reflexive reflection, no longer are the same.

Again, therefore, in the same way that there is a limited inventory for epideictic invention—the displaying and self-displaying artifacts of praise which objectify the phenomenology of an epideictic logos—there is a limited and specifically inflected phenomenality appropriate to the way poetic "invention" in the young man sonnets "bear[s] amiss" (59). When the young man's poet asks, in sonnet 108, "What's new to speak, what now to register,/That may express my love, or thy dear merit," when he complains about the way "I must each day say o'er the very same,/Counting no old thing old, thou mine, I thine," the very asking of the question, the very posing of the problem, is what invites the poet to amplify an imagery that shows the way the "new" and "old" are "now" grotesquely joined together, which is what happens in the sestet, where the poet's "love" appears as a senescent endlessness, as an aged and a protracted sameness condemned to linger over its perpetual endurance:

> So that eternal love in love's fresh case
> Weighs not the dust and injury of age,
> Nor gives to necessary wrinkles place,
> But makes antiquity for aye his page,
> > Finding the first conceit of love there bred,
> > Where time and outward form would show it dead.

Here it is the physical details that work to make eternity into a timeworn, hoary permanence, that make the youth and age of love combine in a disturbing way. In positive terms, the poet says "eternal love" will "make antiquity for aye his page." But, as we imagine this positive claim through the imagery with which it is presented, this means either that love looks backward, as at "your image in some antique book," or that love's aged retainer is called on to perform the duties of a youthful servant. In the first case, love's visionary "eye" seems weary of its sempiternal "aye," and to this extent appears a version of the "eyes of all posterity/That wear this world out to the ending doom" (55). In the second case, we are left with an equally unsettling picture of age dressed up in its bygone puerility, wearing its youth like "golden tresses of the dead." This imagery survives up through and saturates the couplet. We apply these images to "the first conceit of love there bred," which thus calls up a kind of

ancient, wrinkled baby—Cupid as Father Time— who is the procreated equivalent to the way that time will "dig deep trenches in thy
beauty's field" (2) or to "the conceit of this inconstant stay" (15). What
the poet therefore "finds" in the couplet, when he "makes antiquity
for aye his page," is a "conceit" which is "bred," as is "the second
burthen of a former child," in such a paradoxical fashion that in its
very infancy it shows the way that "time and outward form would
show it dead." By the end of the sonnet, despite the sonnet's explicit
eternizing argument, the poet's "prayers divine," precisely because
"I must each day say o'er the very same," have changed into memorial service for the dead.

The same image of an infant whose very being amounts to an
abortion reappears in sonnet 115, and does so in a way that makes
very clear the logic that leads the poet to join themes of epideictic
retrospection and forms of poetic reduplication to imagery of difference. In sonnet 115 the poet begins by talking about the way "those
lines that I before have writ do lie,/Even those that said I could not
love you dearer." The initially playful point of this incipient Liar's
paradox is that the absolute comparison asserted by the remembered superlative—that the poet's previous love was dearest—
implies that the poet's present love is by comparison inadequate.
The conceit (for which there are many Renaissance parallels) is a
variation of the waning-growing conceit developed throughout the
procreation series—"as fast as thou shalt wane, so fast thou grow'st"
(11), or the way "that men as plants increase" but "at height
decrease,/And wear their brave state out of memory" (15)—applied
now, however, to the poet's love and verse, not to the mutable young
man. At the beginning of the sonnet there is something light about
the way the poet's bygone lines thus put an end to themselves by
virtue of their claims to permanence. The increasingly less witty
point of the sonnet, however, is that what holds true for the past
holds true also for the present, for the fullness of any panegyric
present, including the poet's current "lines," will empty out the future. Even as he speaks them, that is to say, the poet's current lines
are already "those lines that I before have writ," and for this reason,
or so it is suggested, they "do lie." (This can be compared to the way
in which in sonnet 17 the poet imagines, in advance, how "the age to
come would say 'This poet lies.'")

Sonnet 115 proceeds to elaborate this paradox regarding both the
poet's bygone and present lying "lines," lines whose eternality is, as
such, ephemeral—like "the lines of life that life repair" (16) or the
"eternal lines to time [in which] thou grow'st" (18)—by describing

reckoning Time, whose million'd accidents
Creep in 'twixt vows, and change decrees of kings,
Tan sacred beauty, blunt the sharp'st intents,
Divert strong minds to th' course of alt'ring things.

It is this particularized description of time that leads the poet in
sonnet 115 to join his present to his past, and this leads in turn, in a
line whose complexity I have already mentioned, to a strong disruption of poetic voice, when the poet, "fearing of Time's tyranny," says
"Might I not then say, 'Now I love you best.'" It is a line whose complicated syntax calls for a rereading or rethinking on the part of the
reader which will sort out the "then" used as a time marker in the
present of the past (i.e., "Might I not have said at that time") from
the "then" which is used as an atemporal "therefore" whose conclusion would unchangingly hold true forever (i.e., "Might I not for this
reason say"). In purely formal terms this confusing syntax serves to
chiasmicize poetic first person, for the grammar of the line—"Might
I not then say, 'Now I love you best'"—serves to locate poetic "I" at
the cross-coupled intersection of deictic "now" and "then," i.e., now
the poet says "then" whereas then the poet said "now." Correspondingly, however, at the level of theme, this syntactic division of poetic
voice leads the poet to a genuinely indeterminate poetic point of
view, for the poet's indirect quotation of himself—when he speaks
about his speaking: "'Now I love you best'"—fits into a larger rhetorical question whose point is that "crowning the present" is precisely
that which "change[s] decrees of kings": "Might I not then say, 'Now
I love you best,'/When I was certain o'er incertainty,/Crowning the
present, doubting of the rest?"

Taken together, the sonnet's formal or syntactic break of poetic
"I" and the sonnet's theme of indeterminacy—"When I was certain
o'er incertainty"—produce a strong counterexample to the *cogito* of
praise. Where Dante developed an ideal poetics and an ideal poetic
self based on the proposition "I praise, therefore I am," sonnet 115
instead establishes and discovers a real difference between the "I" of
a past poetic speech of praise—"'Now I love you best'"—and the "I"
of present poetic being who can only speak about his panegyric
past—"Might I not then say." As the sonnet presents it, this structurally divergent difference between two "Is" which ideally are the same
emerges in the very time required to assert their identity, for the difference between past and present that the line speaks about is experienced, by virtue of the complex syntax, in the very speaking of the
line. It is as though the poet performs his self's postponing in the
same way that the speaker of the Liar's paradox suggested at the be-

ginning of the sonnet performs his own self-belying. The result is
that, in a purely formal way, temporal difference is pressed into the
poet just as, speaking thematically, "Time's million'd accidents creep
in 'twixt vows." This is why the sonnet's initially playful tone grows
darker as the sonnet develops. Temporal difference, or rather self-
difference, is shown to exist in and as the time of unmarked punctuation (for there is no punctuation mark in the Quarto) that links and
separates "Might I not then say" and "'Now I love you best.'" In this
way, syntax and theme both confirm and instantiate the broken "I" of
the poet: we can hear the break in the poet's stuttering voice (when
the sonnet, broaching its Liar's paradox, collapses the difference between language and metalanguage), and we can think it through poetic conceit (when the poet, realizing his belatedness, collapses the
difference between his present and his past).

Both this formally complicated syntax and this theme are characteristically Shakespearean, and the pathos they engender becomes,
as I have suggested and will discuss more carefully in a moment, yet
more emphatic when rendered more explicit in the sonnets addressed to the dark lady, as, for example, "when my love swears that
she is made of truth,/I do believe her, though I know she lies" (138).
The point I want to emphasize now, however, is that both this form
and this theme in turn call up, or are called up by, a specific *material*
image in which the subjective break of the poet's person and love
finds itself objectified. Again, as though this were the necessary
erotic consequence of the poet's experience of difference, sonnet 115
concludes by imagining its "love" with an image that throughout the
young man sonnets is illustration of the way the amplifying "increase" of likeness is attenuated by its own reiteration. What sonnet
108 calls "the first conceit of love there bred," or what sonnet 59 calls
"the second burthen of a former child" reappears in the couplet to
sonnet 115 as an infant "Love" that from its beginning is structurally
noncoincident with itself: "Love is a babe, then might I not say so,/
To give full growth to that which still doth grow."

In a purely formal way this couplet recapitulates the deictic confusions that govern the entirety of the sonnet (again the "then"
which is a deictic marker in the present of the past re-turns—what
the sonnet calls "di-verts"—the "then" that would be a proud
"therefore" were it spoken simply in the simple past). Thematically
the couplet recapitulates the way that any panegyric signifier asymptotically falls short of the ideal it signifies (which is why from
before the sonnet's beginning "those lines that I before have writ do

lie"). But all this is conclusively *imaged* by the "babe" whose "full growth" always "still doth grow," a growing that, *ab ovo*, is permanently stunted because incomparable to itself. Thus conceived and thus conceited, this "babe" is like the tired "love" of sonnet 76, "still telling what is told." In the same way, it is like the ancient sun which "is daily new and old" (76). Of such a "babe" it never can be said "'Now I love you best'" because, as sonnet 76 explains, there is no "best" when "all my best is dressing old words new, / Spending again what is already spent."

This stillborn, ancient baby whose growing is equal to its waning is only one of several images that develop out of the young man sonnets' initial concern with the young man's procreation. Consider, for example, the way

> Nativity, once in the main of light,
> Crawls to maturity, wherewith being crown'd,
> Crooked eclipses 'gainst his glory fight,
> And Time that gave doth now his gift confound.
> Time doth transfix the flourish set on youth,
> And delves the parallels in beauty's brow.
> (60)

or, another example, the way

> my lovely boy . . .
> Dost hold Time's fickle glass, his sickle, hour;
> Who hast by waning grown, and therein show'st
> Thy lovers withering as thy sweet self grow'st.
> (126)

It is structurally equivalent to a self-consuming nourishment— "making a famine where abundance lies" (1) to a "use" which is and is not useless—"That use is not forbidden usury" (6)—to a gift that is best kept by giving—"To give away yourself keeps yourself still" (16)—to a treasure enriched by spending—"Treasure thou some place / With beauty's treasure ere it be self-kill'd" (6). In the procreation sonnets the theme of biological repetition regularly invites poetic devices that stress verbal repetition, and these together regularly call up images whose point is to figure these formal relations in ways that embody the immediate experience of temporal loss. A good example would be the way "a liquid prisoner pent in walls of glass" illustrates in sonnet 5 how "beauty's effect with beauty were bereft." Such images are yet more elaborately developed later on in the young man sub-sequence, as, for example, the "interchange of state" in sonnet 64, which works by "increasing store with loss, and loss with store," or the poet's dwindling fire in sonnet 73, which is "Death's second self" because "consum'd with that which it was nourish'd by." Such images are quite unlike the icy fires of conventional Petrarchan oxymoron. They are different, however, because, relatively consistently and univocally, their equivocations—"still telling what is told"—illustrate the way a second time calls up its difference from the first, the way a copy is unlike the original it remembers. The "violet past prime" that the poet "behold[s]" in sonnet 12, to take a comparatively uncomplicated example, is not an image of something that is simply old. More specifically, it is an image that "calls back the lovely April of her prime" (3); it is an image precisely of "a vanish'd sight" (30), an image of the way the currency of the present, remembering the past, can be what sonnet 45 calls "present-absent" to itself.

What gives these images their specifically literary weight in the young man sonnets is that, whatever else they illustrate, they are first and foremost poetical images, images *of* the poetical, more or less explicitly associated throughout the young man sub-sequence with famous and familiar images of poetical idealization—like the violet, which is a well-known flower of poetic fancy, or the baby, which is a conventional image of literary invention, or the lute, which is the archetypal instrument of lyric poetry itself. The young man sonnets characteristically stress this literary resonance built into the images they employ, but at the same time they show these images to be unlike the way they used to be. These images become images of a changed and different literary likeness: images, on the one hand, that are demonstrably "converted," as are the "eyes" in sonnet 7, which "now converted are," and which therefore "look another way"; images, on the other hand, that are no longer like the ideal vision they look at, as are the dying marigolds of sonnet 25, and which therefore illustrate the way that "in themselves their pride lies buried." It is because conventional imagery of ideal literary likeness in the young man sonnets is thus an imagery of faded and of changing likeness that the young man sonnets rarely unambiguously make "a couplement of proud compare." Instead, images of likeness in the young man sonnets typically will illustrate, "in themselves," a loss brought out by simulation. These images are puffed up with the difference between the way they are and the way they were; they *are* the discrepancy between themselves and that to which they are intrinsically compared.

Nowhere is this more evident than in the poet's most generalized characterizations of the young man. "Their images I lov'd I view in thee" (31), says the poet to the fair young man. But the poet only says this because "thou art the grave where buried love doth live" (31). In this sepulchral image, in this vision of the loss of vision, we see the effective pathos of Shakespeare's epideictic imagery of the ideal: imagery of likeness that functions now as imagery of difference. As the reincarnation of all of that "which I by lacking have supposed dead" (31), the young man is, right now, in the immediacy of his lyric present, the incarnated image of an absent presence. Continually ornamented with this kind of imagery, the young man becomes the palpable embodiment of an insistent lack. In a specifically imagined way he is at once the image and the afterimage of the Mirror of Idea: "The wrinkles which thy glass will truly show,/Of mouthed graves will give thee memory" (77).

These poetic forms, themes, and images all join together in the young man sonnets to build up and example an entirely novel kind of poetic desire, one whose novelty, however, is constitutively derived from and described as the transgressive troping or re-turning of traditional ideality, a desire, therefore, whose motivation and motifs are consistently conceived through the materialized difference now discovered in the sameness of poetic admiration. Hence the force of "stelling" in "Mine eye hath play'd the painter and hath stell'd/Thy beauty's form in table of my heart" (24). Where Dante identifies himself in the final line of the *Paradiso* with the Love that moves *il sole e l'altre stelle*, where Astrophil sees "Stella" when he looks into his heart, the young man's poet instead sees "stelling" printed on his heart. Marked by this marking, by the "crease" which is in "increase," poetic desire is now imagined through an "Ideas Mirrour" that is literally reduced to a graven image of engraving—"I ingraft you new" (15)—an image of ideality whose smooth, steely, glassy surface, being thus an image of its own disruption, functions as an index of the way that "your true image pictur'd lies" (24). It is precisely this stylization of an ideal stylus—a signifier that would ideally be the same as what it signifies, but that is now itself the interruption of such semiotic sameness—that disturbs the ideal, mutually identificatory circles of "now see what good turns eyes for eyes have done" (24). The heart which is thus "stell'd," marked by a "stelling" which is no longer simple image of an ideal homogeneity, is both structurally and materially broken hearted, divided by its own inscription between itself and its specular idealization. Again, "still telling what is told," this is the point of the sonnet's retrospective couplet, where the poet explains the erotic consequence of the failure of his visionary art: "Yet eyes this cunning want to grace their art,/They draw but what they see, know not the heart."

Such a logic, but also such materiality, governs erotic imagination throughout the young man sonnets, and this explains why the homosexuality in these sonnets so regularly elicits from readers so puzzled, even troubled, a response. To many readers the ideality of the poet's relation to the young man seems perversely erotic, whereas other readers instead will strain to see the eroticism of these sonnets as itself ideal. In either case, however, the homosexuality of the sub-sequence presents itself as a problem, as something either moralizingly to regret or sympathetically to overlook. Thus the homosexuality in the young man sonnets will sometimes invite complaints or denials, as when Benson editorially decides to change the "hes" to "shes", just as sometimes it will be treated euphemistically as some version of Platonic love, as when the young man sonnets are read as an example of the literature of heroic friendship. Both reactions, though they are opposed to each other, respond to an erotic ambivalence or uncertainty developed in the sonnets themselves, for the difficult issue raised by the young man sonnets is not whether there is a homosexual desire developed in them, but, rather, what this homosexuality means to and for the poet. This is a question that the young man sonnets seem to raise in order to leave open. Given the poet's love for the young man, and the young man sonnets surely give it frequently enough, the question that remains is just what it is the young man's poet wants.

Sonnet 20 is the *locus classicus* for this discussion, for this is a sonnet whose frankly sexualized vocabulary seems remarkably excessive—"A woman's face with Nature's own hand painted/Hast thou, the master mistress of my passion"—just as the poet's explicit renunciation of the young man seems quite teasingly suggestive:

> And for a woman wert thou first created,
> Till Nature as she wrought thee fell a-doting,
> And by addition me of thee defeated,
> By adding one thing to my purpose nothing.
> > But since she prick'd thee out for women's pleasure,
> > Mine be thy love, and love's use their treasure.

In terms of theme what is distinctive about the sonnet is the way it combines ideality with an eroticism that is nevertheless conceived in a very fleshly way. This combination, half witty and half rueful, belies the chaste conclusion of the sonnet, where the poet, punning on "prick," consigns the young man to the pleasure of women. Even though the bawdiness of sonnet 20 is delivered in the context of a high ideal, this is not at all like the idealized bodily sexuality of Provençal poetry. Neither is the sonnet like other contemporary love sonnets written by a man to a man, none of which evidences this kind of powerfully resonant erotic tonality. Sonnet 20 has nothing in common, for example, with the rather common kinds of memorial sonnets that are addressed to particular men on specific honorific and epideictic occasions—dedications, prefatory announcements, presentations, and the like. Such sonnets often employ Petrarchan motifs and conceits, and they sometimes speak a language of remarkable intimacy. Even so, they always manage modestly to adapt the conventional heterosexual content of their motifs, conceits, and amorous postures to the requirements of an all male context. Sonnet 20, however, does quite the opposite.

More important, sonnet 20 is not high-mindedly homosexual. There is in it none of the ideal carnality that is exhibited in, for example, the verse of Michelangelo. This is significant for, as I have suggested, the sonnet tradition in many ways calls out for, or is amenable to, this kind of idealized homosexuality. Had Shakespeare written a sonnet in this idealizing spirit the result would have been a radical reduction of or extension of, but it would not have been a radical revision of, the homogenizing impulses of the poetry of admiration. As Ficino says, repeating Plato, such a same-sex love is, in its essence, something sexless. Because it is a relation of the same to the same, homosexual desire is already, for this reason, more a spiritual than a bodily desire, a relation of kind to kind that is itself ideal. Understood in this way, in terms of a metaphysics of desire that goes back, like the praise of love, to the *Symposium* and the *Phaedrus,* homosexuality is something higher than heterosexuality in the same way that man is something higher than woman. The one is to the other as sameness is to difference or as unity is to plurality—or, for that matter, as the One is to the Other when the Other is understood as mutable, inconstant variety.[9] If sonnet 20 had been written from such an ideal point of view, there would be nothing puzzling or disturbing about either the poet's erotic object or his erotic motive: in the purest sense the poet's desire would be seen as properly Platonic. By the same token, imagining the alternative, Shakespeare could have written a set of explicitly impure homosexual sonnets—on the order of Richard Barnfield's—and still have raised no fundamental questions with regard to poetic desire. Had he done so, the result might have amounted to something of a scandal, but it would have done so, and it would continue to do so, in a straightforward and nonproblematic way. In an Elizabethan context, such a pederastic sonnet might raise very serious questions regarding the poet's morals, but the reader of such a sonnet would have no difficulty assessing either the object or the motive of the poet's desire.

Sonnet 20, however, is neither the one kind of sonnet nor the other. It expresses a desire that is neither purely spiritual nor impurely physical, nor the two together combined in an exemplary way. Correspondingly, neither is the young man, who is the object of this desire, either purely male or impurely female, or the two of these combined in a harmonious way. On the one hand, it is as a woman that the young man is beautiful: "A woman's face with Nature's own hand painted." So too the young man has "a woman's heart." On the other hand, it is as a man that the young man is a stable and constant ideal, and this specifically in contrast to the generic failure of changeable false women:

> A woman's gentle heart but not acquainted
> With shifting change as is false women's fashion;
> An eye more bright than theirs, less false in rolling,
> Gilding the object whereupon it gazeth;
> A man in hues all hues in his controlling,
> Which steals men's eyes and women's souls amazeth.

This is a relation, neither an opposition nor a sameness, that becomes yet more complicated as the sonnet proceeds. The young man is initially created as an ideal woman, though ambiguously so, given the ambiguity of "for": "And for a woman wert thou first created." However, "Nature as she wrought thee fell a-doting,/And by addition me of thee defeated,/By adding one thing to my purpose nothing." The result of this "addition" is that what marks the young man as a man is precisely that which marks him out for the pleasure of false women: "But since she prick'd thee out for women's pleasure." Developed in this chiasmic way—as both like and unlike a man, but also as both like and unlike a woman—"the master mistress of my passion" does not function as an image of androgynous wholeness or unity. If the young man combines the best part of man with the best part of woman, he does so in a way that distinguishes the one from the other. As subject and object of the poet's love—"Mine be thy love"—and as subject and object of woman's love—"and thy love's use their treasure"—the young man becomes in the sonnet the erotic figure of the difference *between* man and woman. And it is *as* such an intermediate being that the poet addresses him, with an ambiguous and conflicted desire which is half spiritual and half bodily *because* divided between the homosexual and the heterosexual.

This is an ambiguity that sonnet 20 conveys in ways that should by now be recognized as characteristic. There are, for example, grammatical indeterminacies, such as those that I have already mentioned, which work to problematize an ideal visibility, as when the poet praises the young man's "eye": "An eye more bright than theirs, less false in rolling,/Gilding the object whereupon it gazeth." The syntax of the line leaves it unclear whether "gilding the object whereupon it gazeth" modifies "an eye more bright than theirs," in which case "gilding" describes the beautifying luminosity of the young man's vision, or, instead, whether the phrase refers to the way that women's eyes are "false in rolling," in which case "gilding" describes the meretricious duplicity of an artificial brightness. So too the sonnet exhibits formal duplications, again like those that I have already mentioned, whose equivocations work to confuse the univocities they express. Here the obvious example is "a man in hue all hues in his controlling,/Which steals men's eyes and women's souls amazeth," a formula whose collation of the singular and the plural is sufficiently opaque as to have provoked from editors various emendations designed to make the young man's double "hue" make unambiguous sense (e.g., reading "a woman in hue" for "a man in hue"). This is but one of the formal ways in which the sonnet effectively resists the mirroring mutuality of "the lovely gaze where every eye doth dwell" (5). So too there is the large thematic conceit of the sonnet, which once again leads the poet to the zero-sum arithmetic whereby the One, taken by itself, adds up to None, as though there were a continuous logic linking "'thou single wilt prove none'" (8) to the way that Nature "by addition me of thee defeated,/By adding one thing to my purpose nothing."

Finally, however, and in this sonnet most important, there is the image of the young man's "prick" itself, which, as the sonnet presents it, is here not simply a "prick" but a "pricked prick," a disappointing pointer, that is to say, which is conceived and conceited as the same cut and cutting line, scythe and scythed, through which the poet thinks out "stell'd." Marked both as and by this marking— as is Adonis, when "the loving swine/Sheath'd unaware the tusk in his soft groin" or as is Othello when he "smites" the "circumcised dog" which is himself—the erotic body of the young man is again imaged as the physical materialization of a difference in sameness, with the result that the young man's "prick" itself, being "pricked," substantially embodies the desire it provokes.[10] Taking the part for the whole, the "prick" which makes the young man the same as the poet is precisely that which separates him from the poet, just as this same "prick" joins the young man to the women it makes clear that he is not: "But since she prick'd thee out for women's pleasure,/Mine be thy love, and thy love's use their treasure."

This might seem a minor or merely local witticism, the young man's "addition" being, on the one hand, the "one thing" that the poet cannot have because he already has it, and, on the other, the "one thing" that women will eventually receive because they already lack it. The subincised "prick" becomes not only the metonymic part for the whole but, also, the part for the lack. However, since the young man acquires this distinctive organ through the "doting" of "Nature," the same Nature who is traditional synonym for the principle of "kynde," it is fair to say that the sonnet here makes scandalously public the very same "prick" which is hidden in the secret, private parts of Nature, at least as Nature is depicted in Fludd's "Mirror of Integrated Nature": the sickle-crescent moon of Nature which is cut and cutting both at once. More than the finally benignly homosexual theme of the sonnet, this explains why readers find the poet's interest in the young man's "prick" so shamefully perverted. The young man's "pricked prick" is the image—fully anticipated, but heretofore kept secret—of an erotic kind which is unkind. The "one thing to my purpose nothing" that sonnet 20 describes is the organ, now identified as a part, structurally required to illustrate the difference between male sameness and female difference. The young man's "pricked prick" is specifically the image of erotic difference, and, for this reason, it is an image, precisely, of what lies both before and beyond the homogenizing poetics and erotics of ideal admiration. Moreover, to the extent that the poet identifies himself with this "addition," an addition that functions also as subtraction, the "pricking" of the young man's "prick" becomes the image of the way the poet, as a lover, experiences himself as different from himself.

Sonnet 20 is an especially bawdy, but still a characteristic, young man sonnet. As I have argued, the young man who through specular reduplication and repetition is confusingly associated with *his* young man—"Look in thy glass and tell the face thou viewest,/Now is the time that face should form another" (3)—initially appears to the poet in the procreation sonnets as a double "you" and "view," which is why "the lovely gaze where every eye doth dwell" (5) shows nothing to the poet but a personal division: "My glass shall not persuade me I am old,/So long as you-th-and-thou are of one date" (22). The same thing happens in sonnet 20 where the double "you" of the young man becomes a double "hue"—"A man in hue all hues in his controlling"—whose appearance, because both singular and plural, intrinsically exceeds the unitary point of view of visionary art: "A woman's face with Nature's own hand painted." This double "hue" is related in sonnet 20 to the double and cross-coupling homosexual-heterosexual "use" of "mine be thy love, and thy love's use their treasure." But this is the same simultaneously forbidden and idealized "use" that in sonnet 6 both is and is not "usury," or the same "beauty's use" with which in sonnet 2 the aged young man "shall sum my count, and make my old excuse."

In sonnet 20, which is concerned with the specific details of the young man's generative "succession," this doubling and cross-coupling elaboration of "hue," "you," "view," "use," is materially consolidated in the double entendre of the young man's "pricked prick." The same kind of image regularly emerges, however, and to much the same effect, whenever the young man's poet imagines his ideal. The poet's "eternal lines to time" (18) or the young man's "lines of life that life repair" (16) are the same kind of furrows that "dig deep trenches in thy beauty's field" (2), the same kind of "lines" that "Time" will draw "there with thine antique pen" (19), the same kind of lines with which "Time doth transfix the flourish set on youth,/And delves the parallels in beauty's brow" (60). Because imagined as something double, such "lines" always function to "stell" the poet's heart. They are the mark, "an ever-fixed mark," of an eternal beauty which is already figure of its own transience, an eternality traversed and wrinkled by the doubling through which it is conceived: "Those lines that I before have writ do lie" (115). Whenever such an image arises in the young man sonnets, an image *of* difference, its equivocality conveys the poet's univocal sense of poetic, temporal, and sexual loss.

To take one summary example, consider the way the young man's perfect "beauty" is "like a dial hand" in sonnet 104:

> Ah, yet doth beauty, like a dial hand,
> Steal from his figure, and no pace perceiv'd,
> So your sweet hue, which methinks still doth stand,
> Hath motion, and mine eye may be deceiv'd.

The "dial hand" is another disappointing index of the poet's admiration. Like the poet's bygone "lines" in sonnet 115, their truth belied because belated, or like the deictic, time-marking "then" of sonnet 115, which is always after the fact of its own hyperbolic assertion, the "dial hand" of the young man's beauty is here the pointer and marker of a time whose ideal presence is, as such, already past. It is because the poet sees this "imperception," and the way in which it "steals" from what "still doth stand," that the poet, even as he looks at the young man's beauty, doubts the truth of what he sees: "mine eye may be deceiv'd." But this is also correlated in sonnet 104 with the way the poet, as an "I," doubts his presence to himself. Because the young man in sonnet 104 is a double "you" or double "hue"—"your sweet hue"—the poet discovers that he himself is not the same as his "eye" or "I." Instead, what the poet in sonnet 104 sees in the young man is the double, retrospective absence of himself: "For as you were when first your eye I ey'd." And, finally, because the poet in this way doubts both the truth of his vision and the unity of his person, the sonnet concludes by announcing to all future admiration that it inherits nothing but the aftermath of praise: "hear this, thou age unbred:/Ere you were born was beauty's summer dead."

All this is characteristic, or so I have argued, of the young man sub-sequence as a whole, and to the extent that this is the case it becomes possible to understand the various literary peculiarities of the young man sonnets, especially the peculiarity of the person of their poet, as the consequence of a very systematic response to the conclusion of the poetry of praise. The young man sonnets generate division when they redouble the unity and unities of an ideal and an idealizing poetics. They do this formally through the cross-coupling of traditional poetic devices, and they do this thematically by developing familiar Petrarchan conceits and topoi to novel and ambiguous ends. In addition, however, they also do this *materially* when they import difference into the traditional phenomenology of likeness. Insofar as he explains himself by reference to such ambiguous conceits, and insofar as he exemplifies himself with such a novel materiality, the materiality of the "pricked prick," the young man's poet acquires an unusual poetic persona compact of erotic, spatial, temporal, and personal division. As I have argued, in the young man sonnets this division is psychologistically elaborated in various ways, all of them coherently and consistently related to the poet's sense of literary belatedness: in terms of a novel desire that leaves something to be desired (the flawed young man, "that thou are blam'd shall not be thy defect,/For slander's mark was ever yet the fair" [70]); in terms of a claustrophobic and chiasmicized internality that gives both depth and texture to subjective introspection (the "withinness" of "a liquid prisoner pent in walls of glass" [5]); in terms of a present experienced as the immediate duration of "succession" (the unhappy retrospection of "that time of year thou mayst in me behold" [73]); in terms of a first person whose deictic "I" and "eye" are disjunctively related to their vision of an ideal second-person ("'Tis thee (myself) that for myself I praise,/Painting my age with beauty of thy days" [62]).

All this is characteristic of the young man sonnets and character-izing of the young man's poet. However, as I have already argued, not only are the same features—formal, thematic, material—evi-dent in the sonnets addressed to the dark lady, but, in addition, they are yet more prominently featured in the second sub-sequence be-cause there they are explicitly "re-marked." In a way that is far more directly expressed and articulated than in the young man sonnets, the poet in the sonnets addressed to the dark lady advances this kind of differential redoubling—formal, thematic, and material—as the reason *why* his person, his lady, and his verse amount to some-thing altogether different in the history of the sonnet. If the signifi-cance and literary effect of this explicit remarking is recognized, it becomes possible to understand how the sonnets to the dark lady not only register the conclusion or waning of an older poetic tradi-tion, but, more to the point, it becomes possible to understand how the dark lady sonnets inaugurate, over the dead body of a tradi-tional literariness, a new poetics of the person that draws its suste-nance from what Sidney called "poor Petrarch's long deceased woes."

Again it is necessary to insist upon the literary difference that the dark lady sonnets not only express but that they literally *make* when they put explicitly into words what the young man sonnets instead will leave implicit. When the young man's poet looks "with a back-ward look" to see "your image in some antique book" (59) he sug-gests, as I have argued, his retrospective distance from a visionary poetics. When he wonders "what the old world could say,/To this composed wonder of your frame" (59) he suggests, as I have argued, that what he writes is something new because at one remove from writing that is old. Such suggestions are urgent and powerful throughout the young man sonnets. As something oblique and la-tent, as something on the tip of the poet's tongue, they account for the conflicted tonality of the young man sonnets, for the reader's sense that there is something that the poet feels obliged to leave unspoken.

It is not, however, in a muted or an oblique way that the dark lady sonnets will insist that they amount to something novel. In deliberate and emphatic contrast to what happens in the sub-sequence they succeed, the dark lady sonnets begin where the reticent young man sonnets consistently break off, with the dark lady's poet asserting positively what the young man's poet only indirectly intimates between the lines. Thus the first dark lady sonnet officially announces a new epoch in literary history when it develops the difference between "the old age" in which "black was not counted fair" (127) and the poetic present in which "now is black beauty's successive heir" (127). So too with the major images of the dark lady sonnets, images that again example difference in a way that is far more explicitly foregrounded than in the young man sonnets, as when the first dark lady sonnet illustrates the difference between its literary present and its literary past with the oddly double eyes of the lady, eyes whose black and "mournful" beauty both displaces and replaces the fair beauty of "the old age." All this introduces and defines, in a very straightforward way, the literary novelty of the dark lady sonnets, what I have called their para-Petrarchanism, their postidealist and postvisionary poetics. At the same time, however, as happens in sonnet 127, but also as happens characteristically throughout the dark lady sonnets, the dark lady's poet also understands, again in an explicit way, such literary novelties as both the warrant for and the example of his own peculiar speech, as when the poet's "tongue" in sonnet 127 itself becomes the consequence of what the poet speaks about: "Yet so they mourn, becoming of their woe,/That every tongue says beauty should look so" (127).

Two related but nevertheless distinct points are at stake in the thematically self-conscious assimilation by the dark lady's poet of his own eccentric speaking to the eccentricties about which he speaks. To begin with, as the couplet to sonnet 127 says, this enables or sanctions the poet to say things that are unprecedented in the history of the sonnet. In sonnet 127 this means more than simply declaring, in chiasmic fashion, that black is now (in a good way) fair whereas fair is now (in a bad way) black. For this cross-coupling of the ideal old with the novel new—the latter understood as the forswearing repetition of the former—introduces all the thematic innovations that are hinted at in the young man sonnets, leading the dark lady's poet directly to express all the suspicions of a visionary poetics that, without expression, disturb the panegyric postures of the young man's poet. In the young man sonnets there is, for example, the suggestion, forceful but implicit, that the young man is a double "you" and "hue," and this duplication—of an ideal unified sight, of an ideal second person—suggestively evokes the poet's sense of his cross-coupled personal division. In the dark lady sonnets, however, this internal dividing of poetic person—a division that is merely suggested in the young man sonnets by the young man's double aspect—becomes a large-scale narrative frame and a specific lyric theme, as when the dark lady's poet describes "two loves . . . of comfort and despair" (144), the one "right fair" and the other "color'd ill," the two of which together, paired by "despair," cross-couple with each other: "I guess one angel *in* another's hell" (144). So too, where the young man sonnets indirectly characterize the way the first-person "I" of the poet is chiasmically disrupted by the doubling of his "you" (as in the tonally troubled mutuality of the otherwise cheery cuckoldry reported in sonnet 42: "But here's the joy, my friend and I are one;/Sweet flattery! then she loves but me alone"), the dark lady's poet instead proclaims outright the way in which "me from myself thy cruel eye hath taken,/And my next self thou harder hast engrossed:/Of him, myself, and thee I am forsaken,/A torment thrice threefold thus to be crossed" (133). So too, where the "heart" of the young man is "stell'd" by what he sees, the dark lady's poet is quite explicit about the way in which he finds "my heart in thy steel bosom's ward" (133). So too, where the young man's poet only mutedly implies that there is something missing in the way that "thou art all my art" (78), or where the young man's poet only tacitly identifies his person with "a liquid prisoner pent in walls of glass" (5), the dark lady's poet instead describes, and with exact detail, the unhappy and the unfulfilling way in which "I being pent in thee,/Perforce am thine, and all that is in me" (133).

These are all thematic novelties in the poetry of praise. They are as peculiar in, and foreign to, the context of a sonnet sequence as is the dark lady's poet's announced desire for an object he does not admire or his paradoxical encomia of what by his own lights instead should be reviled. As something novel, as something strange and unfamiliar, such themes, as well as the conceits through which they are developed and the images through which they are imagined, would surely elicit a novel response from readers accustomed to the conventional themes, conceits, imagery of the orthodox sonnet.

However, in addition to these literary novelties, the dark lady's poet also offers his own *speaking* as correlative to the various literary innovations that he both speaks and speaks about:

> My thoughts and my discourse as madmen's are,
> At randon from the truth vainly express'd;
> For I have sworn thee fair, and thought thee bright,
> Who art as black as hell, as dark as night.
>
> (147)

And while this kind of collation of speaking with spoken is nothing but a long-familiar sonneteering theme, in the dark lady sonnets it serves to introduce into the genre of the sonnet sequence a novelty whose literary effect is more than merely thematic.

Simply in terms of theme, there is something historically significant about the way the poet associates the nature of his speech with the nature of his lady. By characterizing his own language as something that is false, a "discourse . . . at randon from the truth vainly express'd," the dark lady's poet speaks against the themes of self-validating Cratylitic language that inform the sonnet from the "beatitude" of Dante's "Beatrice," or the self-applauding "laud" of Petrarch's "Laura," up through and beyond the starry light of Sidney's "Stella." Simply in terms of imagery there is also something historically significant about the way the dark lady sonnets regularly imagine their speech as something verbal, not visual, as in "mine eyes seeing this, say this is not" (137). As I have argued, by admitting and expressing this difference between the visual and the verbal the dark lady sonnets, in an unprecedented way, forswear the poetics of idealization, replacing a language composed of visionary "ideas" with a language of "forswearing" words. By themselves such thematic and figural innovations are powerful and decisive revisions of what is central in a perennial and traditional poetics, in the idealizing and self-idealizing poetics of *ut pictura poesis,* of "speaking picture," of "Ideas Mirrour." But these new themes and images acquire an additional and a special force when the dark lady's poet takes seriously the association of the *way* he speaks with *what* he speaks about, when his own "tongue" becomes, as in sonnet 127, example of the way that "beauty" "now" is "sland[ered]" with a "false esteem." To the extent that the dark lady sonnets make this association seem persuasive, the very words the poet speaks become the demonstration and corroboration of the poet's novel, and rhetorically paradoxical, panegyric point of view.

This point can be made—inadequately—by contrasting the implicit Liar's paradox of sonnet 115 with the explicit Liar's paradox of sonnet 138. When the young man's poet says "Those lines that I before have writ do lie," the confession applies, at least initially, only to the past. It is only as sonnet 115 proceeds that the poet's admission of a bygone lie comes more and more to encroach upon the poet's present. In contrast, as I argued in chapter 3, from the very beginning of sonnet 138—"When my love swears that she is made of truth"—the dark lady's poet asserts explicitly the way in which "I do believe her, though I know she lies." The rest of sonnet 138 is designed to show why this might be a reasonable proposition. Whatever one thinks of these two sonnets, the differences between them are not delicate. In the young man sonnet the Liar's paradox that is in the air remains incipient and unspoken, operating in between the lines, as, for example, in between "Might I not then say" and "'Now I love you best.'" Sonnet 115 never actually, or literally, or explicitly, asserts the self-belying it calls up. And because there is an increasingly more palpable resistance or discrepancy between the manifest intention of the sonnet—i.e., how to find a way truthfully to say "Now I love you best"—and the latent implication of the sonnet— i.e., the growing realization that the very assertion of this intention is what renders the assertion false—the sonnet acquires, as it proceeds, an increasingly more serious and more textured tone of conflict and regret. In contrast, in the dark lady sonnet the poet *begins* with the truth of the lady's lies, taking the dilemma thus discovered as a problem directly to be faced. In the dark lady sonnet there is no discrepancy between the manifest and latent levels of the sonnet. The poet means what he says, even though, indeed because, what he says is that he does not mean what he says. Where the young man sonnet acquires its weight by resisting the direct expression of the paradox that haunts it, the dark lady sonnet instead exploits the paradox so as to make it seem a serious kind of truth. Where the young man's poet wants to escape the paradox, the dark lady's poet instead embraces it, and, for this reason, however one interprets "lie," is, as a result, embraced by it: "Therefore I lie with her, and she with me,/ And in our faults by lies we flattered be."

In a purely logical way, the Liar's paradox expressed in sonnet 138 situates the voice of the poet in an altogether different register than that sounded in sonnet 115. If a poet says that what he says is true, then what he says is either true or false. In contrast, if a poet says that what he says is false, then what he says is neither true nor false but both of these together in an irresolvably self-conscious and para-doxical fashion. This is the deliberately trivial and witty logical gam-bit of sonnet 138, distinguished only, as I argued earlier, by the fact that the poet in the sonnet tries to take it seriously. A Liar's paradox, however, because its self-reference involves only a logical, not a rhe-torical, paradox, by itself carries very little literary force. For this reason, it remains, perhaps, an open question whether the poet in sonnet 138 is altogether committed to the "lies" that he invokes. However, this kind of self-canceling self-reference becomes far more consequential and effective when the dark lady sonnets posi-tively associate such self-belying with their own rhetorical proce-dure, which is to say when this kind of paradoxical hyperthematiza-tion of poetic language, conflating rhetorical use with rhetorical mention, appears more literally and more literarily to make its self-denying point.

Thus in sonnet 132 the lady's "mourning eyes become thy face," and for this reason the poet resolves: "Then will I swear beauty her-self is black,/And all they foul that thy complexion lack." Registering the pun on "mourning," whose doubleness displaces the unity of "morning," the poet here literally puts difference *into* words by showing the way that "one thing expressing" *puts in* "difference"— not the merely logical difference of a Liar's paradox, but the rhetori-cal difference of a speaking whose multiple semantic resonations are a demonstration of the way that language by its nature lacks the univocity with which to mean or be the unity it wants to speak. In sonnet 132 what I have called the "languageness" of language, heard as such, in this way becomes the motive and motif of what the poet speaks. This is an example of what I meant earlier when I referred to the mimic or second-degree Cratylism of the dark lady sonnets. By their very speaking, the dark lady sonnets realize their parodic ver-sion of the traditionally idealized correspondence of speaking with spoken, and in doing so they give a reason *why* "then will I swear beauty herself is black."

To take one more example, consider the way sonnet 134 not only renders explicit, at the level of theme and image, what is implicit in the young man sonnets, but also the way in which it supports this explication with the language that it speaks. The sonnet begins with the poet's having "confess'd that he is thine,/And I myself am mortgag'd to thy will." Because the poet's young man is thus pos-sessed, or repossessed, by the lady, the poet proposes an exchange: "Myself I'll forfeit, so that other mine/Thou wilt restore to be my comfort still." The lady, however, refuses this proposal. "But thou wilt not," says the poet, "nor he will not be free," and this because "thou art covetous, and he is kind," and 'the statute of thy beauty thou wilt take,/Thou usurer, that put'st forth all to use." And, as a result, the poet bawdily concludes: "So him I lose through my unkind abuse./Him have I lost, thou hast both him and me,/He pays the whole, and yet am I not free."

At the level both of theme and of image the poet here says quite directly what is consistently suggested in the sonnets addressed to the young man. The coupling of "covetous" and "kind," which represents the double betrayal of the poet, is an unkind "kind" of the sort suggested by the unspoken ambiguities of "'fair,' 'kind,' and 'true' is all my argument" (105). So too the lady's "usury" and the poet's "unkind abuse" pick up the double "use" of "That use is not forbidden usury" (6), just as the coupling of the lady with the man projects the alienating, but implicit, double "yous" and "hues" of the young man sub-sequence into a straightforward narrative relation. The introduction of a third person here doubles the objects of the poet's desire and thereby divides the poet from himself. Because the sonnet is developed in this chiasmic way, through the double dialectic of the financial conceit, through the cross-coupling of the erotic narrative, it makes sense to say, and the sonnet does indeed say, that what the lady possesses is equal to the poet's "loss," or, more abstractly, that the conjunction of the lady with the man is equal to the poet's disjunction.

This is witty and consistent, and it brings out very well the way the poet's heart is broken by its systematic duplication. All this is developed, however, so as to lead to the poet's final pun on "whole," where a "present-absent" double U spells out for the poet the way the erotic "whole" of the young man, when it is placed in the erotic "hole" of the lady, is the same as the affective "hole" within the first-person "whole" of the poet. In terms of imagery, this "(w)hole" within and without the "(w)hole" repeats, though in a far more vivid way, the young man's "pricked prick." So too, in terms of theme and in terms of conceit the double U makes very clear the double "use" exchanged between the poet's double "yous."

But all this is given an additional support by virtue of the difference that is *sounded* in the sonnet's "whole." This sounding, though it stands as warrant for image, conceit, and theme, does not operate at the level of image, or conceit, or theme. It operates instead in a purely verbal, linguistic dimension, in a realm of pure languageness, in which the sound of "whole" becomes a signifier that is significant *because* it is detached from any signified. This *rhetorically* achieved detachment is far more real and more persuasive than the way the speaker of a Liar's paradox is removed, by simply logical translation, to a place beyond the true and false. In sonnet 134 the very sounding of "whole" becomes the literal realization of the difference that the sonnet otherwise merely speaks about. And for this reason, at least in sonnet 134, it is the differential, double "whole" of language that makes the poet's witty, bawdy, but, because of what we *hear* in "whole," profoundly poignant point.

These are small and local examples, the "mo(u)rning" of sonnet 132, the "w(h)ole" of sonnet 134, the "lie" of sonnet 138, the "lack" in "black" in sonnet 127. They are characteristic, however, of the way the dark lady sonnets regularly strive, and quite self-consciously, to make their specifically linguistic effects appear as validating witness to their novel poetic themes, devices, and imagery. This explicit and verifying "bespeaking" of the dark lady sonnets is quite different from the way the verbal undertones of the young man sonnets mutely undercut the young man's poet's ideal point of view. In the dark lady sonnets the language that one is forced to hear—to hear, that is, *as* language—functions as a supplementary and confirming, not a disavowing, gloss on what the poet has to say. This is not a metaphorical way of characterizing the way in which the dark lady sonnets work. After listening to such a "mourning" or to such a "whole," it is no longer possible for us to hear a poet, any poet, praise the brightness of the "morning" or the plenitude of the "whole" without our registering the differentiating echo that the dark lady sonnets literally insert into the very language of the language of praise. And it is this *hearable* reflexivity, active and activating, that gives the dark lady sonnets their novel authority and their novel consequentiality. Because the dark lady's poet speaks a rhetorical, not a merely logical, paradox, he demonstrates in an immediate and palpable way that it is really not the case that "one thing expressing, leaves out difference." And this demonstration sanctions and calls forth the novel terms of the poet's "argument," the "argument," that is, whose point is that poetic discourse is now no longer "'fair,' 'kind,' and 'true.'"

This extra *rhetorical* wrinkle with which the dark lady sonnets inflect their speech is therefore something very significant with regard both to the effect that the dark lady sonnets elicit and to their status in, or significance for, the history of the lyric. The dark lady sonnets are not necessarily more verbally dense or more complex than a good many other poems that might be cited in this context. Indeed, in several respects they are considerably more simple, if only because they abolish a familiar—and, at a certain point, uninteresting—discrepancy between manifest and latent poetic intention. However, because the dark lady sonnets assimilate the peculiar things they say to the peculiar way in which they say them, they are able to make their odd poetic manner serve as guarantee, to be itself the voucher or vouchsafer for, the truth of their poetic matter.

This is important, but it is important precisely to the extent that it is particular. It is necessary to insist upon the specificity of the poetic themes that are *spoken for* by the forswearing speech of the dark lady sonnets, for it is *only* these particular themes—the peculiar, gainsaying, postidealist, paradoxically epideictic assertions of the dark lady sonnets—that the gainsaying languageness of language manifest in the dark lady sonnets can thus positively support. This is why it is fair to say that the perennial poetics of the poetry of praise prescribes in advance the details of its own forswearing, for it is *only* idealism that the language of postidealism has the effective power to displace. On the other hand, this in no way diminishes the significance of Shakespeare's sonnets for later literary history. However much the poetry that precedes them determines the novelty of Shakespeare's sonnets, it remains the case that poets and readers successive to Shakespeare's sonnets, which is to say poets and readers who have heard the languageness of language that is sounded in Shakespeare's sonnets, cannot afterwards forget the significance of the sounds that they have heard.

Again, this is not a metaphorical way of speaking: it is instead a literal characterization of the way in which Shakespeare's sonnets show the inadequacy of a received and orthodox, and the necessity for a new, albeit paradoxical, figure of speech. At the very least, Shakespeare's sonnets register and represent an essential transformation of the nature of poetic language, at least as such language is historically understood, treated, and figured by traditional poetics and traditional poetry. The significance of this transformation cannot be overestimated, for it effectively constrains for post-Renaissance literary history the possible scope of subsequent poetic assertion. In the Western literary tradition, a tradition that begins with and thinks itself through the specular idealization of the literary word, it is necessarily the case that a language characterized as something of the tongue will spell the end of visionary poetics.

Such a verbal poetics will necessarily *enforce* a desire for what is not admired, and in doing so thereby promote a specifically misogynistic, heterogeneous, heterosexual desire for an Other which is not the ideal, homogeneous, homosexual Same. For the sake of its own coherence, such a poetry of re-presentation is *obliged* to represent the loss of presence, so that, for example, the universal present of an ideal time will become a moment whose "Now" is now located in the past, just as the ideal space of epideictic fullness will become a surface whose completely smooth uninterruption is marked by an intrusive scar or gap, or a depth whose deep recesses overflow with the internment of their own internal loss. These are some of the consequences that follow, but that follow by *literary* necessity, from the way Shakespeare's sonnets effectively repeat, but with a difference, the literary language that is spoken by the language of praise. And in this way the gainsaying nature of language that is demonstrated by audition in Shakespeare's sonnets—a language acquired on condition that it speak against itself—exigently dictates, literally predictates, what later poetry can say.

Nowhere is the effect of this linguistic transformation more clearly evident than in the way the dark lady's poet presents his own poetic person. Explicitly introducing himself as a subject of forswearing language, the dark lady's poet invents and acts out the peculiarly conflicted psychology of a "perjur'd eye." Again, given the context and conventions of the traditional sonnet, this psychology presents the reader with a strange and unfamiliar—indeed, with an unprecedented—poetic persona. Again, however, this psychology, its peculiarity stressed and remarked by the poet himself, is made persuasive to the reader by the way the poet speaks. In the dark lady sonnets language itself becomes, *because* it speaks, the spokesman for the poet's unhappy poetic persona: the poet whose very speaking is what leads him thereupon to speak against himself. And the point to insist upon is that this is the case not only for the particular poetic persona who appears in Shakespeare's sonnets. More generally, this defines a fate that is imposed on *any* poetic persona who, situated in the visionary literary tradition of the West, realizes and renders real the fact that what he speaks is speech.

As I have suggested, we can see the way in which this happens, and understand why it happens, in almost all the dark lady sonnets, for throughout the sub-sequence the dark lady's poet is concerned with the personalizing way that "I have sworn thee fair: more perjur'd eye,/To swear against the truth so foul a lie!" (152) It is most

outspokenly exampled, however, in the bizarre dark lady sonnets
wherein the poet plays on "Will," for these are sonnets in which
the relation of poetic subjectivity to forswearing language is
most directly—we can say, following their example, willfully—
expressed. It is true that these "Will" sonnets are not the most universally admired of Shakespeare's sonnets. Indeed, for many idealizing
readers these are sonnets that show Shakespeare at his worst, prepared to let the whole world slide, as Johnson or Christopher Sly
would say, for the sake of a pun. For this very reason, however, precisely because their puns on "Will" so brazenly articulate poetic person, and also as a way of concluding and summarizing the long argument of this book, it will be worthwhile to consider the specific ways
in which the dark lady's poet self-consciously names his name.[11]

The first thing that is striking about the "Will" sonnets is the simple fact that the dark lady's poet goes to so much stylizing trouble to
give himself a name. Again, the difference between this and what
happens in the young man sonnets is instructive and significant. In
the young man sonnets there are several plays on "will"; these, however, are relatively subdued, and the young man's poet does not
make a central issue of the way these "wills" make mention of his
name. Instead, the young man's poet characteristically restricts the
marking of his first person to the system of deictic, I-you, indication
that I have associated with the poetics of epideixis, and whose egocentric mutuality the young man's poet consistently, but again only
implicitly, resists. Thus the poet of the first sub-sequence is an "I"
identified only after the fact with the "you" of the young man—"For
as you were when first your eye I ey'd" (104)—and, of course, a "you"
whose ideal and eternal name we never get to hear. If the young
man's poet tells the young man "your name from hence immortal life
shall have" (81), nevertheless, in what might seem deliberately
"anonymizing" fashion, the young man's poet continues "counting
no old thing old, thou mine, I thine,/Even as when first I hallowed
thy fair name" (108). Correspondingly, even though the young man
sonnets will often speak about their poet's name, the name itself is
never really forcefully pronounced. Quite the contrary, the young
man's poet either explicitly prohibits the speaking of his name—
"When I (perhaps) compounded am with clay,/Do not so much as
my poor name rehearse" (71)—or he speaks of it as something that is
only "almost" spoken, as when "every word doth almost tell my
name" (76). Like the young man's name, which is blemished by the
"canker" that "doth spot the beauty of thy budding name" (95), the

young man's poet's name is typically "stell'd" by the imagery
through which it is conceived: "Thence comes it that my name receives a brand" (111). Even so, the young man sonnets seem deliberately designed to keep their poet's name unspoken.

In emphatic contrast, however, the poet of the dark lady, at least
in the sonnets that play on "Will," not only makes his self-
denomination into a central and explanatory theme—"Make but
my name thy love, and love that still,/And then thou lovest me, for
my name is *Will*" (136)—but also speaks this name in such reverberating and resounding fashion that it becomes, at least at times, a
sound informing almost all the other words he speaks: "Will will
fulfill the treasure of thy love,/Ay fill it full with wills, and my will
one" (136). This intoning of the poet's name, the deliberate excess of
its repetition, calls attention to its purely verbal quality, giving this
verbality a special kind of hearable materiality. By virtue of its
stressed repetition, "Will" turns into a kind of chant, a sound heard
almost purely as a sound, a signifier unrelated in its sounding to any
particular signified. This is an effect, a *naming* effect, that is achieved
despite the fact—more precisely, *alongside* the fact—that "will" also
retains its function in these sonnets as a common noun and familiar
verbal form, as the kind of word possessed of ordinary semantic reference or meaning. In the phrase "Will will fulfill," for example, we
have no difficulty understanding the way in which "Will" "will"
"fulfill," and this will be the case no matter what particular meanings
we assign to "Will" or "will." At the same time, however, in an altogether different semiotic register, one that is at least at one remove
from ordinary meaning, the reverberating, sonar repetition of "Will"
and "will" is what marks them both with the added signature of the
poet's proper name, for it is precisely the verbal surplus that is produced by their insistent repetition that transforms both "W(w)ills"
into mentions of the poet's proper name. Again, it is no metaphor to
say that through this verbal surplus wrought by repetition "Will" or
"will" becomes, as a name, an extraordinary piece of language raised
above or distinct from the ordinary, because merely meaningful,
"wills" on which it is superimposed. (In the Quarto this extraordinariness is indicated by the italicization of "Will," so that "Will," understood as a proper name, literally looks different from, even though it
is the same as, all the other words on the page; the Quarto's typogra-
phy attempts to illustrate or to picture the excessive, surplus language that we hear.)

By insisting on this verbal repetition, therefore, and on the purely verbal surplus that the repetition thereupon calls up, the poet effectively accomplishes in these "Will" sonnets the naming of himself. (We do not, for example, need an outside biographical source to tell us that the poet's name is "Will"; neither would it much matter if we suddenly discovered that the historical author of the sonnets did not really bear the name of "Will".) What is important about the repetition, however, is that by thus intoning this reverberating "Will" the dark lady's poet opens up a new linguistic means or way with which to speak *about* himself, a means that simply does not exist in the epideictic sonnets addressed to the young man. For the "Will" that the dark lady's poet so pronouncedly pronounces is not a merely deictic indication; it is not an "I," that is, whose referential function requires for determination of its referent—who is "I"?—that its speaker be a speaker who is present to his speech. Quite the contrary, the "Will" to which the poet gives voice in the dark lady sonnets is a fixed and stable designation that identifies the poet's individual and individuated self, and does so, moreover, *regardless* of who speaks it. This is a significant difference, for with the naming of his name the poet acquires a referential person, particular and singular, precisely because the poet's person can now, for the first time, in a way that heretofore is unavailable, be spoken *about*. However, while this personal self-reference distinguishes the poet from all other persons, it does so at a personal cost. For if "Will" thus names the person of the poet, it does so in a rather impersonal way, introducing the possibility, the purely linguistic possibility, for the poet meaningfully to be referred to even in his absence. Naming himself, therefore, the poet *to* himself becomes a "he," someone to be spoken about, a third person elsewhere from and different from his first and second person. For this reason, however, even when, and just because, the poet speaks his personal name, the person thus referred to is located in a discursive space of reference in which the poet, as a speaker, necessarily is not. As a result, the poet's name, which designates and thereby fixes person, adduces a distinction between the person who is spoken and the person who is speaking, and the consequence for the poet is that he finds his "Will" at odds with his "I."

Simply in formal terms, this amounts to a significant difference, a difference of discursive kind, between the way the young man's poet and the dark lady's poet can express their sense of self. The young man's poet indicates his person with a deictic, with an "I," that he shares with any other first-person speaker, but an "I" that only gains its referent when its speaker registers his presence to his speech. In contrast, the dark lady's poet will speak about himself with a quite distinctive name that identifies the particularity of his person, but a name whose reference thereby translates person into something functionally *bespoken*. To be sure, this is only a formal difference between deictic and nominal reference, but the dark lady's poet, as a person, as a subjectivity, is thematically subjected to this purely formal difference. For what is most remarkable about the poet's self-denomination in the dark lady sonnets is that when the poet so loudly, almost obsessively, announces his name—a name that only designates the poet and operates as a name when its reiterated pronouncing separates it off from any ordinary meaning— precisely then does the poet say about his alienated person what is only indirectly expressed in the sonnets addressed to the young man. And yet there is nothing really all that strange about this, for it is only when the poet speaks the nominal "Will" that allows him to speak about his person from a discursive referential distance that he possesses the linguistic means with which to say what is indirectly expressed in the sonnets addressed to the young man: namely, that the ideal visionary unity of poetic self, compact of the specular identity of "I" and "you," of ego and ego ideal, is sundered by the very language with which it is expressed. Putting the point as bluntly as possible, we can say that when the dark lady's poet gives voice to his name—again, when he literally gives *voice*, through repetition, to the "Will" which as a name explicitly denominates the specificity of person—precisely then does the poet possess the languageness and language that enables him to speak in a persuasive way about, and in explicit and specific thematic ways about, his distance from himself. In this way the poet's "I," equal to the ideal identity and presence of the poet's first and second person each to each other (e.g., the poet and the young man), finds its unity disrupted by the poet's "Will," which stands as a third person situated in between, as missing copular connection, the poet's "I" and "you." The poet himself, as a subject or a subjectivity, thereby becomes the product of this difference between his being and his name.

To say this is to say that the languageness of language that is realized by and in the poet's reiterated "Will" is not only something that the poet associates with the paradoxically conflicted person that he speaks about. This is also to say that the speaking of this "Will" is the potentiating, necessary, determining, and *realizing* condition of the poet's sense of psychological division. The most obvious example of the way "Will" breaks the unity of the poet would be the straightforward eroticism of the "Will" sonnets, the way they luridly exploit the fact that in Elizabethan slang "Will" refers to both the male and female genitals: "Whoever hath her wish, thou hast thy Will, and Will to boot, and Will in overplus" (135). Recognizing the pun, the sexual denotations of which are elaborately teased out, we might say that the poet's richly resonating name here linguistically performs the copulation that the poet speaks about. Perhaps this is why the "Will" sonnets can speak of sexuality in terms that are so openly assertive, in terms that are, at any rate, far more open and assertive than anything we hear about in the sonnets addressed to the young man. But this explicitness, if it is sanctioned by the verbal "overplus" of "Will," again is purchased at a specific personal price. If the poet thus gives voice to sexual union, he does so at the cost of the loss of the unity of himself. Pronouncing his erotic name, the poet forswears the truth and unity of deixis—"Swear to thy blind soul that I was thy Will" (136)—and this because his intercoursing name denominates the difference that distinguishes his erotic pointer from his erotic pointed, the way the presence of the one is equal to the absence of the other. Thinking back to the young man sonnets, we can say that equivocal "Will" quite literally doubles the double entendre of sonnet 20, and in this chiasmic fashion introduces a heretofore unspoken sexuality explicitly to speech. But the consequence of this equivocation, insofar as the poet identifies himself with the name that designates his person, is that the poet hereafter identifies himself not only with the "pricked prick" of the young man, but also—and the pun is one that Shakespeare does not elsewhere hesitate to make (cf. Malvolio's "These be her very c's, her u's, and her t's," *TN*, 2.5.86 –87)—with the "cut cunt" of the lady: "So thou being rich in Will add to thy Will/One will of mine to make thy large Will more" (135).

As when sonnet 20 plays on "prick'd," the poet's bawdy pun on "Will" might seem a merely local, adventitious piece of wit. But again the pun, though it is surely very witty, opens up a good many other personal explications, not only erotic, of the young man sonnets' implications. The young man sonnets only tacitly suggest that the poet is the missing connection between his first and second persons, they only indirectly associate the poet with the young man's double "hue," or with the "one thing to my purpose nothing," or with an "addition" that is equal to subtraction. The dark lady sonnets, however, by virtue of their polysemic "Will," directly identify the poet not only with the cross-coupling, copulating copula between male and female, but also with what lies between the poet's showing and hiding, between his fair and unfair, between his presence and his absence, between his whole and hole, between his one and none: "Wilt thou, whose will is large and spacious,/Not once vouchsafe to hide my will in thine?/Shall will in others seem right gracious,/And in my will no fair acceptance shine?" (135)

It would be possible to follow out in detail the ways in which these various binary oppositions, which are rendered problematic by the name that dares to speak the poet's love, systematically extract from their play on "Will" a set of personal paradoxes that are only tonally conveyed in the sonnets addressed to the young man. It would be possible to do so, but there is really no need to do so, and this precisely because the poet now is able clearly to say about himself what before he only mutely implies. With his name the poet is able to explain, in a way that requires no elaborate interpretative paraphrase, the logic that turns his person into a something which is nothing and a nothing which is something:

> Will will fulfill the treasure of thy love,
> Ay fill it full with wills, and my will one.
> In things of great receipt with ease we prove
> Among a number one is reckon'd none.
> (136)

In these lines the poet directly summons up the paradoxical class of all classes that does not classify itself (which is the most general formulation of what is paradoxical about the Liar's paradox) and directly applies the paradox to his person. This is why it is with "ease" that the poet's "Will" can "prove" the "hole" in "whole" or the "one" in "none":

> Then in the number let me pass untold,
> Though in thy store's account I one must be,
> For nothing hold me, so it please thee hold
> That nothing me, a something sweet to thee.[12]
> (136)

Moreover, it is not only through such purely logical paradoxes that "Will" conveys the poet's paradoxical psychology. In addition, the themes and images that are employed to characterize the poet's name also materially flesh out the person of the poet, again allowing

the poet explicitly to assimilate to himself what is only indirectly
intimated in the sonnets addressed to the young man. Consider, for
example, the bawdy way in which the poet's "flesh" in sonnet 151
"stays no farther reason,/But rising at thy name doth point out thee/
As his triumphant prize." Here the quarrel between name and deictic is quite vividly enacted. Identified with the language which is at
once the poet's and the lady's "common place," the poet's flesh and
person both become a disappointed pointer, simultaneously waxing
and waning, tumescent and detumescent, precisely because "I call/
Her 'love' for whose dear love I rise and fall" (151). And "Will" also
calls forth the young man sonnets' "still-born" baby, but now as a
straightforward image of the poet's self. In the young man sonnets
"love is a babe" whose "full growth" always "still doth grow" (115).
In the dark lady sonnets, however, it is the poet himself who is such
an exigently frustrate baby, his desire defined as a structurally un-
satisfiable desire *to be* the satisfying desire of an other's desire, to *be*
the desire that the poet *calls* "Will":

> So run'st thou after that which flies from thee,
> Whilst I, thy babe, chase thee afar behind . . .
>   So will I pray that thou mayst have thy Will,
>   If thou turn back and my loud crying still.
> (143)

All this defines the testament of Shakespearean "Will." In the
dark lady sonnets "Will" is an extraordinary piece of language that
hovers over, yet also informs, the merely ordinary language that the
poet speaks. It does so in the same tangential, inside-outside way in
which unspeakable "Jehova" is both apart from and a part of the
wholeness of Fludd's visionary Nature. The only difference between
"Will" and "Jehova" is that the dark lady's poet actually pronounces,
and thereby remarks, the languageness of his name, sounding it out
in an outspoken way, rather than referring euphemistically, as is the
periphrastic custom with "Jehova," to "the Lord" or to "the Name."
But this is a difference that really does make *all* the difference. For
when the dark lady's poet gives voice to his name, he thereby gives
expression to the original verbal difference that the sameness of a
visionary language is committed to leave out. Speaking his name,
therefore, the dark lady's poet speaks a secret that idealizing piety
and poetry prefer to keep in silence. As a result, and perhaps as a
punishment—but a result and a punishment which are prepared for
from before the very beginning of idealism—the poet experiences

at the level of his person the illogic of the *Logos*. He lives out as psychology—particularly as erotic psychology, as "will"—the foundational, constitutive, but heretofore unspeakable paradox that is buried at the heart of, and nestled in between the legs of, orthodox phenomenology, ontology, cosmology, theology. Precisely because he voices the signifier of all personal signifiers, the name which is his "Will," the poet, through the speaking that speaks through him, becomes a person both apart from and a part of his visionary self.

This is the subjectivity that is willed to literary history by Shakespeare's sonnets. And with this subjectivity there comes also a specific literariness. After Shakespeare, all poetry, if it is to be called poetry, will be a poetry of para-Petrachanism not Petrachanism, a poetry of the serious, not comic, paradox of praise, a poetry of representation not presentation, of speech not vision, of name not deixis, of misogynistic heterosexuality not idealizing homosexuality, of heterogeneous difference not homogeneous likeness.

For this "Will" which breaks the person of the poet cannot itself be broken. It cannot be broken because poetry itself—as a theme, as a metaphor, as an image, as an idea, as a word, and also as a practice—necessarily participates in this Shakespearean legacy. Whatever might be different from Shakespeare's poetry of verbal difference would therefore have to find, outside language, another name. Excessive to language, such a hypothetical successor to the Shakespearean would not only be extraliterary, but, in addition, outside history.

Epilogue

This long book on Shakespeare's sonnets was originally conceived as a short, introductory chapter to a book on character in Shakespeare's plays. As it turned out, the discussion of subjectivity in Shakespeare's sonnets took on a life and length of its own and, as a result, any detailed discussion of Shakespearean dramatic character must therefore be postponed. I would like, however, briefly to sketch out the way in which my account of the subject of a "perjur'd eye" helps not only to explain the formation of different subjectivity effects in Shakespeare's plays, but, in addition, how these differences can be correlated, very generally, with generic differences among Shakespearean comedy, tragedy, and romance.

I have argued that in Shakespeare's sonnets a poetics of visionary presentation, associated with the orthodox, idealizing tradition of the poetry of praise, is confronted with and confounded by an unorthodox poetics of verbal representation, the latter understood as a kind of self-consciously mimetic and paradoxical troping of the former. As Shakespeare develops it, the poetics of representation is guilty of its difference from the poetics of presentation. Representation, stressing and registering itself *as* representation, calls up and evokes as something absent the truthful presentation it confesses truly it is not. There is therefore, as Shakespeare develops it, a structural pathos built into representation. The "re-" of representation effects the loss of presentation; it is responsible for that loss because representation is not only achieved over the dead body of the presence it repeats, but, more actively, this very repetition is what transforms such ideal presence into something of the past.

In his sonnets Shakespeare assimilates this structural pathos to the persona of the speaking poet. The sonnets show what happens to poetic subjectivity when a language of visionary presence is replaced and displaced by a language of verbal representation. As a subject of representation, as a character subjected to representation, the subject of a "perjur'd eye" is cut off, because he speaks, from the fullness of subjective self-presence that is regularly held out as a realizable personal ideal by the tradition of the poetry of praise. As I have said, the poet in Shakespeare's sonnets is therefore puffed up with the loss of himself to himself, a loss that is not only asserted by, but is in fact occasioned by, the language that he speaks.

In Shakespeare's sonnets the poet's personal experience of this loss or, rather, the characterization of the personal experience of this loss, is fleshed out through a specific narrative (the poet's relation to the young man and to the dark lady, and his relation to the coupling of the young man and the dark lady each with the other) and a specific set of themes and images (all of which derive their conceptual and material coherence from the way they introduce a paradoxical phenomenology of difference into orthodox themes and images of ideal likeness or sameness). In addition, speaking in the first person, the poet also conveys his own subjective rupture by employing a characteristic and a characterizing rhetoricity (the chiasmicizing rhetoricity of the "cross-coupler" which works its rhetorical effects by repeating with a difference the tropes of dual unity and likeness that are traditionally employed in the poetry of praise).

I have also said, however, that, for all their novelty in the history of the sonnet, this narrative, these themes and images, and this rhetoricity remain faithful to the orthodox literariness they sublate together. Paradoxing the orthodox, troping in an uncanny way the familiar tropes of a perennial poetic tradition, Shakespeare's sonnets reconstitute the ideal *as* that which they succeed, with the result that ideality survives in Shakespeare's sonnets as something palpably bygone. It is in this way that the "re-" of Shakespearean representation, as it calls attention to itself, manages to revive, but as something essentially absent, the traditional ideality of epideictic poetry.

With regard to the person of the poet, this nostalgically citational allegiance to the ideality of a prior poetics works to inform poetic subjectivity with all the authority and force possessed by traditional literariness. The difference is that the poet of a "perjur'd eye" is now inhabited, because he speaks his novel speech of representation, by the presence of his absence (e.g., the "present-absent" letters of sonnet 45); he is continually haunted, as he experiences and responds to the literary belatedness that he himself creates, by the ghost or shade of his ideal vision of himself. For this reason, the language that the poet speaks, though it speaks against itself, works effectively and materially to corroborate the poet's sense of broken person. Presented *as* representation, language points to itself and thereby *realizes* the loss of the poet's personal ideal. In his sonnets Shakespeare coherently develops the psychologistic consequences that follow from this loss, the reality of which is insistently adduced and confirmed by the fact that what the poet speaks is speech. I have spoken, for example, of the complicated misogynistic desire that language forces on the poet, of the fractured interior space and past-present temporality that the poet feels within the "withinness" of his person, of a simultaneously brittle and liquid body ego composed of the phenomenality of difference. All this goes a good way toward defining and determining a specific characterological psychology.

For all its naturalistic detail, however, we must recognize that it is for strictly literary reasons that this psychology comes to possess the novelistic, "characterological" density and texture that is regularly taken to be the distinctive feature of Shakespeare's sonneteering persona. This characterology gains its power from the way the continually rediscovered "insufficiency" of speech establishes traditional literariness as something posthumous. *That* the poet speaks a new kind of literary language is what *proves* the poet's loss. In this self-belying, yet self-reinforcing, way the literary retrospection engendered by representation warrants the psychology of poetic introspection. For this reason it is necessary to realize that if the person of Shakespeare's sonnets amounts to a mutation in the history of literature, this mutation participates within and is conditioned by a larger literary history whose logic sustains and speaks for the coherence of Shakespearean characterology. And it is for this very reason that the particular psychology of Shakespeare's sonneteering first person possesses an importance beyond the history of the lyric up through Shakespeare. I have suggested that to the extent that Shakespeare's sonnets mark the historical conclusion of the tradition of epideictic poetics, to that extent the postepideictic subject of a "perjur'd eye" becomes the governing model of literary subjectivity in literature successive to Shakespeare.

To say that Shakespearean subjectivity is the governing model for subjectivity in literature after Shakespeare is not to say, at least not to say in any simple way, that this is the only instance or type of characterology that can be discovered in literature after Shakespeare. The point is not that authors who come after Shakespeare all read Shakespeare's sonnets and then proceed, when writing, to copy what they read (and here it should be mentioned that, at least up through Malone's edition, Shakespeare's sonnets appear to have been pretty much ignored). Rather, the claim is that Shakespeare in his sonnets drew—and not accidentally at the level of characterology—a fully literary response to the conclusion of the poetry of praise, a response that is fully "literary" because the *only* response to its demise that the perennial tradition of epideictic literariness can continue fully to support even after its conclusion.

This is why it is important to insist upon what I have called specifically literary exigencies that begin before and continue after Shakespeare, for such exigencies explain why Shakespearean characterology has established itself as something uniquely authoritative in the literary history that begins in the early modern period. This also suggests why strong writers who come after Shakespeare, even those authors who might not have read Shakespeare's sonnets, would still be very much affected by the subject of a "perjur'd eye." This Shakespearean subjectivity is authoritative and governing in the sense that, after the poetry of praise, it remains uniquely literary. For this reason, whatever other subjectivities authors might generate in literature after Shakespeare, these subjectivities will be conceived through this Shakespearean subject which functions as a necessary paradigm of literary character, as a master placeholder of literary person, in the aftermath of idealism.

Alternative subjectivities may perhaps be written in reaction to the Shakespearean; they may be imagined as attempts to exceed or to deny the Shakespearean. Nevertheless, to the extent that they are themselves literary, these post-Shakespearean experiments will measure themselves by, and will be measured by, the characterological literary norm to which Shakespeare in his sonnets gives substantial form. This is a norm that, even if Shakespeare had never written his sonnets, would still, as something virtual, control and constrain the subjective possibilities of any literature that understands itself historically to succeed the poetry of praise. It further follows that any literature that understands itself to be yet further successive to this Shakespearean succession, any literature that understands itself to be different in kind from Shakespearean literariness, will be obliged radically to rewrite the themes, tropes, images, and self-conception of literature, to rewrite them, however, to a point at which, on its own terms, practically as well as theoretically, such literature would understand itself to be extraliterary.

This is obviously a very large argument, extending far beyond Shakespeare. The various claims and assumptions made by the argument, including the apparent idealization both of Literature and of Literary History that it seems to depend on, cannot be fully defended in these concluding remarks. There is one way, however, in which this rather global argument concerning all literature returns us to Shakespeare in particular, for it follows from what has been said that what governs authors who come after Shakespeare also governs Shakespeare himself. This is why the discussion of the "perjur'd eye" in Shakespeare's sonnets leads to a consideration of character in Shakespeare's plays. For when Shakespeare comes to construct dramatic character, he too will be subject to the constraints imposed upon him by the literary necessity attaching to the Shakespearean subject fleshed out in the sonnets. This is the case, I would want to argue, from the beginning of Shakespeare's theatrical career to the end, and it explains both the similarities and the differences that obtain among major Shakespearean characters in all the dramatic genres to which Shakespeare turned his hand.

It is perhaps most important to see the operative force of this Shakespearean subject in Shakespearean comedy, for this is a genre in which major characters seem to be immune from the kind of representational pathos to which I have given such emphasis. Certainly the principal figures of Shakespearean comedy tend rather regularly, and not only in the festive comedies, to find whatever they may have lost in the course of their misadventures. So too the comedies only rarely work in any serious way to undercut the machinery of closure by means of which the complications of their plots are harmoniously resolved. For this reason, in terms of the argument I have presented, and as I have already suggested, it is reasonable to characterize Shakespearean comedy as a drama of presentation, a drama in which, as a corresponding consequence, characters arrive at a kind of personal and interpersonal "oneness"—the sort summed up, for example, by the imagery of concordant unity with which *Two Gentlemen of Verona* concludes: "One feast, one house, one mutual happiness" (5.4.173).

There are other reasons to call Shakespearean comedy a drama of presentation. It would be a mistake, however, to understand even the simplest Shakespearean comedy as altogether lacking the personal complexities that are developed in Shakespeare's sonnets, for it is precisely such complexities to which the major characters of the comedies are subjected by the complications of Shakespeare's comic plotting. The mixup of personal identity that occurs in *The Comedy of Errors*, to take a very early example, is organized as an almost diagrammatic acting out of the structure of cross-coupling, and it is only through their experience of such mutually confounded identity that the Antipholus twins acquire what little subjective weight they possess. In *The Comedy of Errors* Shakespeare doubles the single pair of twins given to him by his source, as though this kind of doubling of doubles were the means whereby Shakespeare thinks himself into drama. In later comedies Shakespeare will sophisticate this early double doubling scheme, portioning it out into the two halves of a double plot (e.g., *The Taming of the Shrew*), multiplying it into the serial permutations of pairs of pairs of lovers (e.g., *Love's Labor's Lost*), dividing it into two triangles which share a common, problematic vertex (e.g., *A Midsummer Night's Dream, Twelfth Night*). In all these cases, however, it is the structure of cross-coupling that controls the action of the characters in the play, and that obliges these characters to pass through the very same self-alienations and personal transformations as are developed in the sonnets. (It is worth noting that this chiasmic structure undoes the simpler doubling conventions of medieval allegorical drama in the same way that the cross-coupling rhetoricity of the sonnets redoubles with a difference the two-term figurality of epideictic comparison. Again Shakespeare uses the systematic difference between a convention and its redeployment so as to evoke and to frustrate conventional literary expectations.)

It would be possible to show that in those Shakespeare comedies in which characters are more fully developed than in *The Comedy of Errors* the central themes and images of Shakespeare's sonnets are featured in a very emphatic way. The collision of vision with language is an especially prominent issue in these more personalizing Shakespearean comedies, and this particular theme is directly and frequently associated, moreover, with the relation of presentation to representation (by means, for example, of quite obvious metatheatrical ironies, e.g., the Pyramus-Thisbe play within *A Midsummer Night's Dream*: "Tongue, lose thy light,/Moon, take thy flight" (5.1.304–5)). Characteristically, these themes and images, though they are given a good deal of attention, are either treated very lightly or they are kept at some significant remove from the central characters of the play (as in *A Midsummer Night's Dream*, where the tragedy of Pyramus and Thisbe is staged as something comic, or as in *The Taming of the Shrew*, where the alternative to orthodoxy is couched in terms of relatively familiar epideictic paradox). Because treated lightly or imagined as something alien to the norms of comic life, these themes and images do not impose themselves on Shakespeare's comic characters, and for this reason the comedies can peremptorily, and usually with stressed artificiality, put an end to the personal confusions that are developed by the plot. It remains the case, however, that it is only through or against the recognized possibility of such potentially serious confusion that Shakespeare's comic characters are regularly conceived, and this is why it makes no sense to say that these comedies, or the characters who carry their action, are unaware of that which they so ostentatiously avoid. This is the point of a line like "Cambio is chang'd into Lucentio" in *The Taming of the Shrew,* a line in which, so to speak, language defies language to do its worst. The wit of such a line, like the comedy of Shakespearean comedy, is far from naive, and this is why the major characters at the end of Shakespeare's comedies so often seem to acquire their personal resolutions by surrendering themselves to the dictates of a depersonalizing circumspection. This is why, that is, these characters often seem to know far more than they are either willing or allowed to say.

On the other hand, because Shakespeare's comedies do not present the pathos of representation in an explicitly serious way, neither do they produce very strong subjective effects, and this is why Shakespeare's comic characters so often seem so thin. It happens, of course, that Shakespeare's comedies will sometimes produce especially strong, "characterological" characters. When they do so, however, it is usually the case that the comedy or the comic character begins to exceed the generic scope of comedy—*Twelfth Night,* for example, where representation is taken very seriously, where both Malvolio and Viola are very powerfully "personalized," but a comedy that verges, as many critics have remarked, at least at times, on tragedy. Falstaff, who is well aware of the pathos of representation, would be another example of a fully fleshed-out comic character who is, for this reason, more than comic.

In tragedy, in contrast, Shakespeare is able to assimilate the range of themes and images that are developed in the sonnets more immediately and seriously to dramatic character. So too Shakespeare's tragic characters evince the kind of psychology that I have associated with the "perjur'd eye." In contrast to Shakespearean comedy, the drama of presentation, Shakespearean tragedy, we can say, is a drama of representation, a drama that fully acknowledges the consequential loss of presentation. As a result, Shakespeare's tragic heroes, because they incorporate loss into their person, because they enact in their actions their loss of self-presence, thereby acquire their remarkable subjective density. I have mentioned, for example, the way in which Richard II becomes a realized person when he breaks the mirror of language on which depends his ideal image of himself, or the way Othello, discovering how very truly words are false, passes from being "all in all sufficient" to "that's he that was Othello; here I am." King Lear too learns the folly of his old-fashioned investment in the ceremonial language of praise, and so too the folly of his Cratylitic commitment to "the name, and all th' addition to a king." For this reason, Lear lives to die upon his deictic vision of Cordelia's genuinely postepideictic mouth: "Look her lips,/ Look there, look there!" All these tragic characters live out the unilateral and irreversible effects of Hamlet's translational difference: "Ay, truly, for the power of beauty will sooner transform honesty from what it is to a bawd than the force of honesty can translate beauty into his likeness." All of them experience, in terms of the psychology, themes, and imagery developed in the sonnets, especially the problematic relation of vision to language, that "this was sometime a paradox, but now the time gives it proof." (The moment of maximum personal confusion in *Hamlet*, it can be recalled, occurs when Hamlet names himself in terms of light: "This is one Lucianus, nephew to the king." Thus denominated, the murderer in the play within the play becomes the nephew, not the brother, of his victim— Hamlet becomes Claudius—in a mixup that not only frustrates the revenge plot but also disrupts the presentational aesthetics of a play that is supposed to function as a "mirror up to nature," working by visual likeness to "show virtue her feature, scorn her own image, and the very age and body of the time his form and pressure.")

This is also why the tragedies are more erotically inflected than the comedies. Shakespearean desire, I have argued, requires the loss of presence in order to motivate its yearning. The comedies cannot admit such loss into themselves without thereby transgressing the logic and psychologic of their genre. This is why, for all the bawdy puns, Shakespearean comedy is presexual. It is not simply that the comic marriages are consummated after the conclusion of the play. Rather, desire is structurally foreign to comedy, inadmissible within it, because, being built up out of a constitutive rupture, its presence forecloses the possibility of "oneness." Thus, for example, Sly is anxious for the play performed before him to be over— "would 'twere done"—so that he can go to bed with the page boy he thinks is his wife. If Sly were in fact to consummate his marriage to the page boy, he would learn very well about the likeness in difference and the difference in likeness, for the joke played on Sly is that the pageboy is in drag disguise. But, though this would be a sexy, it would not be a very comic, conclusion to "a pleasant comedy," and this is why Sly's coitus is postponed to a posttheatricality that never occurs. The eroticism of Shakespearean comedy is in this way always promissory: the comic play is always foreplay, titillating but unresolved. In contrast, Shakespeare's tragedies can countenance desire because they are prepared to introduce into themselves the presence of loss. Hence the strong eroticism of Hamlet, Othello, King Lear, an eroticism, however, that can only be constructed in misogynistic terms, and that achieves closure only through its fixed dissatisfaction.

In a rough way, therefore, it makes sense to characterize Shakespearean comedy as a drama of presentation and Shakespearean tragedy as a drama of representation. These generic formulas would no doubt need to be refined when applied to individual plays, but they suggest a general framework within which to correlate Shakespeare's early and middle theatrical production with his sonnets. However, to the extent that this correlation is valuable, it raises the generic question of Shakespearean romance, for this is a theatrical genre chronologically and conceptually successive not only to the sonnets but also to Shakespeare's comedies and tragedies. How is this succession to be understood?

Shakespearean romance very obviously makes reference both to comedy and to tragedy, but it is a genre very different from them both, and one that is very inadequately described as "tragi-comedy." So too, the principal characters of Shakespearean romance possess a very strong subjective weight and force—Leontes and Prospero, to take the best examples—but so too do they seem in a peculiar way to give away the person of their person. A similar peculiarity attaches to the issue of desire in Shakespearean romance, for though these plays seem very knowing about sexuality—the fetishistic voyeurism of *Cymbeline*, for example, or the insistent pressure of incest in the other romances—nevertheless, they focus on the way in which old men might be delivered to the condition of the posterotic. So too these plays are very frank about the discrepancy between vision and language—"Then have you lost a sight which was to be seen, cannot be spoken of "(*WT*, 5.2.42–43)—but they proceed as though this were an issue they can "mock with art" (*WT*, 5.3.18, 68). In all these ways, Shakespearean romance appears to pass beyond the subject of a "perjur'd eye." Romance recognizes loss only on the condition, as *The Winter's Tale* puts it, that that which is lost be found. So too, romance introduces what Leontes calls "this wide gap of time, since first/We were dissever'd" (5.3.154–55), only so as then to plug it up. In terms of the argument I have developed, what is the significance of this apparent exception to the pathos of representation?

Again it is important to recognize that if Shakespearean romance is a literary genre that redresses or resolves the pathos of representation, it does not do so either by ignoring it or in ignorance of it. Quite the contrary, the romances regularly begin by taking tragedy for granted, as though it goes without saying. Prospero's prehistory, what brings him to his island, is the stuff of a familiar Elizabethan or Jacobean tragedy, and is treated as such, which perhaps is why Miranda almost falls asleep when the story is recounted. In the same way, the first three acts of *The Winter's Tale* amount to a miniature Shakespeare tragedy or, rather, they amount to a full-scale tragedy that is acted out before us with a kind of dizzying and somewhat estranging double speed. The various misfortunes suffered by Prospero before his play begins are presented in *The Tempest* as something which, if they are not ordinary, are still to be expected, just as Leontes' erotomania is presented in *The Winter's Tale* as something stipulated and inexorably given, as a kind of necessary human craziness which requires no more explanation than any other fact of nature. Such tragic beginnings are structurally built into romance, for romance is the genre of the twice-told tale. Far from avoiding the tragic, romance requires it as the constitutive beginning to which romance proper is the subsequent response. Hence the characteristic rhythm of Shakespearean romance, where the second part of the play, or even the play as a whole, presents itself as the restaging of a prior tragic story, a repetition that makes up for or redeems original loss.

This is obvious, but it suggests another formula with which to approach Shakespearean romance, one that recalls the elaborate spectacularity of these plays, not only their masques and dances, but also their general atmosphere of self-conscious theatricality. If Shakespearean comedy is a drama of presentation, true to its genre because it swerves away from loss, if Shakespearean tragedy is a drama of representation, true to its genre because its representation presents the loss of presence, then Shakespearean romance is the drama of the representation of representation, and it therefore displays, and wants to present as its generic intention, the loss of loss. The representation of representation is not a trivial conceit, no more so than is the loss of loss. It introduces the idea—central to and explicit in Shakespearean romance—that there "is an art/Which does mend Nature—change it rather; but/The art itself is Nature" (4.4.95–97). If it were necessary to point to one line that conveys the way in which this aesthetic project of Shakespearean romance affects character, I would offer as an example the turning point of *The*

Winter's Tale, when Leontes, obliged to "see what death is doing," responds to the death of his wife and son: "I have too much believ'd mine own suspicion" (3.2.149, 151). From that point forward, all the doubt that comes before this is supposed to be in doubt, and it is this doubting of doubt that the second half of *The Winter's Tale* is supposed to render credible. Admittedly, it is very difficult to imagine what it might mean to suspect suspicion, just as it is difficult to understand what kind of (hyper-Cartesian) faith believes in the doubting of doubt. It is very clear, however, that this is the psychological condition that Shakespeare associates with the human loss of human loss.

At any rate, this is how Shakespeare's romances want to work. Against Alonzo's fear in *The Tempest*—"If this prove/A vision of the island, one dear son/Shall I twice lose" (5.1.175–77)—romance regularly sets the playful vision of a Ferdinand who has "receiv'd a second life and second father" (5.1.195). In this way, if Prospero is to be believed, it becomes possible that we "not burthen our remembrances with/A heaviness that's gone" (5.1.198–99). All this having been said, it remains a question whether Shakespeare ever wrote a successful Shakespearean romance, i.e., a play that manages to forget the memory with which it begins. Regarding Shakespeare's romance strategy, however, there is one thing that cannot be doubted: that it is a response to, and not a transcendence of, the subjectivity that Shakespeare invents in his sonnets.

There is one final way to make this point. At the end of *Romeo and Juliet*, the grieving parents propose to raise two statues "in pure gold" to commemorate the dead lovers, one for Romeo and one for Juliet. We can think of these statues as an image of the way tragic representation elegaically remembers what it causes to be absent: "For never was a story of more woe/Than this of Juliet and her Romeo" (5.3.309–10). In contrast, at the end of *The Winter's Tale*, a not dead statue—"her dead likeness"—springs to life. We are told that this romance statue, which of course does not exist, was "newly perform'd by that rare Italian master, Julio Romano, who, had he himself eternity and could put breath into his work, would beguile Nature of her custom, so perfectly he is her ape" (5.2.96–100). Again the literal level confirms the literary relation. As "Julio Romano" to "Romeo and Juliet," so Shakespearean romance to Shakespearean tragedy: the cross-coupling of cross-coupling.

Notes

INTRODUCTION

1. Aristotle, *Rhetoric*, 1368a,40. I develop this point more fully in chap. 2. References to the *Rhetoric* are to the English translation of W. R. Roberts in *The Basic Works of Aristotle*, ed. Richard McKeon (New York: Random House, 1941), and to the Greek text in the Loeb Classical Library, *The "Art" of Rhetoric*, ed. J. H. Freese (Cambridge: Harvard Univ. Press, 1939).

2. Aristotle, *Rhetoric*, 1358b,2. I cite Aristotle here in part to register the Humanist vogue for the recently translated and disseminated *Poetics*, in part because Aristotle's *Rhetoric* indirectly informs what for the Renaissance is the more familiar rhetorical tradition that stems from Cicero and Quintilian. See Marvin T. Herrick, *The Poetics of Aristotle in England, Cornell Studies in English XVII* (New Haven, Conn.: Yale Univ. Press, 1930), 8–34; Marvin T. Herrick, "The Fusion of Horatian and Aristotelian Literary Criticism, 1531–1555," *Illinois Studies in Language and Literature*, 32, no. 1 (1946):1–113; W. F. Boogess, "Aristotle's *Poetics* in the Fourteenth Century," *Studies in Philology*, 67, no. 3 (1970):278–94. In general (see chap. 2), the characterization of epideictic oratory remains fairly constant from antiquity through the Renaissance. Scaliger, neither accurately nor influentially, disagrees with traditional descriptions of epideictic *ostentatio*: "Quintilian makes an equally bad mistake when he interprets the word *epideiktikos* to mean ostentatious speaking, on the ground that the word usually had this meaning among the Greeks. So far is this from the truth, that the philosophers used it to define the most simple and exact expression." *Select Translations from Scaliger's Poetics*, trans. F. M. Padelford, *Yale Studies in English*, ed. Albert S. Cook (New Haven, Conn.: Yale Univ. Press, 1905):6. Scaliger also disagrees with Aristotle's classification of rhetorical temporalities. For Aristotle, the epideictic orator is concerned with the present, in contrast to the forensic orator who is concerned with the past, and in contrast to the deliberative or political orator who is concerned with the future, *Rhetoric*, 1358b,4. Scaliger, agreeing with Quintilian, though for different reasons, says that the epideictic orator is concerned with the past, ibid., 6. My characterization of epideictic rhetoricity will draw on treatises referring either to oratory or to poetry. For the Renaissance, as is well known, there is much overlap between the two, as in Sidney's *Apology for Poetry*: "But what? me thinkes I deserve to be pounded for straying from Poetrie to Oratorie: but both have such an affinity in this

wordish consideration, that I thinke this digression will make my meaning receive the fuller understanding." Philip Sidney, *An Apologie for Poetrie*, in *Elizabethan Critical Essays*, ed. G. Gregory Smith (London: Oxford Univ. Press, 1904), 1:203; all subsequent references are to this edition. William Ringler, in his introduction to John Rainold's *Oratio in Laudem Artis Poeticae*, c. 1572 (Princeton, N.J.: Princeton Univ. Press, 1940), 20, cites Erasmus: "What especially delights me is a rhetorical poem and a poetical oration, in which you can see the poetry in the prose and the rhetorical expression in the poetry" (*Epistolae*, ed. P. S. Allen, 1:545). The tradition goes back to Cicero, *De Oratore*, 1:70.

3. It might be said that structuralist literary theory inherits this linguistic idealization, for example, the way Roman Jakobson's definition of literariness—as a message that refers to itself *as* a message—implicitly defines literature as that linguistic form whose structurality manifests the structurality of language itself; see "Linguistics and Poetics," in *The Structuralists: From Marx to Lévi-Strauss*, eds. R. and F. DeGeorge (New York: Anchor Books, 1972), 85–122. This becomes yet more explicit in structuralist anthropology, as in Lévi-Strauss, who understands the organizing substructures of cultural life to mimic the macro-structure of language, and for whom cross-cultural investigations conclude when the general structure of one culture vibrates sympathetically with the general structure of another—the sympathy between them again determined by the structurality of language. See, for example, Claude Lévi-Strauss, *The Raw and the Cooked* (New York: Harper & Row, 1969), 1–32. For a discussion of this issue, see Joel Fineman, "The Structure of Allegorical Desire," in *Allegory and Representation: Selected Papers from the English Institute, 1979–80* (Baltimore, Md.: Johns Hopkins Univ. Press, 1981), 26–60.

4. *Non quidem propter Deum, sed propter ipsum laudantem. Summa Theologica*, 2:2, q. 91, art. 1, trans. Fathers of the English Dominican Province (New York: Benziger Brothers, 1947), 2:1509; Latin text in *Summa Theologiae*, Instituti Studiorum Medievalium Ottaviensis (Ottawa: College Dominicain d'Ottawa, 1941), 1903.

5. For a discussion of deictic theory in the Renaissance, see G. A. Padley, *Grammatical Theory in Western Europe, 1500–1700: The Latin Tradition* (Cambridge: Cambridge Univ. Press, 1976), 44ff. For medieval pronoun theory, see G. L. Bursil-Hall, *Speculative Grammars of the Middle Ages: The Doctrine of "Partes Orationis" of the Modistae* (The Hague: Mouton, 1971), 180–95. I emphasize the sense of transition in Renaissance linguistic theory because this seems very much tied up with the way Renaissance literature understands itself to be transitional: the passage from Latin to vernacular poetic performance, the tension between native and learned forms, the way learned forms evolve and are rethought through the doctrine of emulating imitation. It is because transition is so forceful a fact for Renaissance literature that in what follows I do not refer to Michel Foucault's powerful and provocative *Les mots et les choses* (Paris: Gallimard, 1966). Quite apart from its historical inaccuracy (which characterizes as a Renaissance "episteme" what is, if it is anything, medieval), Foucault's account of abrupt, epistemic shifts simply does not ring true to the practice of Renaissance poetry and its self-conscious, retrospective literary sensibility. This is especially the case

with regard to Shakespeare's sonnets whose difference from what precedes them very much lies in the way they register the conclusion of a past poetics as a pressing problem for the present. Again, this would remain a thematic, even if it were not a historical, fact: e.g., the problem of a poet who "makes antiquity for aye his page,/Finding the first conceit of love there bred, /Where time and outward form would show it dead" (108).

6. See Roman Jakobson, "Shifters, Verbal Categories, and the Russian Verb," *Russian Language Project: Dept. of Slavic Languages and Literatures* (Cambridge: Harvard Univ., 1957). Bertrand Russell, *An Inquiry into Meaning and Truth* (New York: W. W. Norton, 1940), chap. 7. For a general account, see Richard M. Gale, "Indexical Signs, Egocentric Particulars, and Token-Reflexive Words," *The Encyclopedia of Philosophy*, ed. Paul Edwards (New York: Macmillan, 1967), 3:151–55. For a detailed account of some related linguistic issues, see Charles Fillmore, "Santa Cruz Lectures on Deixis," mimeographed reprint, Indiana University Linguistics Club, 1975). Emile Benveniste discusses the relationship of pronominal deixis to subjectivity in "Relationships of Person in the Verb," "The Nature of Pronouns," "Subjectivity in Language," *Problems in General Linguistics*, trans. M. E. Meek (Coral Gables, Fla.: Univ. of Miami Press, 1971). For Benveniste, "language is possible only because each speaker sets himself up as a *subject* by referring to himself as *I* in his discourse," 225. According to Benveniste, there is a "correlation of subjectivity" between "I" and "you" which is centered on the "I": "'*you*' can thus be defined as 'the non-*I* person,'" 201. In contrast, both verbally and pronomially, "the 'third-person' is not a 'person'; it is really a verbal form whose function is to express the *non-person*." I will later argue that in Shakespeare's sonnets this absent third person is incorporated into the person of the poet through the medium of "Will": in Shakespeare's poetic first person this absent "he," "she," or "it" is situated *within* the poet when the poet becomes the subject of a proper name, "Will." The point will be that "Will" functions in the sonnets to denominate the subjectivity of a poet whose speaking "I" is found to be both the same as and different from the person thus "bespoken" (when the speaking subject suffers, as Lacan would say, his "Being" being spoken in the discourse of the Other). In what follows I do not take up the vexed relationships, linguistic and philosophical, between deictics and proper names. I am more concerned with the way Shakespeare's sonnets explicitly and implicitly thematize this relationship. This thematization, however, does not occur in a historical vacuum. When relevant, I will note some of this historical context, for example, the idealist prohibition on pronouncing the Name of God, or the way praise paradox characteristically leads to a play on proper names, e.g., Erasmus' play on Thomas More's name, which is developed in the letter to More prefacing *The Praise of Folly* (i.e., *Moriae encomium*).

7. *Non perch' io non m'aveggia*
quanto mia laude è 'ngiurniosa a voi . . .
Onde s' alcun bel frutto
nasce di me, da voi vien prima il seme;
io per me son quasi un terreno asciutto
colto da voi, e 'l pregio è vostro in tutto.
Canzon, tu non m' acqueti anzi m' infiammi

a dir di quel ch' a me stesso m 'inviola;
però sia certa de non esser sola.

The poem is based on the following general conceit: "I hope my pain will be understood there where I desire it to be and where it must be, my pain which in silence I cry out" (*ma spero che sia intesa/là dov' io bramo et là dove esser deve/la doglia mia, la qual tacendo i' grido*). All citations and translations of Petrarch's *Rime Sparse* are taken from Robert M. Durling's *Petrarch's Lyric Poems* (Cambridge: Harvard Univ. Press, 1976), hereafter cited as *RS*. In general, when quoting non-English texts, I will give the original only when the phrasing seems relevant to the point at issue.

8.   "Idea" is, of course, a sonneteering commonplace. J. W. Hebel, in his edition of *The Works of Michael Drayton* (Oxford: Oxford Univ. Press, 1961), cites parallels in de Pontoux's *L'Idée* (1579), in du Bellay, Desportes, Daniel; see 5:13.

9.   This is E. K.'s "glosse" to line 21 of "October," in *The Shepheardes Calender*. E. K. is commenting on Peirce's "the prayse is better, then the price,/The glory eke much greater than the gayne." Unless otherwise noted, all Spenser citations refer to *The Poetical Works of Edmund Spenser*, eds. J. C. Smith and E. De Selincourt (Oxford: Oxford Univ. Press, 1965).

10.   Aristotle, *Poetics*, 1459a,16 –18, "But by far the greatest thing is the use of metaphor. That alone cannot be learnt; it is the token of genius. For the right use of metaphor means an eye for resemblances [*to gar eu metapherein to to homoion theórein estin*]," in the Loeb Classical Library, ed. E. Capps (New York: G. Putnam and Sons, 1927).

11.   Martha Craig, in "The Secret Wit of Spenser's Language," in *Elizabethan Poetry: Modern Essays in Criticism*, ed. Paul Alpers (Oxford: Oxford Univ. Press, 1967), discusses Renaissance interest in Plato's *Cratylus*, which begins with Ficino's introduction to the dialogue in his Latin edition of Plato, and is further enhanced by Ramistic commentary. As Craig points out, two of Spenser's teachers make a great deal of the *Cratylus*: Richard Mulcaster, in his *Elementarie* (1582) and its discussion of "right names"; Richard Wills, perhaps the prototype for "Willye" in *The Shepheardes Calender*, who in his *De Re Poetica* (1573) translates a portion of Ficino's introduction. Etymological Cratylism is a muted version of ontological Cratylism. There are, of course, many medieval precedents; see N. Streuver, "Fables of Power," *Representations*, no. 4 (1983):108 –27. Often the theme is developed playfully, to point up the difference between language in its current fallen state and an ideal past. Even as something playful, however, this kind of correspondence of word to thing is presented as a poetic ideal, especially in the poetry of praise. The point is not that Dante, Petrarch, Sidney, Spenser, et al., were unaware of the difference between words and things; rather, that the panegyric poetics these poets employ leads them, by virtue of its rhetorical logic, to invoke Cratylitic themes in support of epideictic idealization. As I point out in chapter 4, these invocations grow increasingly self-conscious as the sonnet develops.

12.   Unless otherwise noted, all Shakespeare citations are to *The Riverside Shakespeare*, ed. G. B. Evans et al. (Boston: Houghton Mifflin, 1974). Sonnet numbers will be noted within parentheses. In general, I will omit the editors' square brackets, which indicate conjectural emendations. I will

note when I disagree with the editors' emendations and punctuation. Occasionally I will refer to the Quarto's spelling; also to the variants for sonnets 138 and 144 that appear in *The Passionate Pilgrim*. Because punctuation and spelling are somewhat modernized in *The Riverside Shakespeare*, my Shakespeare quotations will contrast rather too starkly with my quotations from the standard editions of Sidney and Spenser. Despite this problem, I use *The Riverside Shakespeare* because it is readily available.

13. See the opening paragraph of E. K.'s dedicatory epistle to *The Shepheardes Calender*, 416.

14. *Othello*, 4.1.265. In chap. 5 I take up briefly the difference between an "all in all sufficient" Othello and the Othello designated by the difference between his first person and his name: "That's he that was Othello; here I am" (5.2.284).

15. Spenser, "An Hymne of Heavenly Love," 1–7.

16. This is Ulysses' paradoxical blazon of a Cressida whose very name—"as false as Cressid"—bespeaks duplicity: "There's language in her eye, her cheek, her lip,/Nay, her foot speaks; her wanton spirits look out/At every joint and motive of her body" (*TC*, 4.5.55–57). Compare this with the sense of retrospective loss in sonnet 106: "Then in the blazon of sweet beauty's best,/Of hand, of foot, of lip, of eye, of brow,/I see their antique pen would have express'd/Even such a beauty as you master now." With regard to the representation of Petrarchanism in the plays, compare with Longaville's sonnet in *Love's Labor's Lost*, which begins: "Did not the heavenly rhetoric of thine eye,/'Gainst whom the world cannot hold argument,/Persuade my heart to this false perjury" (4.3.58–60), or with Romeo in the balcony scene: "She speaks, yet she says nothing; what of that?/Her eye discourses, I will answer it" (*RJ*, 2.2.12–13).

17. The phrase is from the couplet to sonnet 152: "For I have sworn thee fair: more perjur'd eye,/To swear against the truth so foul a lie!" The last two sonnets of the sequence, 153 and 154, are considered spurious by some scholars. If this is the case, then Shakespeare's "perjur'd eye" amounts to the sonnets' final word, the motto of the sequence as a whole. It will be apparent that there is a great difference between the poetic person of this "perjur'd eye" and the poetic person of what Joan Webber calls *The Eloquent "I": Studies in Seventeenth Century Prose* (Madison: Univ. of Wisconsin Press, 1968).

18. *The Vision of William Concerning Piers the Plowman*, ed. W. W. Skeat (Oxford: Oxford Univ. Press, 1968), "Vita de Do-Wel," passus XII.

19. The relationship between "cunt" and the representational mark of difference is a central one for Shakespeare. Compare Maria's forged letter in *Twelfth Night* and the way Malvolio identifies "my lady's hand": "These be her very c's, her u's, and her t's, and thus makes she her great P's" (2.5.86–88). For reasons which will become clearer later, it is significant that Malvolio identifies this "cut/cunt" with "the impressure her Lucrece, with which she uses to seal" (2.5.92–93). The letter itself glosses "Lucrece" thus: "I may command where I adore,/But silence, like a Lucrece knife,/With bloodless stroke my heart doth gore" (2.5.104–6). *Twelfth Night* is also organized around "Will": *or What You Will*.

20. Oscar Wilde, *The Portrait of Mr. W. H.*, ed. Vyvyan Holland (London: Methuen, 1921). The conjecture with regard to "Will Hewes" is first suggested by Thomas Tyrwhitt in 1766, and was later accepted by Malone; see

Holland's introduction, ix. I discuss Wilde and the problematics of literary naming in "The Significance of Literature: *The Importance of Being Earnest,*" *October,* no. 15 (1980): 79–90.

21.   John Marston, *The Dutch Courtesan,* 1.1.105–37; *Drama of the English Renaissance,* eds. Russell Fraser and Norman Rabkin (New York: Macmillan, 1976), vol. 2.

22.   *Fabulae Argumentum.*

23.   *The Dutch Courtesan,* 3.1.4–6. As I point out later, it is for this reason that Woman is a characteristic subject for mock encomium.

24.   However, the play seems concerned to confront the didactic aesthetics of homeopathic imitation with a strong counterexample. What Malheureux learns from the tricks practiced upon him is that it is not the case that "the sight of vice augments the hate of sin" (1.1.172), at least not with regard to "the most odious spectacle the earth can present . . . an immodest vulgar woman" (1.1.168–69). The Prologue insists that "we strive not to instruct, but to delight."

25.   Here again Wilde offers the relevant and sympathetic response, if we recall the subtitle to *The Importance of Being Earnest:* "A Trivial Comedy for Serious People."

26.   George Puttenham, *The Arte of English Poesie,* 1589 (facsimile reproduction, Kent, Ohio: Kent State Univ. Press, 1970), 216.

27.   The crossings here are somehow *too* exact:

28.   For a full account of the way Elizabethan dramaturgy is informed by the rhetorical tradition of arguing *in utramque partem,* see Joel Altman, *The Tudor Play of Mind: Rhetorical Inquiry and the Development of Elizabethan Drama* (Berkeley and Los Angeles: Univ. of California Press, 1978).

29.   *TN,* 3.1.11–20. I will elsewhere discuss the relation in *The Rape of Lucrece* of the "let" to the "letter"; the point is important for *Hamlet's* "let be."

30.   In *The Rape of Lucrece* the structurally inescapable difference between true vision and false language is, in fact, directly thematized in the description of the "skillful painting, made for Priam's Troy" (1367). The tapestry is an especially vivid and vivacious visual representation: "A thousand lamentable objects there,/In scorn of nature, art gave liveless life" (1373–74). One "image," however, is beyond the painter's "imaginary work" (1422), and this is Sinon's "perjury" (1520–24):

> The well-skill'd workman this mild image drew
> For perjur'd Sinon, whose enchanting story
> The credulous old Priam after slew;
> Whose words like wildfire burnt the shining glory
> Of rich-built Ilion.

The painter cannot truthfully display "perjur'd Sinon's" lies for, though he can paint Sinon's false "fairness," the painter, however perfect a painter, cannot represent Sinon's verbal misrepresentations. Lucrece, looking at the picture of Sinon, draws the moral (1530–33):

> So fair a form lodg'd not a mind so ill.
> And still on him she gaz'd, and gazing still,
>   Such signs of truth in his plain face she spied,
>   That she concludes the picture was belied.

It is in this way that a picture of (false) language will point up the limits of (true) vision. *The Rape of Lucrece* relates this unrepresentable feature of verbal representation to the way that language can change itself even as it is spoken. Here again there is connection to the sonnets. In sonnet 145 the poet describes the way the lady can "retract" her speech: "'I hate' from hate away she threw,/And sav'd my life, saying 'not you.'" According to the narrator, Lucrece, speaking of Sinon, does the same (1534–40):

> "It cannot be," quoth she, "that so much guile"—
> She would have said, "can lurk in such a look";
> But Tarquin's shape came in her mind the while,
> And from her tongue "can lurk" from "cannot" took:
> "It cannot be" she in that sense forsook,
>   And turn'd it thus, "It cannot be, I find,
>   But such a face should bear a wicked mind."

It is important to note the way in which, through the description of the tapestry, *The Rape of Lucrece*, Shakespeare's "graver labour" in narrative, more directly broaches the language-vision confrontation than does *Venus and Adonis*. This suggests how Shakespeare, even this early in his career, associates these themes with the specific genre of tragedy. Even so, *The Rape of Lucrece* does not directly assimilate these themes to the psychology of either Tarquin or Lucrece, and this is why, as I have argued, neither of these two figures give off a particularly strong effect of characterological or subjective density.

31.   I speak about a bankrupt poetic tradition because this is how the tradition of idealizing praise is thematized in Shakespeare's sonnets. This is not to say that Shakespeare does not powerfully respond to the vitality of the epideictic poetic tradition he inherits. The same goes, of course, for readers of Shakespeare's sonnets. Throughout, I am concerned with the way literary features of Shakespeare's sonnets, and not only thematic features, are deployed so as give off a subjectivity effect that, speaking historically, is novel and influential in our literary tradition. My argument does not speak to, but neither does it necessarily contradict or argue against, other critical approaches that would take up specific source transmissions or the details of particular biographical Shakespearean context. Such approaches, to the extent that they are successful, will deal with issues which amount to material and efficient causes of Shakespeare's sonnets. I am concerned with more formal causes, to which such material and efficient causes would be instrumentally related.

32. See, for example, Roman Jakobson, "Linguistics and Poetics"; Gérard Genette, "Le Littérature comme telle," Figures I (Paris: Seuil, 1966), 253–65; "Poetic Language, Poetics of Language," Figures of Literary Discourse (New York: Columbia Univ. Press, 1982), 5–102; Michael Riffaterre, Semiotics of Poetry (Bloomington: Indiana Univ. Press, 1978).

33. See, for example, A. J. Greimas and F. Rastier, "The Interaction of Semiotic Constraints," Yale French Studies, no. 41 (1968); A. J. Greimas and J. Courtes, Semiotics and Language: An Analytic Dictionary (Bloomington: Indiana Univ. Press, 1982), 308–11; Paul De Man, "Pascal's Allegory of Persuasion," in Allegory and Representation, ed. Stephen Greenblatt (Baltimore: Johns Hopkins Univ. Press, 1981), 1–25; Jacques Lacan, "On a Question Preliminary to Any Possible Treatment of Psychosis," Ecrits, trans. A. Sheridan (New York: W. W. Norton, 1977), 179–225. With regard to Lacan's "schema L" and also the more elaborate "schema R," it is important also to consider the "punch bar" diagram Lacran draws when discussing the "objet a," Lacan's diamond of desire; see The Four Fundamental Concepts of Psychoanalysis, trans. A. Sheridan (New York: W. W. Norton, 1978), 209.

34. Plato, Parmenides, 130d; this introduces the "third man" argument. I refer generally to Derrida's discussions of the theme of presence in Western metaphysics, in such works as La Voix et le phénomène: Introduction au problème du signe dans la phénoménologie de Husserl (Paris: Presses Universitaires de France, 1972), De la Grammatologie (Paris: Minuit, 1967), La Dissémination (Paris: Seuil, 1972). With regard to theatrical issues, see "Le Théâtre de la cruauté et la clôture de la représentation" in L'Écriture et la différence (Paris: Seuil, 1967). In the context of my discussion of the Shakespearean subject the most relevant works are those in which Derrida explicitly criticizes Lacan, e.g., Positions,trans. A. Bass (Chicago: Univ. of Chicago Press, 1981); "Le Facteur de la vérité," in La Carte Postale (Paris: Flammarion, 1980), 439–524.

35. For example, Jacques Lacan, The Language of the Self, trans. A. Wilden (Baltimore: Johns Hopkins Univ. Press, 1968); also "The Freudian Thing," "On A Question Preliminary . . . ," "The Signification of the Phallus," all in Ecrits. For Freud on "word" and "thing" representations, see "The Unconscious," in The Standard Edition of the Complete Psychological Works of Sigmund Freud, ed. and trans. J. Strachey (London: Hogarth Press, 1953–74), 14:201–4; see also Jean Laplanche and Serge Leclaire, "The Unconscious: A Psychoanalytic Study," Yale French Studies, no. 48 (1972), 118–78.

36. See, for example, Sartre's early work on L'Imagination (Paris: F. Alcan, 1936), or, more elaborate, L'Imaginaire: Psychologie phénoménologique de l'imagination (Paris: Gallimard, 1940); also, the development of this in the discussion of le regard in L'Etre et le néant, essai d'ontologie phénoménologique (Paris: Gallimard, 1943), part 3, chap. 4.

37. Maurice Merleau-Ponty, "Eye and Mind," trans. C. Dallery, in The Primacy of Perception, ed. J. Edie (Evanston, Ill.: Northwestern Univ. Press, 1964), 159–90; The Visible and the Invisible, ed. C. Lefort, trans. A. Lingis (Evanston, Ill.: Northwestern Univ. Press, 1968), esp. chap. 4 and its entrelacs.

38. See The Four Fundamental Concepts of Psychoanalysis, chaps. 6–9. Lacan suggests that Merleau-Ponty, had he lived longer, would have come to the same criticism, 68–69; see also Lacan's obituary for Merleau-Ponty in Les Temps Modernes (1961):184–85.

39. I refer here not only to Lacan's explicit formulations, but also to the development of Lacan's thought, from the early emphasis on visual themes, as in the essay on the "mirror-stage" and accompanying discussions of aggressivity, to the later emphasis on language, anamorphosis, and accompanying discussions of (male) desire, to, finally, as a third term added to the opposition of the Imaginary and the Symbolic, Lacan's emphasis on the "Real," the limits of representation, and accompanying discussions of (female) *jouissance*. Lacan's sense of the Renaissance is colored, however, by a very Catholic and Counter-Reformational—in short, a very French—conception of the Baroque: *"Le baroque, c'est la régulation de l'âme par la scopie corporelle," Encore* (Paris: Seuil, 1975):105, which is why Lacan's comments on Shakespeare are often disappointing.

40. See Derrida's remarks on "the supplement of the copula," in *De la Grammatologie*, part 2.

41. See *The Origins of Psychoanalysis: Letters to Wilheim Fliess*, eds. M. Bonaparte, A. Freud, and E. Kris (New York: Basic Books, 1954), 215–25. For Freud the fact that Shakespeare's Hamlet represses his Oedipal impulses, in contrast to Sophocles' Oedipus, is what makes the play mark, as Freud puts it in *The Interpretation of Dreams*, a new epoch in "the secular advance of repression in the emotional life of mankind," *SE*, 1: 264.

42. Leone Ebreo, *Dialoghi d'amore*, ed. Santino Caramella (Bari: G. Laterza, 1929), 5; cited by J. C. Nelson, *The Renaissance Theory of Love* (New York: Columbia Univ. Press, 1958), 86.

43. Ibid., 207; cited by Nelson, 86–87. Ebreo's collapse of the difference between love and desire stands as a continually nagging challenge to later writers, for example, Robert Burton: "Love, universally taken, is defined to be a *Desire*, as a word of more ample signification; and though *Leon Hebraeus*, the most copious writer of this subject, in his third Dialogue makes no difference, yet in his first he distinguisheth them again, and defines Love by desire." Robert Burton, *The Anatomy of Melancholy*, ed. A. Shilleto (London: George Bell and Sons, 1903), part 3, sec. 1, mem. 1, subs. 2, vol. 3: 10.

44. That desire is death is of course a commonplace, e.g., Ronsard's *"Car l'Amour et la Mort n'est qu'une mesme chose," Sonnets Pour Hélène*, 2, no. 77, in *Oeuvres complètes de Ronsard*, ed. G. Cohen (Paris: Gallimard, 1950), 1:278. What is important is the specifically double way in which Shakespearean revision revives this dead metaphor.

CHAPTER I

1. "'We beg you to tell us wherein this bliss of yours [*tua beatitudine*] now lies.' And I answered her by saying: 'In those words that praise my lady [*In quelle parole che lodano la donna mia*]' . . . Therefore, I resolved that from now on I would choose material for my poems that should be in praise of this most gracious one," *La Vita nuova*, ed. F. Chapelli, *Opere di Dante Alighieri* (Milan: Univ. Mursia, 1967), sec. 18; M. Musa, trans., *La Vita Nuova of Dante Alighieri* (Bloomington: Indiana Univ. Press, 1965). Acting on this resolve, Dante then composes the first *canzone* of *La Vita nuova*, *Donne ch'avete intel-*

letto d'amore, sec. 19, which later, in *Purg.,* 24.49–63, in conversation with Buonagiunta, will be remembered as marking the beginning of *le nove rime* of the *dolce stil nuovo.* All subsequent references to *The Divine Comedy* will be to the translation and edited Italian text of John D. Sinclair (Oxford: Oxford Univ. Press, 1939).

2. Where "Beatrice" is "bliss" itself, "Laura" is "praise" and all that Petrarch associates with it. The assumed etymological connections of "Laura" to "praising" (*laudando*) and "laurel" (*lauro*) are false but popular, and are assimilated to such puns as *l'auro* ("gold"), *l'aura* ("breeze"), *l'aurora* ("dawn"); for example, *RS,* 5, 6, 7, 194, 196, 246, 327, 356. In 5 the punning goes a step further, with "Laureta" broken down syllabically into the essential truth of praise, its reverential silence: *LAU-dare, RE-verire, TA-cere.* According to the concordance, variations on *laudando, laudare, Laura, lauro,* not counting puns, occur forty-seven times, *Concordanze del Canzoniere di Francesco Petrarca* (Florence: A Cura dell'ufficio lessicografico, 1971). Ovid's account (*Metamorphoses,* 1.452–567) of Daphne's translation to a laurel is, of course, a central myth for Petrarch's imagination; see, for example, the longest poem in the *Canzioniere,* 23. Sidney captures the visuality embedded in epideictic Cratylism when in the *Old Arcadia* he names Philisides' beloved "Mira": "And *Mira* I admirde," "Poems from the Countess of Pembroke's Arcadia," no. 73, in *The Poems of Sir Philip Sidney,* ed. William A. Ringler (Oxford: Oxford Univ. Press, 1962), 119. In the *Old Arcadia* Philisides is Sidney's self-portrait. In the *New Arcadia,* where Philisides appears only once, "Mira" is instead addressed as "star." The change helps to date *Astrophil and Stella,* see Ringler, 435. All subsequent citations of Sidney's poetry, including *Astrophil and Stella,* will be to Ringler's edition.

3. Wyatt and Surrey introduce the Italianate sonnet to England in the early part of the century, but the vogue of sonnet cycles, which is as much influenced by French models (Ronsard, Desportes) as by Italian, is sparked by the publication in 1591 of Sidney's *Astrophil and Stella* (written and privately distributed in the early eighties). It is after or against, rather than in, the context of such sonnet sequences as *Astrophil and Stella,* Daniel's *Delia,* Spenser's *Amoretti,* Constable's *Diana,* Lodge's *Phillis,* Barnes's *Parthenophil and Parthenophe,* Fletcher's *Licia,* among many others, all published by 1595, that Shakespeare writes his own sequence, usually dated, though on no absolutely certain evidence, 1593–99.

4. "Praise"—or its variants, "praises," "praising"—appears some thirty-six times in the sequence as a whole, all these in the section devoted to the young man. This does not take into account related epideictic terms such as "hymn," "esteem," "flatter," "slander," "blame," and the like. Moreover, because the sonnets operate within a poetic tradition for which praise is a figure for all of poetry, the sonnets' references to their own poeticality also evoke standard epideictic associations.

5. Taken by itself, the topos is antique, familiar, available to everyone; it is a version of what E. R. Curtius calls "the outdoer," *European Literature and the Latin Middle Ages,* trans. W. R. Trask (New York: Harper & Row, 1963), 162–65. Constable's "To His Mistress" provides a particularly close parallel:

Miracle of the world I never will denye
That former poets prayse the beautie of theyre dayes

> But all those beauties were but figures of thy prayse
> And all those poets did of thee but prophecye.
> Thy coming to the world hath taught us to descrie
> What Petrarchs Laura meant (for truth the lips bewrayes)
> Loe why th'Italians yet which never saw thy rayes
> To find oute Petrarchs sense such forged glosses trye
> The beauties which he in a vayle enclosd beheld
> But revelations were within his secreat heart
> By which in parables thy coming he foretold
> His songes were hymnes of thee which only now before
> Thy image should be sunge for thow that goddese art
> Which onlye we withoute idolatry adore.

No. 4, "To his Mistresse upon occasion of a Petrarch he gave her, shewing the reason why the Italian Commenters dissent so much in the exposition thereof," in *The Poems of Henry Constable*, ed. Joan Grundy (Liverpool: Liverpool Univ. Press, 1960), 133. This is characteristic of the way the praising poet will look backward to the praiseworthy origins from which the paragon of the present is understood genealogically and typologically to derive, as in the address to Elizabeth in the Proem to Book II of *The Faerie Queene*:

> And thou, O fairest Princesse under sky,
> In this faire mirrhour maist behold thy face,
> And thine owne realmes in lond of Faery,
> And in this antique Image thy great auncestry.

(4.6–9)

Notice that Spenser here writes an ideal time *into* his material imagery: "mirr-hour." As will be seen, this vision of temporality is quite different from Shakespeare's "a liquid prisoner pent in walls of glass" (5). For now, speaking of topoi, not material images, the point to notice is that Shakespeare in sonnet 106 proceeds beyond such a conventional "end" of praise, and beyond this conventional epideictic retrospection, and thereby writes a sonnet that genuinely "passes praise."

6.   I should here say something about the vexed question of the order of the sonnets, which, in what follows, I take as fixed and given by the historical response to Thorpe's 1609 edition. From the many errors in Thorpe's text, it seems clear that Shakespeare did not authorize publication of his sonnets. For this reason there is no authorial imprimatur attached to what has become the traditional ordering of the sequence. So too it is possible that the sonnets, or groups of them, were composed sufficiently independently of each other as to make it a matter of debate whether the apparent cast of characters remains the same from sonnet to sonnet. Nevertheless, *because* Thorpe's order is traditional, I accept it as authoritative even if it is not authorial. In what follows I am concerned with the "Shakespearean" rather than with Shakespeare, the former being, at least in principle, a technical term or concept for the analysis of exigencies imposed on and reflected by literary history, the latter being a term that, taken by itself, refers to an object or person of strictly antiquarian interest. By this reasoning, the Shakespearean would retain its critical value for literary history, and remain Shakespearean, even if it turned out that Shakespeare were not the author of the sonnets traditionally attributed to him. Modern attempts to reorder

the sonnets on thematic, narrative, or textual grounds (e.g., B. Stirling, *The Shakespeare Sonnet Order: Poems and Groups* [Berkeley: Univ. of California Press, 1968]) have never been persuasive to the general literary audience, in the same way that Benson's early revision of the sonnets—which involved substituting decorous "shes" for embarrassing "hes"—coincides with the period, up through Malone's edition of 1780, during which the sonnets are almost completely ignored. I assume that the indifference that greets these revisions is itself a fact of literary history, one that reflects an unspoken allegiance to Thorpe's Shakespeare. In this way the very variety of its redactions attests to the normative, however accidental, authority of Thorpe's original sequencing.

I assume the same with regard to the general narrative that has been customarily derived from the sonnets' sketchy details. I accept this Shakespearean story not for want of something better, but, again, because it has already been accepted by literary tradition. In brief, according to the tradition, sonnets 1–126 are addressed to a young man, and they develop the poet's increasingly complicated relationship to this young man whom the poet defines as his beloved ideal. Sonnets 127–54 are addressed primarily to a lady, also an object of the poet's desire, though this is a desire definitively lacking an ideal complexion. Two different narrative crises occur in the course of these two different relationships: (1) the affections of the young man for the poet are challenged by the appearance of a rival poet or poets (sonnets 78–86); (2) the poet's relation to the lady is disrupted by her affair with the ideal young man (133, 134, 144; other sonnets on the lady's duplicity supplement this story); this cuckoldry duplicates, though with more serious consequence, an earlier infidelity on the part of the young man—35, 40, 41, 42—which may itself be but a happier, anticipatory account of the later infidelity with the dark lady. This large-scale narrative and the motifs with which it unfolds can be schematically characterized in terms of a gradual development away from an initial state of identificatory duality toward a more mediated, bifurcated structure of cuckolding triangularity, with the poems about the rival poet(s) and their language of praise serving as a point of modulation:

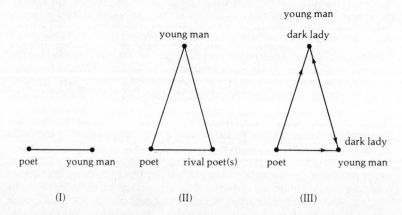

Stage III corresponds to what I will call triangular chiasmus, a situation in which the poet experiences in his person the cross-coupling he observes. It might also be diagrammatically represented thus:

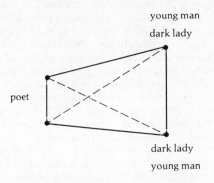

young man
dark lady

poet

dark lady
young man

I rush to say that the point of such diagrams is not to reduce the themes and images of the sonnets to a few diegetic structures, but simply to characterize a general logic through which these themes and images come to be thought. Quite clearly, there is no reason to make the sonnets' narrative the explanation of its particular matter; it might just as well be said that the sonnets' story is adduced as appropriate correlative to the sonnets' various themes and imagery. C. L. Barber properly points out that the sonnets of a sonnet sequence are neither naturally nor pleasurably read all at once; instead, they should be read, as they were written, one or a few at a time, "Shakespeare in His Sonnets," *Massachusetts Review* 1: 4 (1960): 648–72. I will argue, however, that the large frame narrative of Shakespeare's sonnet sequence is immanent in particular and local poetic details, the narrative story being, in specific ways, the projection of Shakespearean *material* imagination.

7.   As she is first presented, the dark lady is both example of and opposite to beauty's "bastard shame." Her "black" is now the proper "name" of beauty because beauty now is "slander'd with a bastard shame." At the same time, "black" is an improper name because it is unlike the "fair" that it "succeeds." I discuss the general poetic logic behind this double articulation later. It is important to realize, however, that several conventional themes are presupposed and conflated here in a novel way. To begin with, the bastard possesses no legitimate name; compare *Lucrece*, "Thy issue blurr'd with nameless bastardy" (522), cited by Stephen Booth, *Shakespeare's Sonnets* (New Haven: Yale Univ. Press, 1977), 434; hereafter cited as Booth. By making the lady's "black" both the proper *and* the improper name of beauty, by making her "black" "successive heir" to a bygone "fair," the sub-sequence to the dark lady therefore begins by repeating and yet perverting the matrimonial logic with which the young man sub-sequence begins. As K. Wilson, among others, has shown, the first seventeen sonnets are closely related to Erasmus' "Epistle to Persuade a Young Gentleman to Marriage," a version of which was available to Shakespeare in Thomas Wilson's *The Arte of Rhetori-*

que (1596), though Shakespeare could easily have found the same argument in many other sources. See K. M. Wilson, *Shakespeare's Sugared Sonnets* (London: George Allen and Unwin, 1974), chap. 4; also *A New Variorum Edition of Shakespeare: The Sonnets,* ed. H. E. Rollins (Philadelphia: J. B. Lippincott, 1944), vol. 1: 7, 18; vol. 2: 124, 192, hereafter cited as *Variorum;* also T. W. Baldwin, *On the Literary Genetics of Shakespeare's Poems and Sonnets* (Urbana: Univ. of Illinois Press, 1950), 183ff. At stake in the blackness of the lady's name, therefore, or in the nominality of this blackness, is the visual logic of familial succession—the legitimate replication of "kinds": "die single, and thine image dies with thee" (3)—which is the logic that guarantees the propriety of names, notably the proper name of the father which succeeds through the generations. This is one of Erasmus' important points: "For if a brother be commaunded to serve up sede to his brother that dieth without issue, will you suffer the hope of all youre stocke to decaye namely because there is none other of your name and stocke, but your selfe alone, to continue the posteritie?" *The Arte of Rhetorique,* 1596 (facsimile, Gainesville, Fla.: Scholars' Facsimiles and Reprints, 1962), 68. Already, then, in the very first sonnet addressed to the dark lady, the theme of cuckoldry is introduced not only as a threat to legitimate familial succession, but also as a threat to the survival of names. This will lead to the puns on "Will." There are established literary conventions which ground the poet's figural equating of poetry with bastardy, e.g., Spenser's dedication to *The Shepheardes Calender:* "But if that any aske thy name,/Say thou wert base begot with blame/For thy thereof thou takest shame." So too the praise of bastardy is a frequent topos of paradoxical encomium, e.g., Donne's paradox, "Why have Bastards best Fortune," *Juvenilia: or certaine paradoxes, and problemes,* 1633 (facsimile, New York: Facsimile Text Society, 1936), or Anthony Munday's "That the Bastard is more to be esteemed, than the lawfully born or legitimate," *The Defense of Contraries: Paradoxes against common opinion* (1593), which is a translation of a collection of paradoxes by Charles Estienne (1553), which is in turn a translation of the *Paradossi* (1543) of Ortensio Landi. See B. Vickers, "*King Lear* and Renaissance Paradoxes," *Modern Language Review* 63, no. 2 (1968):305–14. This tradition of paradoxical praise stands behind Edmund's "Now, gods, stand up for bastards!" (*KL,* 1.2.22)

8. Going back at least to Tertullian's *De cultu feminarum,* cosmetics are a charged topic for the tradition of antifeminist and antimatrimonial literature, their use taken as an infallible sign of female pride and lasciviousness, cf. Donne's fourteenth sermon, *The Sermons of John Donne,* eds. G. R. Potter and E. Simpson (Berkeley: Univ. of California Press, 1955), 295. For the ancient tradition, see M. Turcan's introduction to *La Toilette des femmes* (Paris: Les Editions du Cerf, 1971); Elizabethan arguments for and against women's "painting" are usefully reviewed in C. Camden's *The Elizabethan Woman* (New York: Paul P. Appel, 1975), 173–216. The defense of cosmetics also lends itself to paradoxical encomium, as in Donne's second paradox, "That Women ought to paint," *Juvenilia.* In addition, "Cosmetic" and "cosmos" both mean "ornament" (deriving from Greek *kosmos*) and, as a result, the problem of female "decoration" regularly evokes parallel concerns and ambivalences in speculation about what constitutes a decorous cosmology. So too this cosmeticized cosmolosy informs the language and metaphors with which rhetorical decorum, *exornatio,* will regularly be discussed. As Angus

Fletcher points out, "The history of rhetoric shows a gradual generalization of the term *ornament*, until ornament includes all the figures of speech and all tropes," *Allegory: The Theory of a Symbolic Mode* (Ithaca: Cornell Univ. Press, 1970), 128. The relevant example here is the third book of Puttenham's *The Arte of English Poesie*, "Of Ornament Poetical," which stands as complement to a contemporary treatise on cosmetics such as John Madonese's *The Ornaments of Woemen* (cited in Camden, 203; this is the basis of Giovanni Paolo Lomazzo's *A Tracte Containing the Artes of Curious Painting Carving and Buildinge*, 1598, trans. Richard Haydocke). The familiar question is always whether the ornamental, in woman or in language, is to be despised or prized, whether such an art adulterates or ekes out nature: on the one hand, "a Woman's face with Nature's own hand painted/Hast thou, the master mistress of my passion" (20); on the other, "so is it not with me as with that Muse/Stirr'd by a painted beauty to his verse" (21). The question is frequently posed *in* epideictic literature with regard *to* epideictic literature. In a conventional way Shakespeare regularly figures the rhetoric of praise with imagery that carries this ambivalent cosmetic-cosmological resonance, e.g., "'Tis thee (myself) that for myself I praise,/Painting my age with beauty of thy days" (62), or "Why should false painting imitate his cheek,/And steal dead seeing of his living hue?" (67), or "Thou, truly fair, wert truly sympathiz'd/In true plain words by thy true-telling friend;/And their gross painting might be better us'd/Where cheeks need blood, in thee it is abus'd" (82), or "I never saw that you did painting need,/And therefore to your fair no painting set" (83). The ambivalence of a painterly epideictic rhetoric that deflates because it elevates that which it ornaments also regularly informs Shakespearean misogyny, as in the brothel-nunnery of *Hamlet:* "I have heard of your paintings, well enough. God hath given you one face, and you make yourselves another. You jig and amble, and you lisp, you nickname God's creatures and make your wantonness your ignorance. Go to, I'll no more on't, it hath made me mad. I say we will have no moe marriage . . . To a nunn'ry, go" (3.1.142 – 49). Again, these images of the erotic are also images of the rhetorical. The jigging, lisping, ambling, nicknaming of women corresponds to Puttenham's "figures which we call sensable because they alter and affect the minde by alteration of sense" (188): directly so in "*Asindeton,* or the figure of loose language" (217), "*Metonymia,* or the misnamer" (191), "*Parrisia,* or the licentious" (234); generically so in "*Hipotiposis,* or the counterfait, otherwise called the figure of representation" (245), "*Exargasia,* or the gorgious, otherwise called the bewtifull" (254).

9.   As has often been noted, anti-Petrarchan declarations are regularly issued by poets who just as regularly employ Petrarchan conceits, for example, Sidney, or, for that matter, du Bellay himself. See L. Forster, *The Icy Fire: Five Studies in European Petrarchanism* (Cambridge: Cambridge Univ. Press, 1969) 56ff; also *Variorum* 1:333ff, 2:252ff. From the beginning, strong English poets are comparatively uncomfortable with the foregrounded rhetoricity of Petrarchist manner. This is argued, rather too forcefully, by Yvor Winters when he writes in praise of a native English "plain style," *Forms of Discovery* (Denver, Colo.: Alan Swallow, 1967), chap. 1. Patricia Thomson makes the same point, but more moderately, in her *Sir Thomas Wyatt and his Background* (London: Routledge and Kegan Paul, 1964), esp. chaps. 6, 7.

10.   Compare Petrarch, *RS*, 283: "You have discolored [*discolorato*],

Death, the most beautiful face that was ever seen and extinguished the most beautiful eyes." But "my lady does indeed come back . . . and if I could tell you how she speaks and how she shines, I would inflame with love not only a man's but a tiger's or a bear's heart."

11. On the tradition of *doi Veneri,* see Erwin Panofsky, *Studies in Iconology* (New York: Harper & Row, 1962), 151–69. The origin is Pausanias' distinction in the *Symposium,* 180d sq., between the heavenly and the earthly Aphrodite.

12. For example, Ficino: "As men's bodies are pregnant, as Plato says, so are their souls; and both by the incitements of love are stimulated to give birth. But some either by nature or by habit are better suited to the birth of the soul than of the body . . . The former pursue celestial love; the latter, vulgar love. The former loves males rather than females, and adolescents rather than children: for in them the acumen of the intellect is much more vigorous." Marsilio Ficino, *Sopra lo amore o ver' convito di Platone,* oration 1, chap. 3; cited in J. C. Nelson, *The Renaissance Theory of Love* (New York: Columbia Univ. Press, 1955), 7–71; Nelson gives many more examples, 69–75. This idealized "Platonic love" is ultimately behind the anomalously explicit sonneteering homosexualism of Richard Barnfield, as in *Certain Sonnets* (1595). Marlowe's *Hero and Leander* seems quite different. The most ideal example would be Michelangelo, and not only in the sonnets he addresses to men, for, as has often been observed, the poems about Vittoria Colonna speak about her in the masculine gender.

13. The concept of the ladder and chain of love goes back to the *Symposium* and is a popular topos of Renaissance Neo-Platonism, cf. Bembo's speech in book 4 of Castiglione's *The Courtier.* The regret for former vulgar praise is also conventional, e.g., Petrarch will remember his sonnets as "inane little songs filled with false and obscene praise of females," *Le familiari,* ed. V. Rossi, 10.5; cited in O. B. Hardison, Jr., *The Enduring Monument: A Study of the Idea of Praise in Renaissance Literary Theory and Practice* (Chapel Hill: Univ. of North Carolina Press, 1962), 98.

14. This is very like the argument of, for example, A. Ferry, *All in War with Time* (Cambridge: Harvard Univ. Press, 1975), chap. 1, or J. Bernard, "'To Constancie Confin'de': The Poetics of Shakespeare's Sonnets," *PMLA* 94, no. 1 (1979): 77–90.

15. For Bernard, ibid., Shakespeare's sonnets take this tradition of poetic exemplarism "as in Petrarch's *esempio* or the Platonized theology (exemplarism) of Bonaventua" (89), so seriously that "where Petrarch's lady . . . is merely a resplendent receptacle or *speculum* of divine beauty, Shakespeare's friend is defined as the archetype itself" (81). Bernard says that "Shakespeare intuits in his friend not the mere shadow but the very substance of the divine" (83). As a result, Bernard argues that "in shifting his focus from the friend's moral constancy to the metaphysical constancy of his own 'love,' Shakespeare redefines the latter in terms of poetry's power to capture what is essentially real" (78). Bernard calls such a poetics "figural," meaning to characterize by this a language which is "incarnational" in the sense accorded the term by traditional Christian typological exegesis. While Bernard identifies poetic, metaphysical, religious conventions to which the young man sonnets undoubtedly allude, I will be arguing that it is a great mistake to see these sonnets reiterating so straightforwardly such pious

("Dantesque," 88) themes. To begin with, the fallibility of the young man serves to modify the ideality of the poetry addressed to him just as much as the ideality of that poetry renders the young man ideal. It is important to insist on this fallibility so as to avoid sentimentalizing the sonnets. The relationship of the erring young man to the poet's praise of him is a traditional question *for* criticism of the sonnets, but it is so precisely because this is a question *in* the sonnets themselves. This is a question for criticism to hear and to register *as* a question; the question is evaded or ignored when it is given Bernard's orthodox answer. Far from proclaiming "poetry's power to capture what is essentially real," the young man sonnets display an increasingly poignant suspicion that a traditional poetic ideal, because ideal, is therefore imaginary, constitutively "unreal" insofar as it is poetic. This is an explicit theme in the sequence addressed to the dark lady, though Bernard says "I believe that many of the observations made in this essay are appropriate to the dark lady sonnets as well" (89). In "Poetic Presence and Illusion: Renaissance Theory and the Duplicity of Metaphor," *Critical Inquiry* 5, no. 4 (1979): 597–619, Murray Krieger offers a more theoretically inflected version of Bernard's argument. Again, however, Krieger intends to demonstrate what I will be arguing against: Shakespeare's "absolute commitment to unity, to the dissolution of discreteness, to a constancy which is sustained only by the three-in-one god of love" (618).

16. *Amoretti*, 45; cf. 83. On narcissistic themes in Shakespeare's sonnets, see Barber, "Shakespeare in His Sonnets"; P. Martin, *Shakespeare Sonnets: Self, Love and Art* (Cambridge: Cambridge Univ. Press, 1972); M. Krieger, *A Window to Criticism: Shakespeare's Sonnets and Modern Poetics* (Princeton, N.J.: Princeton Univ. Press, 1964), 80–117.

17. Compare Petrarch, *RS*, 296: "I used to accuse myself and now I excuse, rather I praise myself and hold myself much more dear for the worthy prison, for the sweet bitter blow that I have kept hidden for so many years."

18. Isocrates is usually noticed as the first to claim a didactic purpose for epideictic discourse, though the idea is more than latent in Plato, e.g., *Laws*, 8.829d. Hardison cites Pliny and Julian the Apostate as being especially hypocritical when they defend their servile flattery by reference to didactic intention, *Enduring Monument*, 31. Erasmus will later echo all these arguments: "No other way of correcting a prince is so efficacious as presenting, in the guise of flattery, the pattern of a really good prince. Thus do you instil virtues and remove faults in such a manner that you seem to urge the prince to the former and restrain him from the latter," cited by L. K. Born, "The Perfect Prince According to the Latin Panegyrists," *American Journal of Philology* 55 (1934): 20–35. Besides Hardison, standard accounts of the theory of praise are: T. C. Burgess, *Epideictic Literature* (Chicago: Univ. of Chicago Press, 1902); G. Kennedy, *The Art of Persuasion in Greece* (Princeton, N.J.: Princeton Univ. Press, 1963), 152–203; G. Kennedy, *The Art of Rhetoric in the Roman World* (Princeton, N.J.: Princeton Univ. Press, 1972), 21–23 et passim; Curtius, *European Literature*, chaps. 8, 9; B. Weinberg, *A History of Literary Criticism in the Italian Renaissance* (Chicago: Univ. Chicago Press, 1961), 2 vols., 352–61 et passim; B. K. Lewalski, *Donne's "Anniversaries" and the Poetry of Praise: The Creation of a Symbolic Mode* (Princeton, N.J.: Princeton Univ. Press, 1973). Also useful are A. L. Deneef, "Epideictic Rhetoric and

the Renaissance Lyric," *Journal of Medieval and Renaissance Studies* 3 (1973):203–31; T. H. Cain, *Praise in "The Faerie Queene"* (Lincoln: Univ. of Nebraska Press, 1978); James D. Garrison, *Dryden and the Tradition of Panegyric* (Berkeley: Univ. of California Press, 1975).

19.   Daniel Javitch discusses the relationship between courtly literary manner and the actual conditions of the court in *Poetry and Courtliness in Renaissance England* (Princeton, N.J.: Princeton Univ. Press, 1978). Alan B. Kernan, drawing on Javitch, distinguishes Shakespeare's lyric courtly young man sonnets from what for Kernan are the more realistic and more dramatic dark lady sonnets: for Kernan the latter sub-sequence is evidence of the "failure of patronage" in England and the beginning of an independently funded theatrical literariness, *The Playwright as Magician: Shakespeare's Image of the Poet in the English Public Theater* (New Haven: Yale Univ. Press, 1979). On this topic, see also William Empson, *Some Versions of Pastoral* (New York: New Directions Press, 1974, first published 1935), chap. 3, "They that Have Power." Whatever the actual relation of poet to patron, the Renaissance "image" of the poet remains colored by an ideal, reflexive version of courtliness whose ideal rewards go back to Castiglione. As Spenser has Pierce put it in the "October" eclogue: "Cuddie, the prayse is better, then the price,/The glory eke much greater then the gayne:/O what an honore is it, to restraine/ The lust of lawlesse youth with good advice." "October," *The Shepheardes Calender,* 19–22. Cuddie, of course, for all of his complaints, is, as "The Argument" calls him, "the perfecte paterne of a Poete," just as Spenser, for all his penury, is the poet's poet because he is the courtier's (Sidney's) courtier: nevertheless, this expresses a common sentiment. Foster suggests that Queen Elizabeth consciously encouraged Petrarchan idealization of herself for down-to-earth political reasons, *Icy Fire*, chap. 4. For background, see F. Yates, "Queen Elizabeth as Astraea," *Journal of the Warburg and Courtauld Institute* 10 (1947):27–82; Roy Strong, *The Cult of Elizabeth: Elizabethan Portraiture and Pageantry* (London: Thames and Hudson, 1977).

20.   The idea that Shakespeare's sonnets are imitations or parodies of established literary models is first proposed in the debate as to whether the sonnets are genuinely autobiographical. The impetus for this first "intertextual" reading of the sonnets derives originally from a desire to protect Shakespeare's reputation, for if the sonnets are indeed confessional, then the Bard stands self-convicted both of immorality and of foolishness (e.g., Halliwell-Phillips). Only later, with the scholarship of Sir Sidney Lee, do Shakespeare's imitations of other sonnets and of sonnet conventions become evidence for what is taken to be a deliberately self-conscious literary manner. On this point, however, as the *Variorum* points out, Lee several times changed his mind, 2:144–45. "The Question of Autobiography," as the *Variorum* calls it, is a question which only begins to be asked at the beginning of the nineteenth century. The question is reviewed in *Variorum*, 2:133–65.

21.   Literary precedents for "dark ladies" are reviewed in *Variorum*, 2:242–76. Booth points out that this is part of the Petrarchan tradition: "Tasso played on *negra* and *alba* in praising Leonora, who is both *bruna* and *bella*; Sidney's Stella has black eyes," 434. The principal model comes from *The Song of Solomon*, whose dark desire is the object of considerable mystic and kabbalistic medieval exegesis. For Bruno, who relies on this tradition, the canticle's advice, *Noli mirare, quia nigra sum: decoloravit enim me sol* ("Re-

gard ye me not because I am blacke: for the sunne hath loked upon me,"
Cant. 1:5 in the Geneva translation), is a divine invitation to intellectualize
and to spiritualize desire—this in accord with the false etymology that
transmutes *eros* into *heroes;* see *Giordano Bruno's "The Heroic Frenzies,"* trans.
P. E. Memmo (Chapel Hill: Univ. of North Carolina Press, 1964), 67. The
ideal desire and the ideal sun of *De gli Eroici furori* is intended as a purified
Petrarchanism; Bruno's references to Petrarch in the dedication to Sidney
reflect this intention. This is something quite different, however, from the
discoloring desire and sun developed in Shakespeare's dark lady sub-
sequence. Bruno is so taken with *The Song of Solomon* that he originally
planned to name his own book after it, 62.

22. Gorgias' paradox of Helen eventually becomes orthodox, his ironic
praise taken straightforwardly. Isocrates writes *Busiris* early in his career, but
he considers the form unworthy. See *Isocrates,* ed. L. V. Hook (Cambridge:
Harvard Univ. Press, 1945), 2:100–01. Burgess gives a summary of major
Greek paradoxical panegyrists, *Epideictic Literature,* 165–66. In the Renaissance, the most influential ancient compendium of epideictic paradoxes is
Cicero's *Paradoxa Stoicorum,* though its intentions are more serious than is the
custom for the genre. See H. Rackham's introduction, in the Loeb Classical
Library, *Cicero* (Cambridge: Harvard Univ. Press, 1942), 2:252–53.

23. *"Paradoxon,* or the Wonderer," Puttenham, *The Arte of English Poesie,*
233. To the extent that praise is traditionally visual, the "Wonderer" is a
"sensable figure" that questions visibility, as is brought home in Puttenham's two examples: "I wonder much to see so many husbands thrive,/
That have but little wit, before they come to wive" (233–34), "Now is it not,
a wonder to behold,/Yonder gallant skarce twenty winter old" (234). The
first example has cuckoldry as its theme; the second, the follies of a male
youth. The "Wonderer" is closely related by Puttenham to *"Aporia,* or the
Doubtfull" (234), and is a version of *"Ironia,* or the drie mock" (199).

24. In principle, paradoxical praises will follow the topics and schemes
of regular praise, as set out, for example, by Quintilian, *Institutio Oratoria,*
3.7.1–28. However, as H. K. Miller points out, because ironic praise more
often treats of things than persons, it will most commonly employ arguments "relating to the antiquity, the nobility or dignity, and the utility of the
object praised," "The Paradoxical Encomium with Special Reference to Its
Vogue in England: 1600–1800," *Modern Philology* 53, no. 3 (1956):145–78.

25. Heroic Frenzies, 64–65:

And, by my faith, if I wish to employ myself in defending the nobility of that
Tuscan poet, who showed himself so distraught on the banks of the Sorgue for a
lady of Valclusa, and not say that he was a madman fit to be chained, I shall have to
believe and force myself to persuade others, that for lack of genius apt for higher
things he set himself the task of nourishing his melancholy, and belaboring his wit
in confusion, by analysing the effects of an obstinate vulgar love, animal and bes-
tial, as so many others have done who formerly have sung the praises of a fly, a
beetle, an ass, of Silenus, of Priapus, of apes, and those who have in our time sung
the praises of urinals, of the shepherd's pipe, of beans, of the bed, of lies, of dis-
honor, of the furnace, of the knife, of famine, and of the plague, things which
perhaps give the appearance of being no less lofty and proud by reason of the
celebrated voices of those who sing of them than these and other ladies I have
mentioned are, perhaps by reason of the poets who have celebrated them.

328 • Note to Page 63

Woman is a standard topic for paradoxical praise, e.g., Donne's "In Praise
of Woman's Inconstancie," (*Juvenilia*, first paradox). This is the force of "paradox" in Hamlet's "the power of beauty will sooner transform honesty from
what it is to a bawd than the force of honesty can translate beauty into his
likeness. This was sometime a paradox, but now the time gives it proof"
(3.1.110–14). In the loosest sense, this rhetorically playful misogyny goes
back as much to the *Phaedrus* and Lysias' speech defending the virtues of the
(homosexual) nonlover over the lover as it does to Gorgias' praise of Helen.
That is to say, the connection between praise and eros is already a classical
problem, one that forces Plato, for the sake of metaphysical decency, to revise standard acceptations of both (cf. the *Symposium* and its different
"praises" of Eros). So too the beauty-bawd motif is connected to a kind of
courtship wit that we find in certain sonnet sequences and associated romance conventions whereby the lady is to be both induced and seduced by
high argument to low action—blazoned, as it were, into bed.

Resisting the temptation to identify specific literary antecedents, it is important to realize that the ambiguity of woman, as cultural archetype, perfectly suits the formal requirements of a figure or scheme of speech designed
to show off its own duplicity. This is seen most clearly in theater. Paradoxical
praise is a staple of Elizabethan drama, particularly of witty, intellectual comedy where the verbal fireworks and artificial syllogizings of the figure are
especially appropriate. In drama the introduction of such epideictic irony will
sometimes seem strikingly gratuitous, present solely for the sake of rhetorical
display, as in Dekker's *Satiromastix*, with its alternating set-piece praises of
hair and baldness, or Chapman's *Monsieur D'Olive* with its praise of tobacco.
Equally often, however, in fact more often, playwrights will work hard to
integrate such paradoxical panegyric into their plots, developing the figure
for the sake of the way it can casually set mock-heroic tone or illustrate per-
versity of temperament, as, for famous example, Volpone's opening paradoxical encomium of gold, which does both. However, there is always an especially convenient epideictic plot attaching to praiseworthy female infidelity,
as when Marston presents no less than two formal praises of prostitution in
The Dutch Courtesan (see Introduction) or when Dekker plays with both sides
of the issue in parts 1 and 2 of *The Honest Whore*. A. H. Sackton gives other
examples in "The Paradoxical Encomium in Elizabethan Drama," *University of
Texas Studies in English* 28 (1949):83–104. All these examples presuppose and
invigorate, even if they question, an established rhetorical iconography in
which, however comically the equation is formulated, woman, qua woman, is
a bawd, prostitute by essence, and for this reason speakable only through
paradoxical epideixis.

This is what gives point and rhetorical density to the way Hamlet, immediately after his "paradox," consigns Ophelia to the brothel-nunnery. But it also
allows us to understand why when Shakespeare develops, as he does so often, the traditional association between female sexuality and a kind of femi-
nine sacred—virgin-whore, Madonna-Magdalene—he tends also to invoke a
vocabulary of ironic praise, as though throughout his career he is the false
lover of *A Lover's Complaint*, who "preach'd pure maid, and prais'd cold chas-
tity" (315). Again, in the most straightforward sense, this is simply rhetorically decorous, women receiving, as it were, precisely the loose language they

inspire and deserve. What is striking, however, is the way within this tradition Shakespeare characteristically radicalizes the "decoration" by making
language and woman not only equivalently duplicitous, but also reciprocally
so: the falseness of the one adduced as cause and explanation of the falseness
of the other. Thus it goes without saying that in a world where "every dram of
woman's flesh is false" (*Winter's Tale*, 2.1.138), women's words should not be
trusted, as Hermione complains when forced to answer Leontes' accusation:
"Mine integrity,/being counted falsehood, shall (as I express it)/Be so receiv'd" (3.2.26–28). But it is not only that loose women are "supposed" to lie,
but that this is the way language, even male language, learns its own dissimulation. Again Longaville's sonnet is relevant: "Did not the heavenly rhetoric of
thine eye,/'Gainst whom the world cannot hold argument,/Persuade my heart
to this false perjury?" (*Love's Labor's Lost*, 4.3.58–60). It follows that when a
good woman, if there be such, is genuinely to be praised, it will be in language which, and as something which, exceeds the excess of rhetoric, which,
of course, is precisely the moral Berowne is supposed to draw from the comic
consequences of his own "fair tongue, conceits expositor" (*LLL*, 2.1.72)—
though this is a moral inevitably belied by the inexpungeable rhetoricity with
which it is expressed: "Fie, painted rhetoric! O, she needs it not./To things of
sale a seller's praise belongs:/She passes praise, then praise too short doth
blot" (*LLL*, 4.3.235–37).

We can provisionally observe, therefore, that Hamlet's nunnery is insult-
ingly pornographic directly in proportion to the degree that it is ironically
panegyric. This is a proportion or relationship that remains constant
through the whole of Shakespeare's career, from the Porpentine-Priory opposition of *The Comedy of Errors* to Hermione's chapel at the end of *The Winter's Tale*. Always the topic of mysterious, sacred, and erotic woman will be
colored by the something epideictically "wonderful" built into Puttenham's
sense of rhetorical praise paradox (cf. Marston's *Sophonisba: Or the Wonder of
Women*—derived from Petrarch's *Africa*, with affinities to *Antony and Cleo-
patra*), and almost always this will be formulated in a context defined and
circumscribed by the paradox of women's speech, as in Cordelia's spoken
"nothing" of which nothing comes, or as in the conclusion to *The Taming of
the Shrew* (5.2.188–89):

HORTENSIO: Now go thy ways, thou hast tam'd a curs't shrow.
LUCENTIO: 'Tis a wonder, by your leave, she will be tam'd so.

Whatever the explanation, therefore, for either the ambivalence that
links the idealization of woman to her denigration, or for the paradoxical
language, the rhetorical "wonder," that is correlated with this coincidence of
female opposites, it seems fair to stipulate that with Hamlet's "paradox," or
with the sonnets to the dark lady, we come not only upon a reiterated
Shakespearean topic, but also upon one of the shaping principles of Shakespeare's dramatic imagination: on the one hand, a seducer's language of
dishonest praise, lending itself to anti-Petrarchan satire; on the other, a
cuckold's language of betrayed contempt, where the dishonest praise of
woman turns out to be true with the discovery that its object is false. Moreover, this is a principle that affects the general Elizabethan conception of the
theater, which, as its detractors always and not inaccurately complain, is .

itself a "brothel-house of bawdy," and for this reason a topos or topic that often receives paradoxical praise.

26. Besides Burgess, Miller, Sackton, Vickers, already mentioned, standard authorities on paradoxical praise are: A. E. Malloch, "The Techniques and Functions of the Renaissance Paradox," *Studies in Philology* 53 (1956):191–203; E. N. Thompson, "The Seventeenth Century English Essay," *University of Iowa Humanistic Studies* 3, no. 3 (1926):94–105; A. S. Pease, "Things without Honor," *Classical Philology* 21 (1926):27–42; R. E. Bennet, "Four Paradoxes by Sir William Cornwallis, the Younger," *Harvard Studies and Notes in Philology and Literature* 13 (1931):219–40; W. G. Rice, "The *Paradossi* of Ortensio Landi," *University of Michigan Essays and Studies in English and Comparative Literature* 8 (1932):59–74; Sister M. Geraldine, C.S.J., "Erasmus and the Tradition of Paradox," *Studies in Philology* 61 (1964):41–63. W. Kaiser, *Praisers of Folly* (Cambridge: Harvard Univ. Press, 1963); R. Colie, *Paradoxia Epidemica: The Renaissance Tradition of Paradox* (Princeton, N.J.: Princeton Univ. Press, 1966).

Colie's book, which summarizes much of the above material, is vigorously criticized by Frances Yates for confusing rhetorical with logical paradoxes, *New York Review of Books* 8, no. 3 (Feb. 23, 1967):26–28. Yates's criticism is in good part justified, but the conflation of the syllogistically logical with the discursively rhetorical is one that Renaissance authors themselves regularly indulge in, and not always playfully. For Ramists rhetoric is a part of logic, and, of course, more generally, the medieval *trivium* makes grammar, rhetoric, and logic parts of the same study. Bearing this tradition in mind, Colie's syncretic treatment of Renaissance paradoxes possesses some historical justification; it is only a post-Renaissance sensibility, for which the unity of the *trivium* is something trivial, that decisively separates the art of language from the art of logic. Vickers, "*King Lear*," for different reasons altogether, argues for the serious moral intentions of Renaissance rhetorical paradox, referring to the grave tradition of Cicero; Vickers also associates the genre with the forms of scholastic disputation and with the medieval article. Vickers makes paradox somewhat too earnest a proposition, for the force and seriousness of paradox derives from the way it *first* puts moral as well as rhetorical and logical norms into playful question, e.g., Erasmus, in the letter to More he places as preface to *The Praise of Folly:* "For just as nothing is more trivial than to treat serious matters in a trivial way, so too nothing is more delightful than to treat trifles in such a way that you do not seem to be trifling at all. Whether I have done so others will judge, but unless I am completely deceived by *'Selflove'* [*philautia*], my praise of folly is not altogether foolish," trans. C. H. Miller, (New Haven: Yale Univ. Press, 1979). Compare Marston's epigraph to *The Dutch Courtesan, Turpe est dificiles habere nugas,* and compare the concluding admonitory subtitle of Munday's collection of paradoxes, "only to exercise yong wittes in difficult matters." This "triviality" explains why Sidney disapproves of the genre, *AP,* 181–82.

The defense of paradox by playfully erudite appeals to literary precedent seems almost an inherent, formal aspect of the genre. Thus R. B. McKerrow's gloss of Nashe's list of precedents for "The Prayse of the Red Herring" merely extends Nashe's already formidable enumeration, *The Works of Thomas Nashe* (New York: Barnes and Noble, 1966), 3:176–78; 3:389–95.

Enumeration of detail is a feature of *vituperatio* and *panegyricon*, and thus becomes a part of the paradoxical defense of paradox; this gives mock seriousness to mocking scholarship. Miller, "Paradoxical Encomium," gives a good example of such an "Epistle Apologeticall," by Abraham Fleming (c. 1579): "For, *Lucian* and *Apuleius* wrote of a Asse, *Themison* in praise of the herbe Plaintaine, *Homere* in commendation of Wine, *Ephren* in dispraise of laughing, *Orpheus Hesiodus* of fumigations, or Perfumes, *Chrysippus* of Colewortes, *Phanias* of Nettles, *Messala* made for every severall letter of the *ABC*, a severall booke, *Virgil* of a Gnat, *Ovid* of a nut, *Erasmus* but latelie of the praise of follie, and *Heywood* yet later, of the Spider and the Flie," 155. The scholarship of Bruno's paradoxical account of what for Bruno is Petrarch's paradoxical praise (see n. 25, above) is thus within the tradition.

27.   The young man sonnets, too, will sometimes explicitly blame their object, but always by reference to the ideal that the young man also represents, e.g., "That thou are blam'd shall not be thy defect,/For slander's mark was ever yet the fair" (70); "How like Eve's apple doth thy beauty grow,/If thy sweet virtue answer not thy show" (93). This is to mix praise with blame—according to Menander's epideictic categories, *amphidoxa*—but not, at least explicitly, to mix them up.

28.   "Bi-fold" is Troilus' word when he observes Cressida's duplicity: "O madness of discourse,/That cause sets up with and against itself!/Bi-fold authority, where reason can revolt/Without perdition, and loss assume all reason/Without revolt. This is, and is not, Cressid!"(*TC*, 5.2.142–46). Troilus assimilates this "bi-fold authority" to himself; its folds create within him a space composed of what "is and is not": "Within my soul there doth conduce a fight/Of this strange nature, that a thing inseparate/Divides more wider than the sky and earth,/And yet the spacious breadth of this division/Admits no orifex for a point as subtle/As Ariachne's broken woof to enter" (5.2.147–52). J. Hillis Miller, in "'Ariachne's Broken Woof,'" *Georgia Review* 31 (1977):44–60, sees in "bi-fold authority" an image of utter textual indeterminacy, the proof that there is no "rule in unity itself." I will be arguing, instead, that the "madness of discourse" and the erotics of "orifex" are coordinated by Shakespeare in a very determinate way, and that the two together produce a specific "bi-fold" subjectivity whose authoritative influence in post-Shakespearean literature derives from the way it paradoxically reduplicates the traditional subject and subjectivity of praise.

29.   For suntanning, see Booth, 457–58. Quite apart from the darkness of the dark lady, the theme is not unimportant if we recall, on the one hand, the association of "sun" with "stain" (33, 35), and, on the other, the poet's reference to his own staining, as in the "blenches" of 110, or the (biographically loaded) reference to his "dyer's hand" in 111. That the sun "tans" is, of course, a common Renaissance metaphor, e.g. Spenser's "And face all tan'd with scorching sunny ray,/As he had traueild many a sommers day," *Faerie Queene*, 1.6.35. For E. K., defending Spenser's archaic diction, the poet is "sunburnt" by the brightness of ancient poets; see *Epistle to the Shepheardes Calender*, 416. The image takes on a different rhetorical color, however, in the context of Astrophil's "sun-burned brain" in the first sonnet of *Astrophil and Stella*.

30.   Where Winters opposes a strong "native style" to ornate, aureate Petrarchanism, C. S. Lewis instead, and more influentially, distinguishes a

"drab" traditional poetic style from the Renaissance "Golden" lyric, *English Literature in the Sixteenth Century* (Oxford: Oxford Univ. Press, 1954). Laura is *l'auro* for the same super-naturally imaginary reasons that lead Sidney to distinguish the "brazen" world of nature from the "golden" world of poetry ("Her [nature's] world is brasen, the Poets only deliver a golden," *AP*, 156). These golden themes become satiric when taken literally, as in Volpone's paradoxical encomium of gold. Gold, like light, is either metallic or liquid, as in Spenser's alternately brittle and aqueous light: for example, the imagery associated with the enfeebling water of *Faerie Queene*, 1.7.6, which is "as cleare as cristall glas," as opposed to "the Well of Life" of 1.11.34, from which Redcrosse emerges "as Eagle fresh out of the ocean wave." These conventional associations will determine the way the ideal Shakespearean subject will imagine his own body ego, either in armor or dissolved, in broken pieces (as in *Coriolanus*, 5.6.111) or melted (as in *Hamlet*, 1.2.129). As I argue in chapter V, in the young man sonnets these oppositions determine the way the poet imagines his golden verse: either a rigid edifice liable to collapse (e.g., 55) or a liquid medium of perfume liable to evaporate (e.g., 54).

31. Booth, 187.

32. Riverside, following Gildon, emends Q's "morning" in line 9 to "mourning." But the pun is established by line 5, and the poem is not improved by denying the orthographic consequence of its word play. So too editors have often emended "torment" in line 2 to "torments" so as to make the verb agree in number not with plural, pitying "eyes" but with singular, disdaining "heart." The emendation makes line 2 less complicated by eliminating the confusing admixture of eyes and heart, of plural and singular. But this confusion is the governing logic of the poem, a logic to which the typographical misprint, if that is what it is, authentically responds.

33. Compare "Sometime too hot the eye of heaven shines,/And often is his golden complexion dimm'd (18), or Petrarch, 30: "There never have been seen such lovely eyes, either in our age or in the first years; they melt me as the sun does the snow: whence there comes forth a river of tears that Love leads to the foot of the harsh laurel that has branches of diamond and golden locks." There are innumerable examples of this sun-eye motif in contemporary sonnet sequences; for background material, see M. Bensimon, "The Significance of Eye Imagery in the Renaissance from Bosch to Montaigne," *Yale French Studies* 47 (1972):266–90; Lisle C. John, *The Elizabethan Sonnet Sequences: Studies in Conventional Conceits* (New York: Columbia Univ. Press, 1938), 150–59. The point to notice is the consistency with which the motif evokes particular material associations, for example, in the Petrarch quotation, the progress from eye-sun to melting snow, to river, to diamonds and gold. The progress is conventional: what needs to be explained is why this particular association possesses such poetic force as to have established itself as a convention, for this explains the force of Shakespeare's reworking of the convention. I argue later that these images, which conventionally function to image "likeness" in Shakespeare's sonnets, instead image "difference."

34. Shakespeare plays on the fact that the Morning Star and the Evening Star, Hesperus and Phosphorus, are the same, again an allusion to the double Venus. The paradoxical nominal duplicity of this is again conventional, e.g., Donne's ninth paradox, "Why is Venus-Star Multinominous,

called both *Hesper* and *Vesper*," which I discuss in chapter II; *Juvenilia,* in *John Donne, Complete Poetry and Selected Prose,* ed. J. Hayward (London: Nonesuch Press, 1929), 350 –51. From just this instance of an "identity proposition," modern philosophy, from Frege on, has worried over the question of the propriety of proper names, specifically, whether names have referents and/or senses. If they have only referents, then the proposition "The Morning Star is the Evening Star" is tautological, and yet, unlike a tautology, the proposition conveys new information. On the other hand, it is difficult to understand in what way proper names like "John" possess a connotative, rather than a denotative, sense. I discuss some of this philosophical context in "The Significance of Literature." I discuss the sensuous "sense" of Shakespeare's proper name in chapter V, in connection with the sonnets' puns on "Will." It is worth noting that philosophical discussions of the problem of proper names regularly return to these literary topoi, either to "Phosphorous is Hesperus" or to "Cicero is Tully," as though the philosophical discussion could only be conducted under the aegis of the Queen of Desire (Venus) or the King of Rhetoric (Cicero).

35.   This characteristic Shakespearean feature complicates the alternately dualist or dialectical reading of Shakespeare that, since Bradley, has become increasingly influential. The system of Shakespearean "complementarity," as Norman Rabkin calls it, or the structure of "Renaissance Contrariety," as R. Grudin calls it, whether it characterizes Shakespeare's "mighty opposites" as antipathetic or sympathetic to each other, will regularly interpret those opposites in accord with a binary logic that goes back to Heraclitus and that finds its fullest formal exposition in Hegel, from whom Bradley derived his theory of Shakespearean tragedy in the first place. In this tradition, the "paradoxical" coincidence of opposites is profoundly orthodox. What is novel about the Shakespearean is that it forswears this structure of polarity, not by reconciling contraries within a larger unity nor by exploiting the tension produced by their oxymoronic combination, but, specifically, by reiterating them in such a way as to put the concept and the consequence of polar opposition into question. This is also how Shakespearean drama overflows structures of characterological opposition which are established by the exigencies of medieval theatrical doubling conventions. That is to say, this explains how Shakespeare distances himself from the forms and themes of psychomachian allegorical theater at the same time that he employs them. This is not to say, therefore, that traditional structures of opposition and complementarity are irrelevant to the study of Shakespeare, but, rather, that these are the object of—and are transmuted as a result of—a profound Shakespearean meditation. In the same way that the idealist ideology of Neo-Platonic Humanism is something Shakespeare only deals with in reflective retrospect, so too the revivification of contrariety in the early Renaissance—the speculations of an Agrippa or a Paracelsus, for example—are coded by Shakespeare with a nostalgia that is as moving as it is unsentimental. A parallel would be the Tudor revival of tilting, as a kind of theatrical, festival memorialization of a now-anachronistic medieval joust.

A full bibliography of critics who read Shakespeare in terms of oppositional structures would serve no useful purpose. Bradley, of course, sets a high model for characterological-ethical analysis in *Shakespearean Tragedy*

(London: Macmillan, 1904). C. L. Barber's *Shakespeare's Festive Comedy* (Princeton, N. J.: Princeton Univ. Press, 1959) persuasively relates Shakespeare's comic form to the opposition of holiday and everyday, though here again the point is that an earlier sympathetic magic, now passé, is revived in the register of the imaginary. Norman Rabkin gives a full and valuable synoptic account in his *Shakespeare and the Common Understanding* (New York: The Free Press, 1967). In R. Grudin's "*Mighty Opposites*": *Shakespeare and Renaissance Contrariety* (Berkeley: Univ. of California Press, 1979), there is a useful summary of appropriate Renaissance parallels; also, his first two chapters cite relevant literary studies. M. McCanles offers a rather abstract instance of the mode in *Dialectical Criticism and Renaissance Literature* (Berkeley: Univ. of California Press, 1975). See also M. B. Smith, *Dualities in Shakespeare* (Toronto: Univ. of Toronto Press, 1966). In addition, there are a good many psychoanalytic studies that focus on Shakespearean "ambivalence." An extreme case of binary Shakespeare criticism is René Girard's "Myth and Ritual in Shakespeare's *A Midsummer Night's Dream*," in *Textual Strategies*, ed. Josue Harari (Ithaca: Cornell Univ. Press, 1979), 189–212, which takes up the opposition of difference and no-difference itself. Girard sees Shakespeare repeating and interpreting cross-cultural mythic patterns; see also *Violence and the Sacred*, trans. P. Gregory (Baltimore: Johns Hopkins Univ. Press, 1977); *Des choses cacheés depuis la fondation du monde*, with J. -M. Oughourlian, G. Lefort (Paris: Grasset, 1978). For a version of a "Girardian" reading, see J. Fineman, "Fratricide and Cuckoldry: Shakespeare's Doubles," in *Representing Shakespeare*, eds. M. Schwartz and C. Kahn (Baltimore: Johns Hopkins Univ. Press, 1980), 70–109.

36. For Puttenham's definition, see my Introduction, 37. Puttenham, *Art of Poesie*, 216, offers the following example: "In this figure of the *Cross-couple* we wrate for a forlorne lover complaining of his mistresse crueltie these verses among other. Thus for your sake I dayly die,/And do but seeme to live in deede:/Thus is my blisse but miserie,/My lucre losse without your meede." As Puttenham's example evidences, there is nothing unusual either in Shakespeare's use of the figure of in his application of the figure to Petrarchan complaint. What distinguishes Shakespeare's use of the figure is the seriousness and literalness with which he develops material, thematic, and narrative consequences of cross-coupling.

37. M. Valency summarizes *stilnovisti* eye-heart conventions in *In Praise of Love* (New York: Macmillan, 1958), 230–35; see also John, *The Elizabethan Sonnet Sequences*, 161–65. Bruno repeats Neo-Platonic themes when he comments on his eye-heart sonnet, *alti, profondi e desti miei pensieri*: "All love proceeds from the sight, intellectual love from the eye of the mind; sensible love from the view of the senses. Now the word sight has two meanings. It can mean the visual potency, that is, the power of seeing of the intellect or of the eye; or it can also mean the visual act, the application which the eye or the intellect makes upon the material or intellectual object," *Heroic Frenzies*, 130–31. For specific Plotinian parallels, see M. Bundy, *The Theory of Imagination in Classical and Medieval Thought* (Urbana: Univ. of Illinois Press, 1927) 117–76, also Baldwin, *Literary Genetics*, 158–80.

38. Again Bruno provides a convenient summary: "every contrary is reduced to friendship, whether through the victory of one of the contraries,

or through harmony and conciliation, or by some vicissitude, every discord to concord, every diversity to unity." *Heroic Frenzies,* 67.

39. Petrarch, 174; compare 87, 86. *Le Roman de la Rose,* 1684–87, ed. F. Lecoy, (Paris: Didot, 1914), see notes for background for the motif. The relevant courtly example comes from Castiglione, *The Book of the Courtier, from the Italian of Count Baldassare Castiglione, done into English by Sir Thomas Hoby,* 1561 (London: David Nutt, 1900), 357–63.

40. Browning's scornful response to Wordsworth's sonnet, "Scorn not the Sonnet," is cited in *Variorum* 2:142. From Meres's 1598 reference, in *Palladis Tamia, Wits Treasury,* to Shakespeare's "sugred Sonnets among his private friends," we know that Shakespeare circulated at least some of the poems. From the fact that he chose not to publish any of them—except, possibly, the two printed in *The Passionate Pilgrim* (138, 144)—we can perhaps impute to the sonnets a pointed autobiographical cast, especially since sonnet publication was by now the custom. So too, the striking unconventionalities of some of the poems, the peculiarity and immediacy of some details, suggests at least some dimension of private, personal reference. All this having been said, it remains the case that there is very little autobiography that can be plausibly derived out of the sonnets. There is of course a considerable amount of implausible biography that can be, and has been derived from them.

41. This tradition begins at least as early as 1664, with Margaret Cavendish: "*Shakespeare* did not want Wit, to Express to the Life all Sorts of Persons, of what Quality, Profession, Degree, Breeding, or Birth soever; nor did he want Wit to Express the Divers, and Different Humours, or Natures, or Several Passions in Mankind; and so Well he hath Express'd in his Playes all Sorts of Persons, as one would think he had been Transformed into every one of those Persons he hath Described. . . . there is not any person he hath Described in his Book, but his Readers might think they were Well acquainted with them." *Sociable Letters,* 1664 (Menston: Scolar Press, 1969), no. 123:245–46.

42. See the references to Shakespeare's mimetic mode in N. Frye, *Anatomy of Criticism* (Princeton, N.J.: Princeton Univ. Press, 1957); more particularly, on Shakespearean romance, in *A Natural Perspective* (New York: Columbia Univ. Press, 1965).

43. John Dryden, "Preface to *Troilus and Cressida,*" *Dryden: The Dramatic Works,* ed. M. Summers (London: The Nonesuch Press, 1932), 4:24–25.

44. Cuckoldry is of course a central Shakespearean theme. I have elsewhere discussed the different ways Shakespeare handles the theme in different dramatic genres; see "Fratricide and Cuckoldry, Shakespeare's Doubles." In a larger literary context, Shakespeare's development of the cuckoldry theme, both in the sonnets and in the plays, is significant because it focuses on the betrayed rather than on the betrayer. Shakespeare translates the adventurous cuckoldry story of medieval romance into a story of passive cuckoldry centered on a *mari* who half-welcomes his undoing. This is a shift in narrative focus that will lead directly, as Joyce implies, to Leopold Bloom.

45. Early in the *Rime Sparse,* for example, in a sonnet about erotic entropy, Petrarch questions the conventions of contrariety. The poem's Proustian themes introduce an axiom of literary desire which explains a great deal about the motives of Petrarchan praise (*RS,* 48):

If fire was never put out by fire, nor river ever made dry by rain, but always like is made to grow by like, and sometimes opposite has kindled opposite; Love, you who govern our thoughts, on whom my one soul in two bodies depends, why in my soul, in unaccustomed guise, do you make desire grow less through desiring much?

CHAPTER 2

1. Aristotle, *Poetics*, 1448b,3–1449a,7; Plato, *Republic*, 10:607a. For general accounts of traditional epideictic rhetorical theory, see chapter 1, n. 18. The expansive scope of the epideictic is clearest in Hermogenes, who subsumes history, philosophy, and poetry under "panegyric"; see D. A. Russell, *Criticism in Antiquity* (Berkeley: Univ. of California Press, 1981), 116–17.

2. Aristotle, *Poetics*, 1448b,3–1449a,7. Aristotle imagines the first poetical imitations as being either praise of the high or invective of the low, and he correlates this with the distinction between tragedy and comedy. Aristotle notes that Homer wrote both praise (the *Iliad* and the *Odyssey*) and blame (the satiric *Margites*), which suggests that the same kind of rhetoricity is involved in both genres; Socrates raises the issue at the end of the *Symposium*. Hardison discusses the relation between Aristotle's ideas about epideixis and Renaissance genre theory in *Enduring Monument*, 68–106. Also see Puttenham, *Art of Poetry*, 39.

3. Sidney, *AP*, 160; Hardison rehearses the traditional understanding of the way poetic mimesis induces moral action, *Enduring Monument*, 14–23; see also Wesley Trimpi, "The Meaning of Horace's 'Ut Pictura Poesis,'" *Journal of the Warburg and Courtauld Institutes* 36 (1973): 1–34.

4. S. K. Heninger, Jr. discusses the punctuation problem in *Touches of Sweet Harmony: Pythagorean Cosmology and Renaissance Poetics* (San Marino, Calif.: Huntington Library, 1974), 323.

5. Aristotle, Rhetoric, 1368a,39–40; see also 1367a,28–29.

6. For the relation between comparison and praise in classical rhetoric and rhetorical theory, see Friedrich Focke, "Synkrisis," *Hermes* 58 (1923):327–68, esp. 332–39; Marsh H. McCall, Jr., *Ancient Rhetorical Theories of Simile and Comparison* (Cambridge: Harvard Univ. Press, 1969), passim. For the relations in the Renaissance among praise, amplification, and *comparatio*, see Hardison, *Enduring Monument*, 31ff; Cain, *Praise in the Faerie Queene*, 9ff. Lee Sonnino cites Scaliger on the use of the "comparative mode" in panegyric, *A Handbook to Sixteenth Century Rhetoric* (New York: Barnes & Noble, 1968), 230. Priscian, in his adaptation of Hermogenes' *Progymnasmata*, offers a standard explanation of why "comparisons supply a great opportunity for this kind of oration" (praise):

> Comparison is the bringing together of similar things or different things, or a cross-reference of greater things to lesser or of lesser things to greater. We may also use them in a commonplace, increasing the seriousness of a crime by comparison; it can be used for the same purpose in praise of obloquy . . . always let this principle guide you: be sure that the things you are comparing are alike in every-

thing, or at least in some things. It is a fact that when we criticize one member, we praise the other, as in a comparison between justice and wealth. Also compare your theme to something greater; for instance, if you want to praise Ulysses, you should compare him to Hercules in order to make the lesser of the two seem like the greater in his virtues. But the use of this kind of commonplace demands a superior orator, eloquent and fluent, so that he can make his transference easily.

"Fundamentals Adapted from Hermogenes," trans. J. M. Miller, in *Readings in Medieval Rhetoric*, eds. Joseph M. Miller, M. Prosser, and T. Benson (Bloomington: Indiana Univ. Press, 1973), 63–64.

Puttenham (166) brings out the potential duplicity attaching to epideictic comparison:

As figures be the instruments of ornament in every language, so be they also in a sorte abuses or rather trespasses in speach, because they passe the ordinary limits of common utterance, and be occupied of purpose to deceive the eare and also the minde, drawing it from plainesse and simplicitie to a certaine doublenesse, whereby our talk is the more guilefull and abusing, for what else is your *Metaphor* but an inversion of sence by transport; your *allegorie* by a duplicitie of meaning or dissimulation under covert and darke intendements . . . then by incredible comparison giving credit, as by your *Hyperbole*, and many other waies seeking to inveigle and appasionate the mind.

7. *Astrophil and Stella*, no. 3; hereafter cited as *AS*.
8. *Poetics*, 1459a,18; see Introduction, n. 10.
9. Ibid., 1457b,7–9.
10. The marigold is a common emblematic figure, often used to illustrate the pious relation of the Christian to God, "the light of the world." See Barbara Lewalski, *Protestant Poetics and the Seventeenth Century Religious Lyric* (Princeton: Princeton Univ. Press, 1979), 189. This is also a commonplace figure for poetic devices in general, e.g., John Parmenter, *Helio-Tropes, or New Poesies for Sundials* (1625). Shakespeare characteristically complicates the figure by associating it with loss, as in Perdita's "the marigold, that goes to bed wi'th' sun, / And with him rises weeping" (4.4.105–6).
11. Bruno, *Heroic Frenzies*, 132.
12. Aristotle, *De Anima*, 429a,4.
13. Quintilian, *Inst. Or.* 6.2.29–30; Quintilian relates this to Cicero's "illumination" and *enargeia*, 6.2.32; English translation from the Loeb Classical Library, *The Institutio Oratoria of Quintilian*, trans. H. E. Butler (Cambridge: Harvard Univ. Press, 1921), 433–35. Mazonni cites this passage, see Baxter Hathaway, *The Age of Criticism: The Late Renaissance in Italy* (Ithaca: Cornell Univ. Press, 1962), 358. *Ponimus ante oculos* is a commonplace in epideictic theory; see John W. O'Malley, *Praise and Blame in Renaissance Rome* (Durham, N.C.: Duke Univ. Press, 1979), 63. This is related to traditional faculty psychology, which understands the representations of the "imagination" to render present previous sensible experience, e.g., the way Aquinas distinguishes the interior senses: "for the reception of sensible forms [*formarum sensibilium*], the proper sense and the common sense [*sensus proprius et communis*] are appointed. . . . But for the retention and preservation of these forms, the phantasy or imagination [*phantasia sive imaginatio*] is appointed; which are the same, for phantasy or imagination is as it were a

storehouse [*thesaurus*] of forms received through the senses," *Summa Theologiae,* Part I, Q. 78, art. 4. Aquinas goes on to recall that "Augustine calls that vision spiritual [*spiritualem visionem*] which is effected by the images of bodies in the absence of bodies [*fit per similitudines corporum in absentia corporum*]," *Summa Theologiae,* part 1, q. 78, reply obj. 6.

14. *Summa Theologiae,* part 1, q. 1, art. 9, reply obj. 2.

15. Puttenham, *Arte of Poesie,* 155. Puttenham's description of "*Exargasia,* or the Gorgious,*" which for Puttenham is "the last and principall figure of our poeticall Ornament," illustrates the way this poetic theory calls forth specifically visual imagery with which example to the epideictic fusion of clear mimetic likeness and beautifying metaphoric likeness (254):

> For the glorious lustre it setteth upon our speech and language, the Greeks call it *Exargasia* the Latine *Expolitio* a terme transferred from these polishers of marble and porphirite, who after it is rough hewen and reduced to that fashion they will, set upon it a goodly glasse, so smoth and cleere, as ye may see your face in it, or otherwise as it fareth by the bare and naked body, which being attired in rich and glorious apparell, seemeth to the common usage of th'eye much more comely and bewtifull then the naturall. So doth this figure (which therefore I call the Gorgious) polish our speech and as it were attire it with copious and pleasant amplifications and much varietie of sentences, all running upon one point and one intent.

This is the material imagery through which the copy and the copious join together, "running upon one point and intent." Puttenham's crowning example of *Exargasia* is quite courtly and polished; he cites several severe verses of Queen Elizabeth.

16. On the confusion of *energeia* and *enargia* in traditional rhetoric, see Madeleine Doran, *Endeavors of Art: A Study of Form in Elizabethan Drama* (Madison: Univ. of Wisconsin Press, 1954), 242, 439; see also Forrest Robinson, *The Shape of Things Known: Sidney's "Apology" in Its Philosophical Tradition* (Cambridge: Harvard Univ. Press, 1972), esp. chap. 4; Neil Rudenstine, *Sidney's Poetic Development* (Cambridge: Harvard Univ. Press, 1967) 149–71.

17. Aristotle, *Rhetoric,* 1411b,2.

18. Aristotle, *De Anima,* 418b,11–12. Aristotle rejects both the corpuscular and the emanation theory of vision, e.g., Plato's account, in *Timaeus,* 45b–d, of the way vision is produced by the homogeneous connection—"like to like" (*homoion pros homoion*)—linking eye to object. However, Aristotle develops a similar kind of visionary homogeneity and continuity in his account of the way the color of objects affects and the presence of light actualizes the physical, transparent medium between eye and object. According to Aristotle, the medium acts upon the watery substance of the eye, "moves" it such that it becomes a visible replica of the object. This ocular replica, the part of the eye that is now the image of the object, is what is seen. For discussions of Aristotle's theory of vision, see John I. Beare, *Greek Theories of Elementary Cognition: From Alcmaeon to Aristotle* (Oxford: Oxford Univ. Press, 1906), 9–22; David C. Lindberg, *Theories of Vision from Al-Kindi to Kepler* (Chicago: Univ. of Chicago Press, 1976), 6–9. James Carey relates Aristotle's account of vision to Aristotelian metaphysics in "Aristotle's Account of the Intelligibility of Being," *The St. John's Review,* 35, no. 1. (1984): 40–51.

19. For accounts of classical, medieval, and Renaissance optics, see Lindberg; Vasco Ronchi, *The Nature of Light: An Historical Survey,* trans. V.

Barocas (London: Heinemann, 1970); S. Edgerton, *The Renaissance Rediscovery of Linear Perspective* (New York: Basic Books, 1975), esp. chap. 5. For good bibliographies of specialized studies, see, in addition to Lindberg, A. C. Crombie, "The Mechanistic Hypothesis and the Scientific Study of Vision: Some Optical Ideas as a Background to the Invention of the Microscope," in *Historical Aspects of Microscopy*, eds. S. Bradbury and G. L. E. Turner (Cambridge: W. Heffer and Sons, 1967). The historic shift from a Platonic idealism of forms to an Aristotelian empiricism of categories (related to the traditional distinction in aesthetics between a Platonic imitation of the appearances of things and an Aristotelian imitation of the essences of things) is reflected by the way Latin *species* (from *specere*, "to look at") loses the transcendental connotations of Greek "Idea"; the visual metaphor, however, remains constant. Robert Grosseteste (1168–1253) and Roger Bacon (c. 1220–92) develop the compromise optic theory, which is also a theory of the workings of God's grace, that lies behind Petrarchan intro- and extromissive metaphors of vision: corporeal units of visual energy, "species," radiate out both from objects and from eyes; vision occurs when object species meet eye species; for Edgerton, this is the link between mechanical intromissive optics, as developed by Arab science out of Stoic optics, and the rediscovery of linear perspective by Brunelleschi and Alberti, 74–79. If Drayton had been more an Aristotelian than a Platonist, *Ideas Mirrour* would have been called "Species Speculation"; "Species," however, is still an acceptable late Renaissance translation of Platonic "Idea," e.g., the Cambridge Neo-Platonist Ralph Cudworth: "I suppose, said Socrates, that God and the very Species, Essence or Idea of life will be granted by all to be Incorruptible," *The True Intellectual System of the Universe*, 1678 (cited in *OED*).

On visual imagery in poetic theory, see, besides Hardison, *Enduring Monument*, 51–67, Murray W. Bundy, *The Theory of Imagination in Classical and Medieval Thought*, in *University of Illinois Studies in Language and Literature* 12, nos. 2–3 (1927); Rosemund Tuve, *Elizabethan and Metaphysical Imagery* (Chicago: Chicago Univ. Press, 1947), chaps. 2, 3; R. W. Lee, "Ut Pictura Poesis: The Humanistic Theory of Painting," *Art Bulletin* 22 (1940): 197–269; E. H. Gombrich, "*Icones Symbolicae*: The Visual Image in Neo-Platonic Thought," *Journal of the Warburg and Courtauld Institutes* 11 (1948); R. J. Clements, "*Picta Poesis*": Literary and Humanistic Theory in Renaissance Emblem Books (Rome: Edizioni di storia e letteratura, 1960), chap. 9; Erwin Panofsky, *Idea*, trans. J. Peake (Columbia: Univ. of South Carolina Press, 1968), W. Rossky, "Imagination in the English Renaissance: Psychology and Poetic," *Studies in the Renaissance* 5 (1958). For accounts of the "literary" sense of "imagination," see M. Bloomfield, "*Piers Plowman*" as a Fourteenth Century Apocalypse (New Brunswick: Rutgers, 1961), app. 3; D. Kelly, *Medieval Imagination: Rhetoric and the Poetry of Courtly Love* (Madison: Univ. of Wisconsin Press, 1978), esp. chap. 3; Randolph Quik, "Vis Imaginativa," *Journal of English and Germanic Philology* 53:1 (1954): 81–83; Edmund Gardner, "Imagination and Memory in the Psychology of Dante," *A Miscellany of Studies in Romance Languages and Literatures Presented to Leon E. Kastner*, eds. Mary Williams and James A. de Rothschild (Cambridge: W. Heffer and Sons, 1932), 275–82; Robert J. Bauer, "A Phenomenon of Epistemology in the Renaissance," *Journal of the History of Ideas* 31, no. 2 (1970):281–88; Jay L. Halio, "The Metaphor of Conception and Elizabethan Theories of Imagination," *Neophilologus* 50, no. 4 (1966):454–61; Murray W. Bundy, "'Invention' and 'Imagination' in the Renaissance," *Journal of English and Germanic Philology* 29 (1930):535–45; and, especially valuable for its discussion of "pleasure and morality, artifice and truth," Eugenio Donato, "Tesauro's Poetics: Through the Looking Glass," *Modern Language Notes* 78, no. 1 (1963):15–30. For a useful account of visual imagination in *The Faerie Queene*, see Isabel MacCaffrey, *Spenser's Allegory: The Anatomy of Imagination* (Princeton: Princeton Univ. Press, 1976); also, restricting itself simply to vision, J.-B. Dallet, "Ideas of Sight in *The Faerie Queene*," *English Literary History* 27, no. 2 (1960):87–121; also J. Bender, *Spenser and Literary Pictorialism* (Princeton: Princeton Univ. Press, 1972). There is, of course, an enormous bibliography relating to the motif of vision in poetics and poetry; my citations here are not meant to be exhaustive. I will refer to other individual studies as they become relevant.

20. I summarize here the range of listings in *A Greek-English Lexicon*, comp. H. G. Liddell and R. Scott (Oxford: Oxford Univ. Press, 1966). These listings amount to a thesaurus of Petrarchan motifs and conceits.

21. Aristotle, *Rhetoric*, 1358b,2.

22. Hardison, *Enduring Monument*, 206, cites Quintilian on epideictic oratory: "Its matter is *'ad solum ostentationem compositas'* and its mode is praise *'quae ostentationi componitur,'*" (*Inst. Or* 3.7.1–4); Hardison notes that poetry in general is for Quintilian a *"genus ostentationi comparatum, et praeter id, quad solam petit voluptatem"* (10.1.28).

23. Cited in Baxter Hathaway, *The Age of Criticism: The Late Renaissance in Italy* (Ithaca: Cornell Univ. Press, 1962), 366. Italian text in Jacopo Mazzoni, *Della difesa della Commedia di Dante* (Cesena: Bartolomeo Rauerij, 1587–1688), 1:148. For corrected Greek text, see Plutarch, *De Placitis Philosophorum*, in *Moralia*, ed. G. N. Bernardakis (Leipzig: B. G. Teubner, 1888–96), 900e,17–21.

24. On the mirror metaphor, see Curtius, *European Literature*, 560–62; Hardison, *Enduring Monument*, 52–67. A. Gunn discusses the medieval relation of the mirror to romance erotics, *The Mirror of Love: A Reinterpretation of "The Romance of the Rose"* (Lubbock: Texas Technological Press, 1952), 266–73; Stephen Orgel briefly reviews mirror metaphors applied to theater, *The Illusion of Power* (Berkeley: Univ. of California Press, 1975), 59–60; Edgerton gives references, going back to Aristotle, to the eye as mirror, *Linear Perspective*, 174ff; S. Chew reviews the iconography of the mirror in *The Pilgrimage of Life* (New Haven: Yale Univ. Press, 1962), 61, 97, 192–94. M.-D. Chenu argues that the particular complexity of the medieval concept of an hierarchically organized universe—of which Spenser's *Hymnes* would be a late example—derives from John the Scot's (Eriugena) ninth-century translation of the Neo-Platonic cosmology of (fifth-century) pseudo-Dionysius. According to Chenu, this is the historical conduit for the conception of a metaphysically monistic universe in which the material, sensible world participates in the divine. John the Scot in this way introduces a positive materialism that delights, almost pantheistically, in the things of the world, and this materialism is dialectically at odds with a more orthodox Christian Augustinianism, the semidualist, vestigial Manichaeanism of which retains the familiar Platonic contempt for the material—*contemptus mundi*. According to Chenu, even

though John the Scot was subsequently condemned, his influence extends to the twelfth century and significantly affects the Platonism of the school of Chartres; *Nature, Man and Society: Essays on New Theological Perspectives in the West,* trans. J. Little and J. Taylor (Chicago: Univ. of Chicago Press, 1978), chaps. 1, 2. In contrast, E. Gilson sees Eriugena as the road not taken by the West; *History of Christian Philosophy in the Middle Ages* (New York: Random House, 1955), 111–78; see also H. D. Saffrey, "New Objective Links Between the Pseudo-Dionysius and Proclus," in *NeoPlatonism and Christian Thought,* ed. Dominic J. O'Meara (Albany: State Univ. of New York Press, 1982), 64–74; W. N. Clarke, "The Problem of the Reality and Multiplicity of Divine Ideas in Christian NeoPlatonism," in *NeoPlatonism and Christian Thought,* 109–27. T. K. Seung, following Chenu, argues that the efflorescence of allegory in the twelfth century is directly related to this pseudo-Dionysian revival which makes the things of this world, including man himself, an anagogical "mirror" of a higher reality; according to Seung, this is the major impetus behind the medieval mirror metaphor, for example, the often-noted frequency of "mirrors" in twelfth-century book titles (*speculum naturae, speculum historiae, speculum stultorum,* and so forth), *Cultural Thematics: The Formation of the Faustian Ethos*(New Haven: Yale Univ. Press, 1976), 73; see also Curtius, *European Literature,* 336. Edgerton notes that the flat, lead-backed mirror, "as distinct from the then more common convex glass or imperfect mirror made of shiny metal," is only introduced to Europe in the thirteenth century; this technological novelty, which for the first time allows one to see in a glass clearly, captures the imagination of poets (Dante, for example, mentions it in *Convivio,* 3.9). *Linear Perspective,* 134.

25. Fludd's diagram originally appears in his *Utriusque Cosmi Maioris . . . Tomi Secundi Tractatus Secundus* (1621) and is reprinted in Joscelyn Godwin, *Robert Fludd* (London: Thames and Hudson, 1979), 34. For similar pictures and diagrams, see S. K. Henninger, *The Cosmographical Glass: Renaissance Diagrams of the Universe* (San Marino, Calif.: Huntington Library, 1977). The verse is misnumbered in the picture because Fludd takes the title of the psalm as its first verse.

26. I use the translation of the Geneva Bible (1560).

27. See Introduction, n. 4.

28. *Paradiso,* 33,124–31. It is at this concluding moment of the poem that "power failed the high fantasy" (*all'alta fantasia qui mancò possa*); this is the *fantasia,* as Sinclair notes, that Dante very conventionally defines in the *Convito* as "the power by which the intellect represents what it sees."

29. The diagram originally appears in Fludd's *Utriusque Cosmi Maioris . . . Tomus Primus De Macrocosmi Historia* (1617), and is reprinted in Godwin, *Robert Fludd,* 23. For the relation of this kind of cosmology to this kind of aesthetics, see Leonard Barkan, *Nature's Work of Art: The Human Body as Image of the World* (New Haven: Yale Univ. Press, 1975), esp. chap. 1.

30. According to Macrobius:

Accordingly, since Mind emanates from the Supreme God and Soul from Mind, and Mind, indeed forms and suffuses all below with life, and since this the one splendor lighting up everything and visible in all, like a countenance reflected in many mirrors arranged in a row, and since all follow on in continuous succession, degenerating step by step in their downward course, the close observer will find that from the Supreme God even to the bottommost dregs of the universe there is one tie, binding at every link and never broken.

Commentary on the Dream of Scipio, trans. W. H. Stahl (New York: Columbia Univ. Press, 1952), 1.15.145; A. O. Lovejoy says that this is the principal source of Plotinian cosmology for the middle ages, *The Great Chain of Being* (Cambridge: Harvard Univ. Press, 1971), 63. Macrobius here uses Plotinian terminology; see *Enneads,* 1.1.8. At the level of generality I am concerned with, the point brought out here is what R. Klibansky called *The Continuity of the Platonic Tradition* (London: Warburg Institute, 1939). It should be remembered that, quite apart from those Plato texts which exert an indirect influence even before they are rediscovered, the medieval Latin Plato includes *Timaeus* (abridged), *Meno, Phaedo, Parmenides.* Chaucer summarizes Macrobius' *Commentary* in *The Parlement of Foules* (lines 31–84) and in the same work, when describing the hierarchical order of birds, both refers to and translates Alain of Lille's *De Planctu Naturae* as "the Pleynt of Kynde" (line 316). This is the primary signification of "kind" in Shakespeare's sonnets; see the discussion of sonnet 105's "'Fair,' 'kind,' and 'true'" in chapter 3.

31. John Dee, "Mathematicall praeface," in Euclid, *The Elements,* trans. Henry Billingsley (1570); cited in Heninger, *Touches of Sweet Harmony,* 359. It is important to realize that this general conception of the order of the cosmos is something perennial, as is the imagery with which this order is regularly figured. What Tillyard called *The Elizabethan World Picture,* what Hardin Craig called *The Enchanted Glass: The Elizabethan Mind in Literature,* or the system of resemblance, analogy, and similitude that Michel Foucault in *Les Mots et les choses* calls a Renaissance "episteme" is something that the Elizabethan Renaissance registers as traditional and long standing. Such familiarity is what gives both the idea of Idea and the figures with which this idea is fleshed out their prestige and authority. At the same time, however, it prepares for and gives force to the novel ways in which late Elizabethan literature characterizes this tradition as something old-fashioned and passé.

32. I am concerned with this level of generality because I am concerned with the way a literary genre as large as the epideictic employs motifs as large as vision and language so as coherently to produce generic rubrics on the order of Male and Female. Very obviously, such a level of generality glosses over significant conceptual differences in the history of Western idealism just as it glosses over specific and variously textured material figurations through which this idealism is imagined. Heidegger, for example, who is centrally concerned with the history of metaphors applied to Truth, discusses the way the mediated visuality of Plato is already a falling-off from a pre-Socratic Truth of Nature: "The truth of *physis, aletheia* as the unconcealment that is the essence of the emerging power, now becomes *homiosis* and *mimesis,* assimilation and accommodation, orientation by . . . it becomes a correctness of vision, or apprehension and representation," *An Introduction to Metaphysics,* trans. R. Manheim (New York: Doubleday, 1961), 155. With Aristotle, according to Heidegger, this decline goes further, and the metaphors applied to Truth change accordingly: "Let us now sum up what has

been said of *physis* and *logos:* logos becomes idea [*paradeigma*], truth becomes correctness," 158. In Heidegger's history of metaphysics it is left to the scholastics to work out the consequences, conceptual and metaphorical, of this two-stage "breakdown of unconcealment," which makes of Nature either a Platonic Idea or an Aristotelian *subjectum (hypokeimenon)*, 161; Heidegger discusses "*eidos*" as "look" in *Being and Time*, trans. J. MacQuarrie and E. Robinson (New York: Harper & Row, 1962), 88–90. These differences, conceptual and metaphorical, are significant, for they document the ways in which idealism historically reflects upon itself and its own tradition. On the other hand, given this historical development, it is important to recognize the consistent reappearance of certain central motifs, for this makes it possible to assess the significance of their deployment at various historical moments. The point becomes clearer if we recall, again at a deliberately broad level of generality, the way visual imagery informs the development of language theory up through the Renaissance.

As is well known, from Augustine to Ockham a word's relation either to its referent or to its meaning becomes increasingly attenuated. For Augustine, words are trustworthy signs of the reality to which they intentionally refer. In the same way that God reveals himself through Christ, the incarnate Word, or the way a chance reading of a gospel text providentially leads to Augustine's conversion, so Augustine sees the word as truly—and, despite Augustine's distrust of the visual arts, usually visually—significant of its referent. By the time of Ockham's nominalist critique, words lose this intimate connection to reality just as universals lose their ontological status. The intervening history of medieval linguistic philosophy is therefore a record of decreasing metaphysical Realism (via the incipient nominalism of Abelard, the "moderate realism" of Aquinas) coupled with an increasingly more powerful sense of a semiotic disjunction between signifiers and signifieds. The detailed philosophical history of this development has not yet been written, nor is there a detailed literary history of the metaphors applied to language by medieval linguistic theory. It is certainly the case, however, that the subtle and technical nuances of medieval sign theory cannot adequately be characterized in terms of a simple "likeness" among words, things, and meanings. There are many other ways in which to understand how *Nomina sunt consequentia rerum*, as Dante recites in *La Vita nuova*, sec. 13. Nevertheless, even in technical scholastic sign theory the motif of a specifically mimetic vision continually reappears, so much and so frequently so that Marcia Colish, in her general survey of the subject, subsumes such diverse thinkers as Augustine, Anselm, and Aquinas under the rubric of *The Mirror of Language* (New Haven: Yale Univ. Press, 1968). Colish's large argument is that the *trivium* provides a matrix with which medieval language theory at different historical moments marries words to things. Augustine does this with rhetoric, Anselm with grammar, Aquinas with logic, but in each case the mirror metaphor is appropriate image of the way that words are understood to *mean*. Thus, for example, when words are no longer metaphysically like the things to which they refer, similitude becomes a mediated linguistic or logical relation; even thus demoted, however, similitude, characterized in visual terms, remains the modal explanation of generic kinds, as when Aquinas derives transcendental universals from the anagogical operation of the higher cognitive faculties—judgment, understanding, reason—on the immediate impressions of the senses.

Ideas about language change, therefore, as medieval sign theory passes from realism to nominalism, but the imagery with which these ideas are imagined remains constant. The failure to recognize the discrepancy that thus develops—between linguistic theory and the imagery through which it is expressed—can lead to serious and anachronistic misestimation of the figures and intentions of Renaissance poetics. A great deal of Renaissance literary criticism has committed itself to the general proposition that there is a transition in Elizabethan-Metaphysical lyric from a poetics of the word to a poetics of vision. Joseph Mazzeo, for example, developing the Augustinian background, makes this claim explicitly:

> The war between biblical and classical poetics concerned the surface of the text, so to speak, and not the possibility of allegorical exegesis. Whether or not the text was obscure or clear, the movement of thought was through the words to the realities themselves, from the temporal realities to the eternal realities, from talk to silence, and from discourse to vision.

"St. Augustine's Rhetoric of Silence: Truth vs. Eloquence and Things vs. Signs," in *Renaissance and Seventeenth Century Studies* (New York: Columbia Univ. Press, 1964), 19; see chap. 2 for the application to Metaphysical poetry. Walter Ong, to take a very different example, stressing the Ramistic subordination of rhetoric to logic, as well as the psychosociology of an emerging print culture, says pretty much the same; see "System, Space, and Intellect in Renaissance Symbolism," *Bibliotheque d'Humanisme et Renaissance* 18 (1956); *Ramus, Method, and the Decay of Dialogue* (Cambridge: Harvard Univ. Press, 1958); "From Allegory to Diagram in the Renaissance Mind," *The Journal of Aesthetics and Art Criticism* 17 (1959)—this is the kind of reasoning that leads Forrest Robinson in his *The Shape of Things Known*, to characterize Sidney as a "visual epistemologist." More historically nuanced, but to a similar end, Louis Martz reads the metaphysical lyric in the context of the way the Counter Reformation develops—out of medieval mysticism and Augustinianism (Bernard and Bonaventure)—a set of meditative practices where word and picture profitably meet; as Martz describes it, the connection of Ignatian meditative schemes to the traditional "places" of memory produces a piety and a poetry whose "application of senses" remains primarily visual, *The Poetry of Meditation: A Study in English Religious Literature of the Seventeenth Century* (New Haven: Yale Univ. Press, 1954), esp. chap. 2. Even critics who dispute this kind of "visionary" argument argue against it in equally "imaginary" terms. Barbara Lewalski, for example, whose discussion of Protestant scriptural poetics in the seventeenth century explicitly opposes itself to readings that emphasize idealist poetics, makes her point by eking out Calvin's "mirror of nature" with the "spectacles of scripture," *Protestant Poetics and the Seventeenth Century Religious Lyric*, 164.

All these readings overlook, at least to some extent, the way in which the development of medieval sign theory renders such epistemological, linguistic, and poetic "mirrors" increasingly fragile and brittle. Even in early Humanism, the "mirror of language," if it is not broken, certainly blurs the "perspicuous vision" of a poetics of clear and distinct ideas. The Renaissance is not blind to this failure of vision, and it is not only Shakespearean eyes that "behold and see not what they see" (137). If *The Port Royal Logic* begins by ridiculing the mental "image" of a thousand-sided figure, it does so in response to a medieval revision of intelligible vision the consequences of which are manifest long before the seventeenth century. When Vasari, for example, who gives the Renaissance its name—*il rinascimento*—writes the history of the revival of Italian painting, he begins with Cimabue, who, Vasari says, "originated the use of words in art for the better expression of the meaning—certainly a new and peculiar expedient," *Vasari's Lives of the Artists,* ed. B. Burroughs, trans. J. Foster (New York: Simon & Schuster, 1946), 5. There is, however, nothing new about "the use of words in art." What is new is that Vasari *thinks* this is new, as though word and picture draw together at the very moment when the difference between them begins to be sensed. This is related to the way the emblem's combination of picture and word changes in the development from early Humanism to the seventeenth century, from a collage iconography to a narrative, moralizing mode; see R. Freeman, *English Emblem Books* (New York: Octagon Press, 1970). In literature, this emerging distinction between visual "imagination" and verbal "conception," a difference more delicate than the customary distinction between an ornamental Elizabethan "image" and an intellectual Metaphysical "conceit," prepares the way—long before Lessing theorizes the consequences for aesthetics—for a discursive *poesis* unhappily divorced from the visual *pictura* to which it can never thereafter "correspond." As I argue later, this is what gives historical force to Shakespeare's "perjur'd eye."

For accounts of the rhetorical-logical tradition within which Shakespeare operates, see W. S. Howell, *Logic and Rhetoric in England: 1500–1700* (Princeton, N.J.: Princeton Univ. Press, 1956); G. A. Padley, *Grammatical Theory in Western Europe, 1500–1700: The Latin Tradition* (Cambridge: Cambridge Univ. Press, 1976); J. Murphy, *Rhetoric in the Middle Ages: Rhetorical Theory in the Middle Ages from Saint Augustine to the Renaissance* (Berkeley: Univ. of California Press, 1974); M. Joseph, *Shakespeare's Use of the Arts of Language* (New York: Columbia Univ. Press, 1947); T. W. Baldwin, *William Shakespeare's "Small Latine and Lesse Greeke"* (Urbana: Univ. of Illinois Press, 1944), vol. 2, chaps. 31–37; D. L. Clark, *Rhetoric and Poetry in the Renaissance* (New York: Russell & Russell, 1963). For anticipations of the future, see J. Knowlson, *Universal Language Schemes in England and France: 1600–1800* (Toronto: Univ. of Toronto Press, 1975); M. Cohen, *"Sensible Words": Linguistic Practice in England, 1640–1785* (Baltimore: Johns Hopkins Univ. Press, 1977); Hans Aarsleff, *From Locke to Saussure: Essays on the Study of Language and Intellectual History* (Minneapolis: Univ. of Minnesota Press, 1982). For a broad account of the problem, see R. Fraser, *The Language of Adam: On the Limits and Systems of Discourse* (New York: Columbia Univ. Press, 1977). On Shakespeare's thematizations of language, see T. Hawkes, *Shakespeare's Talking Animals: Language and Drama in Society* (London: Edward Arnold, 1973); L. Danson, *Tragic Alphabet: Shakespeare's Drama of Language* (New Haven: Yale Univ. Press, 1974).

33. In *Paradise Lost,* at the end of book 3, Uriel, "the regent of the sun" (690), one of God's "Eyes/That run through all the Heav'ns" (650–51), "the sharpest-sighted Spirit of all in Heav'n" (691), describes the creation of the

universe to Satan, who is in disguise: "Light shone, and order from disorder sprung" (713). Uriel (3.724–32) explains, in conclusion, how the "borrow'd light" of the "triform Moon," "that opposite fair Star," functions as the difference between day and night:

> That place is Earth the seat of Man, that light
> His day, which else as th' other Hemisphere
> Night would invade, but there the neighboring Moon
> (So call that opposite fair Star) her aid
> Timely interposes, and her monthly round
> Still ending, still renewing through mid Heav'n,
> With borrow'd light her countenance triform
> Hence fills and empties to enlighten the Earth,
> And in her pale dominion checks the night.

John Milton: Complete Poems and Major Prose, ed. Merrit Y. Hughes (New York: Odyssey Press, 1957).

34. The same relations operate in the circle of minerals, where Fludd illustrates the alchemical relation of masculine *Plumbum* to female *Cuprum,* the point being that lead is turned into gold when combined with copper. Copper is named for the copper mines in Cyprus, which are near Paphos, the birthplace of Venus, "the Cyprian Queen"; see *Venus and Adonis,* 1194. Copper participates in the reaction as a principle of "change," the transformation of lead into gold understood as an erotic *translatio.* On the venereal powers of copper, see Lynn Thorndike, *A History of Magic and Experimental Science* (New York: Columbia Univ. Press, 1958), 8:131–32, 136, 389–90.

35. "Her name alone has both little and much kindled your mad passion" (*nomen ipsum nonnichil, imo vel plurimum, furoribus istis addiderit*), *Petrarch's Secret or the Soul's Conflict with Passion: Three Dialogues Between Himself and S. Augustine,* trans. W. H. Draper (London: Chatto and Windus, 1911), 126; Latin text in *Opere di Francesco Petrarca,* ed. Emilio Bigi (Milan: Ugo Mursia, 1963), 628. Also:

> Who could sufficiently utter his indignation and amazement at this sign of a distempered mind, that, infatuated as much by the beauty of her name as of her person, you have with perfectly incredible silliness paid honour to anything that has the remotest connection with that name itself? Had you any liking for the laurel of empire or of poetry, it was forsooth because the name they bore was hers; and from this time onwards there is hardly a verse from your pen but in it you have made mention of the laurel, as if indeed you were a denizen of Peneus' stream, or some priest on Cirrha's Mount [*quis digne satis execretur aut stupeat hanc alienate mentis insaniam, cum, non minus nominis quam ipsius corporis splendore captus, quicquid illi consonum fuit incredibili vanitate coluisti? Quam ob causam tanto opere sive cesaream sive poeticam lauream, quod illa hoc nomine vocaretur, adamasti; ex eoque tempore sine lauri mentione vix ullum tibi carmen effluxit, non aliter quam si vel Penei gurgitis accola vel Cirrei verticis sacerdos existeres*].

Petrarch's Secret, 134–35; *Opere,* 636. Augustine continually objects to Petrarch's Petrarchanism. Defending his love, Petrarch argues that:

> It was she who turned my youthful soul away from all that was base, who drew me as it were by a grappling chain, and forced me to look upwards. Why should you

not believe it? It is a sure truth that by love we grow like what we love [*Illa iuvenilem animum ab omni turpitudine revocavit, uncoque, ut aiunt, retraxit, atque alta compulit espectare. Quidni enim in amatos mores transformarer*]?

Petrarch's Secret, 121; *Opere,* 624. Augustine's response is quite emphatic:

> That woman to whom you profess you owe everything, she, even she, has been your ruin. . . . She has detached your mind from the love of heavenly things and has inclined your heart to love the creature more than the Creator: and that one path alone leads, sooner than any other, to death [*Ista nempe, quam predicas, cui omnia debere te asseris, ista te peremit. . . . Ab amore celestium elongavit animum et a Creatore ad creaturam desiderium inclinavit. Que una quidem ad mortem pronior fuit via*].

Petrarch's Secret, 124; *Opere,* 626. When Petrarch insists that "the love which I feel for her has most certainly led me to love God" *(Deum profecto ut amorem, illius amor prestitit),* Augustine replies with his strongest argument:

> But it has inverted the true order. . . . Because every creature should be dear to us because of our love for the Creator. But in your case, on the contrary, held captive by the charm of the creature, you have not loved the Creator as you ought. You have admired the Divine Artificer as though in all His works He had made nothing fairer than the object of your love, although in truth the beauty of the body should be reckoned last of all" [*At pervertit ordinem. . . . Quia cum creatum omne Creatoris amore diligendum sit, tu contra, creature captus illecebris, Creatorem non qua decuit amasti, sed miratus artificem fuisti quasi nichil ex omnibus formosius creasset, cum tamen ultima pulcritudinum sit forma corporea*].

Petrarch's Secret, 124–25; *Opere,* 626. Augustine's objections, phrased in terms of Christian orthodoxy, reflect Petrarch's anti-Petrarchanism, and this is different from what I have called Shakespeare's para-Petrarchanism. However, if we recall the dramatic nature of Petrarch's private dialogue with Augustine, if we bear in mind, that is, that Petrarch is here arguing *in utramque partem,* speaking both for himself and, ventriloquistically, for Augustine, then the affinities with Shakespeare's paradoxical Petrarchanism are readily apparent.

36. Hayward, *Donne, Complete Poetry and Selected Prose,* 350–51.

37. *TS,* 1.2.69–71; Petruchio alludes here also to the Sibyl, which suggests the daemonic as well as the prophetic register of female speech.

38. The Riverside editors gloss "rope-tricks" thus: "rope-tricks: blunder for *rhetoric* (an interpretation supported by *figure* in line 114) (?) or tricks that deserve hanging (?)." More than their gloss, the editors' parenthetical question marks register the way in which Shakespeare characteristically makes a question out of rhetoric. For while "rope-tricks" manages both to mean and to refer to "rhetoric," it does so in an oddly performative, rather than in a referential or meaningful, fashion. Rhetoric is the signified of the signifier "rope-tricks," but it is so precisely because the disjunction thus disclosed between signifier and signified serves to example rhetoricity as such, rhetoricity understood literally as figurative speech that says one thing and means another: "Rope-tricks" *is* rhetoric because it *is not* "rhetoric." As will be seen, Shakespeare very much enjoys generating this kind of motivated slippage between signifier and signified, and he characteristi-

cally associates this kind of rhetoricity with the paradox of praise—"mourn-ing"-"morning" in sonnet 132 would be another example. Equally character-istic, however, this kind of mimic Cratylism regularly emerges in an anti-visual context, as here, where the "disfiguring" "figure" thrown in Kate's face will leave her "no more eyes to see withal than a cat [Kate]."

39. The proverbial phrase frames the frame story. Sly's final words in the Induction are "Well, we'll see't. Come madam wife, sit by my side, and let the world slip, we shall ne'er be younger;; (*Ind.* 2.142 –44). The logic of *paucas pallabris*—a misquotation from *The Spanish Tragedy*—is straightfor-ward. There are always fewer words than meanings because, through the medium of "translation" (etymologies, false homophones, cross-language cognates, etc.), any given word possesses, at least potentially, a plurality of significations. The "world" "slides," therefore, because the equivocality of the "word" undoes the univocality of the "world." The play that is presented to Sly, which is not the entirety of *The Taming of the Shrew*, stages this para-dox in a comic register, relating the polysemic nature of language to specific sexual representations. I discuss the relation of "translation" to Petrarchan desire in *The Taming of the Shrew* in "The Turn of the Shrew," in *Shakespeare and the Question of Theory*, eds. Patricia Parker and Geoffrey Hartman (Lon-don and New York: Methuen, 1985).

CHAPTER 3

1. Spenser, *Amoretti,* 85.

2. Consider Drayton's "An Elegie upon the Death of the Lady Penelope Clifton":

> If ever any Painter were so blest,
> To drawe that face, which so much heav'n exprest,
> If in his best of skill he did her right,
> I wish it never may come in my sight.
> I greatly doubt my faith (weake man) lest I
> Should to that face commit Idolatry.

The Works of Michael Drayton, ed. J. Hebel (Oxford: Oxford Univ. Press, 1961), 3:221.

3. Petrarch, *RS,* 30.

4. Spenser, *Amoretti,* 61, 54. Spenser's association of "theater" with his "idol"-"idle" pun regularly comes to life in Puritan stage polemic. Consider Stephen Gosson's:

> And William Lodge in that patche pamphet of his wherein he taketh upon him the defence of playes, little perceivinge how lustely the chippes flye in his face, whilst he heweth out timber to make the frame, confesseth openly that playes were con-secrated by the heathens to the honour of their gods, which in deede is true, yet serveth it better to overthrow them the[n] establish them: for whatsoever was consecrated to the honour of the Heathen Gods was consecrated to idolatrie. Be-ing consecrated to idolatrie, they are not of God, if they proceede not from God, they are the doctrine and inventions of the devill. This will be counted new learn-ing among a great number of my gay countrymen, which bear a sharper smacke of Italian devises in their heades, then of English religion in their heartes.

Playes Confuted in Five Actions (1582), in *The English Drama and Stage under the Tudor and Stuart Princes, 1543–1664,* ed. W. C. Hazlitt (London: Wittingham and Wilkins, 1869), 171. Compare this with Phillip Stubb's *The Anatomie of Abuses* (1583):

> There is no mischief which these plaies maintain not. For do they not norish ydleness? and *otia dant vitia,* ydlenes is the Mother of vice. Doo they not draw the people from hering the word of God, from Godly Lectures and sermons? for you shall have them flocke thither, thick and threfould, when the church of God shalbe bare and emptie. . . . Do they not maintaine bawdrie, infinit folery, and renue the remembrance of heathen ydolatrie? Do they not induce whordom and uncleneness? nay, are they not rather plaine devourers of maydenly virginie and chastities?

Reprinted in E. K. Chambers, *The Elizabethan Stage* (Oxford: Clarendon Press, 1923), 4: 223.

For the iconography of idols, and the metaphoric association of idolatry to adultery and whoredom, see J. Nohrnberg, *The Analogy of the "Fairie Queene"* (Princeton: Princeton Univ. Press, 1976), 223–27. It is also customary to associate lechery and blindness, the latter understood as a consequence of the former. This is a medical as well as a moral truth; W. R. Elton cites evidence to this effect from contemporary physiological treatises, *King Lear and the Gods* (San Marino, Calif.: Huntington Library, 1966), 111–12. Elton includes this Baconian parallel to Shakespeare's sonnet 129: "much use of Venus doth dim the sight . . . the cause is the expence of spirits." *Great Instauration,* in *The Works of Francis Bacon,* ed. J. Spedding (London: Longmans, 1876), 2:555–56. This connection is usually picked up in paradoxical praises, e.g., Munday's "Fourth Paradox" ("That it is better to be blinde, then to see cleerely"); B. Vickers, *"King Lear,"* gives other examples, 312–14. These associations are readily assimilated to the conception and characterization of visionary, epideictic poetry. Thus Cuddie complains about the fortune of poetry in the current age:

> So praysen babes the Peacoks spotted traine,
> And wondren at bright *Argus* blazing eye:
> But who rewards him ere the more for thy?
> Or feedes him once the fuller by a graine?
> Sike prayse is smoke, that sheddeth in the skye,
> Sike words bene wynde, and wasten soone in vayne.

"October," *Shepheardes Calender,* 31–36. Here Cuddie imagines the substantive failure of praise, the language of epideixis reduced to "wind." As in Shakespeare's sonnets, this in turn suggests adultery; E. K.'s gloss on this passage reads:

> Argus eyes) of Argus is before said, that Juno to him committed hir husband Jupiter his Paragon Iô, bicause he had an hundred eyes: but afterwards Mercury wyth hys Musick lulling Argus aslepe, slew him and brought Iô away, whose eyes it is sayd that Juno for his eternall memory placed in her byrd the Peacoks tayle. For those coloured spots indeede resemble eyes.

"October," Glosse, 458. This failure of "Argus" affects, through pseudoetymologizing, the idealization of poetic *enargia;* e.g., Puttenham's "that first qualitie the Greeks called *Enargia*, of this word *argos*, because it geveth lustre and light," 155.

5. Constable, "To His Mistresse." See chapter 3, n. 5. The poetics of vision can be developed in this sophisticated and self-conscious fashion because the logic of idealization is associated with, and understood in terms of, the subtle arguments worked out in the course of traditional controversy regarding the value of religious images. It is in the debate around this issue that the ontological and theological consequences of visual imitation receive the most sustained and intense scrutiny. On the tradition of iconoclastic controversy, see P. Alexander, "The Iconoclastic Council of St. Sophia and Its Definition," *Dumbarton Oaks Papers* 7 (1953):37–57; G. Ladner, "The Concept of the Image in the Greek Fathers and the Byzantine Iconoclastic Controversy," ibid., 1–34. Also, E. Kitzinger, "The Cult of Images in the Age before Iconoclasm," *Dumbarton Oaks Papers* 8 (1954):83–150; M. Anastos, "The Ethical Theory of Images Formulated by the Iconoclasts in 754 and 815," ibid., 153–60. For general background, see C. Trinkaus, *In Our Image and Likeness: Humanity and Divinity in Italian Humanist Thought* (Chicago: Univ. of Chicago Press, 1970), esp. 697–98, 746–47.

These doctrinal divisions acquire new urgency in the context of Reformation polemic. Elizabeth's proclamation of 1599, which curtails Marian "popish" practices with regard to religious images, returns the state to the policy of Edward VI and Henry VIII: (1) prohibiting devotional "abuse" of images, (2) tolerating the use of images for strictly commemorative or didactic purpose. See J. Phillips, *The Reformation of Images: Destruction of Art in England, 1535–1660* (Berkeley:Univ. of California Press, 1973), esp. chap. 10. By the 1580s and 1590s, however, this Anglican compromise has itself become an object of increasing controversy, criticized by Puritans as conducive to idolatry, and by traditionary conservatives who value medieval church customs. With James the issue will grow yet more heated and this eventually leads to the victory of Puritan iconoclasm. In this increasingly charged religious atmosphere the tension traditionally attaching to the thematics of idealizing vision acquires increasing literary significance. For example, the Protestant-Catholic debate colors with religious affect what are otherwise conventional word v. picture, poetry v. spectacle, quarrels, e.g., the "Soule of Masque" in (converted Catholic) Jonson's "An Expostulacion with Inigo Jones." In this context, "Soule" is more than a merely technical term from masque theory:

> O Showes! Showes! Might Showes!
> The Eloquence of Masques! What need of prose
> Or verse, or Sense t'express Imortall you?
> You are the Spectacles of State! Tis true
> Court Hieroglyphicks! and all Artes affoord
> In the mere perspective of an Inch board!
> You aske noe more then certeyne politique Eyes,
> Eyes that can pierce into the Mysteries
> Of many Coulors! read them! and reveale
> Mythology there painted on a slit deal!
> Oh, to make Boardes to speake! There is a taske
> Painting and Carpentry are the Soule of Masque.

Hereford and Simpson, *Ben Jonson*, "Ungathered Verse," 8:402–6, lines 39–50. For background, see D. C. Gordon, "Poet and Architect: The Intellectual Setting of the Quarrel between Ben Jonson and Inigo Jones," in *The Renaissance Imagination: Essays and Lectures by D. C. Gordon*, ed. S. Orgel (Berkeley: Univ. of California Press, 1975), 77–101. Jonson's attitude toward the issue of *ut pictura poesis* is, of course, quite complex: "Whosoever loves not *Picture*, is injurious to *Truth*: and all the wisdome of Poetry." *Timber*, 610. This is the context within which to locate the dedicatory poem facing the frontispiece portrait of Shakespeare in the First Folio (1623): "Reader, looke/Not on his Picture, but his Booke."

For a discussion of the relation of Renaissance and Baroque stylistics to the Council of Trent's decision to tolerate the use of images, see W. Sypher, *Four Stages of Renaissance Style* (New York: Doubleday, 1955) esp. 187–88. In general, metaphysical poets tend to emphasize their distance from a purely visual poetics, e.g., Donne, remembering his early verse, "In my idolatry what showres of raine/Mine eyes did waste," *Holy Sonnets, John Donne's The Divine Poems*, ed. Helen Gardner (Oxford: Oxford Univ. Press, 1952), 3, or, for another example, Herbert:

> Who sayes that fictions onely and false hair
> Become a verse? Is there no truth in beauty?
> Is all good structure in a winding stair?
> May no lines passe, except they do their dutie
> Not to a true, but Painted chair?

"Jordan 1," in *The Works of George Herbert*, ed. F. Hutchinson (Oxford: Oxford Univ. Press, 1941). Again, however, the theme is nothing but familiar; for example, the conflict inhering in the correlation of poetic word with poetic picture is already a central thematic issue for Spenser, one that affects his manner as well as his matter, e.g., the complications of Spenser's so-called emblematic stanza. It is important to recognize the way in which this conflict is a perennial literary issue, for this helps partially to explain why, after Shakespeare, the issue loses much of its energy. Consider, for example, the later, domesticated, Protestant emblem tradition discussed by Lewalski in *Protestant Poetics*, chap. 6, or by E. Gilman, "Word and Image in Quarles' Emblemes," *Critical Inquiry* 6, no. 3 (1980):385–410, or by A. Howard, "The World as Emblem: Language and Vision in the Poetry of Edward Taylor," *American Literature* 44 (1972):359–84.

6. Spenser, *The Faerie Queene*, 1.6. 19.
7. The Quarto prints "steeld," which is generally emended to "stelled." For the range of connotations attaching to "stelled," see Booth, 172–73. I argue later that the conflicted ensemble of motifs attaching to "stelled"—visual, metallic, inscriptive—together flesh out the body-ego of the poetics of difference. "Stelled" both describes and *is* what happens when the luminous poetics of "Stella" comes to be marked with difference. There stands behind "stelled" the massive ideality of Dante's *stelle*, which is the final word and image of each canticle of the *Commedia*.
8. Booth, 173.
9. Murray Krieger, "Poetic Presence and Illusion: Renaissance Theory and the Duplicity of Metaphor," *Critical Inquiry* 5, no. 4 (1979):619.

10. Booth discusses the syntactic ambiguity of singular-plural "turns" in sonnet 95; as Booth points out, the grammar "contains a reminder that all that is visible is not all there is," 311.

11. Booth, 197.

12. George Chapman, "Ovids Banquet of Sence," in *The Poems of George Chapman*, ed. P. Bartlett (London: Oxford Univ. Press, 1941), 49–50.

13. Such rhetorical darkness is traditionally understood in terms of the allegorical indirection of epideictic lyric: praise conveys secret philosophical meanings to an elite coterie. Hardison cites Gascoigne as an example, "If I should undertake to wryte in prayse of a gentlewoman . . . I would either find some supernaturall cause . . . or discover my disquiet in shadowes *per Allegoriam*," and relates this to Gabriel Harvey's conception of Petrarch as a poet "whose ditty is an Image of the Sun voutsafing to represent his glorious face in a clowde," 100. Understood in this traditional way, as the instrument of allegorical mystification, darkness remains ideal and idealizing. This is different from a paradoxical praise, such as Shakespeare's, of darkness as such. So too allegory itself begins at this point to be recharacterized as something less than ideal, e.g., Puttenham's description of allegory as "the figure of false semblant," *Arte of English Poesie*, 197.

14. *Romeo and Juliet* develops its tragedy out of an initially comic satire on Romeo's Petrarchan postures. This development parallels in many ways the progress from the young man sonnets to the dark lady sonnets. Especially significant is the way the play associates Romeo's move from Rosaline to Juliet with the discovery of a specifically *novel* desire, one that emerges over the literally dead body of a preceding literariness. As the Chorus explains (2. ind. 1–4):

> Now old desire doth in his death-bed lie,
> And young affection gapes to be his heir;
> That fair for which love groan'd for and would die,
> With tender Juliet match'd is now not fair.

The death of "old desire" is what gives birth to a "young affection" which is more "grown-up" than that which it succeeds.

CHAPTER 4

1. This is related to Petrarch's sense of his own literary novelty, a point that is developed in terms of a tension between the ancients and the moderns (RS, 40):

> If Love or Death does not cut short the new cloth that now I prepare to weave . . . I shall perhaps make a work so double between the style of the moderns and ancient speech [*sì doppio / tra lo stil dé moderni e 'l sermon prisco*] that (fearfully I dare to say it) you will hear the noise of it even as far as Rome.

2. See chapter 2, n. 35.

3.   Stephen Greenblatt, *Renaissance Self-Fashioning: From More to Shakespeare* (Chicago: Univ. of Chicago Press, 1980).

4.   Roger Ascham, *The Scholemaster* (1570), ed. G.G. Smith, *Elizabethan Critical Essays* (Oxford: Oxford Univ. Press, 1950), 1: 3.

5.   Spenser, "Letter to Raleigh," 407.

6.   Dante, *La Vita nuova*, sec. 3.

7.   Ibid.

8.   The procreation series is usually said to conclude with sonnet 17. The theme, however, remains operative in later sonnets as well, and is surely important to sonnet 22. There is no need to set off, as a series all by itself, the procreation sonnets from all the other young man sonnets; however, if there is such a sub-sub-sequence, I would mark its conclusion with sonnet 24.

9.   As an experiment, I have asked naive readers, i.e., readers coming to the sonnets for more or less the first time, to read sonnet 22 aloud after having heard sonnets 1 through 10 recited by others. For what it is worth, I can report that this experiment, conducted five times (in two freshman English courses, two undergraduate introductions to Shakespeare, one graduate course on Shakespeare), produced two stumbling readings of "youth and thou" in sonnet 22 as "you and thou."

10.   Brent Cohen, cited in Booth, 206.

11.   John Donne, "To Sir Henry Wotton," *The Poems of John Donne*, ed. H. J. C. Grierson (London: Oxford Univ. Press, 1933), 159. The closest parallel in Petrarch to sonnets 44 and 45 is *RS*, 168, which also picks up the epistolic conceit:

> Love sends me that sweet thought which is an old confidant between us and comforts me and says that I was never so close as I am now to what I yearn and hope for. I, who have found his words sometimes false and sometimes true, do not know whether to believe him and I live between the two: neither yes nor no sounds whole in my heart [*et vivomi intra due:/né sì né nel cor mi sona intero*].

In Petrarch, however, because "I do not fear that what remains of life may be short," there remains the promise of the promised end. See also *RS*, 113: "Here where I only half am, my Sennuccio" [*Qui dove mezzo son, Sennuccio mio*].

12.   Absent presence and present absence are oxymorons characteristically featured in Petrarchist verse where they are regularly developed through humorous overstylization. Sidney, for example, has Astrophil complain: "Then some good body tell me how I do,/Whose presence, absence, presence is;/Blist in my curse, and cursed in my blisse" (*AS*, 60), or, for another example, "O absent presence, Stella is not here" (*AS*, 106; see also 88, 89, 91). Spenser does the same: "So I her absens will my penaunce make,/that of her presens I my meed may take" (*Amoretti*, 52). However, Shakespeare's "These present-absent with swift motion slide" doubles, or cross-couples, such conventional oxymorons: in sonnet 45 both "presence" and "absence" are equally "present-absent," and at the same time they remain opposed to each other.

13.   Booth, 203.

14. Ibid., 205, 204.
15. Ibid., "The sense here must be 'show thee to me,' but the rhythm (accent on *me*) and the idiom ordinarily dictate 'show me to thee,'" 205. Again, this kind of confusion regularly inflects deictic indication in the subsequence of sonnets addressed to the young man.

CHAPTER 5

1. This material association—a formless, dissolved liquidity that is joined together with an overformed, brittle hardness—is, in effect, a phenomenological description of a mirror. Throughout the young man sub-sequence, this materiality is used to figure the experience of temporal mutation and change, and it is also applied to the poet's verse. Consider the progress from the couplet of sonnet 54 to the opening of sonnet 55: "And so of you, beauteous and lovely youth,/When that shall vade [fade], by [my] verse distills your truth" (54); "Not marble nor the gilded monuments/Of princes shall outlive this pow'rful rhyme,/But you shall shine more bright in these contents/Than unswept stone, besmear'd with sluttish time" (55). This is a constant, material ensemble throughout the plays. Consider the lost, liquid, stony, and temporal eyes of Ariel's song (*T*, 1.2.397–403):

> Full fadom five thy father lies,
>   Of his bones are coral made:
> Those are pearls that were his eyes.
>   Nothing of him that doth fade,
> But doth suffer a sea-change
> Into something rich and strange.
> Sea-nymphs hourly ring his knell.

2. Sonnet 116 argues very strongly, up through the couplet, for the fact that "Love's not Time's fool, though rosy lips and cheeks/Within his bending sickle's compass come." It remains the case, however, that we do not know whether "his" in line 11 refers to Love or Time: "Love alters not with his brief hours and weeks,/But bears it out even to the edge of doom." This is why it is necessary to accept, as a very real possibility, the frightening prospect imagined in the couplet: "If this be error and upon me proved,/I never writ, nor no man ever loved."
3. Petrarch's sonnet 159 can stand as an example: "In what part of heaven [*Ciel*], in what Idea [*Idea*] was the pattern [*l' esempio*] from which Nature copied that lovely face, in which she has shown down here all that she is capable of doing up there?"
4. C. S. Lewis, *English Literature in the Sixteenth Century Excluding Drama* (Oxford: Oxford Univ. Press, 1954), 503.
5. See chapter 1, n. 7.
6. For a discussion of the usury-homosexual relation and its relation to Dante's ideas of language, see Eugene Vance, "Désir, rhétorique et texte," *Poétique* 42 (April 1980):137–55. See also Marc Shell, "The Wether and the

Ewe: Verbal Usury in *The Merchant of Venice," Kenyon Review* 1, no. 4 (Fall 1979):65–92.

7. For the Ovidian parallels, see T. W. Baldwin, *On the Literary Genetics of Shakespeare's Poems and Sonnets* (Urbana: Univ. of Illinois Press, 1950), 267–69.

8. The sun-son correspondence is a common pun, something that Herbert makes a thematic issue of in "The Sonne," where English is commended for the way "How neatly doe we give one onely name/To parents issue and the sunnes bright starre!" For Herbert, the homonymy reflects the teachings of theology, and does so on the traditional model of a language that Cratylitically corresponds to the truth that it bespeaks:

> So in one word our Lords humilitie
> We turn upon him in a sense most true:
> For what Christ once in humblenesse began,
> We him in glorie call, *The Sonne of Man.*

The Works of George Herbert, ed. F. E. Hutchinson (Oxford: Oxford Univ. Press, 1941), 167–68. Herbert writes such poems, however, after the pristine authority of this kind of Cratylitic correspondence of word with meaning or referent is lost, and this is why Herbert's motivated punnings and his other anagrammatic, hieroglyphic efforts to correlate signifier with signified seem always to be written in a wistfully Protestant response to the failure of Catholic iconicism, e.g., the way "The Altar" typologically reproduces a liturgical artifact prohibited by the English Reformation. It is important to stress this point; otherwise one overlooks the tension and conflict informing Herbert's lyric piety. The structure of cross-coupling also informs Herbert's recapitulatory Cratylitic mode. In "Coloss. 3.3.," for example, italicized words running diagonally across the poem form the sentence, *"My Life Is Hid In Him That Is My Treasure."* This diagonal around which the poem is covertly structured illustrates the poem's overt thematic claim: "*My* words & thoughts do both expresse this notion,/That *Life* hath with the sun a double motion," *Works*, 84. Stanley Fish says that with this anagrammatic device "the poem displays not one but (at least) four 'double motions'—its own, and those of the sun, the Son, and the reader, whose experience in this context can be said to approximate an imitation of Christ," *Self-Consuming Artifacts* (Berkeley: Univ. of California Press, 1972), 204. This is true, but the artifice attaching to the device, the strain attaching to the poem's "imitation," disturbs and effectively divides the unity of the poem's "double motion." The reader cannot read the poem and its diagonal both at the same time, and so the reader experiences a difference, not a likeness, in the "imitation" that he reads about; as he reads, the reader acts this difference out.

9. Michelangelo makes this point explicitly in a sonnet to Tommaso Cavalieri. The sonnet distinguishes between a love for men, which attracts one to heaven, and a love for women, which attracts one to earth:

> *Non è sempre di colpa aspra e mortale*
> *d'una immensa belleza un fero ardore,*
> *se poi sì lascia liquefatto il core,*
> *che 'n breve il penetri un divino strale.*
> *Amore isveglia e desta e 'mpenna l'ale,*

né l'alto vol preschive al van furore;
qual primo grado c'al suo creatore,
di quel non sazia, l'alma ascende e sale.
L'amor di quel ch'i' parlo in alto aspira;
donna è dissimil troppo; e mal conviensi
arder di quella al cor saggio e verile.
L'un tira al cielo, e l'altro in terra tira;
nell'alma l'un, l'altr'abita ne' sensi,
e l'arco tira a cose basse e vile.

Michelangelo Buonarroti, *Rime*, ed. Enzo N. Girardi (Bari: Laterza and Figli, 1960), no. 260, p. 123.

> Violent passion for tremendous beauty
> Is not perforce a bitter mortal error,
> If it can leave the heart melted thereafter,
> So that a holy dart can pierce it quickly.
> Not hindering high flight to such vain fury,
> Love wakens, rouses, puts the wings in feather,
> As a first step, so that the soul will soar
> And rise to its maker, finding this too scanty.
> The love for what I speak of reaches higher;
> Woman's too much unlike, no heart by rights
> Ought to grow hot for her, if wise and male.
> One draws to heaven and to earth the other,
> One in the soul, one living in the sense
> Drawing its bow on what is base and vile.

Complete Poems and Selected Letters of Michelangelo, trans. C. Gilbert (New York: Random House, 1965), 145.

The difference between this and, for example, Shakespeare's sonnet 144 is clear enough. Michelangelo praises an ideal, and therefore sexless, desire for a male by distinguishing its "virility" from the vulgar, appetitive desire for a woman. "Woman's too much unlike" (*dissimil troppo*). In contrast, Shakespeare conjoins these two different desires, like with unlike, male with female, not only with each other but *within* each other, as in "one angel in another's hell." As I argue above, in sonnet 20 the erotic imbrication of these two desires each in the other is materially imaged in the "pricked prick." This is quite different from the way the "holy dart" might "pierce" (*penetri*) Michelangelo's liquefied heart. For a discussion of Michelangelo's homosexuality, see Robert J. Clements, *The Poetry of Michelangelo* (New York: New York Univ. Press, 1965), 134–53.

10.   Compare *Love's Labor's Lost:* "Let the mark have a prick in't" (4.1.132); "The preyful Princess pierc'd and prick'd a pretty pleasing pricket" (4.2.56). This is the material logic of Lucrece's glove, whose "needle his finger pricks" (*RL*, 319).

11.   On Shakespeare's "Will," see Margreta De Grazia, "Babbling Will in *Shake-speares Sonnets* 127 to 154," *Spenser Studies* 1 (1980):121–34, and, related to this, Margreta De Grazia, "Shakespeare's View of Language: An Historical Perspective," *Shakespeare Quarterly* 29, no. 3 (1978):375–88. Also useful is Marcelin Pleynet, "*Les Sonnets: volonté et testament,*" *L'infini* (1983):48–61.

12.   For the Aristotelian assumptions behind this familiar arithmetic conceit, see Charles V. Jones, "'One is not a number': The Literal Meaning of a Figure of Speech," *Notes and Queries* 27 (1980):312–14. The traditional notion is that a number is capable of division, for which reason "one" or unity, though it makes number possible, is not itself a number. In sonnet 136 Shakespeare pushes this idea one step further, bringing it closer, we can note, to a more modern (Fregean) conception of number. The sonnet seems to distinguish between ordinal and cardinal numbering: "one" is the "first" *because* it is "none." This ordinal conception sanctions cardinal numbering, "zero" now functioning as a placeholder that warrants counting. It is as though "one" can only be conceived through the nullity, at once the negation and the "not-one," that calls it forth. More striking is the way this reasoning is applied to both the object and the subject of desire, the poet's objective and subjective genitive, genital "Will." As an object, the object of desire is marked by this nothing through which it is counted something. The poet then counts himself, as subject, as this "one" which in its constitution is "none." The subject and object of desire, "Will," become such, therefore, when the "one" in "none" and the "none" in "one" are reciprocally assimilated both to the poet and the lady. The lady's "common place" (137) is, therefore, the placeholder for what the poet and the lady have in common: namely, the "lack," again the "Will," that denomination occasions. This is already implied in the first dark lady sonnet—"In the old age black was not counted fair,/Or if it were it bore not beauty's name" (127)—where the poet makes erotic issue of the "lack" in "black": "Therefore my mistress' eyes are raven black,/Her eyes so suited, and they mourners seem/At such who, not born fair, no beauty lack." It is for this reason that copulation, the joining of "Wills", is what separates man not only from woman but also from himself.

Index

362 · Index